G000154828

£35

NIO

NEW

GREEK SANCTUARIES

GREEK SANCTUARIES

New approaches

Edited by

Nanno Marinatos and Robin Hägg

London and New York

First published 1993
by Routledge
11 New Fetter Lane, London EC4P 4EE

Simultaneously published in the USA and Canada
by Routledge Inc.
29 West 35th Street, New York, NY 10001

This collection © 1993 Routledge; individual chapters © 1993
individual contributors

Typeset in 10/12 pt Garamond by
Florencetype Limited, Kewstoke, Avon
Printed in Great Britain by
Butler & Tanner, Frome and London

All rights reserved. No part of this book may be reprinted or
reproduced or utilized in any form or by any electronic,
mechanical, or other means, now known or hereafter invented,
including photocopying and recording, or in any information
storage or retrieval system, without permission in writing from
the publishers.

British Library Cataloguing in Publication Data
Greek Sanctuaries: New Approaches
I. Marinatos, Nanno II. Hägg, Robin
292.3

Library of Congress Cataloging in Publication Data
Greek sanctuaries : new approaches / edited by
Nanno Marinatos and Robin Hägg.
p.   cm.
Includes bibliographical references.
1. Shrines – Greece. 2.Temples, Greek – Greece. 3. Greece –
Religion. I. Marinatos, Nanno. II. Hägg, Robin.
BL795.S47G74 1993
292.3′5′0938 – dc20   92–30812

ISBN 0–415–05384–6

Contents

CONTENTS

Illustrations

FIGURES

CREDITS

Notes on contributors

Nancy Bookidis, American School of Classical Studies, Athens
Walter Burkert, University of Zurich
Kevin Clinton, Cornell University
Elizabeth R. Gebhard, University of Illinois at Chicago
Helmut Kyrieleis, Deutsches Archäologisches Institut, Berlin
Nanno Marinatos, College Year in Athens
Catherine Morgan, Royal Holloway and Bedford New College, University
    of London
Erik Østby, Norwegian Institute at Athens
Rob W. M. Schumacher, Archeologisch Centrum, University of Leiden
Ulrich Sinn, University of Augsburg
Christiane Sourvinou-Inwood, University College, Oxford

Preface

What were Greek sanctuaries like? Recent scholarship has tended to focus more on social functions and the decoding of religious ritual than on elaborate descriptions of the archaeological remains. Much important work has been done by French scholars. We only mention here the works of J.-P. Vernant, Marcel Detienne, Claude Bérard and the controversial and important book by François de Polignac, *La naissance de la cité grecque* (Paris 1984). There seemed to be a need for something of a general nature designed primarily for English-speaking audiences. This has been provided in the present volume by an international team of authors with an intentional inclination towards Anglo-Saxon scholarship. Some of the contributors are archaeologists, others historians of religion. In the majority of cases, however, the principal issues centre around function and historical development of sanctuaries.

Some papers deal with new material: there are updated syntheses of the sanctuaries of Hera at Samos, Poseidon at Isthmia and of the Kabeiroi at Samothrace. Some essays deal with specific cult functions such as dining at Corinth and the mysteries at Eleusis. A number of papers deal with social function. At the end of the volume a full, up-to-date bibliography should make the book useful for further readings; it will also, we hope, compensate for the sanctuaries that are not treated at all in this volume.

The selection of articles was made by N. Marinatos. The main editing of the volume was done by R. Hägg.

Athens, December, 1991

Abbreviations

AA	*Archäologischer Anzeiger*
AAA	*Archaiologika analekta ex Athenon. Athens annals of archaeology*
AbhBerlin	*Abhandlungen der Deutschen Akademie der Wissenschaften zu Berlin*
ACSMGr	*Atti del Convegno di studi sulla Magna Grecia, Taranto*
ActaAArtHist	*Acta ad archaeologiam et artium historiam pertinentia*
ActaArch	*Acta archaeologica* (Copenhagen)
ActaAntHung	*Acta antiqua Academiae scientiarum Hungaricae*
AIA	Archaeological Institute of America
AJA	*American Journal of Archaeology*
AM	*Mitteilungen des Deutschen Archäologischen Instituts, Athenische Abteilung*
AnatSt	*Anatolian Studies. Journal of the British Institute of Archaeology at Ankara*
AncW	*The Ancient World*
ANET	*Ancient Near Eastern texts relating to the Old Testament,* ed. J. B. Pritchard, 3rd edn, Princeton, NJ 1969
AnnPisa	*Annali della Scuola normale superiore di Pisa*
ANRW	*Aufstieg und Niedergang der römischen Welt,* ed. H. Temporini, Berlin 1972–
AntK	*Antike Kunst*
AntW	*Antike Welt. Zeitschrift für Archäologie und Kulturgeschichte*
AR	*Archaeological Reports*
ArchCl	*Archeologia classica*
ArchDelt	*Archaiologikon deltion*
ArchEph	*Archaiologike ephemeris*
ARV²	J. D. Beazley, *Attic red-figure vase-painters,* 2nd edn, Oxford 1963
ASAtene	*Annuario della Scuola Archeologica di Atene e delle Missioni Italiane in Oriente*

BAR-IS	British archaeological reports, International series
BCH	*Bulletin de correspondance hellénique*
BdA	*Bollettino d'arte*
BE	*Bulletin épigraphique*
BEFAR	Bibliothèque des Ecoles françaises d'Athènes et de Rome
BICS	*Bulletin of the Institute of Classical Studies of the University of London*
BonnJbb	*Bonner Jahrbücher des Rheinischen Landesmuseums in Bonn und des Vereins von Altertumsfreunden im Rheinlande*
Boreas	*Boreas. Münstersche Beiträge zur Archäologie*
Boreas	Boreas. Uppsala Studies in Ancient Mediterranean and Near Eastern Civilizations
BSA	*Annual of the British School at Athens*
Chiron	*Chiron. Mitteilungen der Kommission für alte Geschichte und Epigraphik des Deutschen Archäologischen Instituts*
ClAnt	*Classical Antiquity*
ClMed	*Classica et Mediaevalia. Revue danoise de philologie et d'histoire*
CQ	*Classical Quarterly*
CRAI	*Comptes rendus des séances de l'Académie des Inscriptions et Belles-lettres*
CronCatania	*Cronache di archeologia e di storia dell'arte, Università di Catania*
CSCA	*California Studies in Classical Archaeology*
EAD	*Exploration archéologique de Délos faite par l'Ecole française d'Athènes*
EchCl	*Echos du monde classique. Classical Views*
EPRO	Etudes préliminaires aux religions orientales dans l'Empire romain, Leiden 1961–
FdD	*Fouilles de Delphes*
FGrHist	*Fragmente der griechischen Historiker*, ed. F. Jacoby, Berlin 1923–
FHG	K. Müller, *Fragmenta historicorum graecorum*, Frankfurt 1975 (reprint of 1841–1938 editions)
GGM	*Geographi Graeci Minores*, ed. C. Müller, Paris 1855–61
GöttNachr	*Nachrichten von der Gesellschaft der Wissenschaften zu Göttingen*
GRBS	*Greek, Roman and Byzantine Studies*
Hell.	*Hellenika*
Hephaistos	*Hephaistos. Kritische Zeitschrift zur Theorie und Praxis der Archäologie und angrenzender Wissenschaften*
Hesperia	*Hesperia. Journal of the American School of Classical Studies at Athens*

HomHHerm	*The Homeric Hymn to Hermes*
HomHAp	*The Homeric Hymn to Apollo*
HomHAphr	*The Homeric Hymn to Aphrodite*
HSCP	*Harvard Studies in Classical Philology*
HSPh	*= HSCP*
IG	*Inscriptiones graecae*
IM	Isthmia Museum
IstForsch	Istanbuler Forschungen
IstMitt	*Istanbuler Mitteilungen*
JdI	*Jahrbuch des Deutschen archäologischen Instituts*
JFA	*Journal of Field Archaeology*
JHS	*Journal of Hellenic Studies*
JPR	*Journal of Prehistoric Religion*
JRAI	*Journal of the Royal Anthropological Institute*
JRGZM	*Jahrbuch des Römisch-Germanischen Zentralmuseums, Mainz*
Kernos	*Kernos. Revue internationale et pluridisciplinaire de religion grecque antique*
Klio	*Klio. Beiträge zur alten Geschichte*
Kokalos	*Kokalos. Studi pubblicati dall'Istituto di storia antica dell'Università di Palermo*
LIMC	*Lexicon iconographicum mythologiae classicae*, Zurich and Munich 1974–
MAI	*= CRAI*
MarbWPr	*Marburger Winckelmann-Programm*
Meded	*Mededeelingen van het Nederlands Historisch Instituut te Rome*
MEFRA	*Mélanges de l'Ecole Française de Rome, Antiquité*
MemLinc	*Memorie. Atti della Accademia nazionale dei Lincei, Classe di scienze morali, storiche e filologiche*
MM	*Madrider Mitteilungen*
MusHelv	*Museum Helveticum*
NSc	*Notizie degli scavi di antichità*
OF	Olympische Forschungen
OJA	*Oxford Journal of Archaeology*
ÖJh	*Jahreshefte des Österreichischen Archäologischen Instituts in Wien*
OpAth	*Opuscula Atheniensia*
Palladio	*Palladio. Rivista di storia dell'architettura*
PBF	*Prähistorische Bronzefunde*, ed. H. Müller-Karpe and A. Jockenhövel, Munich
Phoenix	*Phoenix. The Classical Association of Canada*
P.Ox.	*Oxyrhynchus Papyri*, ed. B. P. Grenfell and A. S. Hunt, 1898–

PP	*La parola del passato*
Prakt	*Praktika tes en Athenais Archaiologikes Hetaireias*
RA	*Revue archéologique*
RE	*Paulys Realencyclopädie der classischen Altertumswissenschaft*, ed. G. Wissowa, W. Kroll, K. Mittelhaus and K. Ziegler
REG	*Revue des études grecques*
RendLinc	*Atti dell'Accademia nazionale dei Lincei. Rendiconti*
RGVV	Religionsgeschichtliche Versuche und Vorarbeiten
RheinMus	*Rheinisches Museum für Philologie*
RHR	*Revue de l'histoire des religions*
RivIstArch	*Rivista dell'Istituto Nazionale d'Archeologia e Storia dell'Arte*
RM	*Mitteilungen des Deutschen Archäologischen Instituts, Römische Abteilung*
SicArch	*Sicilia archeologica*
SIG	W. Dittenberger, *Sylloge inscriptionum Graecarum*, 3rd edn, Leipzig 1915–24
SIMA	Studies in Mediterranean archaeology
SMEA	*Studi micenei ed egeo-anatolici*
TransAmPhilSoc	*Transactions of the American Philosophical Society*
Xenia	*Xenia. Semestrale di antichità*
ZPE	*Zeitschrift für Papyrologie und Epigraphik*

1

Early sanctuaries, the eighth century and ritual space

Fragments of a discourse

Christiane Sourvinou-Inwood

This chapter is a self-contained fragment of a wider investigation into early Greek sanctuaries, cult in the Dark Ages[1] and the relationship between Bronze Age and historical Greek religion. Restrictions of space force me to limit its scope to a brief sketch of some aspects of the *Problematik* and to a systematic consideration of one problem which has wide-ranging implications.

Because of the scarcity of the evidence, scholars have often implicitly constructed Dark Age religion with reference to Minoan, Mycenaean and, especially, historical Greek religion. The scant Dark Age data are sometimes studied through filters implicitly shaped by certain (implicit or explicit) perceptions about what Dark Age society and religion 'must have been like'. Since we do not view data neutrally, but through perceptual filters shaped by culturally determined assumptions, this leads to serious distortions, as does any investigation based on model-building on the basis of probabilities and what appear to be reasonable assumptions: for all these notions and their application are inevitably radically culturally determined and any reconstruction which depends on them reflects modern preconceptions rather than the ancient realities. If one asks 'can these (fragmentary and problematic) data fit model A?' it is possible to structure those data in such a way, and, consciously and/or unconsciously, to make such adjustments as to permit an affirmative answer. But this is a different matter from the construction 'A' being the best explanation after a rigorous examination of all the data without *a priori* models and assumptions, and by means of a methodology designed to limit as much as possible the distorting effects of cultural determination.[2] It is therefore crucial to clear the ground of false assumptions and misconceptions, which can become false structuring centres and create false perceptual filters that structure the discourse in insidious ways.

One particularly insidious mode of distortion is the implicit presumption that the limitations of the evidence give licence to downgrade implicitly its importance, as in interpretative discourses which, after systematic analysis, can ultimately be revealed to have been sustained by the deeply hidden assumption that unless a particular thesis can be conclusively disproved – which very rarely happens in this period – it must be presumed to be correct, that if the contrary view cannot be conclusively proven it can be presumed to be wrong even when the, perhaps inconclusive, evidence points in its favour.

One common fallacy, implicit in some recent discussions of early Greek sanctuaries, which creates serious problems for the interpretation of the evidence is the assumption – implicit or explicit – that the forms that eventually became established as canonical (albeit not even then universal) in later Greek religion are the defining characteristics of Greek sanctuaries. This centres the discourse on certain unexamined expectations about what we should find in Dark Age sanctuaries which can seriously distort our reading of the data.

I will now consider a recent hypothesis which, I will argue, falsifies radically the ancient realities. The moderate version was put forward by de Polignac, the extremist version by Morris, who based a wide-ranging theory on it.[3] De Polignac suggested that in the Dark Ages there was a certain spatial indeterminacy in cult, and that the Greek sanctuary as a discrete area for religious purposes emerged in the eighth century. I shall first discuss the objections to de Polignac's thesis and then consider its more extreme version.[4]

A central argument supporting de Polignac's view on sacred space is the Homeric passage *Odyssey* 3.5ff. in which the Pylians are conducting a sacrifice by the sea, on the beach. This de Polignac takes as evidence that there was no sanctuary and no altar, no strictly defined sacred space, that after the rite had ended nothing distinguished the spot where it had taken place from its surroundings. But this interpretation of the Odyssean passage is far from compelling. First, altars by the sea, on the beach, are well known in Homer,[5] as they are in later periods (cf. e.g. *Homeric Hymn to Apollo* 490, 495–6, 508, 516); such altars, like all altars, stood on marked-off sacred ground.[6] Second, *theo d' epi meria ekaion* implies an altar. It is true that the altar is not explicitly mentioned, but this is no detailed description of the sacrifice (the actual sacrifice is only referred to in verses 7–9 and the killing of the animal is not mentioned either). The poet's choices were determined by the flow of the poem and not by the considerations that may appear significant to a modern historian of religion: an element like the altar would have been taken for granted, 'read into' the narrative, by an audience in whose assumptions 'sacrifice' was inextricably associated with 'altar'. This 'omission' is not unique. In *Iliad* 2.427 the altar is not explicitly mentioned either, but we know this is what both poet and audience were thinking in terms of – for there were altars on the beach by the ships (*Iliad* 11.806–8). In *Odyssey* 3.461 too, in the detailed description of Nestor's private sacrifice – in contrast to the communal sacrifice on the beach[7] – the altar is simply alluded to through *amphi* on l.429.[8] It is unclear[9] whether this sacrifice is to be envisaged inside the courtyard enclosure, in which case the sacrifice is taking place at the altar in the house courtyard dedicated to Zeus Herkeios, or outside it, in which case we should visualize something comparable to the Classical altar in front of houses.[10] In *Iliad* 11.773–5 Peleus sacrifices to Zeus in the enclosure of the court at an altar[11] which is not explicitly mentioned; the altar in the house courtyard is mentioned and named as the altar of Zeus Herkeios at *Odyssey* 22.334–6.[12]

What *Odyssey* 3.5ff. does mention is an element unique in Homer which points the interpretation of this passage in the opposite direction from that of the view criticized here: the organization of the Pylians into nine groups of five hundred persons each, with each of the groups providing nine bulls for sacrifice. This has been rightly perceived[13] to reflect an organization into groups for cult activities which was characteristic of the polis. The scholium *ad Od.* 3.7 associates the nine groups with the nine cities of Nestor's kingdom, and it is indeed likely[14] that the author of these verses had in mind the verses of the 'Catalogue of Ships' (*Iliad* 2.591ff.). However, this does not affect the argument, for it is the notion of the communal sacrifice in groups/subdivisions of the polity that pertains to the sacrificial context of the polis. In my view we have a conflation here, on the one hand of polis organization and participation in a communal polis sacrifice of the subdivisions into which the polis is articulated, and on the other of the notion of the nine poleis that made up Nestor's kingdom. This creates the presumption that, far from reflecting some older ritual form, this passage incorporates some of the latest Homeric material, and therefore that the poet and the audience would inevitably have been thinking in terms of an altar of the kind established in their own cultic reality – and deeply embedded in the epics.

That this passage reflects a polis organization has also been suggested on the basis of a purely spatial element. The nine subdivisions of the Pylians in this passage are referred to by means of the word *hedrai* (v. 7). *Hedra* means, of course, 'seat', but also 'place, station', that is, 'seat' in the sense of abode. In this passage (*hedrai* also occurs at v. 31) it is clearly both, seats which form a station in which each group/subdivision of the Pylians is sitting. Kolb[15] takes *hedrai* here to indicate stone seats or benches[16] which form an agora inside a *temenos* dedicated to Poseidon. A sanctuary of Poseidon surrounded by the agora by the sea is also described in *Odyssey* 6.266 (cf. also 8.5), in the polis of the Phaeacians. And at Troy the altars are by the sea in or near their agora (*Iliad* 11.806–8).[17] The fact that the Pylian subdivisions have separate segments of space with seats, and that the groups are referred to through a reference to these 'stations', indicates an organization of the sacred space which may have had some permanent form. Whether or not this is the case, it is extremely implausible that the eighth-century poet (who, whatever traditional material he may have deployed in this passage, operated through filters shaped by, and certainly deployed elements belonging to, the sacrificial context of the polis) was thinking of a sacrifice not conducted at a permanent altar – or that the audience would have so understood it.[18]

The text, then, when perceived through the assumptions of the poet and his contemporary audience, did not entail the absence of an altar and cannot support the notion that in the Dark Ages and the earlier eighth century BC sacred space was indeterminate. In eighth-century eyes the spatial context of the sacrifice in *Odyssey* 3.5ff. would have been either an altar similar to the altars of the Archaic and Classical periods which were set up both in the countryside and within the city in various parts of the public space, or a *temenos* with an altar. The latter is more likely; this sacrifice was probably visualized as taking place in a *temenos* of Poseidon by the sea, like all early *temene* centred on an altar. Sanctuaries and shrines of Poseidon by the sea were well known in the historical period.[19]

The other arguments mentioned by de Polignac in support of the view that Homer reflects above all a state of affairs in which sacred space was indeterminate are as follows. First, that the most common sacred place in the Homeric poems was the sacred *alsos* (grove), which he does not consider to be a strictly defined and organized space, adding that many of these places remained in this wild and little differentiated state throughout antiquity, reserved for a generally more humble or local piety than the 'sanctuaires élaborés pour la collectivité'. He cites as an example the *alsos* of the Eumenides in Sophocles' *Oedipus at Colonus*. He adds that temples are rare in Homer.[20]

However, this picture is not correct. First, with regard to the *alsos*,[21] it is not the case that a cult-place referred to as *alsos* has no altar.[22] In the *Homeric Hymn to Apollo* 384–5, for example, Apollo constructs an altar to himself in an *alsos* by a *krene*. Thus a sacred grove with an altar is a particular version of the altar-*temenos* which was the most common form of early Greek sanctuary. In Homer the altar-*temenos* (*temenos* + altar) is the most deeply embedded type of cult-place, as is shown by the existence of the formula *entha de hoi temenos bomos te thyeeis*.[23] Also altar-*temene* sometimes developed into important historical sanctuaries – like other altar-*temene*. One such important historical sanctuary, which began with a grove and an altar, is the sanctuary of Olympia.[24] In the fully developed *temene* the sacred grove[25] was usually one of the elements of the sanctuary. An example of this development is offered by the sacred grove of Poseidon at Onchestos, mentioned in *Iliad* 2.506 as well as in the Homeric hymns to Apollo and Hermes,[26] which did not contain any buildings until the very latest Archaic times: the earliest phase of the temple is dated to the end of the sixth century BC.[27] As for the grove of the Eumenides in Sophocles' *Oedipus at Colonus*, vv. 6–7 and 171–96 (cf. 39–40; 123–5) make it absolutely clear that the space of the sacred grove is indeed set apart and very clearly defined.

Consequently, the notion that such sacred groves were not sanctuaries in the sense of a strictly defined sacred space set apart, and that this space was somehow indeterminate ritual space, is mistaken, as is the notion that such *temene* are only the objects of humble or strictly local piety. The same is true of cave sanctuaries to which de Polignac[28] compares the sacred groves. That they are not always either humble or local is shown, for example, by the shrine of Pan and the Nymphs at the Corycian cave.[29] Of course, special circumstances pertained at this sanctuary, which functioned in the shadow of the Delphic one; but this simply explains why, it does not alter the fact that, cave sanctuaries could attract that type of devotion. This cult also shows[30] that it is incorrect that 'nature shrines' such as cave sanctuaries are survivals of earlier practices pertaining to humble local piety, since its cult begins in the late seventh century BC.[31] It is not correct that cave sanctuaries do not involve organized, defined space; the positioning of the altar in front of the cave[32] is homologous to the location of the altar in front of the temple.[33]

In Homer, as later, different types of cult-space are found, temples in the city as well as sacred groves.[34] In *Odyssey* 6.7–10 it is taken for granted that when a polis is founded temples are built.[35] But there can be no doubt that the sanctuary with altar – with or without a temple – is the regular, taken-for-granted focus of religious activity. Consequently, the Homeric evidence cannot support the theory of the indeterminacy of religious space. I cannot discuss here the hypothesis that the Homeric poems reflect the world of the eighth century BC only – or that which dates their final version to the seventh century BC. In my view, the poems incorporated material from many periods, perceived, articulated and reshaped through the perceptual filters of the eighth century – as it had been before through the filters of each successive generation of poets who had handled it. But I must stress that this question cannot affect my argument. For I am not using the Homeric evidence positively, to prove something, but only negatively, to show that despite claims to the contrary, there is nothing in the Homeric poems to support the view that sacred space had been indeterminate in the Dark Ages and the earlier eighth century.

I now turn to the extremist version of this theory formulated by Morris, who believes that, while in the Dark Ages cult activity was characterized by spatial indeterminacy, in the eighth century the relationship between sacred space and the living space of men changed, that around 700 BC the living space became 'more sharply differentiated from the sacred space of the gods and the dead', with 'the most obvious change' being 'the rise of the discrete area for religious purposes – the emergence of the Greek sanctuary', which he places from the second half of the eighth century BC onwards. This, he claims, suggests 'that a new system of classification was growing up'.[36] He does admit (1989, 317) that 'there is evidence for a few tenth- and ninth-century shrines, but these are still rare, and generally they were divorced from settlements'. My list of Dark Age shrines (which I cannot set out here) shows that they are not rare and that their number is constantly growing, which suggests that perceptual bias may have been one of the reasons why so few had been identified before.

Morris claims that within settlements cult was domestic.[37] The only plausible candidate for a Dark Age domestic building housing cult is Unit IV–1 at Nichoria which has been mostly interpreted as a chieftain's house.[38] However, there are two parameters of major uncertainty. First, the building's identification as a chieftain's house is far from definite. As we shall see, the presence of domestic-type objects does not in itself demonstrate a domestic, and exclude a cultic, function. Second, even if the building had been a chieftain's house we cannot be certain that the cult practised there had been communal rather than domestic. For we cannot be certain that the focus of the cult, the circular stone platform with a layer of carbonized material on top, did not have a specialized funerary and/or domestic rather than generally cultic use. For the circular stone platform has been identified by Hägg as a cult-structure connected with the cult of the ancestors converging towards the hero-cult.[39] Such platforms were found over graves, but also in settlements – in the Dark Ages also over a Protogeometric apsidal building at Asine – and this could suggest that this was a modality of Dark Age ancestor cult[40] which would have been part, not of community cult, but of a 'domestic' (in the sense of Classical *oikos*-type) cult.

The existence of domestic Dark Age cult does not, of course, invalidate the view that communal cult was practised in a separate space, for the two categories are known to coexist in earlier and later Greek religion – and also in Homer. But the existence of communal cult in a separate ritual space does invalidate Morris's hypothesis, because it shows that the discrete ritual space which that hypothesis necessitates should not exist before the eighth century BC in fact does so. Morris claims (1989) that the (few, as he alleges) existing Dark Age sanctuaries were 'rustic' and 'divorced' from settlements. The implication is that their existence does not invalidate his thesis. I will try to show that he has got his facts wrong on Dark Age sanctuaries and that, even if we were to ignore this, his thesis is in any case untenable.

First, even if we leave aside the sanctuaries that emerged from the late ninth century to *c.* 750 BC, and limit ourselves to the earlier period, it is clear that there were indeed sanctuaries in settlements in Dark Age Greece. The sanctuary of Karphi is, of course, part of a settlement.[41] Morris doubts the identification of the building as a temple, and this raises a very important issue which I hope to develop further elsewhere. His formulation of these doubts in the corrected version (cf. n. 52) of the 1989 paper (p. 318) is slightly more refined than that of the original paper of 1987; he now acknowledges that, as I pointed out in my critique of his article (cf. n. 52), it is wrong to doubt the identification on the grounds that 'spindle whorls, stone tools and a typical domestic assemblage were found here'. For such assemblages *characterize* Minoan and Mycenaean sanctuaries whose identity as sanctuaries is incontrovertibly established,[42] and Karphi is a shrine in the Minoan tradition. In addition, the presence of domestic objects can also be associated with historical Greek sanctuaries.[43] Nor should we forget in this connection that workshops were associated with Greek sanctuaries from an early period.[44] Morris chose to ignore the fact that the evidence for the temple identification includes a low square stone altar in the court.[45]

Since some of the other candidates for the status of intramural sanctuary necessitate lengthier discussions, I will only mention one more Dark Age communal place of worship within a settlement. At Asine[46] near fat, charcoal-filled soil, a pithos was found containing bones of mammals such as ox, sheep, goat and pig; and from the area outside also of donkey, dog, boar, bird, a murex shell. A pit was connected with the pithos, kernoi were found nearby, and generally in that vicinity kalathoi. As Wells convincingly concludes,[47] the condition of the soil in combination with the charcoal and the many bones suggests that sacrifices had taken place to the west of the pithos. The burnt clay bordering the area to the south could then be the lining of a sacrificial area burnt during the cult practices. Kernoi and kalathoi are also associated with religious practices. The pithos then, Wells rightly suggests, had been intentionally set up – a fact to which the ring of stones around it testifies – perhaps as a receptacle for what was discarded from the cult practices, including bones of the sacrificial animals and pottery. It is clear that there are excellent reasons for thinking that in early Protogeometric Asine this was an area set aside for religious purposes in which communal cult activities took place.

We can also be certain that other Dark Age sanctuaries (e.g. the Amyklaion[48] and the sanctuary of Artemis at Mounichia[49] – two cases which do not need further clarification) were not rustic or isolated, but were located either in, or in the vicinity of, a settlement – it is not always clear which. Consequently, it would appear that the Greek sanctuary in all its three forms, intramural, periurban and extraurban, emerged in the Dark Ages.

Moreover, even if no Dark Age sanctuary inside a settlement had been discovered, it would have been methodologically dubious to conclude that none had existed – let alone build grandiose theories on this assumption. *Argumenta ex silentio* are generally of dubious validity, but in this particular instance they are worthless; for the evidence is exiguous and often difficult to interpret. It is not the case that many Dark Age settlements are known and excavated and have produced no evidence of cult-places. On the contrary, despite the difficulties in the identification of cult-units in a period in which, first, various structures are flimsy and thus more easily destroyed or missed, and second, the structures and modalities of cult have not yet crystallized into the forms that will eventually become canonical, so that we cannot be certain of the diagnostic features of early Greek cult-areas and buildings, we do have some evidence for cult-places within settlements; and this, in the circumstances, acquires even greater significance.

Finally, Morris's thesis relies on an entirely arbitrary – and inevitably culturally determined – radical distinction between sanctuaries within the settlement and 'rustic sanctuaries' divorced from settlements. This distinction reflects modern perceptions of space and is not supported by Greek conceptual articulations. All three categories of sanctuary (intramural, peri-urban, extraurban) are found both in historical and in Mycenaean Greece, and what evidence there is suggests that the same was true in the Dark Ages. The status of a sanctuary's location could change without problem, without measures being taken to avoid this happening (thus, for example, the peri-urban sanctuary at Koukounaries came to be enclosed by the relocated settlement).[50]

Consequently, Morris's theory about Dark Age cult-places is untenable. The reality of the evidence is that, strikingly, the image of cult activity suggested by the finds in the sanctuaries coincides with the image reflected in the Homeric epics. The archaeological evidence suggests that most Dark Age sanctuaries consisted of – and all included – a *temenos* with altar. In Homer, we saw, the most deeply rooted type of cult-place is a *temenos* focused on an altar, which suggests that this type of cult-place was most deeply embedded in the material that went into the making of the epics and continued to be common in the eighth century. The same picture is suggested by the archaeological evidence, which shows that the temple is primarily a late ninth- and eighth-century phenomenon – and thus corresponds to the most recent layer of the epic material. I must stress that the cultic situation in the eighth century also moulded the filters through which all Homeric material was shaped by the poet and understood by his audience.

I now turn to Morris's claims that profound changes in practices took place in the eighth century, that

> in the late eighth century the boundaries between the gods, men and the dead began to harden, both physically and conceptually. . . . The living space was more sharply differentiated from the sacred spaces of the gods and the dead and the boundaries emphasized by physical barriers;

and that this alleged change in attitude towards 'the sacred' is the cause of the hardening of the boundaries between the living and the dead, manifested in the cessation of intramural burial and relocation of the cemeteries.[51] The changes concerning cemeteries form a part of the case Morris set up against my own interpretation of a set of very complex phenomena pertaining to the funerary sphere which, I argued, took place gradually over a long period of time; he needed to challenge my thesis in order to defend his own much simpler model of funerary behaviour and attitudes which is based on a schematic and culturally determined structuring of the data.[52] In this

8

endeavour he took the alleged changes in sanctuaries as a given and went on from there.

I had myself argued (see *supra* n. 52) that a hardening of the boundaries between the living and the dead had taken place, though I suggested that it took a very long time and did not crystallize until the Archaic period. I offered an explanation for this phenomenon in terms of a slow, complex and partial change in the attitudes towards the dead, for which there is a lot of other evidence. I will be arguing elsewhere that Morris's interpretation of the cessation of intramural burials cannot stand even if we were to leave aside the fact that the alleged change pertaining to sanctuaries did not take place. But in any case, even if his theory about the emergence of the Greek sanctuary had not been fallacious, his thesis that from *c.* 750 BC onwards the living space of men is more sharply separated and differentiated from the sacred space of the gods, comparably to the establishment of extramural burial, and that both signal a different symbolic articulation of the cosmos, can only be sustained if we ignore entirely a very important Greek cultic modality in Archaic and Classical Greek religion: the presence of the sacred, of cultic foci – such as altars and Herms – all over the living space of the polis;[53] not only the *hestia* and private altars of *oikos* cult in houses, but also in the streets, in public buildings, in gymnasia, and in the agora.[54] Far from there being a greater separation between the spaces of the gods and of men from the second half of the eighth century onwards, in the polis the gods and the heroes were, on the contrary, installed at the very centre of the living space of the polis and its institutions, which are often focused on a sacred structure. I give some examples of this modality, of this interweaving of the sacred and the non-sacred, in the Appendix, pp. 12–13.

Morris could claim that, even though living space and sacred space were intermeshed in both the domestic and the public domain, there had nevertheless been a change in the eighth century, in that one particular type of sacred space was separated from the living space to create a discrete sacred space, the sanctuary. However, even if this were correct – and, we saw, it is not – this theory could not stand for a variety of independent reasons. First, sanctuaries themselves could include non-strictly sacred spaces within their *periboloi*. Second, serious difficulties arise from the notion of a change in the boundedness of space allotted to gods, men and the dead, reflecting a new symbolic classification, which would have affected only one segment of religious behaviour and allotment of sacred space, while the others manifest, if anything, a strengthening of the opposite tendency. Finally, the correlative of this state of affairs would not have been the disappearance of intramural burials; on the contrary, it would have been the existence of both intramural and extramural cemeteries, with intramural burials interspersed in the living space of the polis persisting throughout.

In support of his thesis of change Morris stresses the appearance of *temenos* walls and temples. However, in order to assess whether or not a significant change did take place without relying on our own culturally determined judgements we must first determine what are the important elements, the defining characteristics, of the Greek sanctuary as we know it from the historical period.

First, the *peribolos*, the boundary wall. Throughout the Archaic and Classical periods a *peribolos* that went all the way round was not an essential element of the sanctuary; the sacred space could be marked by a series of marker stones, with entry involving the crossing of an imaginary line between two of them.[55] In some sanctuaries a *peribolos* was built at a later stage in the sanctuary's history – in different periods in the different sanctuaries, so that it is not possible to imagine that the time when *periboloi* were built signals a change in the mentality pertaining to religious space. The demarcation involving *horoi*, boundary stones, is not symbolically different from that through a *peribolos*, but of course the former disappear more easily, and, of course, leave no remains in an illiterate age.[56]

Second, the temple is not an essential religious part of the Greek sanctuary – it is the altar which is essential.[57] Hence most sanctuaries are of earlier date than their temples,[58] and some never acquired a temple,[59] among them sanctuaries housing far from insignificant cults.[60] In general, the *temenos* with an altar and without a temple precedes the 'temple + altar *temenos*'.[61] The latter became the norm quite soon, but as the different rhythms with which different sanctuaries acquired temples (and the fact that some never did) show, the emergence of the temple was not the result of a religious change involving a change in the articulation of sacred space indicative of a change in the relationship between men and the sacred. It was part of monumentalization – and eventual codification – of Greek sanctuaries in the eighth century.

From the eighth century onwards there was a continuous trend towards monumentality in Greek sanctuaries. Though the altar was the most essential cultic element in the *temenos*, it gradually lost its spatial prominence and centrality in favour of the physically more impressive temple.[62] The sacrificial area, originally the space west of the altar up to the west boundary, and later the space west of the altar up to the temple, also changed its position in the course of time in the Archaic *temenos* (through various stages in the different sanctuaries). Thus the altar moved from a central position to an eastward peripheral one, the temple from a westward peripheral to a central one, and the sacrificial area from a westward to an eastward peripheral one.[63] Since we know the respective functions of temple and altar through this period, we know that these changes do not entail a change in ritual or in the perception of sacred space.

A crucial factor affecting the physical appearance of the sanctuary is its worshipping group, the size, needs and aspirations of the (developing) polis and the images of itself it created in the local and the pan-Hellenic sanctuaries. Changes in the size of the sanctuary and its relationship to the surrounding settlement, when there was one, do not signal changes in the perception of sacred space: both changed when the sanctuary needed to expand.[64] Likewise, the presence or absence and number of other buildings (housing offerings, dining rooms and the like) do not involve different perceptions of religious space – nor does their location (whether or not they were in a separate area from that of strict sanctity). Sanctuaries are either simple, consisting of the cultic area only, or composite, including a secondary area containing non-essential buildings – usually an addition to the basic area.[65] This depended on their function (e.g. whether they were local or the seat of pan-Hellenic Games, oracular or not) and popularity.

It is clear, then, that neither *temenos* wall nor temple were essential defining characteristics of the Greek sanctuary. What was fundamental in Greek sanctuaries, what defined a sanctuary in the Greek religious mentality, was that it was a sacred space centred around an altar, sometimes including another sacred focus such as a tree or stone, a spring or cave.

There were indeed observable changes in the eighth century pertaining to sanctuaries. First, many new sanctuaries emerged, some, like Delphi, at the end of the ninth century, others in the course of the eighth. Second, spatial reorganization took place in some earlier sanctuaries. Third, votive offerings became very common everywhere. Finally, we see the beginning of the monumentalization of forms in the sanctuaries, and the emergence of the temple as an element in some sanctuaries – though many sanctuaries did not acquire a temple until much later. This goes together with what can be seen as a certain crystallization of forms, a large topic which I cannot discuss here.

This chapter is a small part of a wider discourse in which I argue that early Greek sanctuaries developed out of the sanctuaries of the Dark Ages through a continuous process of development and change without rupture; that the multifaceted changes observed in eighth-century sanctuaries and the great increase in their number took place in interaction with, in the context, and as a result, of, a set of circumstances of which the emergence of the polis was the most important.

The polis put religion at its centre, forged its identity through religion.[66] This caused some sanctuaries to become a focus for the self-definition of the polis, and thus aggrandized them and monumentalized them. It also led to the foundation of more sanctuaries, to serve specific functions, for example to 'sanctify' a frontier, or to provide for particular needs; the cults were not necessarily new, but they may have been split off, given a separate space (symbolically connected with the old) when there was some need. Also, in this context, in which the significance and symbolic importance of religion were greatly enhanced, votive offerings, which represented a more permanently attested form of worship, acquired increased significance and thus increased very substantially. Second, the greater mobility and interaction within the Greek world and outside it, together with the greater consciousness of a Greek identity and interest in the heroic past, led to a greater interaction between sanctuaries in different places, to the spreading of ideas within the Greek world (for example, from Crete to the mainland and the islands) and from outside it, and to a cross-influence that led to a certain crystallization of forms, further enhanced by the emergence of the pan-Hellenic religious dimension, at the very least in literature such as the Homeric poems and Hesiod, correlative with the perception of Greekness through communality of religion, and perhaps also as a result of the radiation of influence of sanctuaries like Delphi which acquired great prestige all over Greece. In addition, colonization, which created the need to set up new polis-defining sanctuaries in new lands, would have further enhanced this process.

In these circumstances, I submit, out of materially humble beginnings, were the great Greek sanctuaries created over the centuries.

APPENDIX: THE INTERWEAVING OF SACRED AND NON-SACRED SPACE

The agora has religious as well as political and other functions.[67] Sacred space and not strictly sacred civic space are tightly enmeshed, as cultic and not strictly cultic activities cannot be separated radically, either spatially or semantically. One category of agora cults is divine cults, another heroic cults.[68] At Megara Hyblaea the space for the agora, which was laid out in the second half of the seventh century, had been reserved and defined from the very beginning.[69] Its focus seems to have been a sacred space eventually incorporated in the heroon.[70] The excavators suggested that the religious function of the agora may have asserted itself first.[71]

In many poleis the common hearth of the polis, the *koine hestia*, which was also an altar-hearth for Hestia, was located in the prytaneion,[72] a building which was also, though not primarily, religious in character. Its religious function[73] was not limited to its primary association with the *koine hestia* and Hestia; at Naukratis, for example, part of the annual festivals of Dionysos and Apollo were celebrated in the prytaneion. At Kos the hearth-altar of Hestia was in the agora, clearly not in a building, and it was the focus of an important ritual during the festival of Zeus Polieus.[74] In the agora of Pharae a prophetic *hestia* stood in front of the statue of Hermes.[75] Another interesting altar in an agora is the Archaic *eschara* near the altar of the Twelve Gods in the Athenian Agora (whatever its precise function may have been[76]). The altar of Zeus Agoraios in the Athenian Agora originally stood in the Pnyx, the place of Assembly of the Ekklesia.[77] The *lithos*-altar in the Agora, where the archontes swore the oath[78] and on which were set the pieces of a sacrificial victim, is another sacred element with an important role in the Agora.

According to Xen. *Hell.* 2.3.52–5 there was an altar in the bouleuterion in

Athens, referred to as *hestia* in 2.3.52 and *bomos* in 2.3.53, 55. Antiphon 6.45 says there was in the bouleuterion a *hieron* of Zeus Boulaios and Athena Boulaia, where the *bouleutai* prayed as they went in.[79] The altar of Zeus Herkeios stood in front of the Dipylon gate, near the Pompeion.[80] In the gymnasia there were altars and Herms.[81] Indeed the association between gymnasia and cult was clearly close, and in them, at least to some extent, sacred and non-sacred were interwoven. Thus, of the famous Athenian suburban gymnasia, the Lykeion was a cult-place for Apollo Lykeios, a gymnasium for athletes and an exercise area for troops.[82] The Kynosarges gymnasium was associated with the cult of Heracles (though the precise form of the association is not totally clear) to whom the gymnasium was consecrated.[83]

NOTES

I would like to thank Dr Christopher Pelling for his multifarious advice.

1 I shall be using the term 'Dark Ages' to denote conventionally, without any indication of darkness, the period between *c.* 1125 BC and *c.* 800 BC; for the alternative 'Early Iron Age' elides the important differentiation of the eighth century. The Dark Ages correspond to the periods called, after pottery phases, Submycenaean [in Crete Subminoan], Protogeometric, and, in Attic terms, Early Geometric and Middle Geometric I – with variations in other areas that do not concern us.

2 Of course, all reading and interpretation is to a greater or lesser degree culturally determined, but it is possible to limit very considerably cultural determination and its distorting effects. I am discussing this question elsewhere (*'Reading' Greek Culture: Texts and Images, Rituals and Myths* (Oxford 1991), ch. I).

3 F. de Polignac, *La naissance de la cité grecque* (Paris 1984) 27–31; I. Morris, *Burial and Ancient Society* (Cambridge 1987) 189–92; *idem*, 'Attitudes towards death in Archaic Greece', *ClAnt* 8 (1989) 317–18.

4 I hope to discuss elsewhere the theory that in the Dark Ages and in the first half of the eighth century community cult took place in the chieftain's house and that some temples replaced a ruler's dwelling or were transformed from rulers' dwellings into temples (cf. A. J. Mazarakis Ainian, 'Contribution à l'étude de l'architecture religieuse grecque des âges obscurs', *AntCl* 54 (1985) 5–48; *idem*, 'Geometric Eretria', *AntK* 30 (1987) 3–24; *idem*, 1988, 'Early Greek temples: their origin and function', in R. Hägg, N. Marinatos and G. Nordquist, eds, *Early Greek Cult Practice, Proceedings of the Fifth International Symposium at the Swedish Institute at Athens, 26–29 June 1986* (Stockholm 1988) 105–19).

5 See e.g. *Iliad* 11.806–8; *Iliad* 8.238–40. Cf. also *Iliad* 2.305–7 (altars around a *krene* near the sea).

6 See Soph., *Trach.* 237–8 and Sophocles, *Trachiniae*, ed. P. E. Easterling (Cambridge 1982) *ad loc*; cf. also v. 754.

7 See P. Stengel, *Die griechischen Kultusaltertümer* (Munich 1898), 2nd edn, 96.

8 On *amphi* cf. also S. West, A. Heubeck, A. Privitera, eds, *Omero. Odissea* vol. I (libri i–iv) (Milan 1981) 312 ad 429.

9 Ibid. 311 ad 407.

10 Which may or may not have been of the column-/pillar-shaped *bomos agyieus* type (cf. Stengel, *supra* n. 7, 14; M. P. Nilsson, *Geschichte der griechischen*

Religion I (1967), 3rd edn, 203 and n. 7); for a normal type altar in front of a house door see *La cité des images. Religion et société en Grèce antique* (Lausanne 1984) fig. 35.

11 See Stengel (*supra* n. 7) 14 and n. 3; A. J. B. Wace and F. H. Stubbings, *A Companion to Homer* (London 1962) 445–6.

12 On the altar of Zeus Herkeios in the house courtyard see Stengel (*supra* n. 7) 14 and n. 12.

13 Cf. D. Roussel, *Tribu et cité* (Paris 1976) 82 and 86 n. 21.

14 Cf. West, Heubeck, Privitera (*supra* n. 8) 280 ad 7–8.

15 F. Kolb, *Agora und Theater, Volks- und Festversammlung* (Berlin 1981) 13 n. 36.

16 Kolb (*supra* n. 15) 2–3 and n. 9, 5.

17 For R. Martin, *Recherches sur l'Agora grecque* (Paris 1951) 237, the scene took place in Poseidon's federal sanctuary; he saw it as an early example of the historical agorai which appear to be annexes of federal sanctuaries.

18 I should mention that the category 'temporary altar erected for one sacrifice' is not unknown in later Greek religion: see Stengel (*supra* n. 7) 14; and cf. esp. Paus. 9.3.7, where this involves a major official, pan-Boeotian, festival.

19 See e.g. Paus. 10.36.8, 2.34.10, 2.38.4; cf. also Strabo 637. Vv. 30–4 suggest that the poet was thinking in terms of a spatial separateness between the place where Telemachos disembarked and that of sacrifice; this would fit a *temenos*. V. 38 does not argue against a *temenos* hypothesis: the sand is a natural element comparable to other natural elements which form part of sanctuaries.

20 Polignac (*supra* n. 3) 28 n. 14.

21 On sacred *alse*: in Homer see E. T. Vermeule, *Götterkult, Archaeologia Homerica* III.V (Göttingen 1974) V105–6; in general: cf. Stengel (*supra* n. 7) 18.

22 Cf. Vermeule (*supra* n. 21) V106, 108.

23 *Odyssey* 8.363; *Iliad* 8.48, 23.148; see also *HomHAphr* 58–9. See also W. Burkert, *Greek Religion. Archaic and Classical* (Oxford 1985) 87.

24 Cf. A. Mallwitz, *Olympia und seine Bauten* (Munich 1972) 83.

25 On sacred groves in the historical period see F. Graf, *Nordionische Kulte* (Rome 1985) 43 and n. 198.

26 *Iliad* 2.506 mentions a *Posideion aglaon alsos* at Onchestos. *HomHAp* 230 also refers to the *Posideion aglaon alsos* at Onchestos, and *HomHHerm* 186–7 to *polyeraton alsos agnon . . . Gaieochou.* (Cf. also Hes. fr. 219 M-W.) This was a famous sanctuary of Poseidon (Pi., *I.* 4.21, 1.32–3; cf. also Pi., *Parth.* II.46 Snell-Maehler). On the sanctuary and cult at Onchestos: A. Schachter, *Cults of Boiotia*, vol. 2 (London 1986) 207–21. See also Vermeule (*supra* n. 21) V110 and n. 195; W. Burkert, *Structure and History in Greek Mythology and Ritual* (Berkeley 1979) 113 and 199 n. 199.

27 Schachter (*supra* n. 26) 212.

28 Polignac (*supra* n. 3) 28.

29 See P. Amandry, 'Le culte des Nymphes et de Pan à l'antre Corycien', in *Etudes delphiques, BCH* Suppl. 9 (1984) 395–425, esp. 424–5.

30 See also Amandry (*supra* n. 29) 406 no. VI, 408 no. X.

31 The cave had been in use in the Mycenaean period, and then there was an incontrovertible long gap until the 7th century.

32 Amandry (*supra* n. 29) 413–15, 412 fig. 4 (Corycian cave); Paus. 8.42.11 (Phigaleia); and see also the representation *Cité* (*supra* n. 10) 27 and fig. 31.

33 On the cave of Pan in Athens, the introduction of the cult and the organization of its space, see J. Travlos, *Pictorial Dictionary of Ancient Athens* (London 1971) 417.

34 For temples in Homer: Burkert (*supra* n. 23) 88–9; Vermeule (*supra* n. 21)

V106–8; Wace and Stubbings (*supra* n. 11) 446.

35 Cf. C. Mossé, 'Ithaque ou la naissance de la cité', *AION. Archeologia e storia antica* 2 (1980) 8; cf. 7–19 *passim* on Scheria.

36 Morris 1987 (*supra* n. 3) 189; Morris 1989 (*supra* n. 3) 317.

37 Morris 1987 (*supra* n. 3) 189; Morris 1989 (*supra* n. 3) 317–18. In Morris 1987 he states without qualification that it was domestic 'as was perhaps the case in Mycenaean times'. This is corrected in the final version (see *infra* n. 52) of 1989 to 'mainly domestic', the reference to the Mycenaean period has been taken out of the text, and an acknowledgement of the fact that there were urban non-domestic sanctuaries in the Mycenaean period was inserted in n. 133.

38 On Nichoria Unit IV-1: W. D. E. Coulson, in W. A. McDonald *et al.*, 'Excavations at Nichoria in Messenia, 1972–1973', *Hesperia* 44 (1975) 85–92; *idem*, in W. A. McDonald, W. D. E. Coulson and J. Rosser, eds, *Excavations at Nichoria in Southwest Greece*, vol. III: *Dark Age and Byzantine Occupation*, 19–42; cf. also C. Morgan, *Athletes and Oracles* (Cambridge 1990) 73–6; K. Fagerström, *Greek Iron Age Architecture* (Göteborg 1988) 34–5. I shall consider this building in my discussion of Mazarakis's theory (see *supra* n. 4).

39 R. Hägg, 'Funerary meals in the Geometric necropolis at Asine?', in R. Hägg, ed., *The Greek Renaissance of the Eighth Century* BC: *Tradition and Innovation. Proceedings of the Second International Symposium at the Swedish Institute in Athens*, 1–5 June 1981 (Stockholm 1983) 189–93; cf. also V. K. Lambrinoudakis, 'Veneration of ancestors in Geometric Naxos', in Hägg, Marinatos and Nordquist, eds, (*supra* n. 4) 235–45. On the distinction between cult of the ancestors and hero-cult see A. Snodgrass, 'Les origines du culte des héros dans la Grèce antique', in G. Gnoli and J. -P. Vernant, eds, *La mort, les morts dans les sociétés anciennes* (Cambridge 1982) 108.

40 In the case of a major community leader this may also have veered towards something approaching hero cult. It is this type of nexus of attitudes that was perhaps associated with the Lefkandi grave-monument which included a platform of this type (cf. *AR* 1983–4, 17; Lambrinoudakis, *supra* n. 39, 239).

41 On this sanctuary: H. W. and J. D. S. Pendlebury, and M. B. Money-Coutts, 'Excavations in the Plain of Lasithi II', *BSA* 38 (1937/8) 75–6; V. R. d'A. Desborough, *The Greek Dark Ages* (London 1972) 120–9 *passim*; B. Rutkowski, *The Cult-places of the Aegean* (New Haven 1986) 167; *idem*, 'The temple at Karphi', *SMEA* 26 (1987) 257–80. On the settlement cf. also K. Nowicki, 'History, topography and economy of Karphi', in E. Thomas, ed., *Forschungen zur Aegaeischen Vorgeschichte. Das Ende der mykenischen Welt* (Cologne 1987) 25–32.

42 See C. Renfrew, *The Archaeology of Cult. The Sanctuary at Phylakopi, BSA* Suppl. 18 (London 1985) 330; 388; Cf. e.g. Rutkowski 1986 (*supra* n. 41) 146; N. Marinatos, *Art and Religion in Thera* (Athens 1984) 22–4.

43 E.g. cooking pots and the like in *hestiatoria* in sanctuaries (cf. e.g. N. Bookidis, 'The sanctuary of Demeter and Kore: an archaeological approach to ancient religion', *AJA* 91 (1987) 480–1, and in this volume).

44 Cf. e.g. K. Kilian, 'Weihungen aus Eisen und Eisenverarbeitung im Heiligtum zu Philia (Thessalien)', in Hägg, ed. (*supra* n. 39) 131–47.

45 *BSA* 1937–8, 75, pl. XVII.3.

46 See on this B. Wells, *Asine II. Results of the Excavations East of the Acropolis 1970–1974.* Fasc. 4. *The Protogeometric period. Part 2. An Analysis of the Settlement* (Stockholm 1983) 28–9, esp. 34.

47 Wells (*supra* n. 46) 34.

48 On the location of the Amyklaion cf. K. Demakopoulou, Τὸ μυκηναϊκὸ ἱερὸ

στὸ 'Αμνκλαίο καὶ ἡ ΥΕ ΙΙΙΓ περίοδος στὴ Λακωνία (Athens 1982) 93, 95–6; P. Cartledge, *Sparta and Lakonia. A Regional History 1300–362 BC* (London 1979) 107–8.

49 On the sanctuary of Artemis at Mounichia cf. L. Palaiokrassa, Το 'ιερὸ τῆς 'Αρτέμιδος Μοννιχίας (Athens 1991) 90; *eadem*, 'Neue Befunde aus dem Heiligtum der Artemis Munichia', *AM* 104 (1989) 13–14.

50 D. U. Schilardi, 'The temple of Athena at Koukounaries', in Hägg, Marinatos and Nordquist, eds, (*supra* n. 4) 46; cf. also 41 with 45.

51 Cf. *supra* n. 3.

52 My argument is set out in: 'To die and enter the house of Hades: Homer, before and after', in J. Whaley, ed., *Mirrors of Mortality. Studies in the Social History of Death* (London 1981) 15–39; and: 'A trauma in flux: death in the eighth century and after', in Hägg, ed., (*supra* n. 39) 33–49. Morris wrote a critique of my studies, which he withdrew from publication in *JHS* after seeing an extremely brief version of my reply; he has now published a corrected version in *ClAnt* (*supra* n. 3). My reply, reshaped accordingly, will appear in my *Graves, Epitaphs, Charon and Beyond* (forthcoming).

53 See e.g. R. E. Wycherley, *How the Greeks Built Cities* (London and Basingstoke 1962) 87; Stengel (*supra* n. 7) 16.

54 Much of the evidence comes from the later Archaic and Classical periods, but this does not affect the argument, since on Morris's model there should have been progressively more separation between sacred space and living space, as there was exclusion of extramural burials. Moreover, what earlier evidence there is presents the same picture.

55 Cf. e.g. R. A. Tomlinson, *Greek Sanctuaries* (London 1976) 17.

56 Olympia, for example, cautions against taking the presence of a *peribolos* as indicating a new articulation of religious space: it first acquired a boundary wall in the late fourth century (A. Mallwitz and H. -V. Herrmann, eds, *Die Funde aus Olympia* (Athens 1980) 22; Mallwitz (*supra* n. 24) 121), and it is unlikely that there had been a visible boundary before then (cf. Tomlinson (*supra* n. 55) 57). Certainly no traces of one have survived (cf. Mallwitz 121; B. Bergquist, *The Archaic Greek Temenos. A Study of Structure and Function* (Lund 1967) 39).

57 Cf. e.g. Tomlinson (*supra* n. 55) 17.

58 Cf. e.g. the sanctuary of Athena Alea at Tegea: E. Østby, 'The Archaic temple of Athena Alea at Tegea', *OpAth* 16 (1986) 76, 97–102.

59 Cf. e.g. Bergquist (*supra* n. 56) 67, 122; Burkert (*supra* n. 23) 88, 89.

60 One of the latter is the sanctuary of Apollo Delphinios at Miletos, central to the cult of that polis (cf. F. Graf, 'Apollon Delphinios', *MusHelv* 36 (1979) 1–22) which did not acquire a temple until the Roman period (G. Kleiner, *Die Ruinen von Milet* (Berlin 1968) 33–5). On the Archaic altar cf. W. Koenigs, 'Reste archaischer Architektur in Milet', in W. Müller-Wiener, ed., *Milet 1899–1980. Ergebnisse, Probleme und Perspektiven einer Ausgrabung. Kolloquium Frankfurt am Main 1980, IstMitt* Beiheft 31 (Tübingen 1986) 115.

61 Cf. Bergquist (*supra* n. 56) 54, 91; see also 119–20, 132.

62 Cf. Bergquist (*supra* n. 56) 88–9, 79–80, 122.

63 Cf. Bergquist (*supra* n. 56) 88–9.

64 See e.g., for sixth-century Delphi, P. Amandry, 'Chronique delphique (1970–1981)', *BCH* 105 (1981) 721.

65 See Bergquist (*supra* n. 56) 58–61, 104–5; Tomlinson (*supra* n. 55) 19.

66 I have discussed the relationship between religion and the polis in: 'What is polis religion?' in O. Murray and S. Price, eds, *The Greek City from Homer to*

Alexander (Oxford 1990) 295–322; and 'Further aspects of polis religion', *AION. Archeologia e storia antica* 10 (1988) 259–74.

67 See Martin (*supra* n. 17) 164–201, 229–48; Wycherley (*supra* n. 53) 51–2; Kolb (*supra* n. 15) 5 and *passim*.

68 On cults in the agora cf. I. Malkin, *Religion and Colonization in Ancient Greece* (Leiden 1987) 201; Kolb (*supra* n. 15) *passim*, esp. 5–15 (against his views on the *hieros kyklos*: A. Veneri, 'Tra storia e archeologia: il *hieros kyklos* in Omero S 504', *SMEA* 25 (1984) 351ff.), 24–5, 57–8, 81–5). Kolb 5–8, 19 thinks that at first it was heroes and chthonic deities, and not the Olympians, who were associated with the agora. That heroes were closely associated with the agora from the beginning is clear, but not necessarily to the exclusion of Olympians (cf. *Odyssey* 6.256–7). Kolb's definition of chthonic deities (p. 5, n. 5) is not unproblematic and his remarks on Zeus Agoraios (p. 58) not convincing.

69 Cf. G. Vallet, F. Villard, P. Auberson, *Megara Hyblaea I: Le quartier de l'Agora archaïque* (Rome 1976) 388.

70 Vallet, Villard, Auberson (*supra* n. 69) 412.

71 Cf. Vallet, Villard, Auberson (*supra* n. 69) 412.

72 Cf. S. G. Miller, *The Prytaneion. Its Function and Architectural Form* (Berkeley 1978) 13–4; J. -P. Vernant, *Mythe et pensée chez les Grecs* (Paris 1965) 1.150, 165; P. J. Rhodes, *A Commentary on the Aristotelian Athenaion Politeia* (Oxford 1981) 3.v (p. 105); Burkert (*supra* n. 23) 170.

73 On which cf. Miller (*supra* n. 72) 14–16.

74 F. Sokolowski, *Lois sacrées des cités grecques* (Paris 1969) 151A; S. M. Sherwin-White, *Ancient Cos. An Historical Study from the Dorian Settlement to the Imperial Period* (Göttingen 1978) 322–3; Nilsson (*supra* n. 10) 153–4; W. Burkert, *Homo Necans. The Anthropology of Ancient Greek Sacrificial Ritual and Myth* (Berkeley 1983) 138.10; Vernant (*supra* n. 72) 1.155.

75 Paus. 7.22.3 on which cf. Vernant (*supra* n. 72) 1.165–6.

76 Cf. most recently Kolb (*supra* n. 15) 44.

77 Travlos (*supra* n. 33) 466; R. E. Wycherley, 'The Olympieion at Athens', *GRBS* 5 (1964) 162; Kolb (*supra* n. 15) 57.

78 *AthPol* 7.1, 55.5; cf. Dem. 54.26. See Rhodes (*supra* n. 72) 135–6; Martin (*supra* n. 17) 179.

79 For cults in the Tholos in Athens see Travlos (*supra* n. 33) 553.

80 Travlos (*supra* n. 33) 478, fig. 602, D.

81 Cf. C. Bérard, in *Cité* (*supra* n. 10) 29, 30–1.

82 Cf. M. H. Jameson, 'Apollo Lykeios in Athens', *Archaiognosia* 1 (1980) 225–35.

83 Plut. *Them.* 1; cf. S. C. Humphreys, 'The nothoi of Kynosarges', *JHS* 94 (1974) 88, 91; Travlos (*supra* n. 33) 340; *idem*, 'The gymnasium of Kynosarges', *AAA* 3 (1970) 6–14.

2

The origins of pan-Hellenism

Catherine Morgan

INTRODUCTION

The great pan-Hellenic sanctuaries of the Greek world are often characterized as centres of communication and competition, drawing together numerous small states from Italy to the Black Sea to share in a common framework
of ritual activity. Not only did such sanctuaries act as focal points at which
formal relations between communities were established and maintained via
treaties and federal meetings, but inter-state gatherings and institutions
(notably the Delphic oracle) have also been regarded as important in the
reinforcement of ideas and values central to polis organization (such as the
adoption of lawcodes or hoplite warfare).[1] This role was reflected materially
in the creation of monuments to the wealth and achievements of individual
states or leagues, such as treasuries or military trophies, which were designed
to impress and influence visitors from other regions, and it was also expressed in the development of formally regulated athletic and artistic contests, in which rivalries between representatives of different states could be
exercised in a controlled fashion.[2] From late Archaic to Hellenistic times
there is much to be said for this general picture, but it would be wrong to
assume that a pan-Hellenic system of values had early origins, or that pan-
Hellenic sanctuaries were pre-state institutions which continued throughout
the life of the types of state which they helped to foster. The precise nature
of pan-Hellenic values and behaviour has been fully explored elsewhere,
notably by Christiane Sourvinou-Inwood, and whilst the following discussion draws heavily upon her work, it would be futile to attempt to
summarize her complex arguments here. For present purposes, it is sufficient to emphasize that the emergence of pan-Hellenism cannot adequately
be explained by pushing back the values and ideals of a later period.[3]

It is clear that the variety and complexity of evidence for cult activity
during the period *c.* 1100–800 BC precludes simple definitions of 'state' and
'pre-state' forms of sanctuary and perceptions of sacred space (a point made
strongly by Christiane Sourvinou-Inwood elsewhere in this volume).
During the Early Iron Age, there existed almost as many forms of social

organization as regions of Greece, and so almost inevitably, the material expression of religious belief varied greatly according to local social and political circumstances. Compare, for example, the open-air roadside shrine at Isthmia (where there is evidence for dining, but little else, from *c.* 1100 BC onwards) with the first temple at Kommos (perhaps as early as the eleventh century BC). The large votive deposits at Kombothekra and Olympia included bronze and terracotta figurines and tripods, dedicated by communities across western Greece from the late tenth century onwards, and cave shrines such as that at Polis on Ithaka, and the Attic hilltop sanctuary on Mt Hymettos (with evidence for dedication and dining probably connected with the cult of Zeus Ombrios) began in Protogeometric times.[4] As Sourvinou-Inwood shows, many of the forms of shrine and modes of thought often regarded as characteristic of Archaic and Classical polis religion can be observed in earlier times, and it is very difficult to identify any simple dividing line in the development of state religion. In documenting the continual process of invention and re-interpretation of religious structures to suit prevailing social needs and priorities, the nature of activity at sanctuaries is a more sensitive indicator, and in particular, the balance between the representation of the interests of individuals and those of communities in relation to the formal structure of participant state(s).

The eighth century saw the beginning of a long process of state formation in many areas of the Greek world, with changes evident in most areas of cultural and political life, including religious activity. During this period a qualitative and quantitative increase in dedications at a wide range of different kinds of sanctuary suggests that an ever greater proportion of personal wealth was being invested by individuals from a wider range of social groups.[5] Equally, the appearance of temples at a number of widely separated sites, from Perachora to Samos, and Eretria to Ephesos or Aegira (with many more following during the seventh century, including Isthmia, Corinth, Thermon and Delphi), is not only indicative of a growing consensus of opinion on the appropriate monumental development of major community cult places, but also of community investment.[6] From Archaic times at least, the right of temple commission was a prerogative of the state (although individuals, such as the Alkmaionidai at Delphi, often contributed money or materials),[7] and this remained the rule outside the east Greek world until changing concepts of kingship and personal rule during the Hellenistic period encouraged the kind of personal investment evident in, for example, the Philippeion at Olympia (*c.* 335 BC).[8]

It is perhaps understandable that studies of religious development have concentrated upon sanctuaries within state borders, not least because there is an obvious theoretical appeal in looking directly at links between the material expression of religious belief and state formation on a local level; the polis was, after all, *the* community of cult *par excellence*. There is also an important chronological discrepancy in the beginning of monumental construction at sanctuaries inside and outside state territory, since no cult buildings or monuments earlier than the late seventh century have yet been discovered at Delphi (or *c.* 600 BC in the case of Olympia). Priority must have been accorded to the spatial, social and political definition of the state before it could begin to compete consciously within any formal system and invest systematically outside its borders, and the institutionalization of activity at remote sanctuaries would therefore have been low in the priorities of most emergent poleis during the eighth and much of the seventh centuries. It is also no coincidence that many of the earliest states to build treasuries at Olympia and Delphi (largely during the sixth century) were colonies, founded as poleis by settlers with vested interests in the rapid spatial and political definition of their new communities, and thus experiencing fewer of the problems of definition and consolidation evident on the Greek mainland.[9] It is also significant that western Greek (as later eastern) colonies chose to invest in those mainland sanctuaries most removed from the contemporary state structure; and although one should not ignore the relative geographical proximity of Olympia to Italy, the issue of colonial identity is probably more important here. Since colonies owed their existence to the actions of their mother cities, yet their independence to separation from them, dedication at a mainland sanctuary like Olympia would have had the advantage of maintaining general links with the source of a colony's Greek identity, while avoiding the kind of close connection with the mother city which might compromise its independence. Furthermore, the absence of a shared sanctuary in Italy meant that a system which allowed colonies to interact with each other whilst maintaining spiritual links with the mainland had the added advantage of economy.[10] In short, if one discounts monuments attributable to colonies, with their special interests and priorities, the already low level of early monumental investment at the future pan-Hellenic sanctuaries is reduced still further.

Yet this is not to suggest that these sanctuaries were unaffected by the changes evident in all other aspects of life during the eighth century; they too experienced the increase in the number and variety of votive offerings noted earlier. At both Olympia and Delphi, over a century of excavation has produced a rich and well published collection of early votives, including terracotta and bronze figurines, jewellery, and bronze and occasionally iron tripods, and similar evidence also exists at less fully studied sites (Dodona, for example).[11] A substantial part of this chapter will therefore be devoted to examining the way in which these votives represent changes in personal behaviour relevant to the development of pan-Hellenic religious institutions.

OLYMPIA

Perhaps the best documented case with which to begin is that of Olympia, where cult activity can be traced back at least to the end of the tenth century.

The earliest bronze votives (pre-800 BC) mainly come from west Peloponnesian workshops, probably in Messenia and Arkadia.[12] Nichoria, the one extensively excavated settlement site in Messenia, has produced plentiful evidence for the working of bronze, iron, lead and gold, mainly associated with a large, so-called 'chief's', house (see below), and tripods (otherwise rare outside sanctuaries), figurines and jewellery closely similar to items found at Olympia.[13] Equally, the sanctuaries of Arkadia have produced figurines and jewellery of types also found at Olympia.[14]

During this early period, Olympia may be characterized as a meeting place for the petty chiefs of the west, at which they reinforced their status at home and amongst their fellow rulers via the dedication, and perhaps also circulation, of prestige goods.[15] In Messenia, the location of burials and surface remains suggests that the region was divided into a small number of settlement clusters, which reached their greatest extent during the Dark Age II phase (c. 925–850 BC).[16] Detailed evidence of social organization comes from Nichoria, and especially from the exceptionally large central house (units IV–1 and IV–5) which was probably the residence of a local chief, and which contained a small altar and also limited storage facilities for food-stuffs. No other comparable Messenian settlement has yet been excavated, but in one case at least, at Kaphirio, surface remains suggest a site of similar size and perhaps complexity.[17] In a region divided into small scale local hierarchies, probably with a low level of population, there are clear advantages to maintaining a neutral meeting place for local leaders, and since there is no evidence for a pan-Messenian cult place until the establishment of a festival at Thouria during the fifth century, and, with the probable exception of Akovitika (founded late in the eighth century), local shrines mainly date from the Archaic period (after the First Messenian War), it need not be surprising to find Olympia filling this role. Indeed, since the river Alpheios may have formed the northern boundary of the Mycenaean Further Kingdom of Pylos, Olympia might not have seemed such a remote choice.[18]

In Arkadia, by contrast, almost all known archaeological evidence, from Protogeometric times into the eighth century, comes from a scatter of small sanctuaries, reflecting local territorial divisions which are often comparable with the boundaries of the later autonomous cities. Many of these sanc-tuaries were founded during the eighth century, with temples appearing from the late seventh, but in certain cases (notably Tegea) activity began much earlier.[19] The most common early votives are items of jewellery (probably valued personal possessions), figurines (including a few elaborate and unparalleled animal groups which may represent local fertility rituals of some antiquity), and stamp pendants which probably served as seals, real or symbolic, and thus represented the movement of goods, and perhaps even the sanctuary as a context for exchange.[20] This range of votives provides valuable evidence for the nature of activity at Arkadian sanctuaries and for their role as focal points for local communities, where significant events in the lives of individuals were marked, community rituals celebrated (including those linked with fertility), and the exchange of commodities symbolized if not actually undertaken (a role at least in part comparable with that of the chief's house at Nichoria). Although, by the eighth century, the local role of sanctuaries across Arkadia seems fairly uniform, details of material culture (ceramic and metalwork styles, and especially the degree and origin of external influences) vary greatly, suggesting an emphasis upon *local*, rather than *regional*, identity which probably had early origins. The presence of a limited range of Arkadian jewellery and small bronzes at Olympia suggests a very selective use of a distant cult place outside Arkadian territory, perhaps as a meeting place for representatives of various local communities, or perhaps as a special place of pilgrimage in times of trouble or celebration. The fact that Tegea and Mavrikio, in eastern Arkadia, and thus furthest removed from Olympia, show the strongest connections, reinforces this impression of specific purpose, and whatever Olympia's precise role, its place in Arkadian society is confirmed by continuing high levels of dedication throughout the Archaic period in the face of a constant threat from Sparta.[21] Clearly, therefore, *participation at Olympia meant different things to different societies*, but it can generally be understood in the context of local patterns of social organization.

It is generally rare in the Greek world to find types of votives dedicated exclusively to particular deities, and where votives can be said to reflect particular interests, these are more usually those of the dedicator than the recipient.[22] In the case of Olympia, the large-scale dedication of metal (especially bronze) before *c.* 700 BC is particularly significant; breaches in trade relations at the beginning of the Iron Age and an ensuing bronze shortage may have acted as catalysts for the widespread adoption of iron-working, but even thereafter it seems likely that the production, use and distribution of high-quality bronze remained relatively limited, at least until the expansion of trade evident during the latter part of the eighth century. At a number of settlement sites (Nichoria included), metals appear to have been used for only a limited part of their potential range of functions, and although one should not underestimate the problems of recovery, finds of metal goods of all types are largely confined to graves and élite residences. As a relatively scarce resource, access to which may have been restricted, metal would therefore have been an ideal status symbol and commodity for conspicuous consumption.[23] Equally, the presence at Olympia of numerous votives, yet no pottery or wares related to drinking or dining, suggests a material emphasis on display rather than communality, and in this respect, Olympia contrasts markedly with the contemporary shrine at Isthmia.[24] The choice of subjects represented by figurines is also revealing. Bronze and terracotta oxen and sheep may represent pastoral interests, and their dedication may reflect a desire for continued successful husbandry. Indeed, the suggestion that the Olympic festival originated as an agricultural thanksgiving is plausible, if impossible to test (although it would have to have been a very general celebration, since there is no single harvest season in the Mediterranean, and the later festival calendar deliberately avoided periods of intense agricultural activity to allow visitors to attend).[25] Horse figurines became increasingly common during the Early Iron Age, and, along with terracotta wagons and chariot groups, reflect the pursuits of the wealthy; attempts to use chariot figures as evidence for early races are not wholly convincing, however, since in later times horse trappings were often dedicated at sites where races did not occur, and the fact that chariot races were relatively late to appear in the Olympic calendar suggests that they are more likely to reflect sixth century perceptions of the proper conduct of the aristocrat–hero than any genuinely early activity.[26]

Consideration of the origins, subjects and media of votives therefore enables us to establish a general picture of the nature of activity and underlying social interests at Olympia before c. 800 BC. Yet although changes affected all categories of votive during the eighth century, differences in the development of each type of artefact suggest variation in the social interests which they represent, and it is therefore worth examining the eighth-century development of votives category by category.[27] To take figurines first, although they increase greatly in numbers and new regional styles appear (such as Lakonian from c. 800 BC and Corinthian from c. 725 BC), they remained small, simple and essentially unchanged in form, and the technology used in their production stayed the same.[28] These trends therefore represent an escalation in existing dedicatory behaviour rather than the introduction of anything new. Furthermore, the evidence of casting pits, debris and numerous miscastings shows that probably throughout the Early Iron Age, most figurines were cast in situ at Olympia by travelling craftsmen for sale to visitors, and so, strictly speaking, regional styles show the origins of craftsmen but not necessarily of dedicators.[29] This is not to suggest that metalworking for festivals was a full-time job; the fact that the roots of individual wealth and status in the Greek world lay in the possession and working of land (Hesiod, Works and Days 646–94), and craftsmen came low in the social order (Herodotos 2.167.2) would surely be argument enough against abandoning the family farm, even if sufficient work existed to support full-time craft production. Instead, like most other craftsmen (such as architects, builders or potters), metalworkers would have scheduled their various activities to fit in with the agricultural cycle, and here the timing of festivals would have been as important to them as to the ordinary visitor.[30] However, from the eighth century onwards, there is clear evidence that sanctuaries were becoming increasingly important centres of craft production, and especially of metalworking (comparable evidence has been found at a number of sites, including Philia, Kalapodi, Samos and Delphi); and subsequently, during the seventh century, such elaborate items (including orientalizing tripods and their attachments) came to be cast in situ, that visitors may rapidly have acquired the freedom to purchase almost any type of votive, bringing with them only items of particular personal significance.[31]

Tripods, by contrast, increase not only in number but also in size and elaboration, and these changes, combined with the real technological development evident in the introduction of hammered and relief techniques all require greater investment in labour and materials. The real cost of these items therefore rose considerably, as did their value as status symbols for display (as indicated, for example, by literary references to their use as prizes in contests and aristocratic funeral games, see Hesiod, *Works and Days* 654–7, Homer, *Iliad* 23.698–702).[32] Equally, the lack of miscastings and casting debris attributable to the production of tripods suggests that during the eighth century, in contrast to figurines, they were mostly brought to Olympia *from workshops elsewhere* (we have just one mould and one miscasting of this date, and evidence in quantity appears only from the seventh century onwards).[33] These developments in tripod style indicate a real change in dedicatory behaviour unparalleled by figurines. An average visitor might have gained prestige from attending a festival in a remote place, but the kind of figurine he could afford to purchase and dedicate would make little material impression. By contrast, the richer man who could afford a tripod gained greater social rewards for greater material investment; his dedication was seen by his fellows at Olympia, as well as those in his home community, who already knew what kind of man he was and how he fulfilled his material obligations at home, and had seen the commission or preparation of a rich gift for disposal at a remote sanctuary.[34] The development of tripods and figurines therefore reveals a growing social distinction in dedication at Olympia through the eighth century, with different modes of production answering to different patterns of dedication by different social groups.

Additional evidence of sanctuary participation comes with the appearance of archaeological evidence for settlement in Elis from *c.* 730 BC, after a hiatus spanning most of the early Iron Age. From this time, the rivers Alpheios and Peneios formed the nucleus of a dispersed settlement system which lasted until the synoecism of Elis in *c.* 471 BC.[35] That Olympia came to play an important role as the major Elean regional sanctuary is shown, for example, by the presence of pre-synoecism treaty inscriptions between Elean communities, or the way in which Pausanias described the altars in the Altis from an acknowledged Elean viewpoint, according to the order in which the Eleans sacrificed.[36] This continuing relationship between the sanctuary and local communities (albeit not wholly peaceful) probably had early origins and certainly stands in marked contrast to the probably violent dislocation of Delphi from eastern Phokis and its administration by an Amphictyony. From the last quarter of the eighth century, there was a marked increase in the quantity of jewellery at Olympia, exactly the sort of personal possession that one would expect to be offered, especially by women, to mark personal events or life crises like birth, marriage and death. Not all jewellery can be accounted for in this way; miscastings may have resulted from casting *in situ* (and these include a number of pre-eighth century pieces), and a few exotic imports (notably from Italy) may be taken together with tripods as indicative of widening sanctuary participation, but the change with renewed settlement is marked.[37]

A second major development is the appearance of pottery, at first (from *c.* 725 BC) in very small quantities, but increasing greatly from *c.* 700 BC with the beginning of long-running sequences of plainly decorated oinochoai and kantharoi, basic equipment for drinking and dining, which were found packed into the fills of wells dug for the use of visitors each time the games were held. It is always difficult to classify the activities of visitors whilst at a sanctuary (especially when they are as basic as eating and drinking), and so it is impossible to establish whether these vessels were used for a cult meal or just for daily living during the festival; but whatever the case, they are more likely to have been sacralized after use than dedicated *per se*. All of these basic wares were locally produced in Elean fabric and decorated in locally-derived styles, a pattern of local provision of essential sanctuary equipment which is widely paralleled elsewhere (at the Samian Heraion and Isthmia, for example), and which is indicative of the long term economic interests created by a major sanctuary (not only in the provision of dedications and equipment for festivals, but also in offering camping space and food for visitors).[38]

One final aspect of early activity at Olympia, the early festival, has aroused perhaps the greatest speculation over the least evidence. The year 776 BC, the traditional date of the foundation of the Olympic games (or their refoundation, according to Pausanias, 5.8.5), bears little relation to the material evidence.[39] There are obvious attractions in an absolute date (especially for this period), but it derives from later sources, from the fifth-century sophist Hippias of Elis, who compiled the first victor list (transmitted via Aristotle), and the third-century historian Timaeus of Sicily, who first used the Olympic cycle as a framework within which to place historical events. Paradoxically, therefore, one of the few absolute dates available for the Iron Age is of more use to a student of fifth-century Athenian chronology than in reconstructing early activity at Olympia.[40] Early Iron Age athletics are possible but unprovable, and a competition coinciding with either of the stages of escalation of dedication, at the beginning of the eighth century or during the last quarter, is perhaps more likely.[41] However, it is interesting that almost all of the early victors in Hippias' list come from the west and central Peloponnese (joined by Corinth and the Megarid at the end of the eighth century), and that the traditional calendar of events puts the expansion of the games from a single event (the stade race) in the last quarter of the century, with four new events added between 724 BC and 708 BC.[42] In so far as it is possible to trust the historical tradition surrounding the festival, it seems that the general trend of diversification and widening participation evident in the material record may coincide with the development (or institution) of the games.

In conclusion, therefore, the eighth century was a crucial period of transformation, during which Olympia began to develop from a rural cult place serving the petty chiefs of the west to a major festival site. A widening of the range of cult activities may be traced in two stages. First, from c. 800 BC, changes in dedicatory practice reflect an intensification of activity by western visitors combined with participation by the élites of a number of emergent states. If athletic events did not already exist, it is possible that their institution coincided with these changes. Second, from c. 725 BC, the games (if they already existed) expanded, local settlement ensured participation at the sanctuary by Elean communities, and western activity was replaced, at least in part, by the wider involvement of early state élites. This widening participation was particularly crucial to the survival of the sanctuary, since the Spartan conquest of Messenia (by c. 710 BC) not only ended Messenian independence, but resulted in the destruction of most major Messenian settlements and the dispersal of the population across the countryside, thus undermining the social basis of participation at Olympia.[43]

This second stage set the pattern for the development of the sanctuary through the seventh and earlier sixth centuries, and for the growth of the state interests which resulted in the institutionalization of the Olympic festival and its eventual incorporation into a formal, pan-Hellenic, cycle. Two particular aspects of early dedication at Olympia appear significant in this respect. First, the dedication of tripods during the eighth century indicates that the élite of emerging poleis were beginning to exercise their rivalries outside state borders. This must, in time, have made the future pan-Hellenic sanctuaries targets for intervention by states trying to make good citizens of their aristocrats, and to focus their attention on civic interests by suppressing, or containing and marginalizing, potentially threatening areas of traditional élite action (hence, perhaps, the continuing role of pan-Hellenic sanctuaries in the establishment and maintenance of *xenos* relations between citizens of different states).[44] Although there is an important distinction between 'the state' as a decision-making system with institutionalized offices and citizen rights and obligations, and as a group of aristocrats maintaining their position on a basis of personal power, there was no sharp transition between these two conditions (as is shown, for example, by Pheidon's supposed seizure of the Olympic games, probably during the seventh century).[45] Instead, the gradual accretion of functions to the polis involved a taming of the élite, evident in the establishment of a formal role for such traditional pursuits as competitive athletics, equestrian sports or elaborate funerals, and resulting in an institutionalized balancing act between the interests of great families and those of the state or collectivity. Cult developments of all sorts were an important means of achieving this:

Solon's institution of the festival of the Genesia at Athens, for example, drew the celebration of death, previously a purely family matter, into the civic consciousness.[46] Equally revealing are changes in the treatment of the tripod during the Archaic period, a symbol with particular élite associations. At certain sanctuaries (such as Delos) they continued as personal dedications, yet at Olympia, after a brief vogue for orientalizing styles during the first half of the seventh century, tripod dedications declined and disappeared. However at Delphi and in several city centres (Athens included), tripods came to be used mainly as symbols of state or state-approved activities, as choregic monuments for example, or, in the case of the Plataean tripod at Delphi, to commemorate a pan-Hellenic victory. A few personal tripod dedications continued to be made at Delphi, but these often came from citizens of ethne; inscriptions on the rims of Boiotian tripods may be connected with funeral games, for example, and depictions of tripods on Boiotian vases continue long after 700 BC.[47]

Second, the level of consumption of wealth (and especially metal resources) for purely personal ends was a potential area of conflict between aristocratic dedicatory practice at Olympia and emerging state interests. Olympia and other similar sanctuaries were not the only locations of consumption. In Athens, lavish funerary display was first curtailed by Solon's passage of sumptuary laws c. 594/3 BC, and restrictions on personal wealth and expenditure often form part of the codes attributed to early lawgivers (real or legendary) in other regions, Lykourgos in Sparta for example.[48] Equally, the transfer of arms and armour from graves to sanctuaries, which is evident from c. 700 BC, may be taken as an ideological, if not practical, statement of the place of military force in the state rather than the private domain, but it also had the practical advantage of encouraging the dedication of captured items, rather than costly personal equipment which could then be passed from father to son.[49] Behind all of these developments lies a recognition of the necessity of curtailing or diverting expenditure not directed towards the greater good of the community.

DELPHI

So far, discussion has centred on evidence from Olympia, but this site is not unique, and similar developments in dedication can be observed at Delphi (especially during the last quarter of the eighth century). Here, an extensive dump deposit under the Sacred Way has produced a large collection of votives dating from c. 800 BC, and including figurines (mainly Corinthian, Argive and local) and tripods (Argive, Corinthian and, from the end of the century, Attic).[50] In other respects, however, the development of the sanctuary differs markedly from that of Olympia. Most importantly, it grew up in the middle of a village which had been established some 75 years before the appearance of the first votives, and traces of which have been found in the east *temenos* under later buildings, including the temple of Apollo. The pottery associated with early house structures shows that the settlement maintained links with Corinth and Thessaly (probably reflecting its location close to the Doris–Lokris corridor, the main route north from the Corinthian Gulf), and subsequently with the network of small settlements which grew up around the plain of Itea during the last quarter of the eighth century.[51] It is therefore unfortunate that priority has been accorded to the study of sanctuary activity, since although the settlement expanded greatly throughout the eighth century, evidence for cult activity remained very limited, and the sanctuary at Delphi was tiny in comparison with, for example, the nearby Corinthian state sanctuary at Perachora.[52] In their nature, origins and relatively late date (in comparison with Olympia), early votives at Delphi reflect the interests of emergent states more closely than those of the local community. These votives include, in addition to tripods, artefacts with clear aristocratic connotations (such as warrior or horse-driver figurines and chariot fitments), and the rustic themes so common at Olympia are rarer.[53] Furthermore, perhaps the most celebrated feature of the sanctuary, the Delphic oracle, was exceptional from the time of its foundation for dealing with enquiries from a number of states. Divination had probably long been a common means of day to day decision making in many regions of Greece (and continued to be so as, for example, the satires of Aristophanes show, see *Birds* 957–91), but a shared oracle dealing with major community issues was something new.[54]

Contrary to a commonly held picture of the Delphic oracle as an irrational or magical exception to the normal rational conduct of community affairs, recent studies have concentrated upon the function of divination as a regularly-used tool for decision making within state government.[55] As such, the institution of a shared state oracle at Delphi during the eighth century has obvious implications for the changing balance of state and individual interests at the sanctuary. Consideration of responses, as well as cross-cultural analogy, reveals that the basic role of Delphi (as most major state oracles) was to sanction already formulated solutions to difficult, often unprecedented, and potentially divisive problems of past or present community conduct, in order to enable leaders to establish a consensus of opinion for their acceptance. Responses from all periods most commonly took the form of direct answers to simple or alternative propositions, and ambiguity was rare, a last resort to protect the oracle against charges of inaccuracy, or to force a consultor state to reconsider its position on an issue on which no straightforward answer could be given. For example, Herodotos (7.140–3) notes that the Athenians, when enquiring about the best defence against the Persian threat, were told to seek their salvation in wooden walls, an ambiguous response which forced renewed debate on the city's defences, and eventually, the adoption of Themistokles' policy of naval strength.[56] Genuine Delphic responses were not open-ended, nor did they predict the future. The oracle did not bestow divine authority upon rulers, but rather sanctioned their decisions to act upon particular issues. The foundation of the Delphic oracle is therefore an indication of a crisis in political authority which may have been caused by any number of internal factors (including population increase or changes in wealth distribution) or external pressures (such as warfare). In many ways, its institution may be compared to the decision of a number of states later in the Archaic period to appoint law-givers, since in most of these cases, the act of appointing an authoritative individual was as significant to the future development of the state as what he actually said.[57] It is certainly the case that the first states to consult Delphi (Corinth, Chalkis, Sparta and possibly Messenia) did so during periods when they were probably suffering from internal tensions, either because of difficult relations with neighbouring communities which led to war (the Lelantine War and the First Messenian War, which were both regarded as exceptional in antiquity), or because of internal changes (the consolidation of Spartan control of Lakonia, for example, and settlement expansion at Corinth).[58]

The form of the earliest recorded responses from Delphi is more difficult to assess, largely because they dealt with issues of major importance to early states and so were liable to incorporation within local historical traditions, with all the elaboration that that process entails (colonial foundation responses are a particularly clear case of this).[59] However, if one were to discount the received form of responses, and to consider only the historical likelihood that the oracle was consulted over a particular issue at such an early date, one arrives at a list of subjects, including colonization, the adoption of a lawcode, or the prosecution of a war of conquest, all of which are issues of community concern, belonging to the eighth century and no earlier, and probably beyond the collective wisdom of the local élite.[60] The issues of consultation did change over time, and non-religious matters and questions of internal government became increasingly rare through the Archaic period, but since the achievement of consensus in one area almost inevitably opens problems in another, the subjects of consultation mirror the evolution of the polis.[61] From its inception, the oracle was closely tied to the fate of the polis. Powerful *ethne*, like Thessaly, played a leading role in sanctuary affairs (via membership of the Amphictyony, for example), but there is no evidence that they ever consulted the oracle, and it is hard to see how divination would fit with what we know of their decision-making structures.[62] The foundation of the Delphic oracle during the eighth century therefore illustrates the fact that we cannot trace any simple, uniform stages of institutionalization of activity at the future pan-Hellenic sanctuaries, but instead, we find a complex of new activities, ranging from personal pursuits which could be perceived as threatening to the cohesion of the emerging state and therefore as targets for institutionalization (competitive élite dedication, for example), to those which represented the interests of whole communities (such as the oracle) and therefore continued essentially unchanged.

By the end of the eighth century, the complexity of demands put upon the settlement at Delphi (as part of a local exchange system heavily exploited by Corinth and as host to a sanctuary and oracle attracting ever wider participation) must have created a risk of conflict between the local community and sanctuary participants. It is impossible to pinpoint the time at which the sanctuary displaced the settlement, forcing inhabitants to move down the hillside to the site described by Pausanias (10.9.1), but the building of the first temple (covering a number of houses), followed, during the early-mid sixth century, by monuments such as the statues of Kleobis and Biton (or the Dioscuri) and the Naxian Sphinx, may be regarded as a *terminus ante quem*. The construction of the temple may be placed between 650 BC and 600 BC on the basis of comparison with the architecture of the temples at Corinth and Isthmia, and there is no secure evidence for any earlier building; since this is quite early by the standards of inter-state sanctuaries, it is tempting to connect it with the practice of divination, hiding away the oracle and thus enhancing its mystique (although there is no necessity for any connection).[63]

This conflict of interests may be reflected in the legend of the First Sacred War, which resulted in the passing of control of the sanctuary from the local community to the Amphictyony, and the ultimate reduction of the local population to a community of sanctuary servers. It is difficult to accept surviving accounts of the war at face value; a duration of ten years is worryingly reminiscent of the Trojan War, for example, and even if one assumes that the Krisa or Kirrha which opposed the Amphictyony was actually the village at Delphi (since the site of Kirrha has produced almost no material evidence of this period), the imbalance in forces which of necessity must have existed makes it hard to believe that such a long war could have been sustained. Opinion is currently divided over the historicity of the war; some deny that it ever took place, and some accept that it did occur, but that the formalization of local legends into the received account may have occurred relatively late and that fictitious additions may have been incorporated.[64] Nevertheless, it almost seems that if the war had not happened, it would have been necessary to invent it in order to cover the disjunction between sanctuary and community interests. The victory of the Amphictyony marked a turning point in sanctuary affairs, the final separation of the sanctuary from its regional context and the assertion of the inter-state vested interests essential to the development of formalized pan-Hellenic institutions. It was marked by the celebration of the first major (chrematistic) games in 591/90 BC (according to the Parian Marble) or 586/5 BC (Pausanias 10.7.4–5), and these were soon followed (in 582/1 BC) by the first stephanitic festival.[65] Furthermore, the Homeric Hymn to Pythian Apollo, which most probably dates to the early sixth century BC (and would thus be contemporary with, or soon after, the war), deals with such issues as the arrival of Apollo at Delphi, the choice of location for his sanctuary and the establishment of his priesthood from a standpoint almost hostile to local interests. Apollo himself chooses the site and builds his own temple, and having chosen as priests men from as far away as Crete and brought them all the way around the Peloponnese to Delphi (emphasizing the sanctuary's pan-Hellenic role), he demands their obedience under threat of retribution (in implicit contrast to the past behaviour of the local population).[66]

To return to more general issues, it is notable that most pan-Hellenic sanctuaries occupied remote or marginal locations, beyond the borders of the majority of participant states, and usually under the political control of a weak, or subservient, state or institution, and they therefore offered neutral locations for states to meet and compete. In certain cases, these locations may have been determined by the patronage of deities who favoured remote places; Zeus, for example, a weather god (amongst his many roles) and thus fond of rural or mountainous places, was patron at Olympia and Dodona, as well as at purely local shrines such as Mt Hymettos in Attica.[67] Such locations may have proved useful for other reasons in later times, but their initial selection was largely a matter of cult. It is certainly true that for the individual as citizen of the state, going 'beyond the bounds' was a dangerous move, since community boundaries mark the extent of the security and status conferred by group membership.[68] Yet for the individual, it allowed perfect freedom to act in whatever he might deem to be his own interest (and certain of the activities which took place at remote sanctuaries, notably divination, benefitted from this).

One way in which the incorporation of remote sanctuaries into a formal circuit helped to limit the actions of individuals to those acceptable to the city was by reducing the contrast imposed by the presence of civic boundaries for the set period of the festival. Thus the Delphians acted as intermediary proxenoi for the other Greeks who consulted the oracle; on regular consultation days the Delphic polis acted for all the inquirers, whereas on other days, the intermediary role was filled by the Delphian who was proxenos of the enquirer's city.[69]

Yet here also, the formalization of boundaries and the differentiation of space is first discernible within the territories of emergent states from the eighth century onwards (and continued to play a major role in most poleis, for example in determining citizen rights according to the location of residence or birth), whereas, as in the case of monumental building, such perceptions developed later outside state boundaries. In the case of Athens, Peisistratid attempts to consolidate an exceptionally extensive territory included the development of cult sites close to state borders (such as Brauron, Eleusis and Eleutherai), and their systematic relation to cults and festivals in central Athens (Artemis Brauronia and Dionysos Eleutheraios on the Acropolis, and the Lesser Mysteries at Agrai near the Ilissos). In the cases of Eleusis and Brauron, the link was further cemented by the physical movement of people; initiation into the Eleusinian Mysteries (effectively a social obligation for the Athenian aristocracy) involved the procession of candidates along the Sacred Way from Athens to Eleusis, and at Brauron, the Little Bears, daughters of leading Athenian families, performed a fixed period of service at the sanctuary.[70] The scale of Peisistratid activities was exceptional, yet the process continued into the fifth century with the construction of temples such as those at Acharnai, Sounion and Rhamnous.[71] This systematic use of cults was largely *a matter of defining boundaries and encouraging interaction between the centre and periphery* by concentrating the attention of the entire population, however remote, upon the city centre. Yet as expressions of civic values, and thus élite ambitions, came increasingly to be focused on the centres of mainland poleis, so marginal or dangerous activities, or the purely personal concerns of aristocrats, were pushed away from the centre to rural sanctuaries. Hence Ephebic rituals, marking the adoption of adult male status, were celebrated in Athens (as in Sparta) largely in the countryside and at rural sanctuaries, and female rites of passage, including the Arkteia and childbirth (successful and unsuccessful) were celebrated at, for example, Brauron, near the east coast of Attica, and also at Mounichia.[72] The institutionalization of activity at sanctuaries outside state territory may therefore be seen as an extension of the increasingly complex political perceptions of the role of religious space evident within polis territories. It was neither an innovation nor a recognition of some primeval quality of marginality inherent in remote sanctuaries.

IONIAN SANCTUARIES

A further area of potential confusion concerns the archaeological application of the term 'pan-Hellenic'. The appearance of votives from a number of different areas does not necessarily make a sanctuary pan-Hellenic. Perachora, Philia and the Samian Heraion (all state sanctuaries) are not unique in producing a range of eighth and seventh century dedications equally as wide as that at Olympia, and the distinction lies not in the types and origins of votives, but in the human interests they represent.[73] In order to identify these interests, it is essential to trace the place and mode of production of each category of votive (as has been shown in the case of Olympia), and also the nature of the dedicators (their social position and relationship to the community which controlled the sanctuary). At this point it is worth pausing to illustrate this argument by considering the very different case of the major city sanctuaries of Ionia (Didyma, the Artemision at Ephesos, the Samian Heraion and the sanctuary of Athena at Emborio on Chios). Here rich, and often exotic, collections of votives from the period before the Persian conquest have been compared with evidence from the great pan-Hellenic shrines of the Greek world, and in most cases, these dedications are matched by spectacular architectural development within large *temene*.[74] The first temples of Artemis at Ephesos and Hera at Samos date from the early eighth century; the first Artemision was a small rectangular building, with a cult statue which may have been adorned with a rich collection of jewellery (later buried under the statue base), and the first Heraion, a hekatompedon, was rapidly copied at Eretria (perhaps by the same architect). Equally, the earliest stoa at the Samian Heraion is an innovative construction which dates as early as the late seventh century.[75] At most of these sanctuaries, the sixth century was a period of lavish temple building, generally on a large scale, and with elaborate architectural and sculptural detail (the Rhoecus temple at Samos and the second Artemision are cases in point).[76] Much of the wealth invested at Ionian sanctuaries was probably won via the trade for which the region was renowned. Herodotos (4.152) describes the ship-master Kolaios' dedication at the Samian Heraion of a bronze griffin-head cauldron supported by twice life-size kneeling human figures, and claims that it represents only a tithe of the profits from a single voyage; and even if he exaggerates, it is clear that trade, or piracy, offered rich pickings. Many of the exotic luxuries dedicated at Ionian sanctuaries (such as the Phoenician, Egyptian and Cypriot items found at Samos) may also have arrived in this way, yet it is impossible to understand fully the pattern of dedication and its wider meaning without considering local political circumstances.[77]

The high level of expenditure in Ionia on prestigious civic institutions such as sanctuaries must surely be related to the political and social instability evident across the region before the Persian conquest, with frequent changes of city government and constant threats from powerful non-Greek neighbours. Leaders under threat and seeking to assert their own personal status often sought to identify materially with the institutions of the cities they sought to rule. At Miletos, for example, the tyrant Thrasyboulos, who assumed power *c.* 630 BC, was deposed by a party led by Thoas and Damasenor, and their downfall was followed by a period of violent factional strife between the 'wealthy' and the 'populace', which ended only with the award of power by Parian arbitrators to 'those whose land was well cultivated' (Herodotos 5.28–9), presumably some form of aristocratic oligarchy. Furthermore, the fact that the Greek cities of Asia Minor contained alien elements within their populations, and also had to maintain relations with powerful non-Greek neighbouring states, resulted in two distinct levels of foreign sanctuary participation. Alien groups in mixed populations (initially resulting from the foundation of Greek cities in an inhabited region) faced the difficulty of finding an acceptable, non-threatening means of expressing their cultural identity within a Greek community, and the state sanctuary was perhaps the most important place for the resolution of this dilemma.[78] Although Greek patron deities remained supreme, they were often related (formally or informally) to foreign cults (the link between

33

Artemis and the Great Goddess is a case in point), and votives, whilst offered within a wholly Greek framework of practice, could reflect the ethnic origins of their dedicators. Thus, although there is little unusual in the range of objects offered, their styles often reflect a fusion of Greek and foreign traits: for example, a rich collection of ivories dedicated at the Artemision at Ephesos between *c*. 650 BC and 550 BC (and possibly the work of Lydian craftsmen) shows non-Greek influences in style and workmanship, and their subjects include the Hittite-style 'Hawk Priestess' as well as non-Greek figures from daily life.[79]

By contrast, the fewer, but more spectacular, gifts offered by foreign rulers are clear reminders of their power and dominance inside and outside their own kingdoms. The dedication by the Pharaoh Necho of the battle dress in which he was victorious at Megiddo *c*. 609 BC (Herodotos 2.159) is such a case, as are the numerous dedications by Kroisos of Lydia, including property confiscated from a Lydian opponent, the fruits of an internal political dispute which one might otherwise expect to have been commemorated at home (Herodotos 1.92, 5.36). Similar dedications were also offered at sanctuaries elsewhere in the Greek world, notably at Delphi (e.g. Herodotos 1.46–56),[80] but in Asia Minor they were an immediate reminder of the unbalanced political relations between Greek cities and their neighbours, and may also have served as a means of maintaining and smoothing the diplomatic relations essential for the survival of the vulnerable Greek communities. Furthermore, the need to accommodate foreign interests may also help to explain the marginal locations of most major Ionian sanctuaries, up to 4–5 km from their patron city centres and sometimes (as at Samos or Didyma) approached via ceremonial roads, richly adorned with sculpture.[81] Cults did exist in city centres (notably that of Athena Polias, who tended to attract dedications of arms and armour), but the fact that the principal city sanctuaries were some distance away and received most of the dedications associated with foreigners (and also women) may reflect a reluctance to acknowledge in the heart of the city anything potentially threatening to the city's security and Greek identity.[82] In short, votives at Ionian sanctuaries represent a complex of interests which, whilst explicable in terms of local political and social circumstances, are not directly comparable with evidence from future pan-Hellenic sanctuaries elsewhere in the Greek world.

As has been shown in all of the cases so far discussed, there is no simple recipe for identifying the origins of pan-Hellenism in the archaeological record. The range of dedications alone is not sufficient, nor is sanctuary location or even specific types of activity, since a number of events central to the great pan-Hellenic festivals (certain foot races, for example, or, in the case of Delphi, divination) continued essentially unchanged from their inception. Indeed, a checklist of 'pan-Hellenic' traits would be positively misleading, since it is essential to consider the relationship between the social interests underlying dedication or participation in sanctuary events, and the interests of the participant's community or incipient state. Forms of community and forms of community ritual are generally closely related. Although there was no such thing as a 'normal' polis in the Archaic and Classical world, from the eighth century onwards increasingly similar paths of state formation in a number of previously varied and fragmented Early Iron Age societies gave rise to greater investment in community sanctuaries, and also to a growing similarity in religious organization and cult institutions. By the Archaic period at the latest, therefore, the existence of a common framework of cults and forms of sanctuary building reflected a shared need to come to terms with divine and human 'others', and cult places were thus ideal channels for celebrating contacts (friendly or hostile) between states of all kinds. Equally, as noted earlier, the emergence in many poleis of ruling individuals or families who sought to consolidate their own power and exclude their rivals by identifying closely with the cities they led, produced a clearer perception of what constituted the interests of the state; and these interests included discouraging or controlling the private activities of aristocrats, which were at best distractions, at worst threats to the long-term prosperity of the community. It was the coincidence of the existence of these political preoccupations and the common framework of state cults which formed the foundation for the establishment of an institutionalized common structure for religious activity, and for its location outside state borders.

SANCTUARY FESTIVALS AND MYTHS

From the early sixth century, four major sanctuaries, Olympia, Delphi, Isthmia and Nemea, formed the heart of a festival cycle which also included numerous smaller local festivals, of which little or no archaeological trace survives. In contrast to the longer histories of Olympia and Delphi, the inter-state festivals at Isthmia and Nemea were the later creations of controlling patron states. Isthmia, a small Corinthian roadside shrine from Early Protogeometric times, expanded during the eighth century, and became the site of the second monumental stone temple on the Greek mainland during the seventh (built soon after that on Temple Hill at Corinth, probably around the middle of the century), a monumental symbol of Corinthian control of the area around the Isthmus, and, if our assumptions about chronology are correct, perhaps even a Kypselid answer to the Bacchiad temple at Corinth.[83] However, its architectural splendour was not matched by dedications, and until the establishment of the festival in 582/80 BC (Solinus 7.14) there is nothing in the material record to suggest that contests of any kind took place.[84] At Nemea, by contrast, although there is clear seventh century evidence for cult activity, the construction of the first temple, probably c. 600 BC, occurred shortly before the traditional date of the first festival in c. 573 BC, and the development of the sanctuary and the beginning of the festival seem closely connected.[85] The role of Corinth as a political catalyst in the establishment of a festival cycle should not be underestimated. The two sites most closely connected with Corinth, Isthmia and Delphi, established stephanitic festivals on the model of Olympia at approximately the same time, and were rapidly copied by Nemea, initially under the control of Kleonai (nominally an independent city state), but always overshadowed by Corinth's rival, Argos.[86]

These changes were almost immediately mirrored in the creation of a complex body of sanctuary mythology. On a local level, a mutual self-awareness is evident in the parallel mythologies of the young dead heroes whose funeral games were the first festivals at Isthmia and Nemea. Both Pindar and Bacchylides were aware of the legend of the Seven against Thebes' celebration of funeral games for the Nemean child-hero, Opheltes-Archemoros, whose cult was celebrated in a small heroon from the first half of the sixth century onwards, and the legend of King Sisyphus' celebration of games for Melikertes-Palaimon at Isthmia is of similar date.[87] On a more general level, the odes of Pindar are perhaps the most powerful statement of the new pan-Hellenic ideology, celebrating the glory brought by the pan-Hellenic victor upon the city which he represented. This theme is continued in many other ways; for example, the thank-offerings erected on the Athenian Acropolis in the period before the Persian wars reflect the value of victory as a means of establishing social and political status.[88] Equally, a desire to praise the achievements of victors at the new festivals is paralleled by a desire to establish the legitimate place of the periodos as a long established feature of Greek activity. Hence an emphasis on the primeval origins of festivals and sanctuary institutions: for example, the myth of the Delphic succession (which has no archaeological support) served to establish the oracle's antiquity, and therefore superiority, in relation to its rivals (notably Dodona), and is complemented in Delphic mythology by fake oracular responses ordering the foundation of the Olympic games. The common idea that the games were refounded in the sixth century after earlier competitions had lapsed also serves a similar purpose (see Pausanias on Olympia and Solinus 7.14 on Isthmia).[89] The list of similar examples is almost endless, and in the brief space available here, it is only possible to touch upon a very complex subject.

CONCLUSIONS

In conclusion, therefore, the formalized framework of pan-Hellenic cult activity which emerged early in the sixth century may be seen as a political necessity, resulting from a pattern of aristocratic activity which began, or escalated dramatically, during the eighth century, and which is visible in the material record of votives at sanctuaries outside polis borders. A series of parallel changes in attitudes to citizenship, and the role of religion in the state effectively guaranteed that the actions of aristocrats at such sanctuaries would become subject to the state regulation which is central to pan-Hellenic religion. If, as Christiane Sourvinou-Inwood has emphasized, the polis mediated all the religious activities of its citizens, it would surely be impossible for any true pan-Hellenic system to have existed before the eighth century at the earliest; and, if one accepts that pan-Hellenism was more than just the sum of various 'parts' of state religion, one should further distinguish between the emergence of shared community values, and the inevitably later incorporation of these values into an institutionalized ritual programme. Again, I would echo Sourvinou-Inwood's criticisms of the way in which the canonical, defining characteristics of later Greek sanctuaries have been allowed to colour our expectations of Early Iron Age cult places of all kinds, including those which were to acquire pan-Hellenic functions. Our only source of direct evidence for this period is the material record, and, as I have sought to demonstrate here in the case of pan-Hellenic sanctuaries, it offers an essential, independent check upon the multiplicity of models available for the development of institutions which were to become central to the world of the Archaic and Classical polis.

NOTES

1 Treaties/federal meetings: e.g. Herodotos 7.172, 7.175, 8.123; Pausanias 5.12.8, 5.23.4; Plutarch, *Alexander* 14.1; A. M. Snodgrass, 'Interaction by design: the Greek city-state', in C. Renfrew and J. F. Cherry, eds, *Peer Polity Interaction and Socio-Political Change* (Cambridge 1986) 47–58.
2 R. Lonis, *Guerre et religion en Grèce à l'époque classique* (Paris 1979) ch. 9; W. Raschke, 'Images of victory', in W. Raschke, ed., *The Archaeology of the Olympics* (Madison 1988) 38–54; H. W. Pleket, 'Games, prizes, athletes and ideology', *Stadion* 1 (1975) 49–89. Treasuries: *infra* n. 9.
3 Pan-Hellenism: C. Sourvinou-Inwood, 'What is polis religion?', in O. Murray and S. R. F. Price, eds, *The Greek City. Homer to Alexander* (Oxford 1990) 295–322; *idem*, 'Further aspects of polis religion', *AION. Archeologia e storia antica* 10 (1988) 259–74.
4 Isthmia: C. Morgan, *Athletes and Oracles* (Cambridge 1990) 213–15 (hereafter abbreviated *Athletes and Oracles*); *idem*, *Isthmia. The Late Bronze Age Settlement and Early Iron Age Sanctuary* (in preparation). Kommos: J. W. Shaw, 'Excavations at Kommos (Crete) during 1980', *Hesperia* 50 (1981) 236–51; *idem*, 'Excavation at Kommos (Crete) during 1984–5', *Hesperia* 55 (1986) 226–7 (chronology, P. J. Callaghan pers. comm). Kombothekra: K. Müller, 'Artemis-tempel bei Kombothekra', *AM* 33 (1908) 323–6; U. Sinn, 'Das Heiligtum der Artemis Limnatis bei Kombothekra', *AM* 96 (1981) 25–71. Olympia: A. Mallwitz, 'Cult and competition locations at Olympia', in Raschke ed. (*supra* n. 2) 79–109 *passim*; *Athletes and Oracles*, ch. 3. Polis Cave: S. Benton, 'Excavations in Ithaca III', *BSA* 35 (1934–5) 45–73; *idem*, 'Excavations at Ithaca III, the cave at polis II', *BSA* 39 (1938/9) 16–22; *idem*, 'Second thoughts on "Mycenaean" pottery in Ithaca', *BSA* 44 (1949) 307–12. Mt Hymettos: M. Langdon, *A Sanctuary of Zeus on Mt Hymettus*, *Hesperia* Suppl. 16 (Princeton 1976); CAM and ERG in E. R. Gebhard and F. P. Hemans, 'University of Chicago

CATHERINE MORGAN

excavations at Isthmia, 1989:I', *Hesperia* 61 (1992) 9–22 (on the EIA shrine).

5 Discussions of eighth century change are numerous: e.g. papers in R. Hägg, ed., *The Greek Renaissance of the 8th century BC* (Stockholm 1983); R. Hägg, N. Marinatos and G. C. Nordquist, eds, *Early Greek Cult Practice* (Stockholm 1988); A. M. Snodgrass, *Archaic Greece. The Age of Experiment* (London 1980) chs 1 and 2.

6 A. Mallwitz, 'Kritisches zur Architektur Griechenlands im 8. und 7. Jahrhundert', *AA* 1981, 599–642; J. J. Coulton, *Ancient Greek Architects at Work* (Ithaca, NY 1977) ch. 2. Perachora: H. Payne, *Perachora* I (Oxford 1940) ch. 2. Samos: E. Buschor and H. Schleif, 'Heraion von Samos: Der Altarplatz der Frühzeit', *AM* 58 (1933) 150–3; H. Kyrieleis, *Führer durch das Heraion von Samos* (Athens 1981) 78–81; A. W. Lawrence, *Greek Architecture* revised R. A. Tomlinson (Harmondsworth 1983) 4th edn revised. Eretria: P. Auberson, 'La reconstitution du Daphnéphoreion d'Erétrie', *AntK* 17 (1974) 60–8; A. Mazarakis Ainian, 'Geometric Eretria', *AntK* 30 (1987) 3–24. Ephesos: A. Bammer, 'Neue Grabungen an der Zentralbasis des Artemision von Ephesos', *ÖJh* 58 (1988) Beiblatt 1–31. Aegira (Building A): W. Alzinger, 'Aegeira', *ÖJh* 54 (1983) 36–8, fig. 2b; W. Alzinger *et al.*, 'Aegeira', *Klio* 67 (1985) 426–30. Isthmia: O. Broneer, *Isthmia* I: *The Temple of Poseidon* (Princeton 1971) 3–56; E. Gebhard, ch. 8 in this volume. Corinth: H. N. Fowler and R. Stillwell, *Corinth* I (1): *Introduction, Topography, and Architecture* (Cambridge, Mass. 1932) ch. 2; R. Stillwell, R. I. Scranton and S. E. Freeman, *Corinth* I (2): *Architecture* (Cambridge, Mass. 1941) ch. 4; M. C. Roebuck, 'Excavation at Corinth', *Hesperia* 24 (1955) 153–7; H. Robinson, 'Excavations at Temple Hill', *ArchDelt* 26 (1971) B1, 100. Thermon: G. Soteriades, "Ἀνασκαφαὶ ἐν Θέρμῳ", *ArchEph* 1900, 171–211; G. Kawerau and G. Soteriades, 'Der Apollotempel zu Thermos', *Antike Denkmäler* II (Berlin 1908); B. Wesenberg, 'Thermos B1', *AA* 1982, 149–57. Delphi: *infra* n. 65.

7 Herodotos, 5.62.2; Pindar, *Pyth.* 7.

8 Coulton (*supra* n. 6) 17–21; E. Kunze and H. Schleif, *Olympische Forschungen* 1 (Berlin 1944) 1–52; Stella G. Miller, 'The Philippeion and Macedonian Hellenistic architecture', *AM* 88 (1973) 189–218; F. Seiler, *Die griechische Tholos* (Mainz 1986) 89–103. East Greece: S. Hornblower, *Mausolus* (Oxford 1982) 280–93.

9 W. Dinsmoor, *The Architecture of Ancient Greece*, 3rd edn, rev. (London 1975) 115–17: A. Mallwitz, *Olympia und seine Bauten* (Munich 1972) 163–79; P. de la Coste-Messelière, *Au Musée de Delphes* (Paris 1936) *passim*. On western investment in general: E. Kunze and H. Schleif, *Olympische Forschungen* 1 (Berlin 1944) 83–145.

10 W. Dittenberger and K. Purgold, *Inschriften von Olympia* (Berlin 1896) 22, treaty between Selinus and its mother-city, Megara Hyblaea, *c.* 500 BC; I. Malkin, *Religion and Colonization in Ancient Greece* (Leiden 1987) for religious links between colony and mother-city.

11 Olympia: W.-D. Heilmeyer, *Olympische Forschungen* 7: *Frühe Olympische Tonfiguren* (Berlin 1972); M. Maass, *Olympische Forschungen* 10: *Die geometrischen Dreifüsse von Olympia* (Berlin 1978); W.-D. Heilmeyer, *Olympische Forschungen* 12: *Frühe Olympische Bronzefiguren* (Berlin 1979); H. Philipp, *Olympische Forschungen* 13: *Bronzeschmuck aus Olympia* (Berlin 1981). Delphi: C. Rolley, *Fouilles de Delphes* 5(2): *Les statuettes de bronze* (Paris 1969) pt I; *idem*, *Fouilles de Delphes* 5(3): *Les trépieds à cuve clouée* (Paris 1977). Dodona: C. Carapanos, *Dodona et ses ruines*, 2 vols (Paris 1878); metalwork mainly unpublished.

12 Maass (*supra* n. 11) 5–20, 228; Heilmeyer (*supra* n. 11 (1979)) 54–9, 73–6, 136–41.

38

13 W. McDonald, W. Coulson and J. Rosser, *Excavations at Nichoria in South West Messenia* 3: *Dark Age and Byzantine Occupation* (Minneapolis 1983) 273–87; G. Rapp and S. E. Aschenbrenner, eds, *Excavations at Nichoria in South West Greece* 1: *Site, Environs, and Techniques* (Minneapolis 1978) 166–224.

14 M. E. Voyatzis, *The Early Sanctuary of Athena Alea at Tegea and Other Archaic Sanctuaries in Arcadia*, SIMA Pocketbook 97 (Göteborg 1990) ch. 4.

15 *Athletes and Oracles*, ch. 3.

16 W. McDonald and G. Rapp, eds, *The Minnesota Messenia Expedition: Reconstructing a Bronze Age Regional Environment* (Minneapolis 1972) 142–4; W. Coulson, *The Dark Age Pottery of Messenia* (Göteborg 1986) ch. 5; G. Hatzis, "Η πρωτογεωμετρική εποχή στὴ Μεσσηνία', *Acts of the Second International Congress of Peloponnesian Studies* II (Athens 1981–2) 343–7; *Athletes and Oracles*, 68–73. See *Iliad* 2.591–602; Strabo 8.361 for the divisions of the kingdom of Kresphontes.

17 McDonald *et al.* (*supra* n. 13) chs 2 and 6; K. Fagerström, 'Finds, function and plan: Iron Age Nichoria', *OpAth* 17 (1988) 33–50. Kaphirio: Coulson (*supra* n. 16) 38–48.

18 Akovitika: P. Themelis, 'The sanctuary of Poseidon at Akovitika', *AAA* 2 (1969) 356–7 (his 'Protogeometric' pottery equals Dark Age III and probably dates the establishment of the sanctuary); *BCH* 83 (1959) chronique 639–40. McDonald and Rapp (*supra* n. 16) register B includes 24 A(rchaic) or ?A sites, of which eight are shrines.

19 Voyatzis (*supra* n. 14); R. Howell, 'A survey of eastern Arcadia in prehistory', *BSA* 65 (1970) 79–127; M. Jost, *Sanctuaires et cultes d'Arcadie* (Paris 1985); C. Dugas, 'Le sanctuaire d'Aléa Athéna à Tegée avant le IVᵉ siècle', *BCH* 45 (1921) 335–435; *Athletes and Oracles*, 79–85; E. Østby, 'The Archaic temple of Athena Alea at Tegea', *OpAth* 16 (1986) 75–102.

20 Voyatzis (*supra* n. 14); cf. C. Rolley, *Monumenta Graeca et Romana* (Leiden 1967) 2, no. 8, 130–4, 234–6 (cf. J. N. Coldstream, *Geometric Greece* (London 1977) 157, fig. 51b); F. Hiller von Gaertringen and H. Lattermann, *Arkadische Forschungen* (Berlin 1911) 41, pl. 13.3; I. Kilian-Dirlmeier, *Anhänger in Griechenland von der mykenischen bis zur spätgeometrischen Zeit*, PBF 11(2) (Munich 1979) 40–1 (cf. Voyatzis (*supra* n. 14) 185–97).

21 Spartan lead figurines at Tegea: Dugas (*supra* n. 19) 428–9; Voyatzis (*supra* n. 14) 274–81.

22 W. Burkert, 'Offerings in perspective: surrender, distribution and exchange', in T. T. Linders and G. Nordquist, eds, *Gifts to The Gods* (Uppsala 1987) 43–50; R. Hägg, 'Gifts to the heroes in Geometric and Archaic Greece', in Linders and Nordquist (*supra*) 93–9; B. Alroth, *Greek Gods and Figurines* (Uppsala 1989).

23 A. M. Snodgrass, *The Dark Age of Greece* (Edinburgh 1971) 237–9; *idem*, 'The coming of the Iron Age in Greece: Europe's earliest bronze/iron transition', in M. L. S. Sørensen and R. Thomas, eds, *The Bronze Age–Iron Age Transition in Europe*, BAR-IS 483 (Oxford 1989) 22–35; C. Rolley, S. Filippakis, E. Photou and G. Varoufakis, 'Bronzes grecs et orientaux: influences et apprentissages', *BCH* 107 (1983) 111–32; E. Magou, S. Philippakis and C. Rolley, 'Trépieds géométriques de bronze. Analyses complémentaires', *BCH* 110 (1986) 121–36. *Athletes and Oracles*, 194–203.

24 *Athletes and Oracles*, 28–30. Isthmia: Broneer, Gebhard (*supra* n. 6).

25 Zeus as agriculture god: Langdon (*supra* n. 4) 79–87; A. M. Snodgrass, *An Archaeology of Greece* (Berkeley 1987) 205–7; J. Swaddling, *The Ancient Olympic Games* (London 1980) 12. According to E. Simon, *Festivals of Attica* (Madison 1983) 105–8, most Attic festivals originated as agricultural celebrations;

cf. R. Osborne, *Classical Landscape with Figures* (London 1987) ch. 8.

26 Wagons: Heilmeyer (*supra* n. 11 (1972)) 32–55 (including eighth century pieces); Sinn (*supra* n. 4) 67–9. Four-in-hand race introduced at Olympia *c.* 680 BC, two-in-hand *c.* 408 BC (Pausanias 5.8.7, 10–11). Trappings: e.g. Samos: U. Jantzen, *Samos* 8: *Ägyptische und orientalische Bronzen aus dem Heraion in Samos* (Berlin 1972) 64–5, pls 61, 62; Lindos: C. Blinkenberg, *Lindos. Fouilles de l'Acropole 1902–1914* 1: *Les petits objets* (Berlin 1931) 195–202, e.g. cat. 613, pl. 24; Athens Acropolis: H. Lechat, 'Mors antiques en bronze', *BCH* 14 (1890) 385–8, figs 1, 2.

27 *Athletes and Oracles*, ch. 2.

28 Heilmeyer (*supra* n. 11 (1979)) 19–24; H.-V. Herrmann, 'Werkstätten geometrischer Bronzeplastik', *JdI* 7 (1964) 17–71. Cf. Heilmeyer (*supra* n. 11 (1972)) 16–19, 87–92.

29 Heilmeyer (*supra* n. 11 (1979)) 52–3; H. Born and A. Moustaka, 'Eine geometrische Bronzestatuette im originalen Gussmantel aus Olympia', *AM* 97 (1982) 17–23; W. -D. Heilmeyer, G. Zimmer and G. Schneider, 'Die Bronzegiesserei unter der Werkstatt des Phidias in Olympia', *AA* 1987, 239–99, probably eighth century onwards.

30 Osborne (*supra* n. 25) chs 1 and 2 (14–16 on builders); A. Burford, *Craftsmen in Greek and Roman Society* (London 1972) ch. 2; K. Arafat and C. Morgan, 'Pots and potters in Athens and Corinth: a review', *OJA* 8 (1989) 328–9.

31 Olympia: e.g. Heilmeyer, Zimmer and Schneider (*supra* n. 29); W.-D. Heilmeyer, 'Giessereibetriebe in Olympia', *JdI* 84 (1969) 1–28; U. Gehrig, 'Frühe griechische Bronzegusstechniken', *AA* 1979, 547–8 and *passim*; *AR* 33 (1986–7) 21. Philia: K. Kilian, 'Weihungen aus Eisen und Eisenverarbeitung im Heiligtum zu Philia (Thessalien)', in Hägg, ed., (*supra* n. 5) 131–46. Kalapodi: R. C. S. Felsch, 'Zur Chronologie und zum Stil geometrischer Bronzen aus Kalapodi', in Hägg, ed., (*supra*) 123–9. Samos: e.g., G. Kopcke, 'Heraion von Samos: Die Kampagnen 1961/1965 im Südtemenos (8.–6. Jahrhundert)', *AM* 83 (1968) 285, no. 101 (Samian Heraion). Isthmia, Delphi etc.: W. Rostoker and E. Gebhard, 'The sanctuary of Poseidon at Isthmia: techniques of metal manufacture', *Hesperia* 49 (1980) 347–63.

32 Maass (*supra* n. 11) 288; *idem*, 'Die geometrischen Dreifüsse von Olympia', *AntK* 24 (1981) 6–20.

33 Maass (*supra* n. 11) pl. 27, T859; Heilmeyer, Zimmer and Schneider (*supra* n. 29) 266–8. Archaic casting, *supra* n. 31.

34 Mould pairs which relate tripods dedicated at Delphi and Olympia to others from sanctuaries in the home regions of producers: e.g. Maass (*supra* n. 11) 158, B4350, cf. Isthmia IM 295 (in *Isthmia* VI, I.3, cat.15, forthcoming); Maass (*supra* n. 11) 25 n. 30. Early tripod dedications from Argos: *Athletes and Oracles*, 85–9 (cf. C. Morgan and T. Whitelaw, 'Pots and politics: ceramic evidence for the rise of the Argive state', *AJA* 95 (1991) 79–108, including bibliography). For the continuing existence of a substratum of poorer and simpler votives at inter-state sanctuaries: H. Kyrieleis, 'Offerings of "the common man" in the Heraion at Samos', in Hägg, Marinatos and Nordquist, eds, (*supra* n. 5) 215–21.

35 *Athletes and Oracles*, 49–52, app. 1; Osborne (*supra* n. 25) 124–6.

36 Dittenberger and Purgold (*supra* n. 10) nos 10 and 16; Pausanias, e.g. 5.13.10, 5.14.4, 5.15.10–12.

37 Philipp (*supra* n. 11) 1–26. Bronze belts: B. Fellmann, *Olympische Forschungen* 16: *Frühe Olympische Gürtelschmuckscheiben aus Bronze* (Berlin 1984) 109–12; C. G. Simon, 'The Archaic votive offerings and cults of Ionia', (Ph.D. diss. Berkeley 1986) University of California (UMI, Ann Arbor, Michigan). Early Italian imports (including jewellery): Philipp (*supra* n. 11) cat.no. 988, pl. 59,

cat.nos 1031–45, pls 20, 63; K. Kilian, 'Zwei Italische Kannhelme aus Griechenland', in *Etudes Delphiques*, *BCH* Suppl. 4 (Paris 1977) 492–7; H.-V. Herrmann,
'Altitalisches und Etruskisches in Olympia', *ASAtene* 61 (1983) 271–94.

38 J. Schilbach, 'Untersuchung der Schatzhausterrasse südlich des Schatzhauses der
Sikyonier in Olympia', *AA* 1984, 227–30. Wells: W. Gauer, *Olympische
Forschungen* 8: *Die Tongefässe aus dem Brunnen unterm Stadion–Nordwall und
im Südost-Gebiet* (Berlin 1975). Samian Heraion: U. Kron, 'Archaisches
Kultgeschirr aus dem Heraion von Samos. Zu einer speziellen Gattung von
archaischem Trink- und Tafelgeschirr mit Dipinti', in H. A. G. Brijder, ed.,
Ancient Greek and Related Pottery (Amsterdam 1984) 292–7; *idem*, 'Kultmahle
im Heraion von Samos archaischer Zeit', in Hägg *et al.*, eds, (*supra* n. 5) 135–47;
M. S. Goldstein, 'The setting of the ritual meal in Greek sanctuaries: 600–300 BC'
(Ph.D. diss., University of California, Berkeley 1978) 14–16 (Isthmia), 16–23
(Olympia).

39 For a recent review: H. M. Lee, 'The "First" Olympic Games of 776 BC', in
Raschke, ed., (*supra* n. 2) 110–18.

40 E. Lévy, 'Note sur la chronologie Athénienne au VIᵉ siècle', *Historia* 27 (1978)
513–21; T. Lenschau, 'Forschungen zur griechischen Geschichte im VII u. VI
Jahr. v. Chr. IV: Die Siegerliste von Olympia', *Philologus* 91 (1936) 396–411.

41 For example, Mallwitz (*supra* n. 4) 96–103 advocates a starting date of 704 BC.

42 L. Moretti, *Olympionikai. I vincitori negli antichi agoni olimpici* (Rome 1957)
59–63. Calendar: Pausanias 5.8.6; Finley and Pleket (*supra* n. 2) 43.

43 Rapp and Aschenbrenner, eds, (*supra* n. 13) 92–7. McDonald and Rapp, eds,
(*supra* n. 16) register B includes 24 A(rchaic) or ?A sites, of which eight are
shrines, 14 habitation/cemetery, one cemetery, one ?guardhouse. The division of
Messenia into *kleroi* is traditionally associated with Lykourgos; Plutarch,
Lykourgos 8.3.

44 Hence those deprived of citizen rights were also deprived of the right to enter the
sanctuaries of their former polis, with transgression punishable by death:
C. Sourvinou-Inwood in Murray and Price, eds, (*supra* n. 3) 297. Xenia: G.
Herman, *Ritualised Friendship and the Greek City* (Cambridge 1987) see especially 45; Pindar praises *xenoi* alongside the achievements of individuals as
citizens, e.g. Pyth. 3.70–1, 9.82, 10.64–72.

45 G. Huxley, 'Argos et les derniers Téménides', *BCH* 82 (1958) 588–601; cf.
M. Crawford and D. Whitehead, *Archaic and Classical Greece* (Cambridge 1983)
618–9; T. Kelly, *A History of Argos to 500 BC* (Minneapolis 1976) for the
chronology of Pheidon's reign.

46 N. Loraux, *The Invention of Athens. The Funeral Oration in the Classical City*
(Cambridge, Mass. 1986) ch. 1; W. R. Connor, 'Tribes, festivals and processions:
civic ceremonial and political manipulation in Archaic Greece', *JHS* 107 (1987)
40–50; F. Jacoby, 'GENESIA, a forgotten festival of the dead', *CQ* 38 (1944)
65–75.

47 For a full catalogue of orientalizing tripods at Olympia: H.-V. Herrmann,
Olympische Forschungen 6: *Die Kessel der Orientalisierenden Zeit* 1 (Berlin
1966); *idem*, *Olympische Forschungen* 11: *Die Kessel der Orientalisierenden Zeit*
2 (Berlin 1979). P. Amandry, 'Trépieds de Delphes et du Péloponnèse', *BCH* 111
(1987) 79–131; Rolley (*supra* n. 11, *Trépieds*) 147–9, Boiotian tripods cat.nos 267
(seventh century), 268 (*c.* 550 BC). Boiotian pottery: e.g. Athens National
Museum 289, 1119 (unpublished).

48 Plutarch, *Solon* 21.4–5 (cf. Cicero, *de legibus* ii.26.64); Plutarch, *Lykourgos*
27.1–2.

49 Snodgrass (*supra* n. 5) 52–3, 99–100.

50 P. Perdrizet, *Fouilles de Delphes* 5(1): *Monuments figurés, arts mineurs* (Paris 1908) 133–40; P. Amandry, 'Petits objets de Delphes', *BCH* 68–9 (1944–5) 36–51; Rolley (*supra* n. 11 (1969)); *idem* (*supra* n. 11, *Trépieds*).

51 *Athletes and Oracles*, 107–26, app. 2; C. Neeft, 'Observations on the Thapsos Class', *MEFRA* 93 (1981) app. 1. Earliest pottery: L. Lerat, 'Fouilles à Delphes à l'est du grand sanctuaire (1950–1957)', *BCH* 85 (1961) 352–7; P. G. Themelis, 'Δελφοὶ καὶ περιοχὴ τὸν 8° καὶ 7° π.χ. αἰώνα', *ASAtene* 61 (1983) 213–55.

52 E.g. W. G. Forrest, 'Colonisation and the rise of Delphi', *Historia* 6 (1957) 171; J. Fontenrose, 'The cult of Apollo and the games at Delphi', in Raschke, ed., (*supra* n. 2) 121–40. Perachora: I. Kilian-Dirlmeier, 'Fremde Weihungen in griechischen Heiligtümern vom 8. bis zum Beginn des 7. Jahrhunderts v. Chr.', *JRGZM* 32 (1985) 225–30; H. Payne, *Perachora* I (Oxford 1940); T. Dunbabin, *Perachora* II (Oxford 1961).

53 Rolley (*supra* n. 11 (1969)) e.g. 17–26, 38–9, 55–6. Amandry (*supra* n. 50) 49.

54 Magic: G. E. R. Lloyd, *Magic, Reason and Experience* (Cambridge 1979) 10–15 and *passim*; R. Parker, *Miasma* (Oxford 1983) ch. 9; J. D. Mikalson, *Athenian Popular Religion* (London 1983) ch. 6. Cf. Boiotian oracles: S. Symeonoglou, 'The oracles of Thebes', in *La Béotie Antique (Colloquium Lyon-St. Etienne 1983)* (Paris 1985) 155–8; A. Schachter, *The Cults of Boiotia*, *BICS* Suppl. 38 (London 1981) e.g. vol. I, 65–8 on Apollo Ptoion.

55 Irrational view: J.-P. Vernant, 'Parole et signes muets', in J.-P. Vernant, L. Vandermeersch, J. Gernet, J. Bottéro, D. Grodzynski and A. Retet Laurentin, eds, *Divination et rationalité* (Paris 1974) 11–19; R. Flacelière (trans. D. Garman), *Greek Oracles*, 2nd edn (London 1976) ch. 6. Functional view: H. Parke and D. Wormell, *The Delphic Oracle* (Oxford 1956) and J. Fontenrose, *The Delphic Oracle* (Berkeley 1978) are fundamental studies, containing full catalogues of responses. R. Parker, 'Greek states and Greek oracles', in P. A. Cartledge and F. D. Harvey, eds, *Crux. Essays in Greek History Presented to G. E. M. de Ste Croix on his 75th Birthday* (London 1985) 304.

56 G. K. Park, 'Divination and its social context', *Journal of the Royal Anthropological Institute* 93 (1963) 195–209; C. R. Whittaker, 'The Delphic oracle: belief and behaviour in ancient Greece – and Africa', *Harvard Theological Review* 58 (1965) 21–47. 'Wooden walls': Parker (*supra* n. 55) 301; Fontenrose (*supra* n. 55) 124–8.

57 K. Hölkeskamp, review of M. Gagarin, *Early Greek Law*, *Gnomon* 62 (1990) 116–28; *idem*, 'Arbitrators, lawgivers and the "codification" of law in Archaic Greece' (in preparation).

58 *Athletes and Oracles*, 161–71.

59 Malkin (*supra* n. 10) pt 1, ch. 1.

60 *Athletes and Oracles*, 186–90.

61 Parker (*supra* n. 55) (1985) 310–12.

62 Plutarch, *Moralia* 492a–b refers to Thessalian selection of Aleuas the Red as king by means of a lot oracle at Delphi, but consultation of the Pythia was rare: Parke and Wormell (*supra* n. 55) responses 254, 311 and 316. Pausanias 10.16.8, notes that Echekratidas of Larissa dedicated a small Apollo said by the Delphians to have been the first offering to be set up. Thessaly: S. Hornblower, *The Greek World 479–323 BC* (London 1983) 79–83; Snodgrass (*supra* n. 5) 87–90.

63 Temple: C. Le Roy, *Fouilles de Delphes* 2: *Topographie et architecture. Les terres cuites architecturales* (Paris 1967) 21–8; cf. rooftiles from Isthmia and Corinth: Broneer (*supra* n. 6) 40–53; H. Robinson, 'Excavations at Corinth: Temple Hill 1968–1972', *Hesperia* 45 (1976) 231–4; *idem*, 'Roof tiles of the early seventh century', *AM* 99 (1984) 55–66; W. Dinsmoor, *The Architecture of Ancient*

Greece, 3rd edn (London 1950) 71 dates the construction c. 50 years before 548 BC, yet 600 BC must be the latest likely date on the grounds of its hipped roof. Kleobis and Biton: C. Vatin, 'Couroi argiens à Delphes', in *Etudes Delphiques*, *BCH* Suppl. 4 (Paris 1977) 13–22; *idem*, 'Monuments votifs de Delphes', *BCH* 106 (1982) 509–25; T. Homolle, *Fouilles de Delphes* 4 (1): *Monuments figurés, sculptures* (Paris 1909) 5–18, 41–54.

64 W. G. Forrest, 'The First Sacred War', *BCH* 80 (1956) 33–52; N. Robertson, 'The myth of the First Sacred War', *CQ* 28 (1978) 38–73.

65 A. A. Mosshammer, 'The date of the first Pythiad – again', *GRBS* 23 (1982) 15–30; K. Broderson, 'Zur Datierung der ersten Pythien', *ZPE* 82 (1990) 25–31.

66 Homeric Hymn to Pythian Apollo, nb. 244–76, 294–9, 388–544; G. S. Kirk, 'The Homeric Hymns', in P. E. Easterling and B. M. W. Knox, eds, *Cambridge History of Classical Literature* (Cambridge 1985) 114–15 for summary of arguments about chronology.

67 A. B. Cook, *Zeus. A Study in Ancient Religion*, vols II and III (Cambridge 1925, 1940) pt I, ch. 2. Dodona: S. Dakaris, 'Δωδώνη' (Epirus 1978). Mt Hymettos: Langdon (*supra* n. 4).

68 M. Sartre, 'Aspects économiques et religieux de la frontière dans les cités grecques', *Ktêma* 4 (1979) 213–24.

69 Sourvinou-Inwood (*supra* n. 3 (1990)) 297–9.

70 Peisistratids: H. A. Shapiro, *Art and Cult under the Tyrants in Athens* (Mainz 1989) ch. 1; F. Kolb, 'Die Bau-, Religions- und Kulturpolitik der Peisistratiden', *JdI* 92 (1977) 99–138. Dionysos Eleutheraios: T. H. Carpenter, *Dionysian Imagery in Archaic Greek Art* (Oxford 1986) 122–3. Little Bears: C. Sourvinou-Inwood, *Studies in Girls' Transitions. Aspects of the Arkteia and Age Representation in Attic Iconography* (Athens 1988). Cf. L. Palaiokrassa, Τὸ ἱερὸ τῆς Ἀρτέμιδος Μουνιχίας' (Ph.D. thesis, Thessaloniki University 1983); *idem*, 'Neue Befunde aus dem Heiligtum der Artemis Munichia', *AM* 104 (1989) 1–40; L. Kahil, 'Autour de l'Artémis attique', *AntK* 8 (1965) 20–33; *idem*, 'L'Artémis de Brauron: rites et mystère', *AntK* 20 (1977), 86–98; *idem*, 'Le sanctuaire de Brauron et la religion grecque', *CRAI* 1988, 799–813. M. B. Hollinshead, 'Against Iphigenia's adyton in three mainland temples', *AJA* 89 (1985) 426–8. Eleusis: H. Parke, *Festivals of the Athenians* (London 1977) 55–72; G. Mylonas, *Eleusis and the Eleusinian Mysteries* (Princeton 1961) chs 4 and 9.

71 Second temple of Nemesis at Rhamnous: M. M. Miles, 'A reconstruction of the temple of Nemesis at Rhamnous', *Hesperia* 58 (1989) 137–249. Acharnai: W. B. Dinsmoor, Jr, 'Anchoring two floating temples', *Hesperia* 51 (1982) 410–52; Dinsmoor (*supra* n. 9) 181–4.

72 P. Vidal-Naquet, 'The black hunter and the origin of the Athenian ephebeia', *Proceedings of the Cambridge Philological Society* 194 (1968) 49–64. Sparta: J.-P. Vernant, 'Une divinité des marges: Artémis Orthia', *Cahiers du Centre Jean Bérard* 9 (1984) 13–27; F. de Polignac, *La naissance de la cité grecque* (Paris 1984) 49–54, 66–85. Brauron: Euripides, *Iphig. Taur.* 1404–9. Arkteia: Sourvinou-Inwood (*supra* n. 70). Fourth century women's dedications at Brauron: *IG* II, 2nd edn, 1388, 1400, 1514.

73 Kilian-Dirlmeier (*supra* n. 52).

74 Simon (*supra* n. 37).

75 Ephesos and Samos: *supra* n. 6; A. Bammer, 'Gold und Elfenbein von einer neuen Kultbasis in Ephesos', *ÖJh* 58 (1988) 1–23. Eretria/Samos comparison: Snodgrass (*supra* n. 1) 55–6. Stoa: J. J. Coulton, *The Architectural Development of the Greek Stoa* (Oxford 1976) 280.

76 Lawrence (*supra* n. 6) 161–6. Didyma: K. Tuchelt, *Vorarbeiten zu einer*

Topographie von Didyma, *IstMitt* Beiheft 9 (Tübingen 1973).

77 G. Shipley, *A History of Samos 800–188 BC* (Oxford 1987) 54–65; Kilian-Dirlmeier (*supra* n. 52) 235–44, 248–53.

78 Herodotos 1.146, notes that the Ionians who settled at Miletos preferred to marry Carian women than to bring their wives with them. C. J. Emlyn-Jones, *The Ionians and Hellenism* (London 1980) ch. 2, nb 12–17. Ionian migration: J. Boardman, *The Greeks Overseas*, 3rd edn (London 1980) 25–33.

79 R. D. Barnett, 'Early Greek and Oriental ivories', *JHS* 68 (1948) 20–1 (cf. Asiatic iconography on Kanachos of Sikyon's cult statue of Apollo at Didyma: E. Simon, 'Beobachtung zum Apollon Philesios des Kanachos', in K. Schauenburg, ed., *Charites. Studien zur Altertumswissenschaft* (Bonn 1957) 38–46). Artemision ivories: E. Akurgal, *Die Kunst Anatoliens von Homer bis Alexander* (Berlin 1961) 195–209; Barnett (*supra*); J. B. Carter, 'Greek ivory carving in the Orientalising and Archaic periods' (Ph.D. diss., Harvard University 1984) *passim*.

80 H. W. Parke, 'Croesus and Delphi', *GRBS* 25 (1984) 209–323. Cf. Ephesos column base: L. H. Jeffery, *The Local Scripts of Archaic Greece* (Oxford 1961) 339.

81 Samos: Kyrieleis (*supra* n. 6) 118–20. Didyma: J. Fontenrose, *Didyma* (Berkeley 1988) 28–9 for summary and bibliography; K. Tuchelt, *Die archaischen Skulpturen von Didyma*, Istanbuler Forschungen 27 (Berlin 1970) 21–2.

82 Athena Polias: Simon (*supra* n. 37) 23, 54, 61, 64–5, 128, 131–2, 134–5, 159–60, 162–5. Cf. Emborio: *Athletes and Oracles*, 230–3. Cf. C. Morgan, 'Divination and society at Delphi and Didyma', *Hermathena* 147 (1989) 17–42.

83 *Supra* nn. 4 and 6; FPH in E. R. Gebhard and F. P. Hemans, 'University of Chicago excavations at Isthmia, 1989:1', *Hesperia* 61 (1992) 39, pls 13b, c (on the Archaic temple construction date).

84 Athletic equipment appears from around the time of the first festival; e.g. O. Broneer, 'Excavations at Isthmia, fourth campaign 1957–1958', *Hesperia* 28 (1959) 322–3, pl. 73a, jumping weight of *c*.580–75 (dedicatory inscription, W. Peek, 'Archaische Epigramme', *ZPE* 23 (1976) 77–8). Pindar refers to Isthmia as synonymous or closely associated with Corinth, e.g. *Nem.* 4.88; *Ol.* 9.86, 13.4–5.

85 Stephen G. Miller, ed., *Nemea* (Berkeley 1990) 128–32. Stella G. Miller, 'Excavations at the Panhellenic site of Nemea: cults, politics and games', in Raschke, ed., (*supra* n. 2) 141–51, 148 n. 8 for eighth/seventh-century evidence (the archaeological case for a seventh-century cult is stronger).

86 *Athletes and Oracles*, 216–8.

87 Melikertes-Palaimon: Pindar, B. Snell, ed., *Pindari carmina cum fragmentis*, vol. 2, 3rd edn (Leipzig 1964) frag. 6.5(1); Aeschylus, *Athamas*; Euripides, *Iphigenia in Aulis* 625–6. Opheltes-Archemoros: E. Simon, 'Archemoros', *AA* 1979, 31–45; W. Pülhorn, 'Archemoros', *LIMC* II (Zurich 1984); Bacchylides 8.10–14; G. Bond, ed., *Euripides' Hypsipyle* (Oxford 1963) nb. app. V lists relevant scholiasts on Pindar. Heroon: Miller (*supra* n. 87) (1990) 108–10 (cf. 27–9).

88 A. E. Raubitschek, *Dedications from the Athenian Acropolis* (Cambridge, Mass. 1949) includes *c.* 18 securely identifiable examples in his catalogue of 384 sixth/fifth-century pieces. D. Kyle, *Athletics in Ancient Athens* (Leiden 1987) chs 4 and 6.

89 C. Sourvinou-Inwood, 'Myth as history: the previous owners of the Delphic oracle', in J. Bremmer, ed., *Interpretations of Greek Mythology* (London 1987) 215–41. Olympics: Fontenrose (*supra* n. 54) 268–70. Rivalry: H. Parke, *Greek Oracles* (London 1967) 36–9; *idem*, *The Oracles of Zeus* (Oxford 1967) 13–15; Parke and Wormell (*supra* n. 55) 369.

3

Ritual dining at Corinth

Nancy Bookidis

That dining was an important aspect of the ritual practised in celebration of
Demeter and Kore at Corinth is shown by the many dining rooms that cover
the lower zone of their sanctuary on Acrocorinth.[1] At least 14 dining rooms
are known to have existed at the end of the sixth century BC, accommodating
a minimum of 101 people. By the late fifth century that number had grown
to at least 25 buildings, or 30 rooms, with couches for a minimum of two
hundred people (Fig. 3.1). More originally existed in the Archaic period but
could not be fully investigated; furthermore, the east and west limits to the
dining area were never found. Even with the number of rooms we do have,
however, it is clear that dining within the sanctuary was not confined to the
priestly staff but was practised by the celebrating population as well. This in
itself is not an unusual feature, for ritual banquets were commonly held
within the confines of sanctuaries at the culmination of a festival in order to
reaffirm a sense of community through equal distributions of food. To date,
however, no other sanctuary has yielded so many buildings devoted to that
function, buildings whose purpose is clearly established by form, furnish-
ings and contents.

The identification of the sanctuary as one dedicated to the worship of
Demeter and Kore is assured by the graffiti and *dipinti* inscribed on a
number of clay votives. Apart from the information that can be recovered
from the many offerings, we know very little about the cult, for no
Corinthian inscriptions clarify the ritual, and the ancient sources are few.
Those that do exist tell us that at the time of Timoleon's expedition to
Sicily, there were at least two priestesses. When Pausanias visited Corinth,
the cult statues could not be seen. Finally, Hesychius states that at Corinth
Demeter is called Epoikidia, an epithet that is otherwise unattested for
Demeter. If we may associate this epithet with our sanctuary, then we
should expect Demeter to have been concerned with matters pertaining to
the household.

Like many sanctuaries devoted to the two goddesses, ours lies within the
bounds of a city, Corinth, but is removed from the centre, midway up the
north slope of Acrocorinth. For an ancient Greek used to walking, 10 or 15

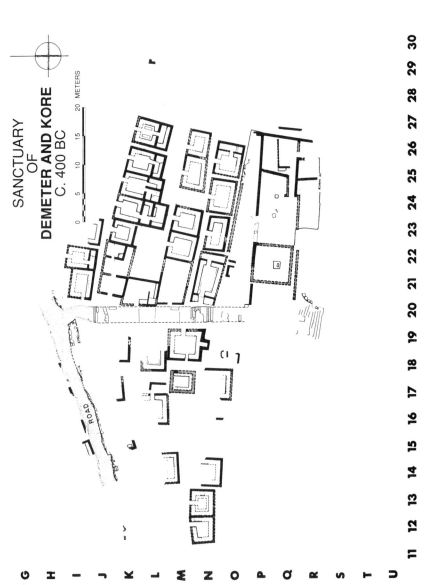

Figure 3.1 Corinth, sanctuary of Demeter and Kore c. 400 BC.

minutes would have sufficed to reach the site from the city centre by means of a dirt road that passed along the lower side of the *temenos*.

The buildings of the sanctuary are organized into three distinct areas – or terraces, as we have called them – on the basis of their function, with access to all provided by a long processional stairway running up the centre of the site. Dining is restricted to the lowest of the three terraces, sacrifice and the dedication of offerings to the middle terrace, and initiation of some sort in a small rock-cut theatre to the upper terrace. Although the dining rooms were the first structures that worshippers encountered as they ascended the hill from the city below, they were probably the last to be used, since the communal banquet could not take place until the sacrifice had been made.

The name for the festival (or festivals) celebrated here is unknown. Consequently, we are also ignorant as to the time of year when it was held. Similarly, we do not know whether the festival lasted one day or more, although several days would seem more likely. Our only conclusion about time can be drawn from the great number of lamps found in the excavations, which indicate that part, if not all, of the festival took place at night. In view of the proximity of the sanctuary to the rest of the city, we might assume that worshippers who were attending a festival of several days' duration did not spend the night there. But this is an incorrect assumption, for during the Thesmophoria in Athens women spent three days and nights within the *temenos*. It is therefore possible that the votaries at Corinth both ate and slept in our dining rooms. But because we cannot reconstruct the festival we can only sketch the basic ritual that would have taken place in those cult places where initiation and dining would have accompanied gift-giving and sacrifice. Limitations of space do not permit us to engage in reconstructing that ritual here. That will be the subject of a future volume in the Corinth series. Here we will confine ourselves to the subject of dining.

As we stated above, our evidence for indoor dining goes back to the third quarter of the sixth century, although worship on the site is attested as early as the middle of the seventh century BC. We assume that communal dining was practised in the earliest period but either in the open air or under temporary shelter. Once the dining room is introduced, its form is remarkably consistent from its inception to its demise in the second century BC, a significant point, since the rooms do not follow the norm for public banquet halls. The only major modifications to the basic structure of the dining halls come about in the fifth century with the addition of facilities for sitting, washing and cooking to the, previously, solitary dining room. Building L-M:28, shown in Figures 3.2 and 3.3, illustrates the arrangements in their most developed, Hellenistic form.

The buildings are small, the dining room proper averaging *c.* 4.50m wide by 5.00m long. Reclining dining was the rule on immovable banquettes of earth, retained by stone walls and plastered with either clay or waterproof stucco cement. Individual couches were marked off by contoured arm rests;

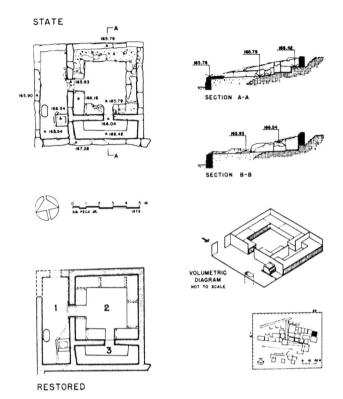

Figure 3.2 Building L-M: 28, plan.

Figure 3.3 Building L-M: 28, from the west.

48

despite the fact that many of these have been destroyed, enough remain to allow us to draw certain conclusions about the process of dining. The total number of built-in couches differs from building to building; nevertheless, seven and one-half may be considered the norm, with as few as five and one-half couches and as many as eight and one-half or possibly nine. Two couches per wall are customary but occasionally there are three. Table 3.1 (pp. 58–9) records the couch lengths in each building, giving the complete lengths or, where incomplete, the estimated lengths. As the table reveals, couch lengths within a single room varied considerably. Because of these variations our buildings have been called 'unplanned', for it is generally assumed that all public dining rooms were laid out according to a regular multiple of one couch length. And yet, an arrangement that has been repeated again and again during the course of two hundred years can hardly be considered unplanned. On the contrary, these variations are so consistent an aspect of the sanctuary dining rooms that we are led to believe that they were intentional. And if these differences were intended, their purpose may have been to distinguish between diners, on the basis of either age or rank.[2] However, they seem to follow no consistent order, and it is not possible to single out a regular position of honour. We have referred to half-couches. These are small units of 0.80 to 1.00m in length, which generally lie next to a door and are too short for normal reclining. Although we have no evidence to support it, we suggest that these places were seats for someone who either supervised the ritual of dining or assisted with the meal. Whatever their purpose, their frequent inclusion takes our dining rooms still further from the realm of canonical public dining settings and places them closer to dining rooms in private houses, where this peculiarity can also be found.[3] Is this an intentional association on the part of sanctuary builders, and has it some bearing on the epithet of Epoikidia recorded by Hesychius? It is tempting to think so. The compact size of these rooms means that the number of people in each unit was very small. If we assume that each couch accommodated only one diner, then five to no more than nine persons shared a room. It is true that Greek vase painting often depicts two people on a single couch, either two men or a man and a hetaira. Attempts to reconstruct this, however, show that a minimum length of 1.75 to 1.80m is needed to fit two adults, more if their legs were to be extended. Since a number of the couches are shorter, although sufficient in width, we can, I think, argue that one person was the norm. Whether two could have used the longer couches is unknown. The atmosphere, nonetheless, would have been intimate, the scale small. As we stated in the beginning, in the late fifth century, the period best attested in the sanctuary, facilities existed for at least two hundred banqueters. Since the limits of the lower terrace have not been found, there were undoubtedly more buildings to accommodate more diners, but surely not enough to house the entire citizenry of Corinth, unless they ate in many shifts. Some process of selection, then, must have limited the number of attending worshippers.

A further indication that attendance was restricted for at least part of the festival is the small size of the theatre at the top of the sanctuary.[4] Eighty-five to 90 people are all that could have fit on the six rock-cut steps that comprise the cavea. In contrast, the capacity of the theatre in the sanctuary of Demeter at Pergamon is estimated to have been eight hundred, while more than two thousand people could be accommodated in the Telesterion at Eleusis. We do not know what was said or done in our theatre but the limited number of participants allows us to postulate initiatory rites of a local character.

In cults of Demeter and Kore for which there is literary or epigraphic documentation the most common basis for selection was that of gender. A few examples should suffice to illustrate this. During the seven-day festival of Demeter Mysia at Pellene in Achaia men withdrew on the third day to leave women to themselves (Paus. 7.27.10). No men were allowed in the temple of Demeter Chthonia at Hermione (Paus. 2.35.8). Only women were permitted at Kos, and during the Thesmophoria in Athens and probably elsewhere attendance may have been further restricted to married women.[5] The Greater Mysteries at Eleusis may have been exceptional in that everyone could attend, including slaves.

At Corinth we cannot argue for the total exclusion of men from the festival for at least five male names appear among the dedicatory graffiti and *dipinti*. Furthermore, 40 or more large-scale statues in terracotta, depicting young men carrying offerings, suggest that youths, at least, played some part in the rites. Most of the dedications, however, point to a strong female presence – objects such as loomweights, jewellery, mirrors and the bulk of more than twenty-three thousand terracotta figurines, many of which represent young female votaries. We are accustomed to think that in mainland Greece men always reclined while respectable women always sat. Accordingly, we should expect our dining couches to have been occupied by men with, at best, women seated at the ends. But because of the strong feminine element expressed in the votives, combined with the restriction in numbers indicated by both the theatre and the dining rooms, and because of the pattern discernible in most other cults of Demeter and Kore, we suggest that at Corinth it was the women who ate by themselves in the dining rooms, that they reclined on the couches like men and engaged in the same sort of lively conversation. Whether this also involved the kind of *aischrologia* attested elsewhere, we cannot tell, but it is certainly possible. Such segregated dining is not unknown in cults of Demeter. It forms a prominent part of the Thesmophoria in every city where the festival was celebrated; it characterizes the Haloa in Athens and is also attested in an inscription from south-west Messenia.[6] What has been missing until now is the physical setting for such meals, and it is this, we suggest, that we have found at

Corinth in the form of traditional banquet rooms with couches for reclining. Nevertheless, an alternative suggestion has been made that would accommodate both reclining men and seated women. According to this theory, use would be made of a small room that frequently adjoins the dining room (Figure 3.2, Room 3). Generally long and narrow, it is no more than 1.30–1.60m wide. Its chief feature is a continuous bench that lines two or three walls. In buildings where space is limited, it can also house washing facilities and even the kitchen. In a normal, three- or four-room building, however, such as Building L-M:28, it is reached through the dining room and is quite separate from the other service rooms. This, according to some, was the women's dining room, where they sat while men reclined next door. As attractive an explanation as this may be, it is impossible for two reasons. First, the sitting room does not appear in every building. This must mean that whatever happened there could be done, if necessary, in the dining room. Second, the room is too narrow to accommodate both seated women and tables for food. We therefore assume that this auxiliary room was used either before or after the banquet – which took place on the couches – as a place for conversation or possibly instruction.

A discrepancy exists between the number of people who could have sat in the theatre – 85 to 90 – and the number of diners – two hundred – who could have been accommodated in the late fifth century BC. We must assume that old as well as new initiates participated in the rites or, less likely, that the initiation rites were performed in at least two shifts.

An interesting question that cannot be answered with the few sources remaining to us is the way in which the votaries were distributed among the many buildings, especially since the number destined for each room was small. Was the division entirely haphazard or were there basic criteria of age, family or tribal association that determined who ate together? It is quite possible that one or more sanctuary officials saw to the distribution. Laconian and Messenian inscriptions frequently refer to an official, titled the *thoinarmostria*, who, by herself or with assistants, was responsible for the organization of the sacrifices and the banquet. It was her duty to see that rules of good conduct were observed and that fines were levied against those who misbehaved.[7] Although the title of *thoinarmostria* is not as yet attested in the northern Peloponnese, it is logical to assume that one or more officials fulfilled similar responsibilities in the sanctuary at Corinth. On the other hand, when one considers the work that must have been required to supervise the operation of 25 or more banquet halls, from the organization of the food to the preparation of the couches and tables and actual direction of the banquet, the staff would have to have been considerable. It may, therefore, be that the operation of the dining rooms was not directly administered by the sanctuary personnel but by private entrepreneurs, who leased the facilities for a fee, much like the leasing of booths or *kapileia* in the sanctuary of Hera at Samos.[8]

An important prelude to the meal must have been washing, for, as we know from many ancient sources, physical cleanliness was closely tied to ritual purity. The importance of this act is shown by the bathing rooms that are attached to most of the dining complexes from the fifth century on. In its simplest form this room was furnished with a slightly elevated cement floor, over 1.00m square, which was drained by a narrow outlet. Where space was limited, the bath stall could be accommodated in one corner of the sitting room or kitchen, as in Room 1 of Building L-M:28 (Figure 3.2). In more spacious examples, such as Room 3 of Building M:16–17, a low bench provided sitting room for waiting participants. To what extent did prospective diners wash? R. Ginouvès has argued convincingly that a room set aside for washing implies a thorough bath, for simple washing of the hands could have been done at the table by means of a pitcher and bowl.[9] Although we have found no bathtubs, clay basins occur in virtually every dining room on the site, and it may be that they were used in conjunction with the bathing rooms. Fragments of *perirrhanteria* are also abundant, many of them predating the bathing rooms, and they may indicate some sort of ritual washing that was done in the open. Since the process of washing in the bathing rooms would have been fairly public, it is a further argument for limiting attendance at the banquet to one sex rather than to both.

As for water, three of the dining buildings were furnished with their own cistern. In Building L-M:28 (Figure 3.2), the cistern lies just opposite the bathing stall. But in most cases the water would have to have been carried from another source, perhaps from either the well or cistern located on the middle terrace.

Nearly every building of Classical and Hellenistic date had some sort of provision for cooking. The presence of such a facility is of considerable importance, for it implies that all or some part of the meal was prepared in each building. The space given over to it varies from building to building. The kitchen could occupy an entire room or a part of a room, as Room 1 on Figure 3.2. In most cases the cooking was done directly on the floor. In two examples, however, the arrangements were more elaborate. In the late fifth century Building K-L:24–5 (Figure 3.1) a raised hearth was equipped with clay burners, which could support at least three cooking pots placed simultaneously above the fire. In Building K-L:23–4 of the same period (Figure 3.1) an elevated hearth occupied the entire west wall of a sizeable room apparently given over entirely to cooking. A further provision of Building L-M:28, where the hearth was not actually found, was a waist-high sink for cleaning dishes (?), placed next to the bath-stall and across from the cistern.

Although no dining room was found with its contents intact, the range of utility and table wares can easily be assembled from the recovered fragments. The types of cooking pots employed are remarkably consistent throughout the sanctuary. Three shapes predominate, namely, the stewpot – both lidded and unlidded types – , the *lopas* or casserole, and the pitcher. Shapes represented by a few fragments are the shallow bowl, the grill – which may, in fact, be of Roman date – and a single brazier. Shapes that are not represented at all are the portable oven, the baking dome, frying pan and bean parcher. The cooking pots therefore suggest that boiling or stewing prevailed over grilling and baking. It is interesting to note the sizes of cooking pots that were used. Figures 3.4 and 3.5 display the range of both unlidded stewpots and pitchers, and Table 3.2 (p. 61) lists their approximate capacities. For purposes of comparison Table 3.2 also lists the amounts of food intended for the Thesmophoria at Cholargos in Attica, as prescribed in an inscription.[10]

Figure 3.4 Typical stew pots.

Figure 3.5 Pitchers and casserole.

Although one might expect the cooking to have been done in one or two large pots, such was clearly not the case, for small pots holding a half litre or less are extremely common. Because it is unlikely that food was prepared in individual portions, the small sizes may reflect some sort of food or sauce that was eaten in small quantities. In addition to the cooking pots, a variety of utility vessels was used, such as mortars for crushing and grinding, mixing bowls in any number of sizes, large clay trays and pitchers for carrying water. That wine may well have been drunk is suggested by the numerous transport/storage amphoras that were also found everywhere. Although local Corinthian types prevail, amphoras from Chios, Thasos, Rhodes and Knidos are also attested.

Drinking was a major feature of the meals, for drinking cups in the form of kotylai, skyphoi and kantharoi probably represent the most common shapes discarded in the sanctuary, discounting the votive miniatures. As for the rest of the table wares, a variety of bowls, plates and small saucers gives us little assistance as to what food was consumed. Pitchers and small aryballoi of blister ware were used for the serving of olive oil. Another vessel common in fourth-century contexts is the so-called baby-feeder, a small spouted juglet with strainer top. Because its fine Corinthian clay is not suited to oil, it must have been used for something else that was both strained and poured out in small quantities. Could this have been vinegar?

Apart from an unusual votive offering, namely, a large terracotta spoon, which bears a painted dedication to Demeter, no implements for eating were recovered and we assume that fingers were used. Iron knives become relatively plentiful in fills that cover the last row of dining rooms that abuts the middle terrace, but because of the situation in which they were found they are probably to be associated with sacrifice rather than with eating.

In trying to reconstruct what was eaten in the dining rooms, we can draw some assistance, albeit small, from remnants of food recovered on the site or from the lack thereof. Beginning with meat, we know that pigs were sacrificed to Demeter and Kore, for pig bones were discovered in a sacrificial pit of early Hellenistic date located on the middle terrace. We might therefore expect that pork was a part of the ritual meal. The total number of bones recovered from the pit, however, is slight, less than 0.22 cubic metres in volume. Such a small amount suggests that animal sacrifice may not have held a prominent part in sanctuary ritual. This is further supported by the almost total absence of bones in the dining rooms, and the complete absence of garbage pits within the sanctuary. Among the 50-odd buildings which we investigated, bones were found on only four floors. In three of the four instances these consisted only of a single small fragment of unidentifiable species; only in the service room of Building N:21–2 were more found, namely, 12 bones of pig, cow and possibly sheep or goat.[11] While it may be argued that even one bone means an animal, these meagre remains can also be interpreted as remnants of sacrifice, disturbed from their original place of deposition, just as votive miniatures and fragments of terracotta figurines are found in virtually every corner of the site. More than 70 sea shells were recovered from the sanctuary as a whole. While most of these occurred in Roman contexts, four sea shells were found in three dining rooms. Among the four are one *murex brandaris*, two *mactra* or *archivades*, and a *patella* or limpet shell – the only example from the site. While these are all edible varieties, the examples are so few that it is difficult to see how they could have formed a part of a communal meal. Indeed, the discovery of a shell made of lead suggests that they were intended as offerings, not as food. More common are the olive pits, which lay on a number of dining room and kitchen floors.

If meat and sea shells were not part of the communal meal, grain in some form was. Our evidence for this is not derived from the many ancient sources that speak of different kinds of cake associated with Demeter but from the grinding stones, found on the site, which indicate that grain was crushed within the confines of the sanctuary. For those not familiar with this implement, the saddle-quern is composed of a rectangular 'board' of andesite, the surface of which is striated to catch the grain. The actual grinding is done by means of an oval stone rubbed over the boards to produce either a coarse meal or finer flour.

In Archaic and Early Classical times barley was more widely grown, while wheat apparently was something of a luxury, but by Hellenistic times wheat was greatly preferred and relatively common. Either could have been eaten in the sanctuary, perhaps even both. Barley, however, requires a preliminary hulling, or pounding, in order to remove the outer husk. This is generally thought to have been done in deep stone mortars, evidence for which has not been found on the site. Therefore, either barley was husked outside the sanctuary, or wheat, because more valued, was the only grain that was dedicated and served.[12]

Once crushed, both could be boiled into a loose porridge or a thick paste. Since no bake-ovens are attested on the site, it is unlikely that wheat-flour was baked into bread, unless it was made into some sort of unleavened bread that could have baked directly on the hearth. A variety of cakes, together with other foods, appear as offerings on clay models of winnowing trays or *likna*. Two examples are shown in Figure 3.6. These need not have been baked but could have been moulded or kneaded from boiled grain. The ancient sources preserve a wealth of names for breads and cakes, many of which were especially popular with Demeter. One of these, called *kollyva*, appears in modern-day Greek usage to denote a wheat-cake served at memorial services for the dead. Its composition must be very close to the sort of food that would have been eaten in the sanctuary dining rooms, consisting as it does of boiled wheat, salt, pomegranate seeds, almonds and other condiments.

In the course of excavation of a Roman temple on the upper terrace we did, in fact, discover a considerable amount of carbonized, unground wheat. This had been discarded behind the building in the late first century AD, for reasons no longer clear to us. Analysis of the grain has shown that at least two, if not three, varieties of naked wheat are represented.[13] All of these could have produced fine white bread if baked, and if we may believe the sources, white bread was always more highly esteemed in antiquity than dark. Since there is no indication that bread was baked in the sanctuary, we must assume that Romans were accustomed to bringing offerings of the best wheat they had; this may also have been the custom in Greek times,

Figure 3.6 Votive *likna* with model cakes.

although we have no such tangible proof in our sanctuary. A study of the inscriptions from Eleusis regarding the grain tithes would certainly be useful in this respect.

In addition to grain, other kinds of foods we might have expected the banqueters to have eaten are varieties of beans, leeks, seeds and nuts, honey, and possibly fresh or dried fruits. Some of these are probably to be associated with objects of similar shape, depicted on the offering trays.

If we have emphasized kitchens and food in our account of dining, it is because food was, after all, central to ritual banquets, and kitchens are apparently where it was prepared. In this respect our account of the communal meal in the sanctuary differs somewhat from the scene set by vase painting.[14] There we see a large cauldron boiling over a fire not far from the altar, sacrificers or mageiroi cutting up animals at low tables, and servants tending spits over the altar fire or rushing off to distribute pieces of meat. The difference between that setting and ours may simply be meat – the presence in one, the absence in the other, if, indeed, we are correct in our conclusion that meat was not eaten in the sanctuary. At the same time, the impression we receive from the Corinth dining rooms is of something closer to a private symposium. The rooms are self-contained units, providing washing, sitting and cooking facilities, in addition to space for eating, for small numbers of people. The sources for the design of our buildings probably lie closer to private houses; the peculiarities of design, which are more numerous than space here permits us to discuss, are undoubtedly due to the specific demands of a localized cult. Nevertheless, the debris found in the buildings is just the sort of material that is lacking from virtually every other banquet hall known to us, either because of ancient looting or early excavation. Such information as can be gleaned from the pottery and other artifacts found in them is extremely important for our fuller understanding of the dining ritual. And if we are correct in our assumption that these rooms were used exclusively by women, we may want to reconsider the way in which such festivals were celebrated throughout the Greek world.

APPENDIX

Table 3.1 records the lengths of individual couches, building by building. Those dimensions marked by an asterisk are actual; the remainder are estimated. We have not included those buildings or rooms for which the couch lengths are entirely unknown. Where the armrests are not preserved, the lengths have been estimated by subtracting the width of one couch and dividing the remaining length of a wall in two. In this way two couches of equal length are reconstructed against each wall. Where two adjacent couches are actually preserved, however, it is clear that these lengths were not identical. The difference between the two couch lengths can generally be explained by overlapping the headrest of one couch onto the foot of the neighbouring one; the result is a difference of 0.20–0.30m between the two.

For purposes of comparison we offer some modern measurements. A person 1.61m tall requires a couch at least 1.46m long in order to recline with legs extended, or 1.22m with legs bent. A person 1.75m tall requires 1.58m of couch for extended legs, 1.30m if legs are bent back. Two people, each c. 1.65m tall, require a minimum of 1.75m, with legs bent back, and 2.08m, if legs are extended.

NOTES

1 For preliminary reports of the excavation of the sanctuary, cf. N. Bookidis and J. E. Fisher, 'Sanctuary of Demeter and Kore on Acrocorinth: preliminary report 5', *Hesperia* 43 (1974) 257–307, with references therein to earlier reports. The first two volumes have appeared of a projected six-volume series on the results of the excavations. These are E. G. Pemberton, *Corinth* XVIII, i: *The Sanctuary of Demeter and Kore, The Greek Pottery* (Princeton 1989) and K. S. Slane, *Corinth* XVIII, ii: *The Roman Pottery* (Princeton 1990). *Corinth* XVIII, iii, on the architectural remains, has been completed and will be followed by *Corinth* XVIII, iv, on the terracotta figurines. Full discussion of the cult will be reserved for the final volume in the series, in order to draw upon all of the finds as well as the conclusions of the various contributing authors. A somewhat more technical version of this paper was presented at Balliol College, Oxford in 1984 at a conference on the Greek symposium and has appeared as N. Bookidis, 'Ritual dining in the sanctuary of Demeter and Kore at Corinth: some questions', in O. Murray, ed., *Sympotica* (Oxford 1990) 86–94.
2 Distinction by gender is not to be considered since husbands and wives did not recline together.
3 Cf. e.g. J. W. Graham and D. M. Robinson, *Excavations at Olynthus* VIII: *The Hellenic House* (Baltimore 1938) pl. 89, houses Aviii1, A6; pl. 94, Avi; pl. 103, Bv1.
4 For the theatre cf. Bookidis, 'Sanctuary of Demeter and Kore on Acrocorinth: preliminary report 4', *Hesperia* 41 (1972) 307–10, fig. 6.
5 Many of the sources are gathered in Th. Wachter, *Reinheitsvorschriften im griechischen Kult* (Giessen 1910) 131–4. For Kos, cf. W. R. Paton and E. L. Hicks, *The Inscriptions of Cos* (Oxford 1891) 1276–7, no. 386. At Mykonos

Table 3.1 Couch lengths in Demeter sanctuary at Corinth.

Building		1	2	3	4	5	6	7	8	9
Sixth century BC										
M-N:20–6:	Room 1	1.85	2.10	2.10	1.85	1.85	2.70	1.95	1.20	
	Room 2	1.75	2.05	2.05	1.77	1.77	1.95	2.08	1.10*	
	Room 3	1.80*	2.08	2.08	1.90	1.90	2.08	1.85	0.75*	
	Room 4	1.90*	1.95	1.95	1.75	1.75	1.85	1.85	0.75*	
N-O:25–6:		1.70–1.90	1.50	1.50	2.00	2.00	1.45*	1.65*	0.75*	
N:12–13	Room 1	1.45	1.45	1.47	1.47	1.77	1.77	1.65	1.65	
	Room 2	1.80	1.65	1.65	1.65	1.55	1.55	1.55	1.00 ?	
L:16–17		1.65	1.87	1.87	2.05	2.05	1.45*–1.50*	1.50*	1.65	
500–450 BC										
J-L:21		1.515	1.515	1.515*	1.65	1.65	1.52	1.52	1.45–1.55	
J-K:22		1.80	1.625	1.625	1.80	1.80	1.625	1.625	1.00	
K:23		1.82	1.52	1.52	1.61	1.61	1.52	1.52	0.40	
K-L:25–6		2.00	1.425	1.425	1.625	1.625	1.425	1.425	0.50	
450–400 BC										
J:23		?	?	?	1.65*	1.85*	?	?	?	
K:23		1.82	1.52	1.52	1.61	1.61	1.52	1.52	0.40	
K-L:23–4		2.00*	1.80	1.80	2.35*	1.80	1.80	0.35		
K-L:24–5		2.00–2.15	1.70	1.70	2.00	2.00	0.35			
K-L:25–6		1.94*	1.81	1.81–1.84	1.31*	1.19*	1.81	1.81	0.48*	
L:26–7		1.80–1.90	1.53–1.58	1.53–1.58	1.62	1.62	1.53–1.58	1.53–1.58	0.90–1.00	
M-N:20–4	Room 3	1.80*	2.08	2.08	1.95	1.95	2.08	2.08	1.10*	
	Room 4	1.90*	1.95	1.95	1.70	1.70	1.85	1.85	0.75*	

Table 3.1 continued

Building		1	2	3	4	5	6	7	8	9
M-N:25–6	Room 1	1.85	1.85	1.75	1.75	2.70	1.80		2.05	
	Room 2	2.05	1.55	1.55	2.40	2.40	1.50	1.50	1.85	1.85
N:21–2		2.00*	1.83	1.83	1.83*	1.35*	1.25	1.85	1.85	
N:22–3		1.90	2.60	2.50	2.50	2.05	1.80*			
N-O:24–5		1.60–1.80	1.85	1.85	1.70	1.70	1.80–1.90	1.80–1.90	0.80–1.00	
L18–19		1.75	1.73	1.73	1.65	1.75*	1.77*	1.70*	0.90–1.00	
M-N:19		1.95	2.00	2.00	2.00*	1.95*	2.00*	2.00*	1.90*	
N-O:12–13	Room 1	1.45	1.45	1.47	1.47	1.77	1.77	1.65	1.65	
	Room 2	1.80	1.65	1.65	1.65	1.65	1.55	1.55	1.00 ?	
400–146 BC										
K-L:21–2	Room 1	1.50	2.40–2.50	1.80	1.80	1.50	1.50	1.10–1.30		
	Room 7	1.77*	2.12*	2.42*	2.27*	1.80*	1.99*	2.33*	2.16*	
L-M:28		1.75*	1.45*	1.80*	1.90*	2.10*	1.95	1.95	1.30*	
M:21–2	Room 1	2.03*	1.85*	1.65*	1.10*	1.85	1.85	0.80–0.90		
	Room 2	1.71*	1.63*							
M-N:25–6		1.65	1.65	1.60	1.60	2.15	2.15	2.10		
N:28		1.80	1.80	1.80	1.15	2.00	1.80	1.80	1.15	
M:16–17		1.75*	1.55*	1.55	1.55	2.215	2.215	1.685	1.685	
N:12–13		2.30	1.87	1.87	1.45	1.80	1.87	1.87	0.80	

* = actual length

sacrifices were made only by women to Demeter, Kore and Zeus Bouleus on the 10th of Lennaion, *SIG.2.* 615.

6 M. N. Tod, 'Notes and inscriptions from south-west Messenia,' *JHS* 25 (1905) 49–53. Reclining female banqueters are also depicted in figurines from the sanctuary of Demeter at Morgantina, as M. Bell III, *Morgantina Studies*, I: *The Terracottas* (Princeton 1981) 83–5, nos 85–95, pls 21–2. This aspect will be discussed more thoroughly in the final volume of *Corinth* XVIII.

7 For a discussion of the *thoinarmostria* and her association with sanctuaries of Demeter and Kore, cf. M. N. Tod (*supra* n. 6) 49–53; *idem*, 'Thoinarmostria', *JHS* 32 (1912) 100–3; Pauly-Wissowa, s.v., 'Thoinarmostria'.

8 C. Habicht, 'Hellenistische Inschriften aus dem Heraion von Samos,' *AM* 87 (1972) 210–25, no. 9.

9 R. Ginouvès, *Balaneutikè* (Paris 1962) 151–9.

10 For the inscription, cf. M. F. Michon, 'Un decret du dème de Cholargos relatif aux Thesmophories', *MAI* 13 (1913) 1–24; F. Sokolowski, *Lois sacrées des cités grecques*, Suppl. (Paris 1962) 208–9, no. 124, would interpret the food as the ingredients of a sweet, but it is difficult to understand what kind of sweet would have been made with wine and garlic.

11 Bone Lot 1965–24. These consisted of a fragment of the posterior mandible, a molar and part of a foreleg bone of a pig; part of a rear leg of a cow, and a rib from a pig, sheep or goat. The pottery associated with this material was sparse and very fragmentary, consisting entirely of fine ware cups, bowls and parts of figurines; utility and cooking wares were completely absent. It is difficult to believe, therefore, that this material represents the contents of the kitchen. Building N:21–2, however, lies on the last row beneath the middle terrace, and it is our general observation that the closer one draws to this area of sacrifice, the greater the number of bones, relatively speaking.

12 A basic source on the subject of mills and grain in antiquity is L. A. Moritz, *Grain-Mills and Flour in Classical Antiquity* (Oxford 1958) with references therein to other sources. For hand-mills and saddle-querns, C. N. Runnels, *A Diachronic Study and Economic Analysis of Millstones from the Argolid, Greece* (Ph.D. diss. Indiana University 1981).

13 The wheat was analysed in two different laboratories. Dr E. H. Everson, Professor of Wheat Genetics at Michigan State University, identified two varieties, namely *Triticum aestivum vulgare*, a soft winter wheat similar to that grown today in the United States, and *Triticum sphaerococcum*. According to Dr G. Wiebe of the United States Department of Agriculture, the two varieties present are *Triticum sphaerococcum* and *Triticum compactum*. It is interesting to note that according to N. Jasny, *The Wheats of Classical Antiquity* (Baltimore 1944) 28, neither of these two last varieties is thought to have existed in the Mediterranean at this date.

The word 'naked' identifies species of wheat which lose their husks on the threshing floor, thereby needing no additional pounding.

14 Cf. e.g. J. L. Durand, 'Bêtes grecques', in M. Detienne and J.-P. Vernant, eds, *La cuisine du sacrifice en pays grecs* (Paris 1979) 133–57.

Figures 3.4 and 3.5 (p. 53) show a series of cooking pots, found, for the most part, in the dining rooms, but not necessarily from the same dining rooms. Below is a list of their approximate capacities, as measured dry with sand. Dimensions are in fractions of litres. For comparison, the amounts of food recorded on the Cholargos inscription are also supplied, following the measurements given by Michon (see note 10).

Figure 3.4 Left to right:

C-1961-432: 5.75l max.   4.95l to base of neck
C-1965-474: 2.15l
C-1971-88: 0.473l
C-1965-438: 0.152l   (= one, 4th-century skyphos)

Figure 3.5 Left to right:

C-1961-385: 3.536l max.   3.38l to base of neck
C-1965-533: 2.075l max.   1.725l to base of neck
C-1968-304: 0.97l

Table 3.2 Capacities of stew pots and pitchers.

Commodity	Greek measurement	Modern equivalent
Barley	½ hektaion	4.377l
Wheat	½ hektaion	4.377l
Barley-meal	½ hektaion	4.377l
Wheat-flour	½ hektaion	4.377l
Figs	½ hektaion	4.377l
Wine	1 chous	3.283l
Oil	½ chous	1.14l
Honey	2 kotylai	0.547l
White sesame	choinix	1.094l
Black sesame	choinix	1.094l
Poppy-seed	choinix	1.094l
Fresh cheese	no less than 2 staters	26.196g ?
Garlic	2 staters	26.196g

4

Three related sanctuaries of Poseidon: Geraistos, Kalaureia and Tainaron

Rob W. M. Schumacher

INTRODUCTION

In his handbook *Greek Religion: Archaic and Classical* (Oxford 1985; original German edition 1977) Walter Burkert pays attention in two places to cult places/sanctuaries: once when he deals with cult places of the prehistoric period (pp. 24–34), and again when he deals with sanctuaries of the Archaic and Classical periods (pp. 84–95). In both cases he devotes almost the same number of pages to this topic. This is remarkable, because the book has more than six times as many pages on the historic period than it has on the prehistoric period. The disproportionate emphasis in the case of sanctuaries is the result of the different source material available for both periods as well as of a different approach.

For the prehistoric period, Burkert deals with caves, peak sanctuaries, tree sanctuaries, house sanctuaries, temples and graves. In other words, the cult places are distinguished according to form, location and function. In his section on the historic sanctuaries his point of departure is the 'normal Greek sanctuary': a *temenos* (a piece of land cut off and dedicated to a god), usually containing a temple housing a cult statue; before the temple stood the altar and the votive offerings were distributed at random in the sanctuary.

Burkert's pages are a reflection of the general line in the study of Greek sanctuaries of the historic period. In many cases attention is focused on major individual sanctuaries and/or on architectural aspects of sanctuaries. It is probably true for most people that when they are asked to visualize a Greek sanctuary, they see a temple. Therefore it is perhaps not superfluous to stress that a temple is only part of a sanctuary and not really necessary (though for us it is of course the most conspicuous element). Like pre-historic Greece, so historic Greece has known sanctuaries in many different forms, with many different functions and on many different locations.

Two recent publications on sanctuaries of the historic period in Greece and Italy[1] are examples of research along the lines I would like to call attention to. They confirm that, with the amount of data available on sanctuaries of the historic period, a shift in emphasis will be rewarding. Stronger attention should, in my opinion, be paid to arranging the material along the lines of form, location and function, be it on a regional or on a thematic basis.

In this chapter the Poseidon sanctuaries at Geraistos (Euboea), Kalaureia (Troizenia), and Tainaron (Lakonia) will be discussed (see map, Figure 4.1). In a compilation of material dating from late antiquity the eponymous founders of these three sanctuaries are said to be brothers. This suggests some kind of relationship; evidence for this has been found elsewhere in the historical and archaeological record as well. The nature of this relationship will be the main theme of this paper. It will be argued that an essential correspondence is the specific function of the sanctuaries and that a distinct relation between function and location can be observed.

Stephanus of Byzantium was a Greek grammarian who probably lived in the sixth century AD. For his *Ethnika*, an alphabetical list of place-names in 60 books containing information on foundation-legends, etymologies, proverbs, etc., he used a variety of sources, sometimes going back as far as Hecataeus (*c.* 500 BC). The work is now lost, but between the sixth and the tenth centuries an epitome was compiled which is extant. Its main value is that it contains material from writers whose works are lost.

In this epitome we find under *Tainaros*: 'polis, [named] after Tainaros, the brother of Geraistos and child of Zeus; who sailed with his brother Kalauros and, having seized a place on the Peloponnese, set up a sanctuary of Poseidon, which is called Tainaron . . .'. In the same work is written under *Geraistos*: 'village on Euboea, in which is a sanctuary of Poseidon, [named] after Geraistos, the son of Zeus . . .'.

We have here Geraistos, Kalauros and Tainaros, three brothers, two of whom were the mythical eponymous founders of sanctuaries of Poseidon; curiously, they are said to be sons of Zeus, not of Poseidon. In view of the major Poseidon cult on Kalaureia, it is not too bold to assume that the third brother, Kalauros, founded the sanctuary there. Since Tainaros made a sailing voyage with Kalauros, it would seem that, according to this mythical representation, the sanctuary at Geraistos was the starting-point from which the Poseidon cult spread to Kalaureia and Tainaron.

PREVIOUS DISCUSSIONS

On the basis of these references, in previous publications, several data have been adduced to explain the connection between the cults in Euboea, Troizenia and Lakonia.

First of all, the spread of the cult from Euboean Geraistos to Troizenian Kalaureia and Lakonian Tainaron seems to be corroborated by the fact that the month name Geraistios, implying the existence of festivals named Geraistia, is attested for Kalaureia and Troizen and the month name

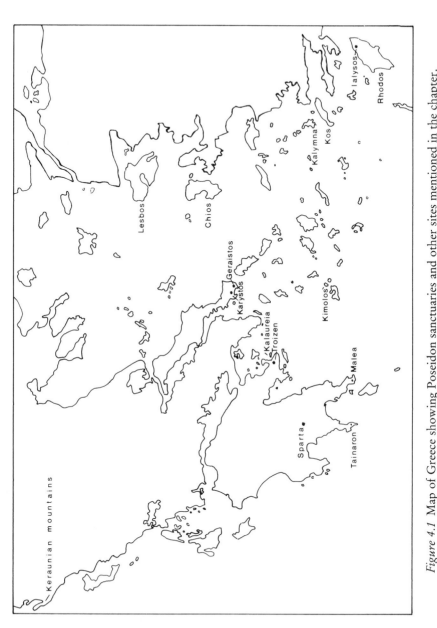

Figure 4.1 Map of Greece showing Poseidon sanctuaries and other sites mentioned in the chapter.

Gerastios (form without *iota*) for Sparta. Elsewhere in Greece we find the month name Gerastios only on Kalymna and Kos. In Sparta, the month falls at the beginning of spring, on Kos it is the last month of the winter period.[2]

We hardly know anything about cult practices. Pindar mentions games on Euboea (*Ol.* 13.112) and the scholiast says that on Euboea the Geraistia are being held for Poseidon by all who live in Geraistos and that a storm around Geraistos was the cause of their institution (Schol. Pind., *Ol.* 13.159b).

From Athenaeus (14.639C) we know of the existence of a festival in Troizen in the month Geraistios, lasting many days; on one day during this festival slaves and citizens played together with knucklebones and masters entertained their slaves. It is a well-known type of festival, in which the social order is temporarily reversed, only to be restored the stronger at the end of the festivities. It acts as a safety valve for possible uncomfortable feelings in society and at the same time it legitimizes the present relationships in authority.[3] Because of the name of the month several modern scholars are inclined to call this festival 'Geraistia' and assign it to Poseidon.

In a Troizenian inscription from *c.* 146 BC, 41 organizations declare their belongings to be at the city's disposal; among them was the clan (*patria*) of the Geraistiastai.[4]

In line with the sea voyage mentioned by Stephanus, several scholars have assumed that a wandering tribe was responsible for the diffusion of the cult of Poseidon Geraistios.[5] This diffusion is thought to go back to pre-Dorian times and Minyans or Dryopians are held responsible. As to the Minyans, special attention is drawn to the Argonaut and Minyan hero Euphemos, son of Poseidon, who was said to have lived around Tainaron (Pind., *Pyth.* 4.43–5). Herodotus (4.145ff.) tells about Minyans on Lemnos, descendants of Euphemos and the other Argonauts, who were expelled from their island by the Pelasgians, sailed to southern Lakonia, sat down on the Taygetos mountain range and were eventually admitted to Lakonian society. The Dryopians were originally a Pelasgian tribe from southern Thessaly, who later occupied southern Euboea. The people in the area around Hermione (just to the south-west of Troizen and Kalaureia) were said to be Dryopians from Euboea; the inhabitants of south-eastern Messenia (west of Lakonia) called themselves Dryopians.

To this account M. P. Nilsson preferred an explanation based on the similar geographical location of the three sanctuaries. He assumed Euboean sea-farers sailing past Kalaureia and Tainaron in early Archaic times, landing often and bringing cult and cult practices to Tainaron, including the festival (from which the month name) and the Poseidonian bull.[6]

The most extensive collection of data has been presented by F. Vian, in whose view the cult of Poseidon Geraistios in Tainaron and Troizen/ Kalaureia was a Mycenaean Euboean addition to already existing Poseidon cults. A critical assessment of his valuable arguments concerning Geraistos was subsequently offered by L. Lerat.[7]

65

Names that are related or similar to 'Geraistos' are also found in other contexts and in different fragments of legendary tradition, and there could well be a common background to them all.[8] But if so, the background must be pre-Hellenic since the words belong to a pre-Hellenic language; and it is difficult if not impossible for us to get a clear picture.[9] Instead, it seems best to argue from evidence of the historic period: in the case of Euboea we are dealing with the name of a place, where a sanctuary of Poseidon was located; his epithet is derived from the place name.

NEW DATA

A category of evidence which can be appreciated more fully now that the first volume of the *Lexicon of Greek personal names* has appeared, is the occurrence and distribution of theophoric names. All names date from the Hellenistic and/or Roman periods.[10] From southern Euboea there is one single instance: an inscription from the Karystia gives the name Geraistion. Elsewhere in the Greek world we find on Kos the personal names Gerastis and Gerastiphanes (attested respectively 9 (or 10) 4 times). On Rhodes and its territory on the mainland a slight variation occurs, the name Geraistis (10 instances). It is of some interest to note that the spelling of the names, with or without *iota*, is consistent on Rhodes and Kos. Furthermore, the names appear to have a very limited distribution in the Greek world: I have not found any other instance anywhere else in the Greek world, which suggests that they are strictly regional.[11] The frequency of the names on Rhodes and Kos is fairly high when compared to other theophoric names referring to Poseidon, like Poseidonios and Poseidippos.[12]

With reference to the names we may suppose that it is possible that Rhodes knew a cult of Poseidon Geraistios too (it should be added that the calendar of Hellenistic and Roman Rhodes is well known and no month name can be associated with Poseidon[13]). This has so far not been documented by independent evidence, though there might be one possible reference. Diodorus Siculus relates that Kadmos in his search for Europa also went to Rhodes. Buffeted by tempests during his sea-voyage, he took a vow to set up a sanctuary for Poseidon and when he was saved he dedicated a *temenos* for the god 'on the island'; when he went away he left some Phoenicians behind to serve as overseers; they mingled with the people of Ialysos and lived among them as fellow citizens, which fact might or might not be an indication of topographical value; and finally it is said that their descendants functioned as priests of Poseidon.[14] In a Greek–Phoenician treaty of 215 BC, 'Poseidon' is the translation into Greek of 'Baʿ al-Saphon', the Phoenician marine storm-god *par excellence*.[15] From Homer onwards the connection between Poseidon and storms at sea is a natural one, and his power is expressed in a positive way in epithets such as 'Asphalios' (Securer) and 'Sosineos' (Saviour of ships). However, there is, to my knowledge, only one other instance in which a storm is given as *aition* in the cult of Poseidon: the institution of the Geraistia in Euboea. Most scholars are inclined to connect this last storm with the death of Ajax, who, on his return from Troy, was killed by Poseidon during a storm at the Gyraean cliffs (Hom. *Odyssey* 4.499–510). The exact location of the cliffs is uncertain; they are variously identified on Mykonos, on southern Tenos or with the dangerous Kapharean promontory, the northern cape on Euboea's east coast.

There is a new fact from Kos. The Orphikidai, an otherwise unknown association, dedicated in the third century BC an altar-plaque to Poseidon Gerastios.[16] This constitutes the first solid evidence for a cult of Poseidon Gerastios on Kos and is in fact the first mention of 'Gerastios' as an epithet of Poseidon outside Euboea. The name 'Orphikidai' has the gentilicial termination -idai, which fact is of some interest in view of the Troizenian clan of the Geraistiastai and theories on the diffusion of the cult by a wandering tribe.[17] On Kos, a month name, theophoric names and the worship of Poseidon Gerastios are now attested. The occurrence of these together within a single region seems to corroborate the fact that the month name on Kos (and elsewhere) is derived from the Poseidon cult and to invalidate the objections to this by von Wilamowitz, Mellink and Lerat.[18] It would seem that the epithet, although originally referring only to a place on Euboea, acquired in time a more independent status.

Of the three sanctuaries which are our main concern here, new evidence has come to light for Geraistos: we now positively know its location and we are informed on a specific function of the sanctuary. These new data may now serve as justification for looking once more at the three sanctuaries and the relation between them.

Some 25 years ago a part of an inscribed marble stele was found not far from the shore in modern (Porto) Kastri; it turned out to be the other half of a stele already known. The inscription dates from *c.* 248–239 BC.[19] It contains two honorary decrees, issued by the inhabitants of the (Dorian) island Kimolos. The Kimolians had requested assistance from King Antigonos Gonatas in settling a number of legal disputes which had accumulated on their island in the later third century BC. Antigonos resolved to send a foreign judge to Kimolos, Charianthos from Karystos (Euboea). Charianthos handled the situation successfully and for this reason the Kimolians wanted to honour him and his secretary.[20] One copy of the stele which recorded the decrees had to be erected in the sanctuary of Athena on Kimolos, and for a second copy 'The ambassador is to request of the Senate and the People of Karystos a place in the sanctuary of Poseidon Geraistios in the inviolable area (τόπον ἐν τῶι ἱερῶι τοῦ Ποσειδᾶνος τοῦ Γεραιστίου ἐν τῶι ἀσύλωι), where it may be set up' (lines 46–9; cf. lines 14–15, 39–41). The editors of the inscription commented that the sanctuary seemed to have become the most important religious centre in the Karystia, if not in the whole of southern Euboea. The word *asylon* seems to have been used here as a substantive which is exceptional; normally it is adjectival and when referring to a place it is in most cases followed by 'sanctuary' (*hieron*), an addition that does not seem appropriate here.

The find of the inscription was a confirmation that modern Kastri was ancient Geraistos, an identification which for a long time was only one out of several possibilities. Still, some doubt was left as to the question of whether the sanctuary of Poseidon too was to be located here in Kastri or had to be identified with, for example, the remains at Elleniko Platanistou, one hour and a quarter to the north (the stele could have been transported in later times). This last possibility seems to have been ruled out by the results of a trial excavation at Kastri in the early seventies: a building from the Late Roman period was found and partly excavated. In the walls, used parts of a Greek building from the fourth century BC were found, including triglyphs and a stone inscribed 'of Poseidon' (Ποσε[ιδῶνος]). The excavation was conducted close to the findspot of the stele from Kimolos and the results make it plausible (though not yet entirely certain) that the sanctuary too was once located at Kastri.[21]

The correspondences between the three sanctuaries which have been stated in earlier publications do not explain their apparent relationship satisfactorily. The reason is that they do not explain why it is these three Poseidon sanctuaries that are taken together to the exclusion of others. If, for instance, the corresponding geographical location is emphasized, Kalaureia does not fit in very well and Sounion and Malea should also have been included (as in Euripides, *Cyclops* 290–5). As Lerat writes: we will have to suppose another kind of analogy, one which could suggest this particular grouping in preference to any other.[22]

I will suggest that there is a specific characteristic which, in combination or not with the possible diffusion of the cult by a tribe, can have led to the grouping of these three sanctuaries. I am referring to a specific function of the sanctuaries: all three had a reputation as an asylum sanctuary. In order to argue this, it is first of all necessary to examine the concept of 'asylum' in ancient Greece.

PROTECTION BY DIVINE AND HUMAN LAW

When dealing with ancient Greece a fundamental distinction has to be made between *asylia* (inviolability) and *hiketeia* (supplication).[23]

Envoys possessed immunity on the basis of their function but inviolability could also be accorded to other individuals: a merchant could obtain *asylia* in order to make it possible for him safely to visit the harbour of a city outside his own state. In this case there is a clear association with the ancient institution of the right of hospitality, which assured protection to the stranger; in content there is a connection with the institution of *proxenia*. The *asylia* could also be accorded to a community: a treaty to this effect

68

between two states led to the discontinuance of the right of reprisal between them. The right of reprisal meant that in the case of a dispute the party wronged could claim the right to use self-help and seize property, not only of the offending party, but also of other citizens and metics of his state. The need for *asylia* has to be seen against the background of the absence of international civil law in the Greek world.[24] A number of documents are preserved, in particular from the Hellenistic period, which inform us of *asylia* between states and of coastal cities (and their territory) being proclaimed 'sacred and inviolable'. A major motive for obtaining *asylia* in this period was that communities were anxious for a safeguard against piracy. In the third and second centuries BC the Cretans and the Aetolians were notorious pirates, and by succeeding in concluding a treaty in which reciprocal *asylia* was guaranteed, a potential danger was averted (clearly the partners in such treaties were of unequal weight). In these cases the acquisition of *asylia* is primarily in the interest of the community, not in that of individuals or outsiders.

Different from the *asylia* is the institution of supplication, the *hiketeia*. The supplication worked in such a way, that everyone who had the symbol of the supplicant and took refuge in a sanctuary, or held on to an altar, became part of the sanctuary and, consequently, 'sacred'. In this way he shared in the inviolability of the sanctuary: it would have been sacrilege to arrest or harm him. Supplication then belonged to divine law and was valid for everyone, stranger and citizen alike. The place used could be qualified as a 'place of refuge'.

In his contribution to this volume (pp. 88–109), U. Sinn studies supplication, while paying attention to, among many other things, the location and spatial organization of sanctuaries where supplication is applied. He demonstrates how in certain sanctuaries with a regional function, and located in an isolated area, the supplicants, who were sometimes in great numbers, were confined to special areas. Measures had to be taken to preserve hygiene, to supply food and water and to assure the continuation of the normal function of the sanctuary.

By late antiquity the concept of asylum had acquired a different meaning, but we can observe a similar concern with the organization and use of space. In the Theodosian legal code is a law dating from 431 AD concerning those who took refuge in the churches.[25] The law is explicit about the spatial arrangements: not only the altar and the inner parts of the temple, but also any space which belonged to the church had the right of asylum. Though at first sight this extension of space might seem generous, it is at the same time a restrictive measure, aimed at keeping the fugitives away from the most sacred places. Those who seek sanctuary are to be prevented by the clerics from sleeping, spending the night or eating inside the very temple of God or at the altars; the clerics are to designate spaces within the ecclesiastical enclosures sufficient for the protection of asylum seekers. Reverence for religion and anxiety concerning pollution make these restrictions necessary; piety is expected from the fugitives. Those who do not obey the clerics are to be driven away, for, as it states, 'reverence for religion must be preferred to humanity' (*praeferenda humanitati religio est*). The law is echoed in a (partly restored) inscription from 578–82 AD, a petition to the emperor to grant the establishment of asylum boundary-stones in an oratory in Phoenicia. Apparently the oratory was used by fugitives, who are distinguished in 'those who fulfil the supplication decently and piously and those who use the sacred precincts unsoundly'. The establishment of a delimited area for the fugitives, supported by the central authority, was to confine their freedom of movement, facilitate control over their behaviour, prevent pollution and guarantee the undisturbed exercise of cult practices.[26]

In principle every sacred place, every altar in ancient Greece was suitable for supplicatory purposes, but there seems to have been a development which led to a concentration in each state of the supplication in one specific place and to a marking out of specific sanctuaries for specific kinds of supplicants. Instead of allowing supplication freely at all altars, certain limiting regulations were imposed in the course of time to obtain a minimum of control over the situation.

Hiketeia and *asylia* have different spatial implications. The usual place for *hiketeia* is the sanctuary, while *asylia* can bear upon entire cities and states. However, *asylia* could be related to a sanctuary as well. In the Hellenistic period a number of large sanctuaries had themselves declared *asyla*, a declaration usually coinciding with the reorganization of a festival including (pan-Hellenic) games. The *asylon*-declaration was sought in order to assure potential participants, visitors and merchants that their safety was guaranteed. The recognition of the right of asylum meant that within the boundaries of the sanctuary acts of reprisal were forbidden; it was aimed at strangers. Without such a recognition the festival would attract far fewer visitors, provide far less revenue (e.g. from port taxes) and remain a purely local affair. Boundary stones were put up to mark out the *asylon* area of a sanctuary. At the same time, however, the sanctuary could be a place of refuge for supplicants: in an inscription from the end of the third century BC the sanctuary of Apollo Pythaios in Chalcedon is, on authority of the Delphic oracle, declared to be 'inviolable and a place of refuge' (*asylon* and *phyktimon*), while the area is marked out by boundary stones.[27]

The relation between *hiketeia* and *asylia* is a complex one and some reports by ancient writers suggest that the Greeks themselves sometimes had difficulty distinguishing them.

PROTECTION IN POSEIDON SANCTUARIES

A number of sanctuaries of Poseidon must have served as places of asylum in one way or another; our sources mention several instances. In Sophocles' tragedy *Oedipus Coloneus* (1156ff.) Polyneikes sits down as a supplicant at the altar of Poseidon Hippios in his sanctuary at Kolonos Hippios (Attika) in order to force Oedipus to receive him. No example of this function of the sanctuary is known from historical sources.

In the pan-Hellenic sanctuary on the Isthmos the Isthmian Games were held every two years, one of the four 'Sacred Games' in the Greek world. For the duration of the games a sacred truce (*ekecheiria*) existed, a temporary cessation of hostilities between the poleis, enabling participants and visitors to come to the games (see Xen., *Hell.* 4.5.1ff. for the (un)certainty of the truce). The Isthmian sanctuary is mentioned, together with, among others, the sanctuaries at Tainaron and Kalaureia, by Plutarch in his enumeration of not-to-be-violated-nor-to-be-trodden (*asyla* and *abata*) sanctuaries which, nevertheless, were plundered in the first century BC by pirates (Plut., *Pomp.* 24.6). A sacred truce is also recorded for the Poseidon sanctuary, a grove full of wild olive trees, at Samikon (Triphylia); it was a sanctuary with an important regional function.[28] In both these cases the asylum function was said to be valid only for a certain period, but we may assume that the sanctuaries were appropriate places for supplication throughout the year.

On a winter's night in 373 BC the city of Helike (Achaia) was destroyed by an earthquake and subsequently submerged by a tidal wave. The disaster was the outcome of divine wrath: not long before, the people of Helike had killed Ionian envoys in the sanctuary of Poseidon. The sources telling this story differ slightly and it is not completely clear whether the sacrilege was committed against Ionians who had simply claimed personal immunity as envoys or whether, in addition to this, they had sat down as supplicants in the sanctuary. Another case of sacrilege in this sanctuary is the treatment by the priests of the supplicant Themisto from Oiantheia.[29]

At the end of the fourth century BC the sanctuary of Poseidon and Amphitrite on Tenos was founded. In the first half of the third century BC the state (*koinon*) of the Phokians, later followed by other states, declared the sanctuary and the island *asyla*, a declaration sanctioned by the pan-Hellenic authority of the Delphic god. The institution of the right of asylum coincided with the institution of games, sacrifice and festal assembly: the *asylon*-declaration helped to assure the success of the festival, the Posideia. The amount of building activity in the sanctuary is one of the indications that it was successful. In the decennia around 200 BC Tenos was a religious centre in the Aegean, second only to Delos. Tenos was one of the states whose right of asylum was tested for its legitimacy by the Roman Senate in 22 AD (Tacitus, *Ann.* 3.63).[30]

In the cases recorded above we see examples of protection by divine and by human law, places of refuge for supplicants and sanctuaries declared inviolable for the sake of festivals. The sanctuaries of Poseidon at Tainaron and Kalaureia were widely known for their use by supplicants, probably from an early period onward. The discussion of them will be followed by that of Geraistos, which was, in my opinion, inviolable as well as a place of refuge.

TAINARON, AN EXEMPLARY SANCTUARY[31]

In 464 BC Sparta was hit by a severe earthquake: hardly a single house, at the most five houses (Pausanias versus Aelianus), was left standing. The cause adduced was, as usual, divine wrath. Poseidon had taken revenge on the Spartan ephors, who had dared to drag helots away from Poseidon's sanctuary at Tainaron, where they had taken refuge as suppliants; after that they had killed them. This sacrilege put a curse (*agos*) on the Spartans, which was well remembered by the Greeks, and especially by the Athenians. A few years before, a slave of the Spartan king Pausanias had claimed a supplication in the sanctuary at Tainaron; for this purpose he built himself a hut in the sanctuary. In 241 BC the Spartan king Kleombrotos II and his family took refuge in a sanctuary of Poseidon, probably the one at Tainaron. The sanctuary is mentioned by Polybius among the asylum sanctuaries destroyed by the Aitolian Timaios in *c.* 240 BC, and by Plutarch among the asylum sanctuaries attacked by pirates in the first century BC.[32]

Pausanias' slave claimed supplication. For this purpose he went all the way from Sparta to Tainaron, instead of using a sanctuary in or near the city: an indication that the sanctuary at Tainaron was especially assigned as a place of refuge for slaves. The supplication of Kleombrotos could be seen as an exception (though it is not absolutely certain that he used the Poseidon sanctuary at Tainaron), but is more probably simply an indication of the growth of the reputation of the sanctuary. Attention has also been drawn to the fact that one of Sparta's sacred ambassadors of the third century BC bore the revealing name Taenarius.[33]

The special relation between Tainaron and helots is attested by several other pieces of evidence: a scholiast commenting on a verse by Aristophanes in the Dorian dialect refers to helots crowning Poseidon; in Sophocles' satyr-play *Herakles at Tainaron* the choir was made up of helots; the *temenos* of Poseidon Pontios ('of the sea') is mentioned in a fragment of Eupolis' play *The Helots*. There are four stelai dating from the fifth and fourth centuries BC which were set up at Tainaron and on which the release of slaves is recorded: they had a most appropriate setting in this sanctuary with its Helotic background and its special reputation as a place of refuge. Also related to this reputation, and to the isolated location, seems to be the presence of mercenaries in this area. In the Hellenistic period Tainaron was well known as a recruiting base, as a huge man-market where at certain times thousands of mercenaries were awaiting recruitment on ships which would have landed at the harbour of Porto Kayio further to the north.[34]

The sanctuary at Tainaron must date at least from the time that the helots were still independent; after being subjugated by the Spartans, they kept a special relation with this sanctuary. The official name of the god, as attested by evidence from literature and inscriptions, was 'Poseidon at Tainaron'; in literature we find (probable) references to him as 'Pontios' and 'Asphalios' (the Securer).

The crowning of (the statue of) Poseidon by the helots may have been part of a festival. The festival was called Tainaria(s) and the participants Tainaristai. Elsewhere mention is made of a feast with sacrifices which lasted three days and nights and included dances and games at the beach.

Though they could be the same as the Tainaristai, the Tainarioi should for the sake of clarity be distinguished from them. The Tainarioi occur in three inscriptions dating from the first century BC from Sparta.[35] Sparta had, probably from the time that Tainaron was independent from her, a *temenos* of Poseidon Tainarios, located just outside the city. The Tainarioi were the participants and in part organizers of a feast, which included a procession in which the statue of the god was carried by one of them, and the usual sacrificial meal. Near the racecourse in Sparta Pausanias saw the *mnema* of Tainaros.

Pausanias and Strabo differ in their description of the sanctuary. Strabo writes that the sanctuary stands in a sacred grove and that the cave is nearby; Pausanias tells us that there is a temple that looks like a cave, with a statue of Poseidon in front of it. The cave was well known in antiquity, since it had a reputation as one of the entrances to the Underworld, namely the one through which Herakles had fetched Kerberos from Hades' realm. The cave and the sanctuary have been located at the head of a small bay, half an hour to the north-east of the most southern point of the peninsula. The largest part of the cave is exposed to the open air. On the north side of the cave entrance a series of stelai cuttings has been identified: the place for the stelai recording the release of slaves and other inscriptions. West of these are traces indicating a large rectangular structure of uncertain nature. The cave and the structure shield a small pebble beach. In the immediate surroundings are numerous rock-cut foundations. Most recently these have been interpreted as traces of the equipment for accommodating the sometimes numerous suppliants in the sanctuary: they provided space for building huts.[36] From different sources we know of the existence at the sanctuary of stelai, of votive bronzes of bulls and horses (votives reported but never seen since) and, reported by Herodotus, of a bronze votive-gift of the poet Arion (a dolphin with a man, Arion, on his back), but proper excavations have never been carried out.

At about 60m to the south-west of the cave, on top of a hill, stood a rectangular building, dating perhaps from the Hellenistic period, later turned into a chapel for the Ayios Asomato ('the bodiless saint'), that is, the archangel Michael. Not too long ago the archangel was still reported seen with drawn sword 'passing to and fro at the mouth of the caves of Tainaron'. This saint is among other things the modern version of Hermes

Psychopompos, the god who escorts the souls of the dead. In antiquity
Tainaron had, according to Plutarch, a Psychopompeion: should the building be related exclusively to this function or was it once a temple for
Poseidon? Plutarch (first century AD) writes that the murderer of the poet
Archilochos (seventh century BC) was sent by the Pythia to Tainaron to
reconcile himself to the soul of the poet. A relation between the Delphic
oracle in the centre of the world and this oracle of the dead at the end of
the world also seems to be indicated by the history of the exchange of the
ownership of these sanctuaries between Poseidon and Apollo.[37]

In ancient Greek the general word for 'sanctuary' is *hieron*; this word,
according to the philologist A. Motte, suggests the idea of an intermediary
zone between the divine and the human world, a space with a numinal
charge, suitable for communication between both worlds. The social anthro-
pologist E. Leach, followed by the archaeologist C. Renfrew, has plotted
this symbolic order graphically: two circles represent This World and The
Other World, which are conceived of as separate topographical spaces; they
overlap slightly. The area where they overlap is the liminal zone with
qualities of both worlds; this ambiguous boundary zone is the focus for any
ritual activity.[38]

In the case of Tainaron this symbolic boundary location is manifest in
more ways than one. In the first place the sanctuary functioned, just like any
other, as a place for communication between humans and gods. Furthermore
it was a zone between this world and that κατ' ἐξοχήν other world, the
Underworld. It is a sanctuary on the boundary of land and sea (in ancient
Greece entrances to Hades were preferably located at or in the sea), in the
margin of the polis, even seen as located at the very edge of the Greek world:
Plutarch writes on Greeks exiled by Antipater 'being driven out of Hellas
beyond the Keraunian mountains [in the extreme north-west of Epirus] and
Tainaron' (Plut., *Phocion* 29.3). As has been stated above the sanctuary was
especially used by marginal groups from the Lakonian community and its
specific function assured it of a legal order different from the rest of society.

A sanctuary, then, at the edge of a polis, at the end of the (Greek) world,
on the boundary with the Underworld, functioning as an asylum, used by
helots, slaves and mercenaries: how marginal can you get?

MOST SACRED KALAUREIA[39]

The function of the Poseidon sanctuary on Kalaureia, an island just off the
coast of Troizen, as a place of refuge is well known, since the sanctuary once
received a distinguished supplicant. In 322 BC the politician and orator
Demosthenes, champion of the Athenian democracy, fled to this sanctuary;
his supplication is recorded by Plutarch in particular. It was the second time
that Demosthenes had to leave Athens. This time he, Hypereides and other
anti-Macedonian politicians whose extradition was demanded by Antipater,

who ruled Macedonia after the death of Alexander the Great, first went to the Aiakeion on Aegina. Demosthenes did not feel safe there and crossed over to Kalaureia. Antipater sent Archias to capture Demosthenes and, on his arrival at the sanctuary, Archias, accompanied by soldiers, tried to persuade Demosthenes to give up his supplication by alternately flattering and threatening him. The orator asked permission to write a last letter to his family and used this delay to commit suicide by administering poison to himself. According to Plutarch Demosthenes went into the temple to write the letter; while he was there, soldiers were standing on guard at the doors. When the poison had almost finished its work he stumbled out of the building in order to show his piety towards Poseidon and not to pollute the sacred place with his death: he collapsed just outside the building near the altar. Though in point of fact we hardly know what range of activities could take place inside a Greek temple, we may suppose that the use of the building by Demosthenes as his office is mainly a product of Plutarch's imagination. According to Pausanias Demosthenes' tomb was inside the enclosure.[40]

Clearly, Demosthenes was a supplicant (*hiketes*), and he is described as such in the ancient sources. Nevertheless Strabo refers in this connection to the *asylia* of the sanctuary, which seems not entirely correct. On the other hand sanctuaries where supplication is applied (including Tainaron and Kalaureia) are more than once referred to by ancient writers as *asyla hiera*: the concepts of inviolability and supplication do not seem to have had a clear boundary line at all times.

Supplicants other than Demosthenes are not known for Kalaureia, but two other indications for this function of the sanctuary can be mentioned. The first is that of the several names of the island which preceded the name 'Kalaureia' the oldest was apparently 'Eirene', meaning 'peace', a condition which metaphorically equals 'inviolability'. The name is therefore probably related to the asylum function of the sanctuary.[41]

Second, the sanctuary of Poseidon on Kalaureia was once the seat of an Amphictyony, a fact that is connected too with its asylum function. The members of this league were Hermione, Epidaurus, Aegina, Athens, Prasiai, Nauplion and Minyan Orchomenos. The (at least) seven members shared in a joint sacrifice in the sanctuary. The evidence for the league is meagre and opinions on its date, purpose and importance differ. It probably dates from the ninth or even the late tenth century BC; usually it is assumed to have had mercantile and military aims. Yet, if one stresses the maritime character of the league, it seems a little odd that it chose as a meeting place a sanctuary located in the centre and in the highest parts of an island, instead of one nearer to a harbour. The sanctuary is situated 190m above sea level and half an hour from Vayionia bay (but the best harbour in all of Greece is situated on the other side of the island). However this may be, we can in any case stress the need for neutral places which provided opportunity for different kinds of allies to meet. In the aristocratic society of early Greece, festivals must have been important occasions for political and other consultations between members of the nobility from the many different Greek cities. The places for such festivals were of course sanctuaries: sanctuaries, preferably the ones located outside any major power-centre, must have been the junctions in the nobility network of early Greece.

The sanctuary was excavated at the end of the nineteenth century. Pottery indicates the existence of graves in the Mycenaean period; cult activity probably started in Early Geometric times. The excavation did not produce a large number of finds and information about the nature of the cult activities is scarce. According to Pausanias the service in the sanctuary was performed by a girl till she was old enough to wed. In the last quarter of the sixth century BC the sanctuary acquired a temple, of which nothing except the foundation trenches now remains; an altar stood in front and a *temenos* wall surrounded the area. To the west and south-west of this sacred centre a number of buildings, mostly stoai, were raised: one in the last quarter of the fifth century BC, four in the course of the fourth century BC and two at the beginning of the third century BC. The buildings belonged partly to the sanctuary and partly to the adjoining village or city.

The original Amphictyony seems not to have lasted very long and will not have been connected in any way with the (much later) building activities in the sanctuary. These may have partly resulted from the wish to provide accommodation for visitors and supplicants (see the chapter by U. Sinn in this volume, pp. 88–109), but the building activities will also have been a consequence of the sanctuary's role in the region of Troizenia. Poseidon was worshipped under different epithets in Troizen and in one source he is referred to as 'Poliouchos' (protecting the city). It has been suggested that the Poseidon of Kalaureia was the Poliouchos of Troizen.[42]

The old Kalaurian Amphictyony had a short revival in the Hellenistic period. In the intervening centuries Kalaureia's reputation as a safe place remained intact. In fact, as Strabo remarked, even the Macedonians seemed to acknowledge the inviolability of Poseidon's sanctuary (though later, in the first century BC, pirates committed ravages here as well as in the Isthmian sanctuary, Tainaron and elsewhere). For while Archias, without hesitation, violated sanctuaries on Aegina and in Hermione to capture and kill Demosthenes' fellow democratic politicians, in the case of Demosthenes on Kalaureia he had recourse to persuasion. Of course it may have been the reputation of Demosthenes rather than that of the sanctuary which led him on this course, but nevertheless the Poseidon sanctuary seems to have provided a higher degree of protection: all sanctuaries are sacred, but some sanctuaries are more sacred than others.

GERAISTOS, PLACE OF REFUGE

Geraistos is first mentioned in the *Odyssey* (3.176–9). On their way home from Troy Nestor, Diomedes, Menelaos and their men sail from Lesbos and, after crossing the open sea, land in the night at Geraistos, where they sacrifice many bulls as a thanks-offering to Poseidon. The site is mentioned by several other ancient authors, especially because of its harbour. Geraistos was important as a harbour since it was the only safe one along the rugged eastern coast of Euboea. During storms the channel between Andros and Euboea was dangerous for sailing ships and besides Geraistos the Euboean coast had only cliffs to offer.

Odyssey 3.169–72 records a discussion among the Greeks, who had come from Troy to Lesbos via Tenedos, about whether they should sail in the direction of Geraistos or Chios. Arrian (*Anab.* 2.1.2) informs us that on Lesbos the usual approach for merchant ships from Chios, Geraistos and Malea was by Cape Sigrion. Cape Sigrion is the south-western cape of Lesbos; north of the cape is a good natural refuge harbour.[43] Sigrion is part of the territory of Eresos;[44] according to Kallimachos (fr. 39 Pfeiffer) Poseidon was worshipped in Eresos as 'Mesopontios' (amid the sea): a reference to the sea-route?[45] It can be observed that the harbour at Sigrion would have been well situated as a transit-camp for Nestor and the others, the point at which the decision on which route to take could no longer be postponed.

Literary references show that at all times Geraistos attracted ships which came from or went to the east. In the time of Homer the route from Lesbos to Geraistos was already in use, and in 428 BC one did not have any problem finding a merchant ship at Geraistos bound for Mytilene (Thucydides 3.3.5).[46] The Athenians seem to have acquired Geraistos around 470 BC, when it was an important station on the grain-route of their ships. It was this importance which probably caused them to settle a cleruchy there. After their defeat by the Spartans they stayed on at Geraistos: in 375 BC it was a major Athenian recruiting centre. In the period in between, the Spartans seem to have had a garrison at Geraistos. In 396 BC their King Agesilaos, before sailing to Ephesos to wage war against the Persians, had his troops assembled at Geraistos. According to Procopius, a historian from the sixth century AD, a stone ship was dedicated at Geraistos to Artemis Bolosia (the epithet is usually given to the goddess of birth, Eileithyia); an inscription stated that it was a dedication by Agamemnon. Wallace has suggested that this gift, if real, could well have been a dedication from Agesilaos, with his ambitious notions of himself as the new Agamemnon leading the Greeks a second time against the barbarian peoples of Asia Minor.[47] Demosthenes complains of Philip of Macedon, who, among other things, seized the shipping at Geraistos and levied untold sums: an indication that normally ships had to pay (lower) port taxes. For Athenians, Romans, Macedonians and traders of every possible provenance Geraistos must have been a station in sailing from or to the east.[48]

We may wonder about the part played by Karystos, the town nearest to Geraistos: did the Karystians control this harbour? On Karystian coins from 230 BC onwards we sometimes see Poseidon's head on the obverse, his trident on the reverse; imperial coins from the time of Nero and Trajan usually have Poseidon's head on the reverse. These symbols undoubtedly refer to Poseidon Geraistios.[49] Furthermore it was left to the Senate and people of Karystos to decide on the exact place in the sanctuary for the stele from Kimolos.

On the other hand there is the evidence for Athenian, Spartan, Macedonian and Roman control of the harbour. Geraistos is never mentioned as 'the harbour of Karystos': it may be significant that in a fourth-century source Euboea is described as having four cities: 'Karystos, Eretria with harbour, Chalkis with harbour, and Hestiaia with harbour' (Ps.-Skylax, *Periplus* 58 [*GGM* I, 47]). Probably the harbour was too vital in times of tension to leave to the locals and every state that came to power tried to exert its control. Moreover, the area is rocky and mountainous and communications overland between Karystos and Geraistos must have been difficult. Today, on the dirt road along the coastline or through the interior, it is a walk of at least four hours. Though in normal circumstances the Karystians must have controlled Geraistos, it seems also to have been a harbour with a national, if not an international mark (see Livy, who refers to Geraistos as *nobilem Euboeae portum* (Liv. 31.45.10)), often controlled by the power of the day, well known for its transit function and its sanctuary of Poseidon.

In some topographical descriptions Geraistos is mentioned as the name of a promontory, for which reason it has sometimes been identified with present day Cape Mandhili, the southernmost point of Euboea, roughly 5km to the south-west from the harbour. We may assume that the name could be used to refer to the harbour as well as to its region.

The harbour of Kastri cuts into the land in a north-western direction and is protected from the storms coming from the north-east by a promontory.[50] Its conclusive identification was due to the find of the inscription and the trial excavation mentioned earlier. Remains of a mole, a sarcophagus, unopened graves and sherds were observed in the nineteenth century. The site was visited during the British survey of Euboea (surface finds from medieval, Late Roman, Classical and Early Helladic periods) and has recently been surveyed by members of the Southern Euboea Exploration Project.[51]

Though Geraistos is mentioned many times, as a harbour, as a promontory, as the site of a sanctuary of Poseidon, we rarely get more information. Strabo (10.1.7 (446)) refers to the mention by Homer, who, he writes, plainly indicates that the place is conveniently situated for those who are sailing across from Asia to Attika; it has a sanctuary of Poseidon as the most remarkable local attraction, and a settlement (*katoikia*[52]) worthy of mention.

Throughout the year the harbour must have been bustling with activity in the sailing season, when ships came and went, and must have looked very different in the non-sailing season. All normal sailing activity in ancient Greece took place in summer and a few weeks before and after it; during autumn and winter the harbours went into hibernation to await the early sailing season of springtime. On Kos and in Sparta the month Gera(i)stios fell at the end of the winter/beginning of spring. Arguing from here we may put forward the hypothesis that the Euboean Geraistia took place at this time of the year, at the beginning of a new sailing season (cf. the Isthmian Games, which also took place at this time of the year, in April). In view of this 'renewal' it is tempting (though probably too speculative) to extend this hypothesis to the festival in Troizen.[53]

The exact location of the sanctuary has not yet been established; we do not know what it looked like (there are some uncertain indications for the existence of a temple and a statue[54]) or when it was founded. It will be noted that in the *Odyssey* only a sacrifice is mentioned, not the sanctuary; the possibility that the sanctuary came into being as a result of the lines by Homer cannot be excluded a priori. From the Hellenistic inscription we know that there was an *asylon* area. One can see in the sequence place–sanctuary–*asylon* (in lines 46–9 of the inscription) a broadening-out of the place where the stele had to be set up and assume that the sanctuary was part of a bigger area declared inviolable. In that case, however, the addition 'in the *asylon* area' seems redundant in an instruction concerning the place for setting up the stele. The *asylon* area was therefore probably a separate part of the sanctuary. In view of what has been said earlier on sanctuaries declared '*asyla*' and in view of the time and the place in question, this might suggest that an attempt has been made to raise the Geraistia above the level of a local festival. But still, why the addition 'in the *asylon* area' in this inscription? A possible explanation is that the stele, recording a small contribution to the improvement of interstate relations, would now find a place in an area where (on authority of the Delphic god?) reprisals were forbidden and where it could safely be seen and read by Kimolians and other strangers. At the same time this area will have been a place of refuge: it seems naturally suited for such a function. Moreover, Geraistos' (*supra-*)regional function and peripheral location meet some important requirements for regional refuge sanctuaries. Like the sanctuary of Apollo Pythaios mentioned earlier, Geraistos too might well have been a sanctuary that was both *asylon* and *phyktimon*. In Euripides' *Cyclops* 290–5, Odysseus enumerates Poseidon sanctuaries the Greeks have retained in Greece's most remote corners: Tainaron, Malea, Sounion and 'the Geraistian places of refuge'. The word 'place of refuge' (*kataphyge*), can be used in a general way (Eur., *Cycl.* 197) or to indicate an asylum place (Eur., *Suppl.* 267–8). It is tempting to consider the possibility that concerning Geraistos Euripides was thinking of its natural as well as its social function.

In modern times Kastri/Geraistos is still a refuge harbour. Connected with this function is the fact that there are telephone facilities, in spite of the fact that there is no formal settlement:[55] it only consists of a limited number of houses and a church and it does not have any official public building (it is – definitely now, it seems – part of the community of Karystos). Port taxes are no longer levied at Geraistos and it has lost its international reputation, but it still is a *katoikia* with a *hieron* and functioning as a place of refuge.

CORRESPONDENCES IN FUNCTION AND LOCATION

In spite of the fact that a number of correspondences between Tainaron and Geraistos or between Tainaron and Kalaureia can be enumerated, it is only the, historically attested, functional correspondence which gives a connection between all three of them. The sanctuaries at Geraistos, Kalaureia and Tainaron were asylum sanctuaries, generally recognized and with an international reputation. For Kalaureia and Tainaron the evidence of their function as a place of refuge leaves little doubt about this reputation. The *supra*-regional function of Kalaureia is attested furthermore by the fact that it once was the seat of an Amphictyony. In the case of Tainaron and Geraistos this international aspect can also be seen in their function as markets, be it of men or of goods. Tainaron's function in the Hellenistic period as a fixed rallying-point for soldiers in want of employment has already been referred to and there can be no doubt about Geraistos' function as a commercial harbour. In addition we may wonder if Geraistos was a recruiting base for soldiers as well. The evidence makes it clear that already in Homer's time as well as in the subsequent centuries all kinds of soldiers spent shorter or longer periods at the harbour and it certainly would have been well situated for such a function. Tainaron and Geraistos were situated, together with Malea (see Diod. 16.62.3: Malea as a recruiting base) and Sounion, in the most remote corners of Greece, as Euripides put it (see above, p. 79): perhaps that is where one ought to look for mercenaries, and it certainly must have been where the established powers, when not in need of them, wanted them to be.

There is another point in connection with the specific function that should be emphasized: the location of the sanctuaries. All three have an isolated topographical position, lying on the fringes of the polis, and not being easily approachable.

The isolated location of Tainaron is well known and has in fact played a major part during the entire history of the region. The area is (very) rocky and mountainous and access to the sanctuary was difficult, at least overland.[56] We can observe this characteristic also on Kalaureia and in Geraistos. Being an island there is limited access to Kalaureia; moreover the sanctuary is located on higher ground, in the saddle between the highest hills of the island. Since it was not lying on any normal route or in a very populated area, one really needed to have a particular reason to visit the sanctuary. Geraistos was a transit-station and though its location on a sea-route occasioned the attraction of merchants and other visitors during part of the year, at the same time the mountainous character of southern Euboea assured its isolation (to the present day) and interfered with the approach by land.

For these three sanctuaries, location and function seem to go together: just as the supplicants find themselves on the margin of the legal order of the polis-society, similarly the sanctuaries are lying on the topographical margin of the polis-area. Their typical location must have been an important factor in determining their specific function, and vice versa. We may wonder whether a sanctuary got its specific function because of its location, or whether, inversely, the need for an asylum sanctuary led to the establishment of a sanctuary in a suitable location. Perhaps it is reasonable to assume that both situations could occur, in which case it can be concluded that an interdependency between location and function of asylum sanctuaries existed more than once.

Of course asylum sanctuaries are not always located in marginal areas: the historical record gives enough counter evidence. Nevertheless, a distinct relation does seem to present itself. As has been said, this relation between function and location is also stressed by Sinn, who adds a characteristic concerning the form of refuge sanctuaries: he argues that the remains indicating occupation at Perachora, Kalaureia, Tainaron and elsewhere should be connected directly with this function. At Geraistos similar traces are absent.

The three eponymous founders are said to be sons of Zeus, a fact for which no explanation could be given in previous publications. It seems an illogical choice, because one would expect them to be sons of the god to whom the sanctuaries they founded are dedicated, Poseidon. However, the elements of correspondence emphasized in this chapter suggest an explanation. For the asylum function can be readily connected with the figure of Zeus: Zeus is the one and only Greek god who especially protects the supplicant, the *hiketes*; he is virtually the only god with the epithet 'Hikesios' (for supplicants).[57]

CONCLUSION

The first correspondence between Geraistos, Kalaureia and Tainaron is that they are all sites which have a sanctuary of Poseidon. The entries in Stephanus indicate the assumption by the Greeks that the cult in early (pre-Dorian?) times was diffused from Geraistos to Kalaureia and Tainaron, arriving there by sea. It is hard to decide if there is any historic reality behind this diffusion; Minyans and Dryopians are shadowy figures lurking in the background. With the present material available, we can hardly get any further than assuming this to be a possibility, while awaiting new evidence to come to light. But there is another correspondence which distinguishes them sufficiently from other Poseidon sanctuaries: all three, located in an area with a low approachability, had a special reputation as an asylum sanctuary; their function and location are interdependent. Rather than singling out one single characteristic, it was perhaps this combination of factors which gave occasion at some point in the historic period to present their eponymous founders as brothers and as sons of Zeus.

And what about Poseidon? Where does he come in? The asylum function is recorded for sanctuaries dedicated to different gods and there is no reason to assume any special relation to Poseidon. However, the situation is slightly different when we look at the aspect of location.

In studies on other gods of the Greek pantheon a relation between a god and the location of his/her sanctuaries has been observed. Sanctuaries of Zeus, god of the heavens, are often found on mountain peaks. Sanctuaries of Demeter, goddess with an agrarian function, are more than once located on a hill just outside the city. The god Pan is very strongly connected with a typical kind of landscape: to him belongs the marginal land, all that the Greeks call the *eschatiai*, the 'edges'; Pan rules the frontier of human space and has a violent antipathy to civic space.[58]

These examples suggest a relation between the physical location of sanctuaries, the general notion of a god and the function of his/her cult in a particular community. The typical landscape for a Poseidon sanctuary is often assumed to be a promontory, a one-sided view, which can easily lead to the mistake of assigning a sanctuary to Poseidon only because it is located on a promontory (the 'just-like-Sounion' argument).[59] To be sure, a number of Poseidon sanctuaries were actually located on promontories; these cases probably concern relatively modest sanctuaries, consisting only of an altar – or sometimes perhaps not even that: a cape can simply be called 'Poseidion'. In this case the relation with the god of the dangerous sea, worshipped on sites important for sailors, is an obvious one. But as a matter of fact we find sanctuaries on promontories also dedicated to other gods, just as we find Poseidon sanctuaries also in other kinds of landscape: in a plain, on a hill or on a mountain(side).

Apart from looking at the landscape, the aspect of location can also be studied by looking at the relation city–sanctuary. In this respect it is noticeable that in those cases where we can establish a topographical relationship between Poseidon sanctuary and city, the sanctuaries are remarkably often located outside the city (by shorter or longer distances). If we see the city as the centre of society, we can observe a consistency with general traits in the god's character: Poseidon is a god of elemental powers, who was never closely associated with the high achievements of the polis-society, and dissociated from moral values, intellectual advance or technology. This last aspect is best illustrated in his relation to Athena: Poseidon creates the horse, but Athena invents the bit; Poseidon is lord of the seas, but Athena invents the first ship. Consequently, sanctuaries of Athena can be found in the centre of society and it is no wonder that Poseidon sanctuaries are not.[60]

On the one hand we see a relation between the asylum function of sanctuaries and their peripheral location, on the other hand we see that sanctuaries of Poseidon are located remarkably often outside cities and more than once in marginal areas. As a kind of minimal conclusion we can perhaps say that it comes as no surprise that the two have sometimes met, though there is clearly no internal relation between them.

NOTES

I am grateful for the advice and encouragement (and patience) of H. Geertman, N. Marinatos, U. Sinn, F. T. van Straten and H. S. Versnel. E. J. Bakker kindly corrected the English text of this paper; E. van Driel drew the map (Figure 4.1). The research for this paper was supported in part by the Faculty of Letters of the University of Leiden and in part by the Foundation for Archaeological Research, which is subsidized by the Netherlands Organization for Scientific Research (NWO).

1 F. de Polignac, *La naissance de la cité grecque. Cultes, espace et société VIIIe–VIIe siècles avant J.-C.* (Paris 1984); I. E. M. Edlund, *The Gods and the Place: Location and Function of Sanctuaries in the Countryside of Etruria and Magna Graecia (700–400 BC)* (Stockholm 1987). Of course there are also older examples, e.g. B. Bergquist, *The Archaic Greek Temenos. A Study of Structure and Function* (Lund 1967).

2 Kalaureia: *IG* 4.841.12. Troizen: Athenaeus 14.639c. Sparta: Thuc. 4.119.1 (see ibid., 118.12: in 423 BC 12 Gerastios in Sparta equals 14 Elaphebolion in Athens; see A. W. Gomme's commentary on Thucydides, vol. 3 *ad loc.* and pp. 711–13 and A. E. Samuel, *Greek and Roman Chronology* (Munich 1972) 92–4 for calendar problems). Kos and Kalymna: Samuel 1972 (*supra*) 111–13; S. M. Sherwin-White, *Ancient Cos* (Göttingen 1978) 185 n. 63, 193–4, 298 with references. On Kos the year is divided into a winter period of six months and a summer period of six months. On Kalymna the name was changed to 'Tiberios' in imperial times.

3 See for this type of festival F. Graf, *Nordionische Kulte* (Rome 1985) 90ff. and the index; H. S. Versnel, 'Greek myth and ritual: The case of Kronos', in J. Bremmer, ed., *Interpretations of Greek Mythology* (London and Sydney 1987) 121–52.

4 *IG* 4.757.B 12–13; cf. Polybius 38.15.6 (39.8) and F. W. Walbank's commentary *ad loc.*

5 G. F. Unger, 'Die Isthmientag und die Hyakinthien', *Philologus* 37 (1877) 34–40 (he argues that the Isthmian cult also originated from Geraistos); S. Wide, *Lakonische Kulte* (Leipzig 1893) 40–5; O. Waser, 'Tainaros', in W. H. Roscher, ed., *Ausführliches Lexicon der griechischen und römischen Mythologie* vols I–VI (Leipzig and Berlin 1884–1937) vol. 5 (70. Lief. 1915) 8–14; W. R. Halliday, *The Greek Questions of Plutarch* (Oxford 1928) 106.

6 M. P. Nilsson, *Griechische Feste* (Leipzig 1906) 67–9; Waser 1915 (*supra* n. 5); F. Schachermeyr, *Poseidon und die Entstehung des griechischen Götterglaubens* (Bern 1950) 46, 162.

7 F. Vian, 'Les Géants de la mer', *RA* 22 (1944) 97–117; L. Lerat, 'Geraistos et les Geraistai', *RA* 25 (1946) 196–203; F. Vian, 'Génies des passes et des défilés', *RA* 39 (1952) 129–55.

8 Harbour Geraesticus on Teos: Livy 37.27–8; see Lerat (*supra* n. 7) 197. There were in Attica Geraistai Nymphai Genethliai, on Crete nymphs called Geraistiades, and in Arcadia there was a place called Geraistion. All these cases point to kourotrophic nymphs who were said to have swathed and taken care of the child Zeus. Geraistos was also the name of a Cyclops: on his grave the Athenians slaughtered the daughters of Hyakinthos (Paus. 2.2.2 mentions an altar of and sacrifices to the Cyclopes in the Isthmian sanctuary of Poseidon, their only known place of worship). For references and discussion on the nymphs and the Cyclops see Lerat (*supra* n. 7); Vian (*supra* n. 7 (1952)); M. Mellink, *Hyakinthos* (Ph.D. diss. Utrecht 1943) 59–64; M. Ervin, 'Geraistai Nymphai Genethlai and the hill of the nymphs. A problem of Athenian mythology and topography', *Platon* 11 (1959) 146–59 (she identifies the Cyclops' grave with the Hill of the Nymphs in Athens; cf. U. Kron, 'Demos, Pnyx und Nymphenhügel. Zu Demos-Darstellungen und zum ältesten Kultort des Demos in Athen', *AM* 94 (1979) 49–75); M. Jost, *Sanctuaires et cultes d'Arcadie* (Paris 1985) 243–4, 248–9.

9 E. Schwyzer, *Griechische Grammatik* I (Munich 1939) 66, 276, 503; Lerat (*supra* n. 7) 203 n. 2–3; E. J. Furnée, *Die wichtigsten konsonantischen Erscheinungen des Vorgriechischen* (The Hague 1972) 335–6. The name Hephaistos seems related (Vian (*supra* n. 7, 1952) 139 n. 2). His cult originated on Lemnos, the island from which, according to Herodotus, the Minyans were driven away by the Pelasgians.

10 All references in: P. M. Fraser and E. Matthews, eds, *A Lexicon of Greek Personal Names* 1: *The Aegean Islands, Cyprus, Cyrenaica* (Oxford 1987) under Geraistion, Geraistis, Gerastiphanes, Gerastis.

11 After consultation of the indexes of *IG* and the regular epigraphical publications and available prosopographical studies. W. Pape and G. E. Benseler, *Wörterbuch der griechischen Eigennamen* (Braunschweig 1911³) under Gerastios: name of a man in a Doric inscription in the stoa of Hadrian at Athens. No publication reference is given (the name was an addition by Professor Kumanudas, Athens: see p. vii (Benseler's preface from 1862)).

12 Poseidonios on Kos: three or four times, on Rhodes: 11 times. Poseidippos on Kos: one instance, on Rhodes: two instances (from *Lexicon of Greek Personal Names* (*supra* n. 10) under Poseidippos, Poseidonios).

13 On the Rhodian calendar Samuel (*supra* n. 2) 107–10; Chr. Börker, 'Der rhodische Kalender', *ZPE* 31 (1978) 193–218 with *BE* 1979, 310.

14 Diodorus Siculus 5.58.1–2. Phoenician presence in Ialysos archaeologically attested from *c.* 750 BC: J. N. Coldstream, 'The Phoenicians of Ialysos', *BICS* 16 (1969) 1–8; R. Hope Simpson and J. Lazenby, 'Notes from the Dodecanese III', *BSA* 68 (1973) 132. On Kadmos and Phoenician settlements in the Aegaean: R. B. Edwards, *Kadmos the Phoenician* (Amsterdam 1979) 179–85.

15 Polybius 7.9; M. L. Barré, *The God-list in the Treaty Between Hannibal and Philip V of Macedonia* (Baltimore 1983) 80–2. Ba᷄ al-Saphon is later known as Zeus Kasios; a possible Poseidon Kaseos in Kyzikos: I. and Th. Pekáry and E. Schwertheim, 'Kataphraktos und Zweireiher. Zu einer Stele mit Schiffsdarstellung aus Mysien', *Boreas* 2 (1979) 76–86; *BE* 1980, 426.

16 The altar-plaque is an ineditum mentioned in Sherwin-White (*supra* n. 2) 167 n. 81.

17 Vian compares the Geraistiastai with the Tainarioi/Tainaristai (Vian (*supra* n. 7, 1952), 135).

18 U. von Wilamowitz-Moellendorff, *Der Glaube der Hellenen* I (Berlin 1931) 214

n. 3; Mellink (*supra* n. 8) 61; Lerat (*supra* n. 7) 201.

19 T. W. Jacobsen and P. M. Smith, 'Two Kimolian dikast decrees from Geraistos in Euboia', *Hesperia* 37 (1968) 184–99 (date of inscription: *c.* 250–225 BC). M. Wallace, 'The history of Karystos from the sixth to the fourth centuries BC' (Ph.D. diss. University of Toronto 1972 (unpubl.)) 306 no. 57, dates it to 248–239 BC.

20 Though L. Robert, *Opera minora selecta* 5 (1989) 153, writes 'Des juges de Carystos . . .'.

21 A. K. Choremis, Ἐιδήσεις ἐξ Εὐβοίας', *AAA* 7 (1974) 28–32; *idem*, Γεραιστὸς (Καστρὶ) Καρυστίας', *ArchDelt* 28 (1973 (1977)) *Chron.* 305–6. Cf. C. Bursian, *Geographie von Griechenland* 2 (Leipzig 1872) 434–6 on the village Platanistos ('eine Art Oase in dieser sonst durchaus rauhen und wilden Gebirgswelt') and the ancient remains nearby. Excavation of the building at Platanistos: G. A. Papavasileiou, ''Ανασκαφαὶ ἐν Εὐβοίᾳ', *Praktika* (1908) 101–11 (I owe this reference to D. R. Keller).

22 Lerat (*supra* n. 7) 201 with n. 1.

23 Only a few of the main developments are indicated here. For *asylia* one is especially referred to Ph. Gauthier, *Symbola* (Nancy 1972) 209–84, for *hiketeia* (and for all references to ancient and modern literature) to U. Sinn, 'Das Heraion von Perachora. Eine sakrale Schutzzone in der korinthischen Peraia', *AM* 105 (1990) 53–116; I am grateful to Ulrich Sinn for sending me in advance a copy of his article. See also Sinn's contribution to this volume, pp. 88–109.

24 On the right of reprisal see B. Bravo, 'Sulân. Représailles et justice privée contre des étrangers dans les cités grecques', *AnnPisa* 3.10 (1980) 675–987; review of this study by Ph. Gauthier, *Revue historique de droit français et étranger* 60 (1982) 553–76.

25 *Cod. Theod.* 9.45, esp. § 4; transl. in English by C. Pharr (Princeton 1952). See the contribution by E. Schwartz, in F. von Woess, *Das Asylwesen Ägyptens in der Ptolemäerzeit und die spätere Entwicklung* (Munich 1923) 253–72. Cf. for (restrictions to) the right of asylum in Ptolemaic Egypt, F. Dunand, in *Hommages à la mémoire de S. Sauneron* II (Cairo 1979) 77–97.

26 A. Dain and G. Rouillard, 'Une inscription relative au droit d'asile, conservée au Louvre', *Byzantion* 5 (1929–30) 315–26. Cf. L. Wenger, ''Οροι ἀσυλίας', *Philologus* 86 (1931) 427–54.

27 L. Robert, 'Borne de l'asile d'Artémis', *Hellenica* 6 (1948) 33–42.

28 Strabo 8.3.13–20,27 (343–7, 351); Paus. 6.25.5–6; E. Meyer, *Neue Peloponnesische Wanderungen* (Bern 1957) 74–9.

29 Diod. Sic. 15.49; Strabo 8.7.2 (384–5); Paus. 7.24.4–7; E. Meyer, 'Helike', *RE* Suppl. 9 (1962) 79f. Polyain., *Strat.* 8.46.

30 Phokians: *IG* 9(1) 97; cf. R. M. Berthold, *Rhodes in the Hellenistic Age* (Ithaca 1984) 142–4, 221–2; for further references see R. Etienne and J. -P. Braun, *Ténos* I: *Le sanctuaire de Poséidon et d'Amphitrite* (Paris 1986).

31 For discussion and references to various ancient and modern sources see G. Lippold, 'Sparta', *RE* 3A (1929) 1503–5; F. Bölte, 'Tainaron', *RE* 4A (1932) 2030–46; L. Moschou, 'Τοπογραφικὰ Μάνης', *AAA* 8 (1975) 160–77; N. D. Papachatzes, 'Ποσειδῶν Ταινάριος', *ArchEph* 1976 (1977), 102–25; W. Cummer, 'The Sanctuary of Poseidon at Tainaron, Lakonia', *AM* 93 (1978) 35–43.

32 Earthquake and helots: Thuc. 1.128.1; Aristoph., *Ach.* 509–11 with scholia; Paus. 4.24.5ff., 7.25.1; Aelianus, *Var. Hist.* 6.7. Slave: Thuc. 1.133. Kleombrotos: Plut., *Agis* 16 (cf. *idem*, *Cleomenes* 22). Devastations: Polyb. 9.34.9; Plut., *Pomp.* 24.6.

33 P. Cartledge and A. Spawforth, *Hellenistic and Roman Sparta. A Tale of Two Cities* (London and New York 1989) 47–8. The Minyans who came from Lemnos

to Lakonia according to Herodotus (4.145ff.; see above, p. 65) 'sat down' on the Taygetos mountain range: as supplicants? They had chosen Lakonia because of genealogical connections. See Sinn (*supra* n. 23 (1990)) nn. 68 and 69 on terminology and on genealogical arguments concerning supplication.

34 G. T. Griffith, *The Mercenaries of the Hellenistic World* (1935; repr. Groningen 1968) 259–60. Cartledge and Spawforth 1989 (*supra* n. 33) 21, 25, 30.

35 *IG* 5(1) 210–12. Cf. F. Poland, *Geschichte des griechischen Vereinswesens* (Leipzig 1909) 67 (also on Geraistiastai) 71–2; Cartledge and Spawforth (*supra* n. 33 (1989)) 99.

36 Sinn (*supra* n. 23 (1990)) and see his contribution to this volume, pp. 88–109. In another recent interpretation the cuttings are identified by F. Cooper as marble quarries and the cave is located elsewhere (F. A. Cooper, in N. Herz and M. Waelkens, eds, *Classical Marble: Geochemistry, Technology, Trade* (Dordrecht 1988) 69–70). Cooper is probably referring to the natural cave on the western side of the cape which is nowadays locally known as 'the entrance to Hades': see the description by P. Leigh Fermor, *Mani* (1958) ch. 10.

37 Poseidon exchanged with Leto Delos for Kalaureia and with her son Apollo Delphi for Tainaron; according to another source Poseidon exchanged with Apollo Delphi for Kalaureia. On the stories of these exchanges, which refer to cults with similar elements but regarding gods representing opposite values, see R. Ginouvès, *Balaneutikè* (Paris 1962) 342; C. Sourvinou-Inwood, in Bremmer, ed., (*supra* n. 3) 215–41.

38 A. Motte, 'L'expression du sacré dans la religion grecque', in J. Ries, ed., *L'expression du sacré dans les grandes religions* III (Louvain-la-Neuve 1986) 117ff.; E. Leach, *Culture and Communication* (Cambridge 1976) 33–6, 82; C. Renfrew, *The Archaeology of Cult. The Sanctuary at Phylakopi* (London 1985) 16–17.

39 For discussion and for references to ancient sources: S. Wide and L. Kjellberg, 'Ausgrabungen auf Kalaureia', *AM* 20 (1895) 267–326; U. von Wilamowitz-Moellendorff, 'Die Amphiktionie von Kalaurea', *GöttNachr*, Phil.-hist. Kl., 1896, 158–70; L. Bürchner and H. von Geisau, 'Kalaureia', *RE* 10 (1919) 1550–1, 2535–41; G. Welter, *Troizen und Kalaureia* (Berlin 1941); Th. Kelly, 'The Calaurian Amphictiony', *AJA* 70 (1966) 113–21; Bergquist (*supra* n. 1) 35–6; A. M. Snodgrass, *The Dark Age of Greece* (Edinburgh 1971) 402; C. Sourvinou-Inwood, *Theseus as Son and Stepson* (London 1979) 20–1.

40 Main sources: Strabo 8.6.14 (373–4); Plut., *Demosthenes* 28–9; Paus. 1.8.2–3, 2.33.2–3. Welter tentatively identifies a heroon for Demosthenes: Welter (*supra* n. 39) 52.

41 Plut., *Quaest. Graec.* 19 = Aristot. fr. 597 (Rose) = *FHG* II, 136 fr. 95; Steph. Byz. and Harpocration under Kalaureia; K. Philippson and O. Waser, 'Eirene', *RE* 5 (1905) 2128, 2130.

42 Plut., *Theseus* 6; E. Meyer, 'Troizen', *RE* 7A (1939) 650. Cf. von Wilamowitz (*supra* n. 39) 164

43 A. Philippson and E. Kirsten, *Die griechischen Landschaften* IV (Frankfurt 1959) 234.

44 R. Koldewey, *Die antiken Baureste der Insel Lesbos* (Berlin 1890) 32–3, 37–8, 62.

45 Cf. Hom. *Od.* 3.174: the god urged Nestor and the others 'πέλαγος μέσον εἰς Ἐύβοιαν τάμνειν'. A different interpretation of the epithet: H.-G. Buchholz, *Methymna* (Mainz 1975) 200, 204.

46 In 336 AD the orator Libanius, imitating Nestor, crossed the open sea and landed at Geraistos (Liban., *Or.* 1.16). On the association Lesbos–Geraistos see also: Schol. Eur., *Or.* 990 (Oinomaos is said to have been a king on Lesbos, and

Myrtilos killed by Pelops at Geraistos); Sappho, fr. 96 Lobel–Page, 33.

47 Procopius, *De Bellis* 8.22.27–9; Wallace (*supra* n. 19) 332–4. It is not said that the dedication stood in the sanctuary.

48 For all references and discussion: F. Bölte, 'Geraistos', *RE* 7 (1910) 1233–4; Wallace (*supra* n. 19) 31 n. 29, 147–8, 172, 219–20.

49 B. V. Head, *Historia numorum* (Oxford 1911^2) 356–7; Wallace (*supra* n. 19) 337–69.

50 A photograph of the site in: D. Müller, *Topographischer Bildkommentar zu den Historien Herodots: Griechenland* (Tübingen 1987) 413–14. See A. Philippson and E. Kirsten, *Die griechischen Landschaften* I.2 (Frankfurt 1951) 629.

51 A. Baumeister, *Topographische Skizze der Insel Euboea* (Lübeck 1864) 34–5; L. H. Sackett *et al.*, 'Prehistoric Euboea: contributions toward a survey', *BSA* 61 (1966) 80–3. In 1984 it was surveyed by the Southern Euboea Exploration Project, directed by D. R. Keller and M. Wallace (not yet published). See for the project *EchCl* 32 (1988) 151–7 with references. I am grateful to Donald Keller for discussing and visiting the site with me.

52 L. Robert, 'Strabon et la katoikia de Pergame', *BCH* 109 (1985) 483–4 on *katoikia* in Strabo.

53 L. Casson, *Ships and Seamanship in the Ancient World* (Princeton 1971) 270–3; Hesiod, *Erga* 663ff., 678ff.; cf. Vian (*supra* n. 7 (1944)) 102–3, 12; *idem* (*supra* n. 7 (1952)) 155; N. Robertson, 'Poseidon's festival at the winter solstice', *CQ* 34 (1984) 1–16, dates a number of festivals of Poseidon at the winter solstice.

54 Acceptance of the emendation of 'νεῶν ἕδρας' into 'ναῶν ἕδρας' in Eur., *Cycl.* 290 would indicate that the sanctuary had a temple. Perhaps an implicit reference to a Poseidon statue with a trident in Lucianus, *Iupp. Trag.* 25.

55 Observed by Sackett *et al.*, (1966) (*supra* n. 51) 81 n. 136.

56 See Edlund (*supra* n. 1) 137 on the approaches to sanctuaries.

57 O. Jessen, 'Hikesios, Hikesia', *RE* 8 (1913) 1592–3; H. Schwabl, 'Zeus', *RE* 10A(1972) 316–17. Evidence for the worship of Zeus is not attested for Geraistos and Tainaron. On Kalaureia in an inscription from the third century BC a widow issues instructions for sacrifices on the altar before the statue of her deceased husband for Poseidon and Zeus Soter ('Saviour'): *IG* 4.840–1; F. Sokolowski, *Lois sacrées des cités grecques* (Paris 1969) 58–9; L. Robert, *BE* 1974, 244. The epithet is a rather general one (cf. *RE* 10A (1972) 362–4). Pausanias (2.31.10) mentions a sanctuary of Zeus Soter in Troizen, allegedly founded by King Aetios, a grandson of Poseidon.

58 Zeus: H. Schwabl, 'Zeus', *RE* Suppl. 15 (1978) 1045–6. Demeter: N. J. Richardson, *The Homeric Hymn to Demeter* (Oxford 1974) 250–1; Burkert 1985 (*supra* p. 62) 85, 159–61. Pan: Ph. Borgeaud, *The Cult of Pan in Ancient Greece* (Chicago and London 1988; original French edition 1979) 59–61.

59 No doubt the sanctuary on Cape Sounion has made an important contribution in creating this image. On the sanctuary at Sounion see now U. Sinn, 'Sunion. Das befestigte Heiligtum der Athena und des Poseidon an der "Heiligen Landspitze Attikas"', *Antike Welt* 23 (1992) 175–90. Cf. also Edlund (*supra* n. 1 (1987)) 48–9 on sanctuaries on promontories.

60 Cf. Burkert 1985 (*supra* p. 62) who concludes: 'Poseidon remains an embodiment of elemental force' (p. 139). I hope to discuss aspects of location and function more extensively in my thesis on sanctuaries and cult of Poseidon (in preparation).

5

Greek sanctuaries as places of refuge

Ulrich Sinn

If a person in Greece found himself in a threatening situation he had the option of taking refuge in a sanctuary.[1] At first glance the ancient sources do not create the impression that sheltering people seeking asylum was one of the everyday responsibilities of the sanctuaries. We learn about personalities in political life who turned to sanctuaries seeking help when they had been stripped of office or had fallen into disfavour among the people.[2] The sources name victims of war and civil war in particular as making use of the protection provided in sanctuaries.[3]

We consistently hear about the sanctuaries as places of refuge in exceptional situations. This naturally led scholars to compare the protection afforded by Greek sanctuaries with modern institutions officially recognized as places of refuge, such as Christian churches, diplomatic missions or universities; in practice only occasional use is made of the privilege of guaranteeing protection enjoyed by these present-day institutions.

Thus it is readily understandable that this topic, which apparently played a rather minor role in the everyday life of the Greeks, attracted little interest among scholars. The right of sanctuaries to grant asylum is, indeed, counted as an exemplary feature of the Greek social order, but how this idea worked in reality has hardly been explored.

It does in fact seem as if it were hardly possible to find concrete evidence of how the protection afforded by sanctuaries worked in practice. In the ancient sources, and especially in pictorial representations, the action of seeking sanctuary takes place among objects which in any case are the obligatory components of a sanctuary: at the altar (Figure 5.1) or at the image of the god (Figure 5.2). It seems that there are no specific arrangements for looking after suppliants which the archaeologist could find by means of excavation and could analyse.

Under these circumstances would one then be justified in considering that protection offered in sanctuaries – in theory such an august institution – is in fact nothing more than an occasional obligation, which the sanctuaries rather casually fulfilled?

Our views on the right of sanctuaries to grant asylum have been thrown

Figure 5.1 Suppliants on the altar. The daughters of Danaos in the Argive sanctuary. Main scene on a volute krater in Ruvo (inv. no. J. 494).

Figure 5.2 Suppliants at the image of the god. The daughters of Proitos in the sanctuary of Artemis Hemera at Lusoi (?). Main scene on a volute krater in Naples (inv. no. 1760).

off balance by the reports written by ancient historians, mentioned above. In accordance with the genre, they focus on the lives of outstanding figures and tell us almost exclusively about spectacular individual cases. On the other hand many different aspects of the daily life of the normal citizen are mirrored in ancient drama, in the texts of the orators or in philosophical treatises. These types of literary evidence mention the protective function of sanctuaries much more often than do the works of the historians – but mostly by allusion and indirect implication, rather than by outright statements.

Taking into consideration sources which have not been properly evaluated up until now, we gain a much broader spectrum of the ways in which sanctuaries were invoked for protection – especially in the realm of private life: for example, girls turned to sanctuaries for help in order to escape a forced marriage.[4] We also hear about a woman who became a suppliant because she had left her husband and wanted to reach her lover.[5] Orphans were placed under the protection of a guardian by means of action taken by a sanctuary.[6] Members of a family who had been cast out tried to bring about a reconciliation with their relatives in the same way.[7] The same sort of thing also occurs in public life: diplomatic missions, the personal safety of whose members was already guaranteed (see below), placed themselves under the protection of a sanctuary at their destinations in order to make it difficult for the negotiators on the other side to reject their requests.[8]

These examples serve to show that the concept 'asylum' is not a suitable term for characterizing the sort of protection the Greek sanctuaries were in a position to offer. It is true that the ancient world had the institution of asylum (*asylia*), but this should not be confused with the specific form of guaranteeing protection afforded by the sanctuaries. This important distinction must be briefly elucidated.[9]

Ancient Greece was broken up into many independent towns and districts. There was no law code valid for all of the Greeks. Here the institution of *asylia* provided some sort of compensation. It limited the consequences bound to result from the lack of a common set of laws by means of a network of contracts and agreements between the various states. *Asylia* (literally translated: 'prohibition against stealing') guaranteed safe conduct for all those who, acting in the interests of their home towns, crossed the city–state boundaries and therefore were outside the jurisdiction of local justice. Those who profited from *asylia* were envoys – as mentioned above – and especially negotiators, but also artists and athletes whose professions involved travelling around. This kind of protection was effective only when it had been previously agreed on or when it had been formally granted to individuals as an honour.

Sanctuaries are involved in this kind of *asylia* only insofar as the agreements and documents were usually publicly displayed in sacred places which acquired greater effectiveness through the authority possessed by the sanctuary.

But the sanctuaries themselves were protected by *asylia*. One of the basic tenets of Greek religion was that everything inside sacred territory was owned by the god – and the possessions of divinities were of course taboo for human beings. Hence every sanctuary had the status of an inviolable precinct (*asylon hieron*). The inviolability of the sanctuaries guaranteed pilgrims and festival participants security. In the same way it served to protect the often valuable votive offerings. The sanctuaries were predestined to fulfil other functions by virtue of the security afforded by *asylia*. For example they could perform the function of banks. The sanctuary of Artemis in Ephesus is the most noteworthy example of this. Thanks to its status of inviolability the Sacred Island of Delos became one of the most important trading centres of the Mediterranean.

It is important to make a distinction between this general guarantee of protection and the granting of a specific type of protection, the avowed aim of which was to help people in their daily need. The inviolable precincts were the most suitable places for this purpose too. They did not have to be limited to sanctuaries; according to old beliefs the gods were also present in the fires on the hearths of private houses, so that they also counted as *asyla hiera*. And of course this also held true of images of the gods and altars in civic institutions, as in the bouleuterion or the agora. But one most often sought refuge in sanctuaries.

If a person in trouble entered a sanctuary, he was protected by *asylia* as explained above. But his trouble would not be solved simply by staying in a sanctuary. If someone were being pursued on account of a misdeed, he could of course attempt to hide in a sanctuary, but in the long run that was of no help. We know from regulations governing conduct in sanctuaries that anonymous stay on sacred land was not tolerated. For example, whoever wanted to enter the Amphiaraion at Oropos had to hang a wooden tablet with his name clearly visible at the entrance of the sanctuary.[10]

If someone really wished to avail himself of the protection of a sanctuary he had to appear openly and set forth the reasons for his coming. After such a presentation the sanctuary was in turn obliged to work towards a solution of the problem, as a rule by undertaking the role of go-between. This assistance was set in motion through a fixed ritual. This is the rite of *hiketeia* according to which the person in need of help sat down on the altar or at the image of the god holding a certain symbol identifying him as a suppliant, either a freshly broken off twig or a strand of wool (Figures 5.1 and 5.3). From this moment on he was no longer an ordinary visitor to the sanctuary. He had acquired the status of suppliant (male: *hikétes*; female: *hikétis*) and thus had a claim to special treatment, mentioned above. This was the decisive moment for the person in trouble. That is why one used the short-hand phrase 'he sat down in the sanctuary' for a person who sought refuge in a sanctuary. This is also the reason, of course, why artistic representations reduced the subject matter of sacred protection to the motif of settling down at the cult monument (Figures 5.1–5.3).

If the person in trouble had become a suppliant, he now had a legal adviser in the person of the priest. This was not always an easy assignment. Since criminals, even convicted murderers, had the right to perform the rite of *hiketeia*,[11] it was all too often a matter of calming emotions running high, hindering acts of revenge, and instead setting in motion orderly criminal proceedings – since the suppliant could not avoid paying for his crime. The priest's obligation was particularly ticklish when the claim for protection was politically motivated and that was doubtless very often the case. Rejecting a person begging for protection counted as sacrilege. The demand

Figure 5.3 Warriors threatening two suppliants at the altar. Main scene on an amphora in St Petersburg (Hermitage).

for entry into the sanctuary on the part of the person seeking protection could bring about retaliatory measures from the political opponents, and expose the sanctuary and/or the town to which it belonged to great danger. This burden on the priests was in fact the weak point in the system of sacred immunity. Complaints over breakdowns run like a red thread through the ancient literature on the protective function of sanctuaries. The suppliants, as we shall see later on, drew their own conclusions and acted accordingly.

Historians record only examples where the law of sacred immunity was disregarded. It is blood-curdling to read how suppliants are forcibly driven out of sanctuaries, starved to death in sanctuaries, massacred or burnt to death. Scenes such as these have also been represented on vases (Figure 5.3). Over and over again the priests were not able to endure the pressure and strain and found ways of hypocritically circumventing the sacred law. Many a suppliant was the victim of malicious deception. When a sanctuary wanted to rid itself of an undesirable suppliant, there was, for example, a much favoured method of pretending to ask an oracle how to deal with the suppliant. The oracular answer was, as a rule, ambiguously formulated and could be interpreted at will as being unfavourable to the suppliant. Faced with reproach for having left the suppliant in the lurch, one could talk one's way out by claiming to have misunderstood the oracular response. This happened, for example, in Kyme after the oracle at Didyma had been hypocritically consulted.[12]

Athens, which prided itself on being the 'bulwark for all suppliants' is no exception. Just at the time when Euripides has one of his actors say in the *Heraclidae*: 'Here suppliants are not driven away as they are elsewhere', (i.e., in the second half of the fifth century BC) the Athenians put up a police station at the entrance to the Acropolis with the clear aim of keeping undesirable suppliants away from the sanctuaries in the fortress.[13] In Athens, too, it could happen that a priest would not scruple to guarantee a supliant safe conduct to the borders of the state and that once across the border he would be caught at once by his pursuers, who had been tipped off by the priest as to the route by which the suppliant was to be sent 'to freedom.'[14]

Many similar accounts have played a decisive role in influencing scholars to adopt the present consensus, namely that the protection afforded by sanctuaries was effective only in the early period, if at all, and that this institution had lost its effectiveness by the fifth century BC at the latest.[15]

The emotional laments over failures to provide sacred protection could, nonetheless, be explained in quite another way: that every violation against this indispensable institution was recorded with misgivings and at the same time branded with sharp disapproval, whereas all mention of the cases with positive outcomes were omitted because they were normal. This way of interpreting the sources is supported by the fact that reports of bad treatment of suppliants always have moralistic undertones. The great number of legends that grew up around instances where sacred protection was either disregarded or abused are evidence of the unremitting struggle to preserve the effectiveness of sacred protection. The legends give awe-inspiring accounts of the gods mercilessly punishing sacrilege: when Kleomenes, the king of Sparta, went mad in his old age it was considered to be punishment for having ordered thousands of suppliants in Argos to be put to death.[16] A crime against suppliants was thought to be the cause of Sulla's stomach troubles.[17] When an earthquake and a tidal wave buried the town of Helike on the north coast of the Peloponnesus together with all of its inhabitants in 373 BC it was thought to be the response of the gods to a crime committed shortly before against suppliants in the Poseidon sanctuary of the town.[18] And elsewhere in Greece natural catastrophes and military defeats were directly linked to preceding mistreatment of suppliants, for example in Sparta, Sybaris, Metapontum, Croton and Aegina.[19]

These dramatic legends are evidence that the institution of *hiketeia* was deeply rooted in popular belief. The harshness of the divine retribution is a measure of how highly the institution of sacred protection was valued by the people – a measuring stick also for the tenacity with which people continually claimed the right to sacred protection.

Considering how strongly people were aware of the protective function of sanctuaries, it is not surprising that politicians exploited the popularity of *hiketeia* for their own purposes. The topic was well suited for stirring up emotions both in a positive and in a negative sense: thus the Spartans claimed superiority for the law code of Lykurgus because, among other things, they glorified the lawgiver as a man who valued the observance of sacred protection more than his own life.[20] The historian Xenophon praised the same attitude in the Spartan general Agesilaus whom he esteemed so highly.[21] Even the Romans attempted to set themselves up as champions of the right of protection in order to worm their way into the good graces of the Greeks.

This occurred in 192 BC in a speech held at Corinth by the Roman general Flamininus.[22] In the same way hate could be whipped up against political opponents. On the eve of the Peloponnesian War the chief rivals, Athens and Sparta, went through the pretence of conducting negotiations long after they had decided on war because they still had to deal with the problem of convincing their own citizens and allies who were unwilling to fight to back them up. One of their methods in this situation was to summon up remembrance of times when the opponent had disregarded *hiketeia* – coupled with the rhetorical question, whether it is conceivable that one would enter into a peaceful agreement with such evil-doers.[23]

Even this selective glance at the sources serves to show that the institution of *hiketeia* was an ever-present factor in the thinking and dealings of the Greeks. And one could expand the list of examples by pointing out the great number of legends and anecdotes clustered around this topic. *Hiketeia* appears as the main theme for plots not only in drama but also in comedy and even in erotic farce. There was even a code of behaviour advising suppliants how to behave towards hesitant priests: the suppliant should lay claim to compassion and give an impression of humility, but at the same time show unequivocally that he is determined to take his life on the spot, should his call for help be rejected[24] – a powerful means of exerting pressure, for suicide under these conditions would have meant terrible disgrace for the priest himself and the sanctuary in his care.

The everyday routine in activating sacred protection shows up just as it actually was with no retouching in the information referred to above. Mention has already been made of the evil tricks used in the sanctuaries to get rid of undesirable suppliants, while ostensibly keeping to the letter of the law. These reports, reflecting raw reality, are very important documents for determining that the function of granting protection, brought about by means of the rite of *hiketeia*, was not merely an idea up in the air, but was really put into practice – though subject to breakdowns through human weakness – and it can be shown that it was practised far into the period of Roman rule in Greece.

Just as each person had to reckon with having to rely at some point on the protection given by sanctuaries, so the sanctuaries must have held themselves in readiness to respond to the appeals of suppliants. How did the sanctuaries prepare for these continual claims on their hospitality?

In order to answer this question it is sufficient to recall that protection in a sanctuary was put into effect by means of a rite; that the granting of protection and help from the priest as an intermediary was a matter of practising a cult, comparable with proclaiming an oracle, holding musical or athletic contests or taking care of sick people. And so, just as it was taken for granted that lodging inside the sanctuary would be temporarily provided for pilgrims to the oracular shrines, for athletes and artists competing in contests and for patients in sacred places of healing,[25] in the same way it was also taken for granted that suppliants would live in sanctuaries, until a solution to their problems was brought about.

There are several different indications that suppliants and other cult participants lived side by side in the sanctuaries. In this case too, sources outside official histories have proved to be particularly revealing.

For example, the poet Alcaeus bewails his lot in one of his poems[26] as being politically persecuted and having to seek refuge in a sanctuary, but he at once adds that his status as suppliant has the advantage that he can enjoy watching the ritual ring dances performed by the girls of his homeland every day. It is clear that he lived among the other pilgrims. Herodotus tells the story of how three hundred suppliant boys were rescued in a Samian sanctuary of Artemis: when their pursuers threatened to starve them to death in their place of refuge, the Samians simply included the refugees in the cult ceremonial involving meals – once again we see the suppliants mixed together with the other participants in the cult.[27]

Such testimonia indicate how natural it was for pilgrims and suppliants to be together, and there were also several regulations for Greek sanctuaries giving us more definite information about this question. There is an inscription from the Demeter and Apollo sanctuary in Andania, Messenia, dating to 92 BC, in which the organization of the cult ceremonies is regulated to the last detail. One of the sections pertains specifically to suppliants living in the sanctuary – which is, by the way, an uncommonly strong indication that suppliants continually stayed in sanctuaries. The rule is laid down that participants in the cult and suppliants are to be separated for the duration of the cult festival (celebration of mysteries!). We may infer that for the rest of the time pilgrims and suppliants were sharing the living quarters of the sanctuary.[28] One may infer from an inscription from the Heraion on Samos that the suppliants – except those who were slaves – are allowed to frequent the eating places and lodgings in the sanctuary and even to accept temporary employment.[29]

This information leads us to the further question, where exactly inside the sanctuary were all of these long-term guests living? We do not need to consider the suppliants alone. We can now say that it is a matter of the infrastructure for taking care of all the pilgrims living for longer periods in the sanctuaries.

An extensively excavated sanctuary such as Olympia lends itself particularly well to an investigation of the arrangements for lodging and feeding cult participants. Guest houses, bath installations and even shops have been cleared right around the Altis at some distance from the temple and altar (Figure 5.5). In most of the literature about Olympia it is stated that these structures lay outside the sacred precinct. But this formulation is not correct. We are able to state this with such certainty because we have an authentic testimonium about the sacred territory in Olympia. The poet Pindar, in one of his victory odes, recounts the legend of how Herakles founded the sanctuary.[30] Herakles first marked the bounds of the smaller sacred precinct. Pindar speaks of the 'Altis'. He is referring to the precinct, bounded by a low wall with a few entrances, where later the temples of Hera and Zeus were built, and where the treasuries and the masses of statues were erected. But a further passage in Pindar's text shows that the sacred area extended far beyond the area enclosed with a wall; marking off a large area destined for visitors to live in was part of the foundation ceremony. In Pindar's words 'and he set apart the plain right round as a resting-place for the banquet'.

Excavations in Olympia show that the land around the Altis was, in fact, used in this way. By the early seventh century at the latest, hundred of wells had been dug, from which the visitors to the sanctuary could draw water (Figure 5.4).[31] Household wares and bones were found in many of these wells, remains of the meals mentioned by Pindar. After a short period of use these wells were filled in and the dumped fillings contained a great number of votive offerings that had been discarded. This provides proof that the land around the Altis (first occupied by wells, later on by practical structures) was sacred, because according to Greek sacred law votive offerings were inalienable possessions of the divinity and even after they had been discarded could be deposited only inside the sanctuary.

The division into a smaller and larger precinct, as exemplified by Olympia, is an absolutely typical feature of Greek sanctuaries in general as may be demonstrated by a basic review of cult sites everywhere. As a rule the inner precinct with the altar, a temple (if there is one) and votive offerings is separated off from the outer precinct. This can be achieved by means of a low wall, as in the case of Olympia, or by a large artificial terrace, as in the case of the sanctuary of Aphaia on Aigina (Figure 5.6).[32] As a rule one took advantage of the natural terrain to separate the two areas, siting the sacred centre at the top or on the slope of a hill with the larger area spreading out below. The Zeus sanctuary on Mt Lykaion is an outstanding example. The place of sacrifice is on the second highest peak of Lykaion, 1400m high, while the subsidiary sacred structures, including the facilities for the athletic contests, are located on a highland plateau 200m below. Strabo's description of the Apollo sanctuary at Actium also fits into this scheme: the temple stands on a hill; down below in the plain is a grove with all facilities for conducting the sacred contests held in Actium.[33] A variant of this canonical topography is to be found, for example, at the Heraion at Perachora[34] or at the Artemis sanctuary in Arcadian Orchomenos where the lay of the land necessitated placing the temple precinct below the utilitarian area above.

Strabo's description of the Apollo sanctuary at Actium has already been mentioned. Livy further documents our definition of the topography of Greek sanctuaries as conditioned by function: in reporting Flamininus' campaign against Antiochos III, Livy mentions how the Roman soldiers, before the outbreak of the war, paid a visit to the sanctuary of Apollo (Delion) at Tanagra.[35] In passing, Livy gives a short description of the sanctuary for his Roman readers and says that it consists of a temple precinct and a grove like all Greek sanctuaries. Livy expressly adds that both parts are equally sacred and therefore inviolable (*asyla*).

In this context the significance of a passage in Aeschylus becomes clear. At the same time this text takes us back to our initial question concerning the arrangements for lodging suppliants. In the *Suppliants* Aeschylus describes the whole procedure of requesting protection taking place in the world of myth. In the course of events he also deals with the moment where the initial rite of *hiketeia* is performed at the altar and the priest takes up his role as intermediary. Because the negotiations are so difficult, there is no way of getting around a long stay in the sanctuary for the more than one hundred suppliants. The mistrustful suppliants are loath to abandon their secure place at the altar, but the priest cannot permit something so detrimental to the sacrifices continually being performed. He sends them to a grove situated away from the altar. The suppliants are afraid that there they are no longer safe from attacks by their pursuers; the priest explains that when they are in the grove they are just as much under the protection of the sanctuary as they are at the altar. Aeschylus in line 509 calls the grove '*bébelon alsos*' which means something like 'profane grove'. However, since sacred protection is spoken of in the same breath, this name is not to be taken literally. 'Profane' is here clearly meant in distinction to the 'Holy of Holies' (*hieron alsos*), the nucleus with the altar for sacrifices and the cult image. The profane-sounding name simply mirrors the character of the adjacent area used for various purposes, among other things joyful cult celebrations attended by ritual dances and feasts.

These subsidiary areas had an infrastructure with a water supply and either permanent structures or simply shady places for temporary shelters, that is, huts made of branches or tents. Thus all Greek sanctuaries, with their subsidiary areas indispensable for cult requirements, were in a position to put up large numbers of cult participants – and therefore suppliants too – for a long period of time on sacred ground (Figures 5.4, 5.5, 5.7, 5.9, 5.10).

The protective function of Greek sanctuaries was not associated with any one particular divinity. As guarantor of the concept, Zeus was accorded the epithet '*hikesios*', just as he guarded the rights of guest-friendship as Zeus Xenios and the validity of an oath as Zeus Horkios. In Greece there were no sanctuaries which were specifically sanctuaries for asylum, in contradistinction to the practices of the Jews and Egyptians.[36] The rite of *hiketeia* could be performed in any sanctuary, no matter what kind of sanctuary it was or to whom it was dedicated. The right and the duty of extending protection was valid for all sanctuaries without distinction. As the result of bitter lessons, however, suppliants always attempted, if they had the time, to reach sanctuaries they trusted. The effort to choose a sanctuary which would favour the best possible mediation by priests is a recurring theme in drama. One

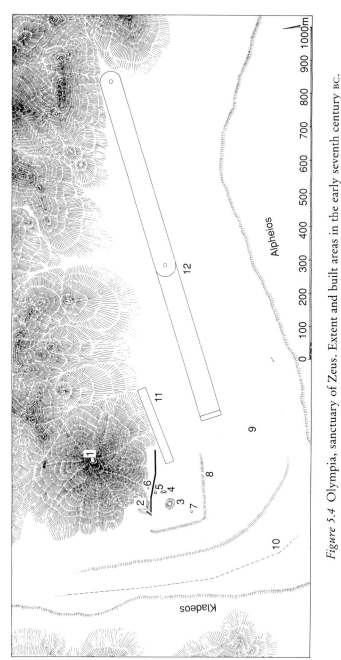

Figure 5.4 Olympia, sanctuary of Zeus. Extent and built areas in the early seventh century BC.

1 Kronos Hill
2 Shrine of Gaia
3 Pelopion
4 Altar of Zeus

5 Altar of Hera
6 Altar of Herakles
7 Sacred olive tree
8 Slope delimiting the Altis (altar precinct)

9 Outer sacred precinct
  (still without permanent
  buildings, while used for
  cooking pits and wells)

10 Wall along the bed of
   the Kladeos stream (?)
11 Stadium
12 Hippodrome

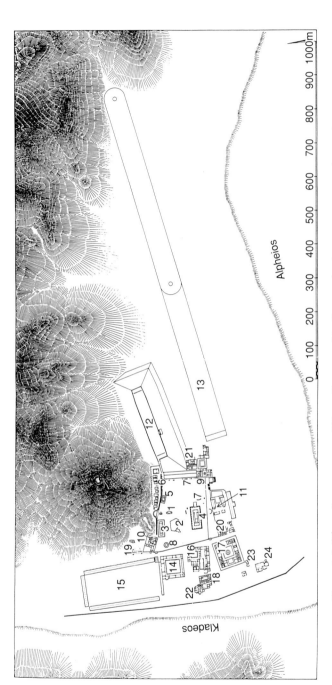

Figure 5.5 Olympia, sanctuary of Zeus. Extent and built areas in the Roman imperial period.

a) in the Altis (the altar precinct)

1 Altar of Zeus
2 Pelopion
3 Temple of Hera
4 Temple of Zeus
5 Temple of Meter
6 Terrace of the treasuries
7 Statue bases

8 Philippeion
9 Sanctuary of Hestia and
  gathering place of the council
  ('Prytaneion')
10 Sanctuary of Hestia and
  Prytaneion in Roman
  times

b) in the outer sacred precinct

11 Bouleuterion
12 Stadium
13 Hippodrome
14 Palaestra
15 Gymnasium
16 Building for the administration
  of the sanctuary

17 and 18 Guest houses
19 Dining pavilion with bath
20 Shops and bath
21 Multi-purpose complex with meeting-
  hall, dining rooms and baths
22 and 23 Baths
24 Club building of athletes (?)

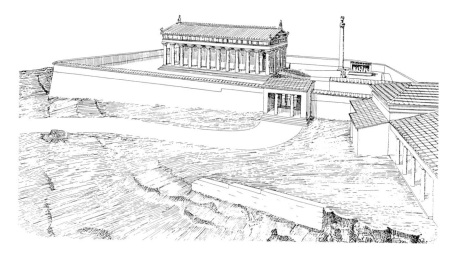

Figure 5.6 Aigina, sanctuary of Aphaia. View of the separate temple precinct on the podium.

preference shows up clearly: if at all feasible the suppliants turned to the main sanctuaries of the towns or districts.

It is easy to make out the reasons for this preference. The psychological factors should not be underrated: the aversion encountered by the suppliants in the sanctuaries has already been described. The risk of being rejected was much lower in the larger sanctuaries. For one thing there was a certain awareness of what went on in these well-frequented cult centres making it less easy for a priest to avoid fulfilling his responsibilities. An observation in Euripides' *Heraclidae* (l. 44) indicates that the presence of other visitors to the sanctuary was reassuring. In *Oedipus Coloneus* (ll. 47f.) Sophocles suggests that in a small sanctuary not frequented by the public it could easily happen that a suppliant could be driven out of the precinct.

The religious centre of a town or region offered the further advantage, especially for a political fugitive, that the priest was backed up by the authority of a whole town or even a whole district. The demand of a political opponent, coupled with threats, to surrender a suppliant would have less effect. We encounter this argument too in Classical drama.[37]

The chief sanctuaries of the towns and districts, where a large general public regularly came together for common cult ceremonies, offered much more favourable conditions for a stay lasting some length of time. The areas set aside for the convenience of visitors in these religious centres were more extensive, the infrastructure was doubtless of a higher standard in respect to hygiene and maintenance. But this consideration is still not sufficient to explain why the suppliants were so powerfully drawn to the main sanctuaries.

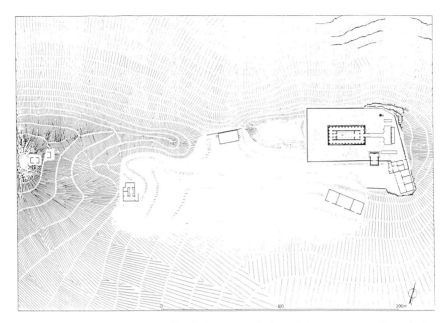

Figure 5.7 Aigina, sanctuary of Aphaia. Ground plan of the sanctuary. Dotted: the temple precinct; white: the outer precinct.

Figure 5.8 Perachora. View of the Perachora peninsula from the east, with the sacred precinct on the rocky spur at the tip.

One turns to consider the known phenomenon that the main sanctuaries of a town or region were often situated far outside the inhabited areas. One may profitably enquire if there may not be some causal connection between the site of a sanctuary and its function as a place of asylum. Of course one has to take into consideration the fact that within the settlements there would have scarcely been enough land available for the necessarily extensive subsidiary areas of the religious centres. But if a question of space were the only reason for siting the sanctuaries outside of the settlements, the distance between town and sanctuary need not have been so great as it actually is in most cases. It is not only a question of measurable distance. The geographical placement of many of these sanctuaries is striking: they are sited on particularly exposed spots remarkably often.

The sanctuary of the Messenian League is sited on the edge of the Messenian plain on the steep ridge of Ithome 700m high. The Arcadians had their joint sanctuary at an even more remote place on the peak of Mt Lykaion 1400m high. The inhabitants of the Epidaurian region gathered together for the common cult ceremonies in the sanctuary of Apollo Maleatas far inland on the edge of a highland plain enclosed by mountains far inland. The temple of Apollo at Bassae in its oft-mentioned mysterious lonely mountain setting belongs in this category. The main sanctuary in Phigalia, just as in the case of so many other regional cult centres, is sited on the highest mountain of the region – and occupies the whole peak.[38]

The exposed position of these sanctuaries was an advantage with regard to their function as potential places of asylum, as the example of the sanctuary of Apollo at Thermon (Figure 5.9) clearly indicates. The historian Polybius has some very suggestive observations to make concerning the sanctuary of the Aetolian League.[39] He emphasizes the fact that the site of this sacred precinct is on a highland plain enclosed by mountains and difficult of access and describes this as the ideal place for a sanctuary under whose protection the inhabitants of a large region come together for their religious festivals, their political gatherings and their annual trade fair. Polybius explicitly states that in times of war the Aetolians were accustomed to deposit their personal belongings and a supply of food in houses maintained in their so well protected league sanctuary. Because the site served a protective function, the sanctuary of the Aetolian League was also called 'the Acropolis of all Aetolia'.

For the same reasons sanctuaries were sited at the tip of capes or peninsulas or on an island close to the mainland. For example, the sanctuary of Poseidon at Cape Taenaron (the religious centre of the Laconian helots) or the sanctuary of Athena and Poseidon at Cape Sounion (Figure 5.10), which had had the descriptive name of 'holy land's end of Attica' since the time of Homer.[40] The island of Kalaureia with its sanctuary of Poseidon, highly esteemed by all the Greeks as a place of asylum, lies directly off the coast of Troizen.[41]

Just as information about Thermon demonstrates that sanctuaries in out-of-the-way hill districts are specially well suited as places of asylum, so testimonia on the sanctuary of Hera at Perachora (Figure 5.8) provide striking information about sanctuaries at the ends of capes being specially suitable for guaranteeing protection. Xenophon reports that in times of danger the inhabitants of the entire peninsula of Perachora were accustomed to hasten to the sanctuary on the cape.[42] On these occasions they even drove all of their flocks into the sanctuary. This was nothing unusual in an agrarian region. In times of danger, the inhabitants of the Chelmos region in Arcadia used to drive their flocks, their most valuable possessions, into the sanctuary of Artemis at Lusoi. During their stay there the animals, like the suppliants, belonged to the god.[43] Xenophon's report on how the Heraion at Perachora was used is so important for our investigation because excavations have made it possible to show what additional practical arrangements were made in a sanctuary so that it could serve as a place of refuge. Extensive subterranean cisterns and wells were installed in order to provide men and animals with water. In addition some houses were constructed here, as in Thermon, either as storerooms for food supplies or as lodgings for people who could not be expected to live out in the open or in temporary dwellings.

The living arrangements that are comparatively well attested at Thermon and Perachora may reasonably be assumed to have existed at those sites where the historical sources inform us that protection was extended on a large scale. Without such living arrangements it would not have been possible for thousands of Messenians to hold out as suppliants in the sanctuary of Zeus on Ithome in the 460s BC until they finally obtained safe conduct to their new home at Naupactus.[44] A few years earlier the sacred precinct on Mt Lykaion had served as a collecting point for the inhabitants who had been driven out of the town of Ira and who were distributed among various localities in Arcadia from there.[45] In the early fifth century BC, when the people of Phigalia decided to abandon their town in the face of Laconian superior power, they doubtless took this decision knowing that they could temporarily settle in their cult centre on Mt Kotilion.[46]

It surely would not be right to consider the exposed position of these sanctuaries as a measure adopted for strategic reasons. The unassailable sanctuary of Zeus on Ithome is certainly an exception. If religious awe no longer acted as a deterrent, then geographical isolation would not hinder a determined opponent from attacking sacred land. Not even if the sanctuaries were enclosed within fortification walls, as for example on the Acropolis of Athens, the sanctuary of Apollo at Thermon (Figure 5.9), the Athena-Poseidon sanctuary at Sounion (Figure 5.10), or at the Demeter sanctuary at Lepreon. But as long as one had it in one's power to choose the site where people would come together to practise the rites of a cult, then why not consider the conditions under which the site could function as effectively as possible as a place of refuge.

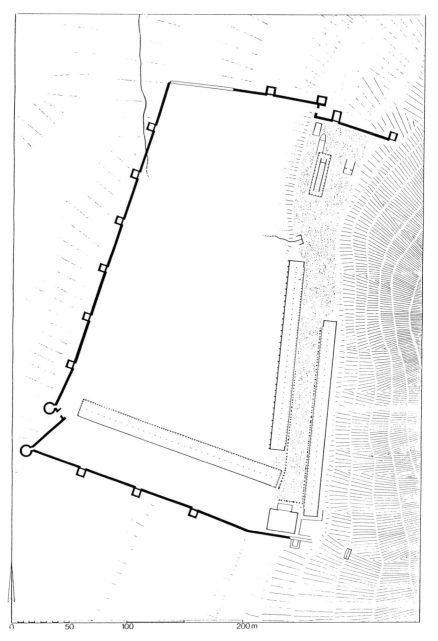

Figure 5.9 Plan of the fortified sanctuary of Apollo at Thermon. Dotted: the temple precinct; white: the outer precinct.

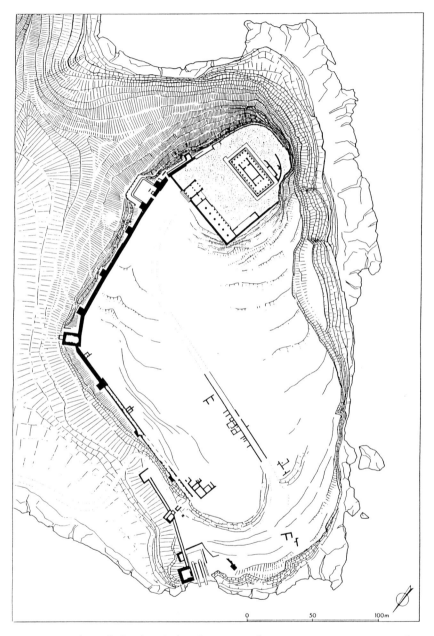

Figure 5.10 Plan of the fortified Athena–Poseidon sanctuary at Cape Sounion.
Dotted: the temple precinct; white: the outer precinct.

105

In reading the literary sources, one becomes aware of a further reason for the often very sharp separation of inhabited areas from sacred places of refuge: there is a passage in Thucydides' history where no attempt is made to conceal the strong sense of unease aroused by the presence of politically motivated suppliants in a sanctuary in the midst of a town.[47] The scene is set in the town of Corcyra which was plagued by an intense civil war in the 420s BC. While the balance of power was constantly shifting back and forth, the democrats on one occasion got the upper hand and the whole group of oligarchs, more than four hundred fighting men, removed themselves to the sanctuary of Hera in the middle of the town. The democrats saw danger in having their enemy concentrated in a small space in the centre of town. They were afraid that the oligarchs could use the sanctuary as the basis of operations for a military counter offensive (as had actually occurred at that time in the Delion near Tanagra![48]). So the Corcyrans declared themselves ready to make allowances for the suppliants on condition that they would transfer the site of their *hiketeia* to a place outside the town. The suppliants were then interned on one of the islands lying in front of the town. If a sacred precinct was not available, a suitable substitute was created.

Several Spartan kings driven out of office owed their survival to the fact that they avoided the sanctuaries inside the town and instead chose a distant sanctuary as the place for their *hiketeia*: Leotychides II[49] and Pausanias II[50] in Tegea, Kleombrotos II at Cape Tainaron,[51] and Pleistoanax at Mt Lykaion.[52] King Agis behaved differently.[53] He did not give up his political ambitions and ostentatiously remained in the sanctuary of Athena in the town, thus arousing the mistrust of the new rulers. So he courted his own fate, he was tricked by an extremely sophisticated ruse and met his death.

The Greek towns were repeatedly confronted with the situation in which members of the political opposition came over to their side. On the one hand this was welcomed because it meant that the opponent was weakened. On the other hand the presence of such suppliants attracted the opponents like a magnet, possibly leading them to take revenge on the town sheltering the suppliants. In these circumstances it was understandable that the town-dwellers would be easier in their minds if a suitable place for *hiketeia* could be found far removed from where they lived. This is what the Athenians did in the early fifth century BC when an uprising which they had masterminded on the island of Aegina collapsed. The Athenians of course provided their Aeginetan collaborators with a place of refuge – but not in Athens. They sent the fugitives out into the Attic countryside to a place which was as far away from Athens as possible: Sounion.[54]

Herodotus uses the simile that suppliants are naturally to be found in sanctuaries, just as birds are accustomed to make their nests there.[55] Later on Aelian[56] recorded a very popular fable in which the idea of sacred immunity was transferred to the animal world: there were safety zones in the woods which provided absolute security. Once one was inside the boundary the pursuers came to an abrupt halt and the hounds were thrown off the scent. In the middle of these safety zones everything was arranged most satisfactorily for the animals.

The image used by Herodotus and the parable handed down by Aelian both arose from efforts to create more respect for the institution of sacred immunity. But when one plucks these ancient testimonia out of their contexts, they reinforce the notion that is nowadays so popular, to the effect that Greek sanctuaries were retreats where peaceful quiet and greatest harmony reigned – a notion that naturally springs to mind over and over again when one visits the sites of the once heavily frequented places of refuge on capes washed by the waves of the sea, or in quiet bays or in remote mountain landscapes. This point of view so charged with emotion hardly does justice to the true significance of the Greek sanctuaries: the sacred precincts lead us straight into the everyday world of the Greeks. The very existence of these sacred precincts with their specific rights was what made it possible for the Greeks to master the crises of daily life with its private needs and general hazards.

(Translated by Judith Binder.)

NOTES

1 The topic of Greek sanctuaries as places of refuge has been treated *in extenso* by the author; see U. Sinn, 'Eine sakrale Schutzzone in der korinthischen Peraia', *AM* 105 (1990) 53–116, hereafter abbreviated: Sinn, *Perachora*.

2 For example the Athenian statesmen Kylon (*c.* 630 BC, Herodotus 5.71; Thucydides 1.126.10–11) and Demosthenes (after 322 BC, Arrian (*FGrHist* 156 F 9.13); Strabo 8.6.14; Pausanias 1.8.2f., 2.33.2f.). Members of various Greek royal families availed themselves of the protection afforded by sanctuaries: Queen Deïdameia of Epirus (Polyain. *Strat.* 8.52), King Perseus of Macedonia (Livy 44.45.5–45.6.10) and Cleopatra IV (Justin 39.3.10–11). For Spartan kings seeking asylum, see nn. 49–53 below.

3 For example the inhabitants of Plataia sought refuge in a sanctuary when the Spartans captured their town (427 BC, Thucydides 3.58.3) and so did the Thebans when Alexander the Great took their town (335 BC, Arrian, *Anabasis* 1.8.8 and 1.9.6–10; Diodorus 17.8–15).

4 Flight to a sanctuary in order to get married or for escaping the unwanted attentions of a lover is a common topic in ancient drama, even in tragedy (Aeschylus, *Suppliant Women*), as well as in burlesque (Plautus, *Rudens*); see also Pausanias 8.5.11f.

5 The legend about the local Naxian heroine Polykrite originates in the tale of the Milesian Neaira, who falls in love with the Naxian Promedon, follows him to Naxos and, pursued by her husband, takes refuge there in the sanctuary of Hestia (Parthenios, *Erotica patemata* XVIII (= Theophrastus); Plutarch, *Moralia* 254 B.-C. *de mul. vir.*).

6 This convention is mentioned in ancient commentaries in connexion with a myth about Medea (Kreophylos in Didymos in: Schol. Eur., *Med.* 264).

7 In *Oedipus at Colonus* Sophocles describes such a case (ll. 1158ff.): Polyneikes is a suppliant at the altar of Poseidon in Athens in order to force his father, who has cursed him, to speak to him.

107

8 Thucydides (1.24.3–7) describes this use of sacred protection in Corcyra. The events that took place in the sanctuary of Zeus in Olympia in 428 BC are particularly informative. After Mytilene had left the Athenian League the Mytileneans wanted to be taken into the Peloponnesian League; this was deliberated in a session of the League, which convened at the Olympic Games (sic!). Realizing that their position as former partners of Athens was weak, the Mytileneans, at the end of the speech in which they request membership, interpose the observation that, in view of the fact that they are convening in Olympia, they are basically suppliants of Zeus, so that reverence for the god should hinder rejection of their application for membership (Thucydides 3.14.1; F. E. Adcock, *Thucydides and his History* (London 1963) 8).

9 This differentiation is extensively set forth and the earlier, basic literature cited in Sinn, *Perachora*, 71–83.

10 *Inscriptiones Graecae* VII (Berlin 1892) no. 235 ll. 39ff.

11 In *Ion* (ll. 1312f.) Euripides has one of the actors utter a complaint (such as we are accustomed to hearing nowadays) about the allegedly over-liberal regulations of right to asylum.

12 Herodotus 1.159.

13 *Inscriptiones Graecae* I (Berlin 1924) Suppl. 26A; K. Wernicke, 'Die Polizeiwache auf der Burg von Athen', *Hermes* 26 (1891) 51–7.

14 Euripides, *Heraclidae*, l. 257.

15 J. Gould claims a virtually complete failure ('Hiketeia', *JHS* 93 (1973) 101); so does H. Schaefer, *Staatsform und Politik* (Leipzig 1932) 46ff.

16 Herodotus 6.75.3.

17 Pausanias 1.20.7.

18 Pausanias 7.25.1.

19 For a collection of such legends, see Sinn, *Perachora*, 115f. (Appendix III).

20 Plutarch, *Moralia* 227 A.B.

21 Xenophon, *Agesilaus* 11.1.

22 Diodorus 29.1.

23 Thucydides 1.126–8. For a collection of passages in which mistreatment of those seeking asylum is exploited for propaganda, see Sinn, *Perachora*, 113f. (Appendix III.)

24 Aeschylus, *Suppliants*, ll. 194ff.; cf. Aeschylus, *Eumenides*, ll. 415ff., 443ff.; Sophocles, *Oedipus Coloneus*, ll. 237ff.; Plutarch, *Agis* 16–18, is clearly referring to the code of behaviour in Classical drama when he describes the request for protection made by the Spartan kings Kleombrotos II and Chilonis in the sanctuary of Poseidon at Tainaron.

25 Inscriptions show that patients in healing sanctuaries were actually termed suppliants; see e.g. R. Herzog, *Die Wunderheilungen von Epidauros* (Leipzig 1931) 9ff.

26 *P. Ox.* XVIII 2165 fr. 1 col. II 9–32.

27 Herodotus 3.48.

28 H. Sauppe, 'Die Mysterieninschrift aus Andania', *Abhandlungen der königlichen Gesellschaft der Wissenschaften zu Göttingen* 7 (1859) 253, 265f.; F. Sokolowski, *Lois sacrées des cités grecques* (Paris 1969) 120ff. no. 65.

29 Chr. Habicht, *AM* 87 (1972) 210ff.; G. Thür and H. Taeuber, *Anzeiger der Österreichischen Akademie der Wissenschaften* 115 (1978) 205ff.

30 Pindar, *Ol.* 10, ll. 42ff.

31 A. Mallwitz, 'Cult and competition at Olympia', in *The Archaeology of the Olympics*, Wisconsin Studies in Classics (Los Angeles 1988) 79ff.

32 U. Sinn, 'Der Kult der Aphaia auf Aegina', in R. Hägg, N. Marinatos and G. C.

Nordquist, eds, *Early Greek Cult Practice, Proceedings of the Fifth International Symposium at the Swedish Institute at Athens (26–29 June, 1986)* (Stockholm 1988) 154ff.

33 Strabo 7.7.6, p. 325.

34 Sinn, *Perachora*, pl. 11 and Beilage 4.

35 Livy 35.51.1–4.

36 For the regulated right of asylum among the Jews, see L. Fuld, 'Das Asylrecht in Alterthum und Mittelalter', *Zeitschrift für vergleichende Rechtswissenschaft* 7 (1887) 102ff.; M. Siebold, *Das Asylrecht der römischen Kirche mit besonderer Berücksichtigung seiner Entwicklung auf germanischem Boden*, Universitas–Archiv, Historische Abteilung, Band 4 (1930) 9ff.

For the right of asylum in Egypt in which the government played a role, see F. v. Woess, *Das Asylrecht Ägyptens in der Ptolemäerzeit und die spätere Entwicklung*, Münchner Beiträge zur Papyrusforschung und antiken Rechtsgeschichte 5 (Munich 1923); L. Wenger, 'Asylrecht', in *Reallexikon für Antike und Christentum* I (1950) 838ff.

37 For example in the *Suppliants* of Aeschylus and in the *Heraclidae* of Euripides.

38 The author is preparing a full treatment of the geographical position and the topography of these and other sanctuaries under the title: 'Die griechischen Heiligtümer, Funktion – Organisation – Topographie.'

39 Polybius 5.7–8.

40 Homer, *Odyssey* 3.278ff. On the names of the cult precincts and for the topography of sacred territory on Cape Sounion, see U. Sinn, 'Sunion. Das befestigte Heiligtum der Athena und des Poseidon an der "Heiligen Landspitze Attikas"', *Antike Welt* 23 (1992) 175ff.

41 Strabo 8.6.14.

42 Xenophon, *Hellenica* 4.5.

43 Polybius 4.18.10–12, 4.19.4. On this topic, see U. Sinn, 'The "Sacred Herd" of Artemis at Lusoi', in R. Hägg, ed., *The Iconography of Greek Cult in the Archaic and Classical Periods*, Proceedings of the First International Seminar on Ancient Greek Cult, organized by the Swedish Institute at Athens and the European Cultural Centre of Delphi (Delphi 16–18 November 1990). Kernos, Suppl. 1 (Liège 1992) 177ff.

44 Thucydides 1.101–3; Diodorus 11.84.8; Pausanias 3.11.8, 4.24.7. For the historical event, see F. E. Adcock, *Thucydides and His History* (1963) 123f.; H. Bengtson, *Die Staatsverträge des Altertums* II (Munich 1982) 138.

45 Pausanias 4.6ff. For the sources used by Pausanias in his treatment of the Messenian Wars, see L. Pearson, 'The pseudo-history of Messenia and its authors', *Historia* 11 (1962) 397ff.

46 Pausanias 8.399.3f.; also F. Cooper, *The Temple of Apollo at Bassai* (New York and London 1978) 17ff.

47 Thucydides 3.75.5 – 81.3.

48 Thucydides 4.97f.

49 Herodotus 6.72; Pausanias 3.7.9f.

50 Xenophon, *Hellenica* 3.5.25; Strabo 8.5; Diodorus 14.89.1; Pausanias 3.7.

51 Plutarch, *Agis* 11, 16–18.

52 Thucydides 2.21.1, 5.16.3; Plutarch, *Pericles* 22.3.

53 Plutarch, *Agis* 16–21.2.

54 Herodotus 6.90.

55 Herodotus 1.159.3.

56 Aelian, *De natura animalium* 11.6.

6

The sanctuary of Demeter and Kore at Eleusis

Kevin Clinton

> Many are the sights to be seen in Greece, and many are the wonders to be heard; but on nothing does heaven bestow more care than on the Eleusinian rites and the Olympic games.
>
> (Pausanias 5.10.1.)[1]

In the fifth century BC Eleusis and the sanctuary of the Two Goddesses were very much a part of Athens. At the end of the sixth century, as a result of the democratic reforms, the town of Eleusis had become one of the many demes making up the Athenian polis. In spite of this well-known fact, modern works often refer erroneously to Athens and Eleusis as if they were separate cities, as if the territory of Athens comprised only the area immediately around the Acropolis – ignoring the fact that the Athenian polis extended to the borders of Megara and Boeotia in the west and north and to the sea on all other sides.[2] In size, therefore, Eleusis constituted just a tiny part of Athens.

No one would deny that at least from the *middle of the sixth century* BC, the town of Eleusis, though not yet a deme in the later sense, was already part of the polis. But there are differing opinions on the relation of Eleusis to Athens prior to this time. The question is of great importance for our understanding of the early history of the Mysteria, Athens' most famous festival, which was celebrated in the sanctuary of Demeter and Kore at Eleusis (Figure 6.1).

The notion that Eleusis was independent of Athens until the early sixth century is based partly on the fact that the *Homeric Hymn to Demeter*, probably composed around the end of the seventh century,[3] sets much of its story in Eleusis but says nothing about Athens, and also on the fact that, shortly after 590 BC, Solon, as quoted by Herodotus (1.30.5), refers to 'a battle that the Athenians fought with their neighbours, at Eleusis'. However, historians have pointed out that the passage in Herodotus probably refers not to a battle between Athens and Eleusis but to a battle fought *at Eleusis* between Athens and its neighbours the Megarians.[4] In addition, Thucydides gives us good reason to think that Eleusis was not independent of Athens in the seventh century: he discusses Athenian traditions about the early

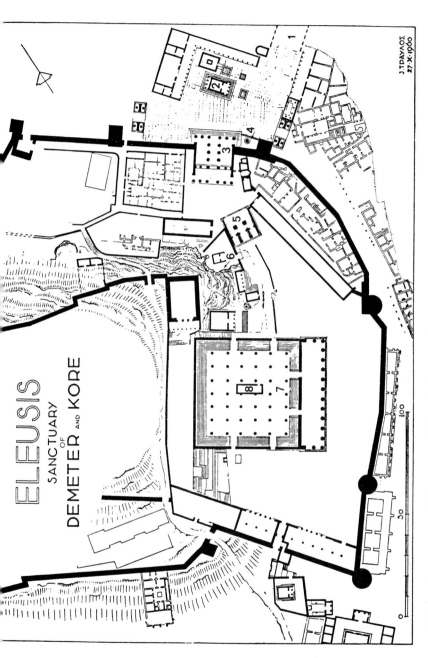

Figure 6.1 Eleusis, sanctuary of Demeter and Kore in the second century AD: 1. Sacred Way; 2. Temple of Artemis; 3. Greater Propylaea; 4. Callichoron Well; 5. Lesser Propylaea; 6. Mirthless Rock; 7. Periklean Anaktoron; 8. Interior structure.

'history' of Attica at some length, but says nothing that would suggest that Athenians believed Eleusis was independent as late as the seventh century. As Russell Meiggs put it succinctly: 'Had Eleusis remained independent into the seventh century Thucydides should have mentioned it.'[5]

Furthermore, there is, in Athenian law and political institutions, evidence which sheds some light on the relation of the sanctuary to the polis in this period, and it corroborates the picture we get from Thucydides. Andocides, *On the Mysteries* 111, refers to a 'law of Solon' regulating a matter concerning the Mysteries. From this fact we can infer that the sanctuary and its festival were firmly under Athenian control by the time the Solonian law code was passed, in the late 590s. This in turn suggests that the festival probably belonged to Athens long enough, at least several years, for legal deficiencies in the administration of the festival to make themselves sufficiently felt to require Solon's intervention.[6] And there is more. The Aristotelian *Athenaion Politeia* (57.1) informs us that the *basileus*, the *archon* who inherited the religious functions of the old king of Athens, was in charge of the administration of the Mysteries.[7] It goes on to tell us (57.2) that the *basileus* administered 'all ancestral (πατρίους) sacrifices,' whereas earlier it stated (3.3) that the eponymous *archon*, on the other hand, administered 'none of the ancestral matters (πατρίων) like the *basileus* and *polemarch* but merely those matters added later (τὰ ἐπίθετα)'. In fact, when the eponymous *archon*'s religious functions are later described in some detail (56.3–5), we are told that he was in charge of the contests at the Greater Dionysia, contests which we know were instituted no earlier than the second half of the sixth century, and also of the procession at the Mysteries to Asclepius, first held in 420 BC (or the following year).[8] In principle, then, Athenian control of the Mysteries ought to have preceded the year of the first known annual eponymous *archon*, viz. 683/2 BC. This may press the notion of 'ancestral' too much, but it is not at all impossible. At any rate it is clear, all things considered, that Athenian control of the Mysteries in the person of the *basileus* ought to go back long before the law code of Solon (late 590s) and the *Homeric Hymn to Demeter* (c. end of the seventh century).

Therefore we must conclude that the *Homeric Hymn to Demeter* ignores Athens not because Eleusis was independent but evidently because the author of the *Hymn* felt no compelling reason to mention Athens; for some reason he simply had no interest in its relation to Eleusis.[9] This conclusion is of great importance, because it compels us, in assessing the *Hymn* as evidence for the Mysteries, not to pursue political interpretations but to concentrate our attention on religious issues.

In the *Hymn* the position of Eleusis itself is curious. Demeter's stop there on her wanderings is completely unmotivated (96). In general, the Eleusinian setting seems to be rather loosely superimposed onto the more basic story, widespread throughout Greece, of the rape of Kore and her return.[10] But what has captured the imagination of modern readers is a set of events in the

Hymn that seems to reflect events in the cult of the Mysteries: Demeter's fasting (200); Iambe's efforts to amuse Demeter (202–5);[11] Demeter's drinking the Kykeon (206–11);[12] Demeter's nursing Demophon and immersing him in fire (219–55). That these are reflections of cultic events seems to be confirmed at the end of the story, when Demeter establishes the festival of the Mysteries (473–82). Therefore it seems to follow that the *Homeric Hymn to Demeter* is primarily concerned with the cult of the Mysteries.

However, in many respects, the *Hymn* relates poorly to the Mysteries: in the names used for Kore (usually Persephone in the *Hymn* but Kore or Thea in our documentation for the Mysteries) and for Pluto (Hades or Aidoneus in the *Hymn* instead of the correct Pluto or Theos); in the place of her abduction (Nysa instead of Eleusis); in the conspicuous role accorded to Hekate (non-existent in the Mysteries); in the treatment of Eumolpus, the ancestor of the priestly clan which controlled the major priesthood of Mysteries; and in the absence of any reference to the important role which Triptolemus played upon the consummation of the Mysteries (disseminating the grain).[13] To this may be added the absence of any mention of Eubuleus, a principal god in the Mysteries and co-equal with Triptolemus,[14] or of the Mirthless Rock (Ἀγέλαστος Πέτρα), where, according to the myth of the Mysteries, Demeter sat when she arrived in Eleusis.[15] Yet the events in the story that I listed earlier do have the flavour of cultic events. If the cult in question is not the Mysteries, then which cult is it? And if it is not the Mysteries, why does the author of the *Hymn* bother to introduce the Mysteries at the end of the poem?

A clue is given by a certain type of sacrificial ritual practised at Eleusis. In the course of a study of Eleusinian sacrificial ritual, my attention was drawn to several pit-like structures attached to the foundations of the porch of the Telesterion (Figure 6.2 a–e).[16] They are built of the same poros stone as the foundations; they extend to bedrock, but their function is not structural. In fact, they are not mentioned in the building inscription that gives the architectural specifications for these foundations. In the central pit the excavator found a remarkably black soil reminiscent of compost, and in two of the pits he discovered animal bones. The pits must be the so-called *megara*, into which piglets were thrown, both at the Mysteries and at the women's festival of the Thesmophoria. At the Thesmophoria women called 'bailers' went down into the pits, fetched up the rotted remains of the piglets and piled this material on the altars of the sanctuary. People came and took small portions to mix with their grainseed before sowing, in order to render it more fertile; and fertility was imparted also to the women who took part in the festival.[17] It had long been suspected that the Thesmophoria were held at Eleusis, as in other demes of Attica, and now the pits provided archaeological confirmation of the sparse but clear testimony of other sources.[18] There can be no doubt that the sanctuary was the scene of the Thesmophoria in addition to the Mysteries (and other festivals).[19]

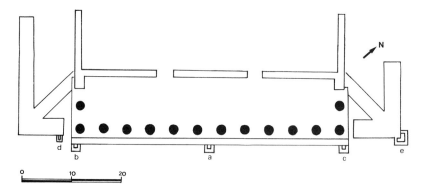

Figure 6.2 The *megara* in the sanctuary at Eleusis.

Of Greek festivals the Thesmophoria were the most widespread and among the oldest.[20] The Mysteries, too, it is sometimes thought, went back to the prehistoric period[21] – a view based in large part on the existence of Mycenaean remains beneath the Telesterion. However, in an important recent study of these remains P. Darcque concluded that they offer no evidence for a Mycenaean proto-Telesterion and are of no relevance to our understanding of the later Telesterion.[22] Even so, we cannot completely dismiss the possibility that 'Megaron B'[23] with its unusual stairway and front platform served some religious purpose, despite the lack of positive evidence of cult.[24] At any rate, the fact remains that we have no evidence that the Mysteries went back to the Mycenaean period. Indeed, their uniqueness and several other considerations tend to suggest that they are a more recent phenomenon than the very old and widespread Thesmophoria.[25]

The women in the Thesmophoria probably saw themselves, to some extent, as imitating the myth of the Rape of Kore. On the first day of the festival they watched the piglets fall into a chasm, and so too did Kore descend. On the second day, the *Nesteia* (the day of 'Fasting'), they in sadness and fasting behaved like Demeter, sitting on the ground, submitting to be targets of ritual mockery (*aischrologia*). On the third day, *Kalligeneia* (the day of 'Fair Birth'), they effect the return of the piglets from the earth,[26] piglets now transformed into earth, ensuring fertility of womb and land; and this, like the return of Kore to her mother, is a joyous event, a triumph of maternity. With this last day, which looks toward childbirth and nursing, we should probably associate the goddess Kourotrophos (nurse of children), one of the gods of the Thesmophoria to whom the heraldess in Aristophanes' *Thesmophoriazusae* (260) urges the women to pray.

The *Homeric Hymn to Demeter*, as mentioned earlier, relates poorly to some events of the Mysteries, but we can see that it fits the known features of the Thesmophoria quite well. First, *Nesteia*: fasting and sadness (of

Demeter in her search for Kore); sitting on the ground next to a well; *aischrologia* (Iambe episode). Second, *Kalligeneia*, featuring Kourotrophos (Demophon episode: Demeter's awesome powers of nursing are highlighted and stymied by distrust).[27] One ancient author, in recounting the Rape of Kore, specifically links the Iambe episode not to the Mysteries but to the Thesmophoria: 'Because of this they say that the women in the Thesmophoria make jokes.'[28] In addition, Hyginus, after recounting a version of the myth in which again the episode of Demeter's nursing a boy is the central element, concludes the story with the founding of a cult: the Thesmophoria.[29] So the ancient festival reflected in the main story of the *Hymn*, which also puts nursing at its centre, is surely the Thesmophoria.

It now becomes possible to propose answers to the questions raised earlier. First, why are the Mysteries mentioned in the *Hymn* at all?

We should keep in mind that the Mysteries are not necessary to the story: it could just as well end without mentioning them, that is, it could end with the Return of Kore and the rebirth of the grain. This more recent festival (the very newness of the Mysteries receives emphasis in the *Hymn*) is Demeter's generous gift to the Eleusinians for the return of her daughter. This homage to the Mysteries, piously appended by the poet to a traditional story that reflects the ancient Thesmophoria, allows him also to honour the newer cult without making significant alterations to the traditional story or taking the risk of betraying secrets.[30]

The Mysteries are similar to the Thesmophoria in that they too are directed toward agrarian prosperity (Ploutos), but they aim to fulfil for the initiate a hope which is largely irrelevant to the Thesmophoria: a better lot in the underworld. In the course of the Mysteries worshippers viewed a myth enacted in dramatic form – a phenomenon foreign to the vast majority of Greek cults, including the Thesmophoria. The outline of this myth has been the subject of much modern debate, for ancient authors, not unexpectedly, have little to say about it. Some early Christian writers were eager to disclose it, but their testimony must be used with great caution. Fortunately Athenian vase painters and sculptors did not feel subject to the same constraints as writers, and from their abundant images of Eleusinian scenes we get glimpses of the myth – in none so clearly as in a polychrome relief hydria in St Petersburg, the so-called Regina Vasorum.[31] The scene (Figure 6.3) consists of an array of figures, arranged symmetrically around a central pair that represent the happy end of the myth: Demeter (no. 5) greeting Kore (no. 6) upon her return. A goddess on the far left (no. 1) and another on the far right (no. 10) represent the beginning of the myth: on the left Demeter sits on the Mirthless Rock, despondent after her wanderings; on the right, the goddess is Thea (as Kore was called in the underworld), sitting in sorrow on her seat in Hades. To the right of Demeter on the Mirthless Rock and facing her stands Iacchus (no. 2), the god who leads the initiates to Eleusis; on the other side, to the left of Thea and facing her is Eubuleus (no. 9), the Eleusinian god who leads her from Hades to Eleusis, back to her mother's embrace. To the right of Iacchus and to the left of Eubuleus respectively sit Triptolemus (no. 3) and Athena (no. 8), who together symbolize the magnanimous invitation of Athens to all Hellenes to participate in this Athenian festival; and between them and the central Demeter and Kore are the most famous divine initiates, Dionysus (no. 4) and Heracles (no. 7, holding a piglet). This finely crafted scene shows us that in the Mysteries the drama begins not with the rape of Kore (for it had already taken place) but with the separation of mother and daughter. In the beginning Demeter sits on the Mirthless Rock, as the initiates (here indicated in the person of their special god, Iacchus) approach her.

A major expectation of the initiates was a happy lot in the afterlife, as, for example, the *Homeric Hymn to Demeter* (480–2) proclaims: 'Happy is he who has seen these things, but he who is not initiate in the rites, who does not share in them, he does not have a lot of like things when he is dead in the dank gloom.' In the Mysteries the initiate experiences the feelings of the Two Goddesses in their progression from grief to joy. In contrast to most Greek cults, this is truly extraordinary. Two gods are in pain, and are displayed to the worshippers in this state. The initiates share their pain and, in the end, their relief and joy.

It will be most convenient to outline the events of the cult day by day:[32]

Boedromion 14 the day before the festival. The ephebes escort the *hiera* (the sacred objects) from Eleusis to the City Eleusinion.

Boedromion 15 Agyrmos: the first day of the Mysteries. The hierophant had the sacred herald make the announcement, *prorrhesis*.[33] Later the command ἱερεῖα δεῦρο ('Hither the victims') was given, and a sacrifice was performed.[34]

Boedromion 16 Halade Mystai ('To the sea, initiates!'). The initiates bathed in the sea off Phaleron with their piglets.[35]

Boedromion 17 Epidauria.[36] The day commemorates Asclepius' late arrival at the Mysteries (his cult was, in fact, introduced in Athens on this day in 420 BC),[37] and the day was reserved for late arrivals. Following a procession there was a second major sacrifice and all-night celebration (*pannychis*) in honour of Asclepius.

Boedromion 18[38] apparently a day of rest.

Boedromion 19 procession (πομπή) to Eleusis.[39] In the πομπή the ephebes, priests and magistrates escorted the *hiera* to Eleusis.

Boedromion 20 escort of Iacchus.[40] The great crowd of initiates set out, led by their special god, Iacchus, whose statue was carried by the Iakchagogos.[41] The walk from Athens to Eleusis covered approximately fourteen miles. It was a considerable effort, and many of the initiates must have likened the journey to the toils of Demeter, wandering in search of her daughter. At some distance from Eleusis they were joined by the ephebes who came out from the sanctuary to provide an escort for the rest of the

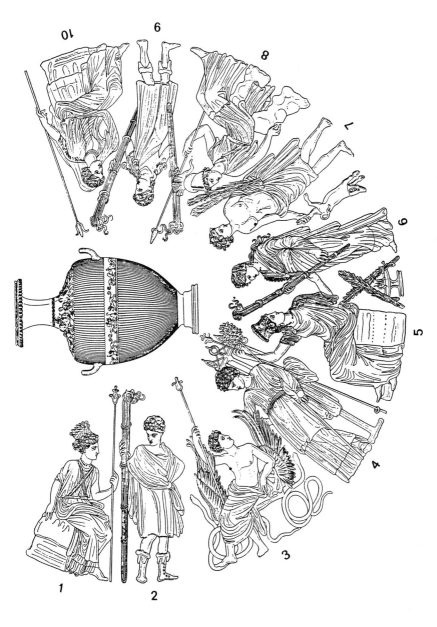

Figure 6.3 Regina Vasorum. St Petersburg, Hermitage.

way. On the outskirts of the deme, as they crossed the river Cephisus, the marchers were subjected to ridicule by a group of people standing by the bridge (the so-called *gephyrismos*). When, near dusk, they arrived at the sanctuary, the magnificent Reception of Iacchus took place. The initiates danced by the Callichoron Well (the Well of the Beautiful Dances) in honour of Demeter and her daughter,[42] while the goddess sat nearby on the Mirthless Rock ('Αγέλαστος Πέτρα). The Callichoron Well was the closest they could approach her without entering the sanctuary.

The Mirthless Rock was just inside the sanctuary, within the cave that looms to the right of the entrance. In it there is a natural seat which is most likely the very spot where the goddess was believed to have sat. (The area has traditionally been called a Ploutonion, but the testimony taken in support of this idea has been misunderstood.)[43]

Boedromion 21 the τέλη.[44] The day is spent in rest. The secret rites take place in the evening. In reconstructing them there are few sure guideposts, and the following attempt relies on a good amount of speculation.[45]

When it is completely dark, the initiates file into the sanctuary, the wall on their right blocking from view the area of the Mirthless Rock. When they reach the doorway in this wall, perhaps they are able to look in as they pass and see at the back of the cave, by flickering torchlight, a deeply unsettling sight: the goddess sitting on the rock in sorrow. In any case they hear lamentations coming from this cave precinct. They pass by, and walk on up to the Telesterion. There they evidently deposit their piglets in the *megara*.[46] Then they wander about outside the Telesterion (or Anaktoron, as it was usually called)[47] in search of Kore, confused and disoriented as they stumble in the dark, their eyes apparently blinded by a hood, each initiate guided by a mystagogue. All the while the hierophant keeps sounding a gong, summoning Kore.

Kore's return naturally cannot be seen by the initiates. In the cave below she emerges, guided by Eubuleus, through an opening just opposite where Demeter is sitting.[48] After embracing Demeter, Kore leaves the cave together with her mother, and they take the path up to the Telesterion, in the company of Eubuleus. When the gods reach the Telesterion, they pause, and the Epoptai (second-year initiates) catch a glimpse of mother and daughter reunited. The Two Goddesses and Eubuleus then enter the Anaktoron.

Moments pass. Suddenly the Anaktoron opens, and the hierophant stands in the doorway, silhouetted against a brilliant light streaming from the interior. The initiates enter, passing from darkness into an immense space blazing with extraordinary light, coming from thousands of torches held by the Epoptai.

Within the Telesterion the goddesses were probably again visible to the initiates, but now displayed on a structure which served as a platform (the structure which has usually been called the Anaktoron).[49] Divine initiates, such as Heracles and Dionysus, we may imagine, appeared as well, and of course Triptolemus. The basic scene is presented often enough in painting.

After the current year's initiates left the Anaktoron, a special vision was revealed to the Epoptai. A Christian writer speaks of a display of grain and the birth of a child. It seems rather doubtful that a birth was literally depicted in the rite.[50] The child cannot be Iacchus. In art Iacchus is always depicted as a man (often beardless, carrying one or two torches), and in any case it is he who led the initiates to the Mirthless Rock (and perhaps to the Anaktoron as well). The child must be Ploutos. In art he appears as an older boy (in modern terms, from eight to 12 years old), usually naked, holding a cornucopia and wearing a wreath of grain. As he makes his epiphany, presumably from within the structure at the centre of the Anaktoron, it is probably at this moment that the hierophant displays the ear of grain mentioned by a Christian author.[51]

Boedromion 22 a day of sacrifice and festivity. Bulls were officially sacrificed to Demeter and Kore, and many other animals, especially pigs, were sacrificed by individual participants,[52] on the altars of Demeter and Kore, located in the forecourt of the sanctuary.[53] Thus at the Mysteries the main sacrifices of the traditional sort took place outside the sanctuary – a rather unusual location for sacrifice but one which makes sense for this cult. It allowed everyone, both those who did and those who did not attend the secret part, to participate in this joyous culmination of the rite.[54]

Boedromion 23 the initiates return to Athens. The final day of the festival was called Plemochoai, when two vessels called by this name were poured out, one facing east, the other west, evidently into the *megara* attached to the Telesterion.[55] The initiates presumably returned to Athens on the 23rd, for on the 24th the Boule met in the City Eleusinion, its traditional session on the day after the Mysteries.[56] The final day, the Plemochoai, ought therefore to be the 23rd.

At the heart of the Mysteries lies a drama, and we can at least surmise its general shape: an overall progression from sadness to joy, from the sorrow of the separated mother and daughter to their joyful reunion. At its conclusion perhaps the most important object shown was an ear of grain.[57] The secrets, thus told, inevitably appear, like all such secrets, relatively trivial. But knowing them still leaves us a world apart from the experience. It was the experience, not knowledge, which was at the heart of the rite, as Aristotle (fr. 15) emphasized.[58] Of this experience Cicero (*De legibus* 2.36) left us an eloquent and stately impression. But we have a poetic expression that comes a bit closer to the mood at its conclusion in an epigram by Crinagoras of Mytilene (*A.P.* 11.42):[59]

Even if your life is sedentary and you never sailed the sea or walked the highways of the land, go nevertheless to Attica to see those nights of the great Mysteries of Demeter: your heart shall become free of care while you live and lighter when you go to the realm of the majority.

The Mysteries represent a transformation of the much older Thesmophoria and similar cults open only to women. Several elements and themes of the older cult remain in the new creation – sorrow, fasting, a sacred well, ritual mockery, deposition of piglets in *megara*, agrarian prosperity – but now these are given different emphases, arranged in a rite that has a divine drama at its centre, and which looks toward death and the afterlife. The initiates suffer as the Goddesses suffer and finally share in the Goddesses' extraordinary joy. And so they enter into a special relationship with each of them and naturally with Kore's other self, the Thea in the underworld, who will look after them in the life to come.[60] The cult is no longer limited to women; it becomes increasingly more accessible, eventually open to all adult Greek speakers. And it becomes increasingly more popular: the sanctuary and Anaktoron, as the remains reveal, were expanded from time to time, to meet the rising demand.[61] As centuries pass, the Mysteries inspire and influence many other cults of similar type and, in the end, leave their mark on Christianity.

NOTES

The most complete treatment of the cult with full documentation can be found in Foucart, *Mystères* and Burkert, *Homo Necans*, 248–93; for the archaeology of the sanctuary, see Mylonas, *Eleusis*.

Abbreviations

Burkert, *Homo Necans*: W. Burkert, *Homo Necans* (Berkeley 1983).

Burkert, *Mystery Cults*: *idem*, *Ancient Mystery Cults* (Cambridge, Mass. 1987).

Clinton, 'Author': K. Clinton, 'The author of the Homeric *Hymn to Demeter*', *OpAth* 16 (1986) 43–9.

Clinton, *Iconography*: *idem*, *Myth and Cult: The Iconography of the Eleusinian Mysteries*, Skrifter utgivna av Svenska Institutet i Athen, 8°, 11 (Stockholm 1992).

Clinton, *Sacred Officials*: *idem*, *The Sacred Officials of the Eleusinian Mysteries*, *TransAmPhilSoc* 64.3 (Philadelphia 1974).

Clinton, 'Sacrifice': *idem*, 'Sacrifice in the Eleusinian mysteries', in R. Hägg, N. Marinatos and G. C. Nordquist, eds, *Early Greek Cult Practice, Proceedings of the Fifth International Symposium at the Swedish Institute at Athens, 26–29 June, 1986*, Skrifter utgivna av Svenska Institutet i Athen, 4°, 38 (Stockholm 1988) 69–80.

Deubner, *Feste*: L. Deubner, *Attische Feste* (Berlin 1932).

Deubner, 'Weihehaus': *idem*, 'Zum Weihehaus der eleusinischen Mysterien', *AbhBerl*, Phil.-hist. Klasse, 1945/6, no. 2.

Foucart, *Mystères*: P. Foucart, *Mystères d'Eleusis* (Paris 1914).

Graf, *Eleusis*: F. Graf, *Eleusis und die orphische Dichtung Athens in vorhellenistischer Zeit*, *RGVV* 33 (Berlin and New York 1974).

Mylonas, *Eleusis*: G. E. Mylonas, *Eleusis and the Eleusinian Mysteries* (Princeton 1961).

Richardson, *Hymn*: N. J. Richardson, *The Homeric Hymn to Demeter* (Oxford 1974).

Travlos, 'Anaktoron': J. Travlos, τὸ ᾿Ανάκτορον τῆς ᾿Ελευσῖνος, *ArchEph* 1950–1, 1–16.

In general, for iconographical matters not fully explained here, discussion of the *Homeric Hymn to Demeter*, the Thesmophoria and the secret part of the Mysteries, the reader should consult my book, *Iconography*.

1 Translation: W. H. S. Jones and H. A. Ormerod, Loeb edition (1918).

2 Such an 'Athens' often appears on maps. But this part of Athens, the central area, was simply the part known as the Asty (τὸ ἄστυ; cf. *AthPol* 21.4 and P. J. Rhodes, *A Commentary on the Aristotelian* Athenaion Politeia (Oxford 1981) on 21.4.

3 See the excellent edition and commentary by N. J. Richardson, *The Homeric Hymn to Demeter* (Oxford 1974). A penetrating and stimulating literary analysis: J. S. Clay, *The Politics of Olympus: Form and Meaning in the Major Homeric Hymns* (Princeton 1990).

4 Cf. Clinton, 'Author', 47.

5 J. B. Bury and R. Meiggs, *A History of Greece to the Death of Alexander the Great* (London 1975) 525; cf. now S. Hornblower, *A Commentary on Thucydides* (Oxford 1991) vol. 1 262–5.

6 It is sometimes supposed (cf. e.g. D. MacDowell, *Andokides, On the Mysteries* (Oxford 1962), *ad loc.*) that Andocides' attribution of the law to Solon is incorrect. It is claimed that the law stipulates that the Boule meet in the Eleusinion in the City on the day after the Mysteries, but the existence of both Boule and Eleusinion in the time of Solon is unlikely. However, even if they did not exist, there is no reason to question the existence of a Solonian law about a meeting of this sort, i.e., a meeting of a civic body on the day after the Mysteries to review the conduct of the festival. The officiating body and the location could have been changed in a later law, which still would be called a 'law of Solon'; on this way of referring to Solonian law see my article, 'The nature of the late fifth-century revision of the Athenian law code', in *Studies in Attic Epigraphy, History and Topography Presented to Eugene Vanderpool, Hesperia* Suppl. 19 (Princeton 1982) 27–37, esp. 29–30. But there is in fact evidence that the Boule existed in Solon's time: *AthPol* 4.3 (with P. J. Rhodes, *A Commentary on the Aristotelian* Athenaion Politeia (Oxford 1981) on 4.3). And it is not impossible that the Eleusinion also existed. M. Miles, 'The temple of Triptolemos in the city Eleusinion', *AJA* 86 (1982) 276 (paper read at Archaeological Institute of America annual meeting) reports 'walls and entrances dating from the mid-sixth century BC', which leaves open the possibility that they replaced earlier structures, or they represent an expansion of the sanctuary, which is largely unexcavated. It stands to reason that if Athenian control of the Mysteries preceded the time of Solon, then the Eleusinion or something like it must have existed, in order to house the sacred objects when they were brought to Athens in preparation for the procession to Eleusis.

7 *AthPol* 57.1; K. Clinton, 'A law in the City Eleusinion concerning the Mysteries', *Hesperia* 49 (1980) 258–88, esp. 263–4, ll. 29–37 and commentary.

8 Contests at the Dionysia: A. Pickard-Cambridge, J. Gould and D. M. Lewis, *The Dramatic Festivals of Athens* (Oxford 1990) 101–2; cf. W. R. Connor, 'City

Dionysia and Athenian democracy', *ClMed* 40 (1989) 7–32, who would date the establishment of the City Dionysia late in the sixth century. Procession to Asclepius at the Mysteries: *IG* II² 4960, with forthcoming article by K. Clinton 'The Epidauria and the arrival of Asclepius in Athens', in R. Hägg, ed., *Ancient Greek Cult Practice from the Epigraphical Evidence* (Stockholm 1993). It should be noted that the *AthPol* does not expressly state that the eponymous *archon* oversaw the entire Dionysia, though one might draw this conclusion from the loosely worded sentence summing up this section ('He is in charge of these festivals.'). The preceding description states that he oversees (1) the procession to Asclepius at the Mysteries, (2) the procession at the Greater Dionysia, (3) the procession for the Thargelia and (4) the procession to Zeus Soter; and he administers the contest of the Dionysia and that of the Thargelia. Certainly some parts of the Thargelia must have been ancestral, as perhaps were also some sacrifices at the Dionysia (to which the contests were added in the late sixth century).

9 On the author's lack of interest: Clinton 'Author'. 'The Epidauria and the arrival of Asclepius in Athens' (1993).

10 Clinton, 'Author'. This conclusion is now opposed by R. Parker, 'The *Hymn to Demeter* and the *Homeric Hymns*', *Greece and Rome* 38 (1991) 1–17; his arguments are discussed in my book, *Iconography*, ch. I.

11 Specifically stated to be a cultic act.

12 Here too, line 211, there is reference to a rite; cf. Richardson, *Hymn*, on l.211.

13 For a full discussion: Clinton, 'Author'. This article now needs to be revised, as the conclusions of *Iconography* show. In the article the term 'Eleusis' usually refers, as is customary in modern discussions of Eleusinian religion, to the Eleusinian Mysteries, but results of the investigation in *Iconography* show this to be too restrictive, as will also be clear in the discussion below. 'Local legend', undefined in my article but usually taken to indicate the myth that was enacted in the cult or a version close to it, is, I see now, too vague to be useful.

14 Clinton, 'Sacrifice'; *Iconography*, chs II–III.

15 *Iconography*, ch. I.

16 See full description in Clinton, 'Sacrifice'.

17 See discussion in 'Sacrifice'. There I stressed the connection between depositing the pigs in the pits at the Mysteries and fetching them up at the Thesmophoria; but we must not overlook the deposition at the Eleusinian Thesmophoria, for it was the primary one: cf. *Iconography*, ch. II, n. 203.

18 See discussion in 'Sacrifice' and Aeneas Tacticus, *Poliorcetica* 4.8.

19 Haloa: Deubner, *Feste*, 60–7. Probably also the Kalamaia, ibid., 67–8.

20 M. P. Nilsson, *Griechische Feste von religiöser Bedeutung mit Ausschluss der Attischen* (Leipzig 1906) 313–16; cf. Clinton, *Iconography*, 29.

21 Mylonas, *Eleusis* 23–54; J. Travlos, *Bildlexikon zur Topographie des antiken Attika* (Tübingen 1988).

22 'Les vestiges mycéniens découverts sous le Télestérion d'Eleusis', *BCH* 105 (1981) 593–605.

23 Mylonas, *Eleusis*, fig. 11.

24 Mylonas, *Eleusis* 47.

25 *Iconography*, ch. I.

26 The day on which they were retrieved is uncertain; Deubner, *Feste* 59, would put this event on the second day.

27 See full discussion in Clinton, *Iconography*, ch. I.

28 Pseudo-Apollodorus, *Bibliotheca* 1.5.1.

29 Hyginus, *Fab.* 147.
30 The suspicion arises that the addition of the Mysteries may have been inspired by the Eumolpidae, since virtually all the kings in the poem are Eumolpid ancestors or the objects of Eumolpid cult (Clinton, 'Author' 48). In view of the fact that the main story is in all probability an *aition* of the Thesmophoria and not the Mysteries, I no longer preclude the possibility that the author is from Attica.
31 Full discussion in Clinton, *Iconography*, ch. III.
32 For the scheme see in general S. Dow, 'Athenian decrees of 216–212 BC', *HSCP* 48 (1937) 113; J. Mikalson, *The Sacred and Civil Calendar of the Athenian Year* (Princeton 1975) 54–60.
33 Cf. Clinton, *Sacred Officials* 81.
34 For the view that both *prorrhesis* and *hiereia deuro* took place on this day, see K. Clinton, 'The Epidauria and the arrival of Asclepius in Athens' (1993).
35 Foucart, *Mystères* 314–17.
36 For the assignment of the Epidauria to this day, Clinton, op. cit. (*supra* n. 34).
37 Full discussion, ibid.
38 For the assignment, ibid.
39 Clinton, 'Sacrifice' 69–70.
40 ibid.
41 The Iakchagogos: Clinton, *Sacred Officials* 96–7. The escort of Iacchus: Clinton, *Iconography*, ch. III; Graf, *Eleusis* 51–8.
42 Cf. *Iconography* 27–8.
43 On the Ἀγέλαστος Πέτρα and the Ploutonion see *Iconography*, ch. I.
44 No name is attested for this day; τέλη is one term used of the secret rites: Sophocles, fr. 837.
45 For the evidence for this description see *Iconography*, ch. III; for a different view of some of the same evidence, Graf, *Eleusis* 126–39.
46 Clinton, 'Sacrifice' 72–9.
47 The building we call the Telesterion was commonly called Anaktoron in antiquity: Deubner, 'Weihehaus'; Clinton, *Iconography*, app. 7, 'The name of the Telesterion'. The structure near the centre of the building has been called 'Anaktoron' ever since Travlos's excavation of it (see Travlos, 'Anaktoron'), but this designation is incorrect; its actual name is unknown, and its function needs to be re-assessed.
48 *Iconography*, ch. III, 87–9.
49 See *supra* n. 47.
50 The evidence for a birth is practically non–existent; see *Iconography*, ch. III.
51 For the Epopteia, *Iconography*, ch. III.
52 Clinton, 'Sacrifice' 71 and n. 24.
53 'Sacrifice' 71–2.
54 Clinton, 'Sacrifice' 72.
55 'Sacrifice' 78; *Iconography*, ch. III.
56 On the Solonian law, above, p. 112; on the day, Mikalson (*supra* n. 32) 60–1; Clinton, 'Sacrifice' 71, n. 28.
57 Perhaps the other objects were simple agrarian instruments, such as the mortar and pestle; cf. Burkert, *Homo Necans* 272–3.
58 On the experience in general see Burkert, *Mystery Cults*, ch. IV, 'The extraordinary experience' 89–114.
59 A. S. F. Gow and D. L. Page, *The Greek Anthology: The Garland of Philip and Some Contemporary Epigrams* (Cambridge 1968) 218–19, Crinagoras 35.

60 Cf. the initiates in Aristophanes' *Frogs* 399–401, 444–59: they head towards the Thea (i.e., Persephone) to be under her protection: 'in the holy circle of the Thea' (445).
61 See Mylonas, *Eleusis* 55–137.

7

The Heraion at Samos

Helmut Kyrieleis

The Heraion at Samos, one of the great centres of ancient Greek religion, received only a short, incidental mention from Pausanias. Our understanding of this great sanctuary would be enormously facilitated if only Pausanias had given an account of the island in his famous description of Greece, just as he had done for the sites of mainland Greece and the Peloponnesus. The lack of a text by Pausanias on the Heraion at Samos makes us so keenly aware that the detailed descriptions of buildings, history and cult, collected by the periegete at other sites, constitute fundamental invaluable help for modern investigations of sites such as Delphi, Olympia and the Acropolis of Athens. Only a very little information about the Heraion at Samos has come down to us in the literary sources. The most important is from Herodotus who mentions the Hera sanctuary at Samos several times and provides us with some important pieces of information. Otherwise there are only a few scattered mentions which partly contradict each other, and whose reliability as sources is hard to evaluate because they are mostly so late, many centuries after the *floruit* of the Hera cult on Samos. With the exception of the great temple of Hera and the altar of Hera, no ancient structure in the Heraion is named in the ancient sources. Since the ancient sources mainly pass over the Samian sanctuary in silence, we must rely almost exclusively on the results of archaeological excavations if we wish to form an idea of the significance, the character, the history or the individual features of the cult in this sanctuary.[1]

Perhaps this important ancient Greek religious centre would remain undiscovered even today, if Herodotus had not described the temple of Hera as the largest Greek temple of his time and if a half of a temple column were not still standing upright, fortuitously preserved in the course of a long history of destruction. For the site of the sanctuary, 6km away from the ancient town in a marshy river basin near the sea, is everything but a landmark in the Samian landscape. Since the ancient buildings in the sanctuary had been used as a stone quarry from the Middle Ages onward and had been dismantled right down to the foundations, the ruins of the sanctuary had disappeared below ground long before the present day excavations; the lonely column shaft of the temple was the sole witness of former greatness.

(Probably it had purposely been left standing so that the cargo ships transporting the ancient stone material across the sea could more readily find the anchorage along the flat coastal plain.) Thus, ever since ancient times there has never been any doubt as to where the site of the Heraion was.

The first modern explorer of the Heraion was Joseph Piton de Tournefort, the French doctor and natural scientist who was commissioned by Louis XIV to travel in Greece and the East; he visited Samos in 1704 and obviously had not the slightest difficulty in identifying the place. The first published drawing of the ruins was made by de Tournefort. During the eighteenth and nineteenth centuries various learned travellers visited the Heraion and investigated the slight remains of the temple still visible above ground. Short stretches of the foundations were also cleared but to no great depth. These early attempts at investigating the site failed because of obstacles, some of which still have not been entirely overcome. For one thing there were massive deep deposits of silt from a series of floods. But the main obstacle was the dense vegetation that repeatedly blanketed the cleared remains of structures and excavated areas with reeds and thickets of blackberry bushes.

The first real archaeological excavations in the Heraion were carried out in 1890–2 by P. Kavvadias and Th. Sophoulis under the auspices of the Greek Archaeological Society in Athens. These excavations contributed some important information about the great temple, but its full dimensions had not yet been determined. The temple itself and substantial portions of the whole sanctuary were not cleared until the large-scale excavations of 1910–14 directed by Theodor Wiegand under the auspices of the Königliche Museen zu Berlin. The temple (Figure 7.1) proved to be a Late Archaic building of colossal dimensions, 55.2 × 108.6m, originally having 155 columns outside and inside. Earlier architectural material reused in the foundations indicated that there must have been a predecessor temple of approximately the same dimensions. Furthermore, the following structures were recognized: the northern boundary of the precinct, buildings of the Roman imperial period in the temple forecourt, a group of smaller temple-like buildings north of the forecourt and the paved 'Sacred Way' leading into the sanctuary from the north-east, that is from the direction of the ancient town.

In 1925, after a long interval, the German Archaeological Institute in Athens began excavations directed by Ernst Buschor and these continued until the outbreak of the Second World War. In 1951 this work was resumed, at first under the direction of Buschor until 1961, then under Ernst Homann-Wedeking until 1975. These excavations provided important information, especially for the early period of the sanctuary. In particular the general lines of the development of the main temple and its altar were clarified over a historical time span of one thousand years (see plan, Figure 7.2): the first temple of Hera was constructed as early as the eighth century BC, a long narrow structure typical of that time, 100 ft long (c. 33m). This 'Hekatompedos' was replaced by the gigantic dipteral temple built before the

Figure 7.1 Heraion at Samos. Later Archaic temple of Hera. In the foreground the
base of the cult image in the Late Geometric Temple.

middle of the sixth century BC. The so-called 'Rhoikos temple' must have
been destroyed shortly after completion. Its successor was a somewhat
larger temple, shifted about 40m further west, started in the Late Archaic
period. The column still standing in place up to mid-height belongs to this
temple which was under construction for hundreds of years into the Roman
period and never finished. The tremendous unfinished ruin was apparently
judged unsuitable for housing the cult statue in the long run and a new
temple of Hera was erected in the Roman imperial period further to the east,
quite near the altar. This new temple was much smaller, of an odd design,
and used column types clearly linked to the Archaic temple of Hera; this
temple must have stood until the Hera cult came to an end in the fourth
century AD. In the fifth century a Christian church was built beside this
temple, largely of material taken from it. The way in which a Christian cult
immediately started up at the site of a pagan cult is a phenomenon which
may be frequently observed in Greek sanctuaries. The excavations also

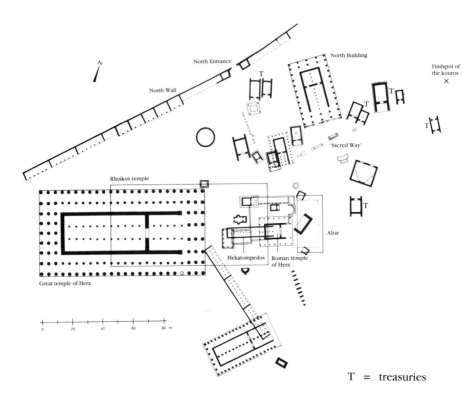

Figure 7.2 Heraion at Samos. General plan of the sanctuary including buildings and monuments ranging in date from the eighth century BC until Early Christian times (sixth century AD).

produced evidence for the historical development of the altar of Hera, the true centre of the cult in the sanctuary. The inconspicuous beginnings of the altar may perhaps date back to late Mycenaean times. A series of construction and extension phases culminated, together with the Rhoikos temple, in a huge monumental altar, about 40m long, that stood for centuries until it was so worn down by weathering that it had to be renewed once more in the Roman imperial period. A further important discovery made during the excavations directed by Buschor and Homann-Wedeking was that an extensive Early Bronze Age settlement lies below the northern area of the ancient Heraion.

Seven decades of excavations conducted in the Heraion provided evidence for both the beginning and the end of the Hera cult and also for its history over a period of one and a half millennia. This picture is certainly still very incomplete and thrown off balance by the random nature of the finds. But in the last analysis that is typical of all sources for historical enquiry. In any case it is now securely established that the *floruit* of the Heraion was in the Archaic period, the seventh and sixth centuries BC. The evidence for this is provided by the architecture which did not assume truly monumental dimensions until the sixth century BC, but chiefly by the Archaic votives which in both quantity and quality far surpass those of the earlier and later periods. But in the Classical period, when Samos was at times completely under Athenian domination, not a single new building went up and important votives are almost entirely lacking during this time. In the Hellenistic period the sanctuary appears to have had a brief revival, as indicated by many inscriptions and many important honorary statues set up in the sanctuary. It is characteristic for the role of ancient sanctuaries in Hellenistic times and also for the history of Samos at this time that the subject matter of the inscriptions is mainly political and the dedications of statues tend to be political statements rather than genuine votive offerings. Samos belonged to the province of Asia in the Roman Empire and as such played only a modest role. From time to time, however, the sanctuary seems to have enjoyed the patronage of some of the emperors, an assumption based on the inscriptions and minor temple buildings, and also the costly paving of the 'Sacred Way' carried out at the beginning of the third century AD.

Samos was not a pan-Hellenic sanctuary such as Olympia or Delphi. Although the buildings and the finds amply attest its great importance, it was always a local island sanctuary. The administration of the sanctuary and of the cult, the financing of the great temples and dedications of monumental votives were all carried out exclusively by inhabitants of the island. Thus the history of the city-state of Samos is reflected in the development of the Heraion as worked out from archaeological research. The rise and decline of the sanctuary coincide precisely with the historical development of Samos and much may be learned about the special character of Samos as a marine trading centre from a study of the votives found in its main sanctuary.

The rich harvest of knowledge reaped in earlier excavations is the result of patient work accomplished by several generations of scholars. An area as large as the Heraion, which has in places highly complicated building phases one on top of another and disturbed levels from various periods, cannot be thoroughly investigated from one day to the next, especially in view of the obstacles created by mother nature. Apart from external conditions and the amount of work necessary to do the job, it is also a question of evolving scientific procedures in such a long-term enterprise. At the beginning it is virtually impossible to formulate the goals of the exploration with any precision. The line of investigations swerves over and over again, following the track of whatever is (often quite unexpectedly) encountered. Most of the questions, and the excavations opened up to answer these questions, resulted

from analyses of earlier excavation work. In addition, the aims and methods
of archaeology have in the course of time become much more precise, thus
causing progress in actual excavation to become correspondingly slower and
more painstaking. In 1976 when we undertook to continue the excavations,
the work of clearing the Heraion was thought to be largely completed.
Nevertheless it seemed reasonable to plan at least a limited programme of
excavation in order to solve certain topographical problems merely touched
on by previous investigators, and also, where possible, to add a few more
props to the scaffolding of stratigraphically guaranteed chronology by
digging in various hitherto unexplored spots. Considering the very limited
aims of the campaign begun in 1976, it is all the more surprising to see what
varied and interesting results and finds came to light. A selection from the
bounty of the past 15 years is briefly presented here. In this connection we
would like to stress the fact that almost each new find and each newly
discovered structure in this sanctuary not only enriches our understanding
and answers hitherto open questions, but also raises new questions the
answers to which will come, if they come at all, only by further investigations in the future.

First a few new observations concerning topographical questions and
some of the buildings of the sanctuary: since it was far away from the ancient
town, the main connecting road, the 'Sacred Way' (Figure 7.3), was surely,
along with the altar and the temple, one of the most prominent topographical features of the sanctuary. This is evident because the majority of the
votive statues and the largest ones are set up along the 'Sacred Way' and
some of the smaller buildings are oriented towards this road. This broad
processional way, which in the third century AD was provided with costly
stone paving, was not, however, part of the sanctuary from the start. The
stratigraphical sequence recorded in the excavations of 1980/1 showed that
the street was not laid out until the late seventh century BC.[2] When the street
was laid out, a branch of the river Imbrasos, which had formerly blocked the
route between sanctuary and town, had to be rerouted and the marshy tract
had to be made passable by means of a dam of dumped fill. Before the
'Sacred Way' was laid out, the main entrance to the sanctuary seems to have
been from the south-east, from the coast. Other more recent observations,
to be discussed below, also point in this direction. The 'Sacred Way' was
evidently constructed at the time when the first large secular building in the
sanctuary was erected, the so-called South Stoa, 60m long. The rebuilding of
the hekatompedos and the first monumental architectural version of the altar
of Hera were probably carried out at the same time. Thus the new arrangement for the main approach to the sanctuary appears to be associated with
the first sizeable building programme that, in accordance with the growing
importance of the sanctuary, gave the Heraion a new, although still rather
modest, architectural form.

Another part of our investigations focused on a large building to the north

Figure 7.3 Heraion at Samos. The 'Sacred Way' leading towards the sanctuary.

of the 'Sacred Way'; its foundations had been cleared earlier on by Theodor Wiegand (Figure 7.4). The form, the function and the date of this so-called North Building were, until now, largely obscure. Finding the answers to these problems was difficult, since long stretches of the foundations had been robbed out and in many places had been cut through by deep foundations for later houses. Only a fairly small patch above the north-east corner of this building had remained unexcavated. Fortunately, the state of preservation at this spot was sufficiently good for crucial observations to be made. This excavation, taken in conjunction with a careful investigation of all the preserved material from the building, has made it possible to reconstruct the main lines of the history and original plan of the North Building.[3] It has the architectural form of a temple. Two building phases may be clearly distinguished in the foundations. The first phase dates to the mid-sixth century BC, a large cella measuring 13.75 × 29m, with two aisles divided by a row of central columns; at the back the northern section was separated off as

131

Figure 7.4 Heraion at Samos. The North Building.

an *adyton* (Holy of Holies). The south side from which the building was entered was set off by a portico. This temple was surrounded by an earth podium with a terrace retaining wall. In the last third of the sixth century BC the temple was given a peripteral colonnade with two rows of columns front and back, now measuring 25.8 × 41.2m The preserved column bases and fragments of column shafts and capitals show that the temple was in the Ionic order; nothing is otherwise known of the superstructure. But knowledge of the essential features of the second largest temple in the sanctuary of Hera has been retrieved. This temple was begun at about the same time as the main temple for Hera which raises the question: to what divinity was this temple dedicated and is it, in fact, a temple?

There is the same problem with all the other temple-like buildings in the Heraion. The Archaic Heraion had ten other buildings which, to judge by the ground plan, could have been temples.[4] Not a single one of these buildings, however, had its own altar as one would normally expect for Greek temples. On the other hand, most of these temple-like buildings are, strikingly enough, orientated towards the great altar of Hera. One might interpret this by assuming that the great altar served all the temples in common, instead of having a separate altar for each temple. It is not a priori unreasonable to suppose that several temples were dedicated in the sanctuary of the goddess Hera, founded by leading families or rulers. Other sanctuaries of Hera, such as Paestum, Perachora or Stymphalos, are known to have had two or more contemporary temples of the goddess. On the other hand, at least some of the smaller temple buildings were surely so-called treasuries, that is buildings to protect and exhibit especially valuable votives, just as in Delphi or Olympia. That is clear from the way in which they have been placed on the main routes through the sanctuary, in the immediate vicinity of votive sculpture. Alongside the great dedications of sculpture, particularly valuable votives, made of precious metals, ivory or other costly materials, protected from the weather by buildings, were set up here as representative gifts to the great goddess of Samos by the local aristocracy or foreign donors.

Nevertheless, it is hardly possible to draw a clear line between temple and treasury in the Heraion, since the ancient literary sources and inscriptions leave us completely in the dark about this and since only the ground plans of most of the buildings in question have been preserved. There is no decisive difference between the architectural form of a treasury and that of a small temple. The truth is that we know almost nothing about what cult procedures took place in the Greek temple and how temples differed from similar buildings in respect to legal status and function. It does appear to be certain that the main temple of a sanctuary contained the cult image of the divinity, but such a temple could surely also fulfil the function of a 'treasury'. Thus, Herodotus, for example, reports seeing in the great temple of Hera two statues offered by the Egyptian pharaoh Amasis, and Strabo describes this temple as a Pinakotheke (a place where older votives are kept). Besides, as mentioned above, other sanctuaries had several temples of the goddess, only one of which could have been the main temple with the cult statue. We simply do not know what functions, related to cult or otherwise, the other temples had. Perhaps one should picture a situation like that on the Acropolis of Athens with its Athena temples: the ancient cult statue of Athena Polias stood in the Old Temple of Athena, later on in a chamber of the Erechtheion. The much larger and more important Parthenon with the chryselephantine statue of the goddess by Phidias was not the real cult temple of the Athenian Acropolis, but seems rather to have functioned as a 'treasury' of the Athenian state. The North Building in Samos could have served a similar function as a 'treasury temple'; and the same holds true of the 'South Building' in the southern part of the altar forecourt, a slightly smaller peripteral temple, also built in the sixth century BC.

During the last excavation campaign an old problem was, to a great degree, solved, namely the dating and building phases of the first and second *dipteros*, the main temple of Hera. The first dipteral temple, the so-called Rhoikos temple, was the first and earliest in the series of colossal Ionic temples; as the model for later temples it must have had central significance for the development of monumental Ionic architecture. Some of its

133

architecture was reused in the foundations of its successor and was thus preserved. The gigantic size of this second dipteral temple is in itself enough to make this temple a landmark of Greek architecture, apart from the high quality of the partly preserved architectural ornament. Hence it is all the more regrettable that when the remains were cleared no stratigraphical observations were made that could have contributed to a more precise dating of the two colossal temples. Until now attempts at dating ranged over a relatively long time span and were, in part, wildly divergent.

The supplementary excavations carried out by Hermann Kienast in the pronaos of the second peripteral temple in 1989 have, to a great degree, provided clear answers to these essential questions. It turns out that the Rhoikos temple will have been begun in the first or early second quarter of the sixth century and completed c. 560 BC. This temple could not have been standing for any length of time, since its successor was begun in the second half of the sixth century. Presumably the marshy building site and insufficiently sturdy foundations are to blame for making this first marvel of Ionic architecture so unstable that it had to be dismantled. Furthermore, we now know that the second dipteral temple was not erected in a single operation, but that first the cella foundations were laid during the time of Polykrates. But the foundations of the outer colonnades and the pronaos could not have been laid before the end of the sixth century. Hence it has become clear that the columns of the temple are to be dated later than has hitherto been generally assumed.

Along with a common language, religion is the strongest cohesive agent linking the Greeks to each other. But even though all the Greeks worshipped the great Olympian gods and even though in some sense a poetically ideal pantheon of Greek gods had been in existence since the time of Homer and Hesiod, nevertheless there was never any form of religious practice universally valid and binding for all of Greece. Instead, the idea of the Greek gods is built up from local myths and differing traditions and forms of cult practices. In spite of a common ground of belief, the idea of Greek gods in the individual states and territories of Greece is in some cases so strongly coloured by local traditions and cult forms that to our modern way of thinking the great figures of the Olympian gods almost convey the impression of being local gods. Understanding and interpreting these local manifestations of Greek religious belief in relation to the pan-Hellenic pantheon is one of the most fascinating, yet difficult, problems of Greek religious history. The ancient written sources provide us with relatively little information on this subject. This means that we are all the more dependent on archaeological research enabling us to reach certain tentative conclusions concerning cult practices and the individual character of a sanctuary through a study of its buildings, inscriptions and votive offerings. The individual nature of the Heraion at Samos is also clearly recognizable. Here the cult of Hera differed, in some ways, from that in other Greek sanctuaries of Hera in respect to both content and form. The results of our recent excavations have again confirmed this observation by providing at least glimpses of specific customs of making sacrifice and offering votives. But before presenting a brief account of several of these phenomena let a single example serve to illustrate the necessity for maintaining utmost caution when proceeding to interpret archaeological finds in order to get at the history of a cult.

The core of the legend concerning the foundation of the Heraion seems to have been that this place was regarded as the birthplace of the goddess. According to local tradition the goddess was born under a *lygos* tree (*Vitex agnus castus*), a tree or bush common to the Imbrasos plain. At the annual festival of Hera, which is named in some ancient sources as the Toneia (binding ceremony) the cult image of Hera was wound around with *lygos* branches and symbolically bound. The *lygos* tree was clearly the sacred tree of Samian Hera and the cult probably centred around this tree beneath which the goddess was born. The tree is still pictured on coins of the Roman imperial period and Pausanias (8.23.5) mentions that the *lygos* in Samos was the oldest tree in his time. Thus during the excavations of 1963 great significance was attached to the find of a large tree stump directly behind the altar (Figure 7.5) in the paving of an earlier phase of the altar. The findspot at the altar and at a depth indicating an early level left little room for doubt that this was Hera's sacred tree. The cult landmark and thus the nucleus, so to speak, of the Samian Heraion had definitely been found, so it seemed. An investigation carried out in 1985 showed that this beautiful discovery had been a mirage.[5] A sample of the wood taken from the tree stump showed that it was not a *lygos* at all but a juniper tree. According to the Carbon-14 method, the tree dated to between 750 and 450 BC, but a count of the tree rings showed that this tree could not have lived longer than eighty years. The tree probably belonged to a sacred grove, mentioned in an ancient source; the grove will have been east of the altar. At best the tree serves to indicate that the altar lay directly at the edge of the grove.

Finds from recent excavations yield interesting indications as to the special nature of the cult of Hera on Samos, especially in respect to the Early Archaic period. In particular the excavation campaigns of 1977, 1983 and 1984 in the area between the great altar and the coast have provided much new and interesting material. There was no ancient building activity in this area. Today the ancient layers all lie below the ground water level, because here the land has subsided since ancient times. This situation causes considerable technical problems; excavation can be done only with pumps working to keep the constantly flowing ground water from flooding the excavation area. On the bright side, organic materials such as wood or plant remains are especially well preserved, shielded from exposure to air in the permanently wet soil.

We found three wells in our excavations, one rectangular (Figure 7.6),[6] the other two round; the wells are remarkable in respect both to the manner of

Figure 7.5 Heraion at Samos. The altar of Hera. The tree stump wrongly thought to be the *lygos* tree is seen in the paving next to the altar.

construction and to their function. Starting from the ancient surface level they were dug right through a watertight layer of clay into a layer of sand that conducts water. The walls of the well shaft were sheathed with limestone slabs and the floor was paved with limestone slabs with an opening into the ground. Just as in the case of an artesian well, the water under pressure in the gravel layer streamed in through the opening at the bottom of the well all the way up to the top, where it flowed through an opening in the well-kerb into limestone gutters. That is to say, we have here a kind of artificial spring, constantly flowing. As we cleared these wells they began functioning again just as they had in ancient times; without further ado we drank the crystal clear drinking water as it burbled up. To judge from the dumped deposits of gravel laid down alongside these wells, they were at the side of a path leading from the sea to the sanctuary. This is a further indication that in the early period the main entrance to the Heraion was from the coast, where ships and boats could easily land on the flat shore. Evidently the wells provided those who wished to enter the sanctuary with water for drinking and purification. The wells were surrounded by limestone paving which shows, among other things, that the ground here had already become swampy at the time these wells were dug and had to be given

Figure 7.6 Heraion at Samos. Rectangular well.

a firm surface. The filling inside the wells consisted of potsherds, whole pots and broken votive offerings. These fillings, as well as the layers below the paving of the wells, can be dated by means of the Corinthian pottery. Thus it can be shown that the wells were constructed in the late seventh century BC and were soon afterwards filled in by the early sixth century BC. All the finds from these contexts date to the seventh or, at the latest, sixth century BC. The many animal bones, pieces of charcoal and iron cooking spits show that the wells were filled with debris from the sanctuary. The votives found in the wells had either been damaged or had become unsightly before they were discarded or buried. These finds, taken as a whole, offer an extremely interesting cross-section through the contents of the sanctuary in the seventh century BC.

An analysis of the many animal bones, virtually all of which must come from slaughtered sacrificial animals, affords us interesting glimpses of sacrificial customs in the Heraion.[7] They evidently belong to the debris from feasts eaten by those who had participated in sacrificial ceremonies in the Heraion. Bovines were by far the most common sacrificial animal, fully grown animals, mostly cows. Sheep came second in far smaller numbers, and pigs were third. There were strikingly few goat bones. Several fallow deer bones show that, contrary to widespread opinion, wild animals could also be sacrificed in Greek sanctuaries. Surprisingly enough, no animal thigh bones were found at all, in contrast to comparable finds of animal bones in settlements or in other sanctuaries. The best and most sought after parts of the sacrificial animals were evidently not consumed at the sacrificial feasts, the remains of which we are dealing with here. This surely points to a sacrificial custom attested in Homer and elsewhere, namely that the delectable thighs of a sacrificial animal receive a ritual treatment different from the other parts of the animal. During the sacrifice the thighs were wrapped in fat and burnt on the altar. It is still an open question whether only the thigh bones were burnt up or if the meat was included. It is also conceivable that the priest was entitled to the thighs as his share of the sacrifice. In any case, the excavation finds verify the special treatment of the thighs (*meria* in Greek) in Greek animal sacrifices and sacrificial feasts.

The bones found in the excavation show not only the customary practice of sacrificing animals in Greek sanctuaries but also another, extremely peculiar, aspect of the Samian Hera sanctuary. There was an entirely unexpected, unique find: skull fragments from a 5m long Egyptian crocodile (*Crocodylus niloticus*) as well as skull and horn fragments from two African antelopes (*Alcelaphus uselaphus*). These exotic animals could hardly have been living on Samos, not even in captivity. It is reasonable to assume that these animals, or perhaps only the heads, were brought by travellers from Egypt, as trophies of the chase for instance and as such dedicated to the Samian goddess. These bones of exotic animals, taken together with artworks imported from Egypt and other countries, reflect the far-flung trade connections that Samos had in the Early Archaic period.

To return to sacrificial practices in the Samian Heraion, there are yet more insights to be gleaned from the new finds at the wells. As mentioned above, remains of plant life were particularly well preserved in the soaking wet ground. Grape seeds and olive pits were, for example, easily recognizable with the naked eye and show, of course, what fruits were consumed during the Hera festival. The following case is of interest with reference to basic assumptions concerning the ritual connection between the natural object and the representation thereof.[8] Strikingly many terracotta pomegranates and terracotta or ivory poppy pods (Figure 7.7) have been found in the Heraion. A terracotta pinecone was also found. The feature shared in common by these fruits is that they are rich in seeds and there can be no doubt that this must be seen as a special element of Hera's divinity as a great fertility goddess. The replicas in clay and ivory are, so to speak, durable artistic substitutes for the perishable natural objects, which likewise have a symbolic function. The finds now provide excellent evidence that this is so: among the remains of plant life found in our excavations many pomegranate seeds and poppy seeds have turned up, and also several well-preserved pine cones, which could not possibly have been growing in this spot, but must have been brought into the sanctuary as simple votive offerings. They were, after all, true votives, gifts for the goddess, differing from the grand dedications made out of marble, metal or other precious materials only in regard to material

Figure 7.7 Ivory pomegranates and poppies from the Heraion. Inv. nos E 119, E 113, E 106, R 108.

worth, but not in spirit or purpose. It is scarcely possible to draw a line between what is purely a votive offering and what is sacrificed or eaten at a ritual banquet, certainly not in the case of pomegranates which were presumably not only offered as votives, but also consumed during the sacrificial feasts.

In a slightly different context the same holds true for the pottery table ware and drinking cups found in and around the wells in large quantities and partially in a very good state of preservation. It consists of plainly painted but elegantly profiled vessels, including drinking goblets, cups and mugs, as well as plates and amphoras, which are clearly to be identified as a kind of cult dining equipment on the basis of the vast quantities (which would alone define their function) but also because of the contexts.[9] They must have been used for sacrificial meals and then left in the sanctuary according to the sacred regulation, commonly valid in Greek sanctuaries, forbidding removal of all objects once they had been brought inside the sanctuary.

One kind of pottery stands out among the thousands of finds: the pieces on which the letters D and H are painted. This combination of letters was formerly read as an abbreviation for *demosion* meaning 'public property' or 'belonging to the state', so that this pottery was taken to be state-owned property which the Samian state made available for the sacrifice. This

Figure 7.8 Statuette of limestone
from the Heraion.

interpretation, however, has little to recommend it, because it is difficult to imagine that the political concept *demosion*, which appears later on in connection with democratic governments in the Greek city-states, existed in the aristocratic society of the Archaic age when this pottery was made. A new possibility for another interpretation of these *dipinti* opened up when several pots came to light in our excavations bearing the letters HRH, that is, Hera, written in the same way as the earlier ones. Here the connection between the goddess and her sanctuary is explicit. This suggests that the *dipinti* consisting only of the two letters *delta* and *eta* or vice versa also have to do with Hera's name and cult. The letters could be an abbreviation of the goddess' name where what seems to be a *delta* is actually a *rho* which is written in a closely similar manner in many other examples. There is other evidence that these labelled pots are directly linked to the cult of Hera: they are found nowhere else outside of the Heraion. The sole parallels are from the sanctuary of Hera in Naukratis in Egypt. But the Heraion in Naukratis is a branch sanctuary of the Samian Hera in Egypt, founded by Samian merchants in this trading centre in the Nile delta and maintained by several East Greek towns. This typical cult equipment for Hera, used only, as mentioned above, in the sanctuary of Hera, was most likely produced and sold in the sanctuary itself. Finds from recent excavations prove that there were pottery workshops in the area of the Archaic Heraion.[10]

The plain inconspicuous finds in an excavation are often just the ones to reveal aspects of worship apt to be overlooked because attention is focused on the more spectacular works of art. Thus our excavations constantly produced pieces that one might best describe as 'votives of the common people', that is to say objects that on the one hand were certainly votives, but on the other hand point to a lower class of donors because of their rustic style or low commercial value.[11] There are, for example, not only primitive inartistic statuettes of limestone (Figure 7.8), terracotta and wood, but also plain wooden bowls and plates, probably carved by the dedicator himself. There were also rare and strange natural objects, for instance: a branch of coral, a piece of a stalactite, and chunks of rock crystal, probably dedicated to the goddess as curiosities.

The Archaic wooden objects found in the Heraion of Samos are in a class by themselves in the annals of Greek excavations. They were preserved in the permanently waterlogged earth in and around the wells and thanks to modern methods of conservation they can be preserved indefinitely.[12] Since wood is a highly perishable substance, disintegrating rapidly when exposed to air or in normal soil conditions, little or no wood has been found in other excavations in Greece. Although written and pictorial sources inform us that much Greek sculpture, furniture and utensils were made of wood, nevertheless this aspect of Greek art and cultural history is still, to a considerable degree, *terra incognita*. Hence the wooden objects found in the Heraion are, even though largely fragmentary, of invaluable significance for the archaeology of Greece. They display a wide range of types and artistry, from simple utensils and well-crafted furniture all the way to masterpieces of wooden sculpture (Figure 7.9). These finds give us at least an inkling of how precisely and inventively Greek cabinet-makers of the late seventh century worked and let us see, as if through a keyhole, what excellent artistic attainments the carvers of wooden figures were capable of achieving. At the same time these finds convey a marvellously interesting picture of the wealth of richly varied votive offerings brought together in this sanctuary. Here, too, certain unusual types of frequently recurring votives attract attention; they seem to have been made specifically for the Samian Heraion.

One striking example is the many representations of little boats (Figure 7.10), on average about 40cm long. These 'models' reproduce the elegant shape of Greek warships and trading vessels in simplified form. Until now a total of 40 of these has been found. Since only a fraction of the original votives has been recovered, it is safe to assume that hundreds of such ships were dedicated in the Archaic Heraion, and it is tempting to think of them as offerings from seafarers. But if this were so, it is strange that all the votive ships are of wood, none made out of other materials, such as the clay or bronze ships found at other sites. Another striking feature of these wooden ships is that they are virtually abstract forms, reduced to a few basic elements – the hull is barely recognizable. If they were really votives one would expect a greater variety and also more details, such as masts, superstructure,

Figure 7.9 Kore statuette of wood from the Heraion. Inv. no. H 100.

Figure 7.10 Wooden 'models' of ships from the Heraion. Inv. nos H 93, H 94, H 95.

structure, rudder etc., as is the case with other miniatures of ancient ships. Perhaps these oddly abstract little boats point to a peculiarity of the Samian cult of Hera hitherto unknown to us.[13] Their appearance is reminiscent of toy ships and the occasionally rough unfinished-looking workmanship might suggest that these boats played a role in the ritual of festivals of Hera as a kind of symbolic cult object. In this connection a custom, harking back to ancient times in Magna Graecia, still practised nowadays, may prove illuminating: there is a chapel in the sanctuary of Hera in Foce del Sele which is dedicated to the Madonna del Granato who, by virtue of her epithet and the attribute of a pomegranate, must be the Christian successor of the ancient Greek goddess Hera. Even now there is an annual festival in honour of the Madonna del Granato in which little decorated ships of the simplest form are carried in procession, although nowadays the inhabitants have nothing to do with seafaring. It is thought that the custom goes back to ancient times when the sanctuary was not yet so far distant from the sea. The pomegranate too is an ancient symbol that played a great role in the Heraion, as we have seen. In itself there is nothing unusual about Christians adopting ancient pagan customs.

Archaic terracotta figurines from the Hera sanctuaries in Tiryns and Perachora provide further evidence: they show the goddess holding a little boat decked with flowers. These are, at the very least, strong indications that representations of ships functioned as a symbol or cult object in the ritual of Hera's festival. Aetiological explanations for certain features of local legends concerning the cult should also be taken into consideration in interpreting the boat as a symbolic object used in the largely unknown ritual of the Hera cult. According to Athenaeus (XV 671) Tyrrhenian pirates attempted to carry off the cult image of Hera in their ship; but the goddess intervened, the ship remained motionless as if nailed to the water, whereupon the pirates returned the cult image to its place with all speed. According to another variant of the tradition cited by Pausanias (7.4.4) the image of Hera was brought to Samos on the ship Argo. Even though the exact meaning the little boats had in the cult of Hera escapes us, nevertheless there is a significant accumulation of information pointing to a link between the ship symbol and the Hera cult. This symbolism cannot, of course, be separated off from the major importance of seafaring for Samos in general, manifested in other ways: a real boat was set up as a votive offering next to the altar of Hera; the later coins of Samos still display the representation of a ship. Everything that held special significance for people, in their lives and in the way they saw themselves, was translated into the special features and local peculiarities of their divinities.

Peculiarly shaped little wooden stools (Figure 7.11)[14] must also be ranked among the typical votive objects in the Heraion because of their relatively frequent occurrence. They are put together out of plain boards decorated with carved figures. The sides are schematic horses carved from thick

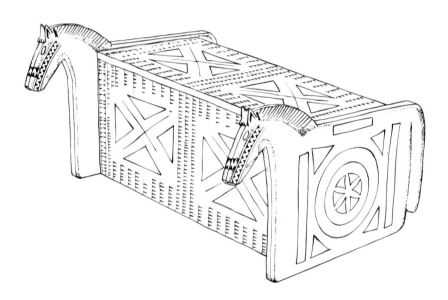

Figure 7.11 Wooden stool from the Heraion. (a) Side piece. Inv. no. H 108. (b) Reconstructed drawing.

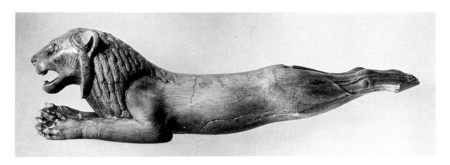

Figure 7.12 Egyptian lion of ivory, Ramessid period, found in the Heraion. Inv. no.
E 133.

boards. Because of their small size they could hardly have been used as real furniture, as footstools, for example. The largest ones are on average 35cm wide, others considerably smaller. Most likely they would have served as pedestals for votive figures made out of wood or clay. Representations of standing or seated gods on pedestals, supported by lions, bulls or sphinxes, frequently occur in Near Eastern art from which early Greek art received many stimuli. A bronze statuette of this Near Eastern type has been found in the Samian Heraion, hardly a mere coincidence. Laconian bronze mirror supports, figures of women on a stand held up by two little horses on either side, provide Greek examples of this type of representation. Archaic votive figures may well have been similarly set up in the Heraion. Since, as far as we know, only horses served as stool supports, they must be associated with the cult of Hera on Samos in some way not yet understood. It is interesting to note in this connection that remarkably many of the bronze finds consist of bridles or harnesses for horses. In no other Greek sanctuary have so many horse trappings been found as in the Heraion at Samos. Since in early Greece ownership of horses, riding and horse-drawn transport were the prerogatives of the nobility, it is reasonable to assume that votive horsetrappings were signs of a privileged, aristocratic way of life. At the same time these votives reveal a special trait of Samian Hera – the concept of Hera as protector of horses and riders, to some degree an aristocratic aspect of the goddess in the Early Archaic period.

The high percentage of imported items from foreign countries, especially from Egypt and the Near East, among the early finds from the Heraion at Samos is a striking phenomenon. No other archaeological excavation in Greece has, in fact, produced anything like the number and variety of imports found in the Archaic sanctuary of Hera in Samos.[15] This is even more fully borne out by our investigations of the fillings of debris from sacrifices and votives at the wells, which yielded important finds, three of which may be cited: a splendid Egyptian ivory carving, a lion from the

Ramessid era (Figure 7.12), originally decorating a piece of pharaonic furniture, is one of the most beautiful animal figures that has come down to us from antiquity.[16] Since the lion was brought to Samos about six hundred years after it was made, one could hardly assume that it reached Samos via a direct route from the court of the pharaohs in Egypt. Perhaps a Greek in Egypt acquired the lion as an antiquity so to speak. A comparison with the present day art market is not altogether irrelevant because we know from ancient Egyptian legal documents that as early as the second millennium BC grave robbers systematically plundered pharaohs' tombs stuffed full of possessions which they naturally will have sold.

Two closely similar bronze figures of bearded men, each accompanied by a dog, are interesting from the point of view of the history of religion (Figures 7.13–7.14).[17] They come from Babylonia where they are associated with the cult of the mother- and healing-goddess Gula whose main centre of worship was in the town Isin. In this case eastern visitors to Samos may have been the donors who saw in Hera the same goddess known to them at home under the name of Gula, a perfectly plausible hypothesis in the light of what is known about the nature and individual character of these two goddesses. In general, the equation of Greek and Near Eastern divinities is a well-documented phenomenon in the history of Greek religion.

A trapezoidal bronze relief served to protect and adorn the forehead of a war-chariot horse (Figure 7.15). The relief depicts a winged sun, beneath which a group of four naked girls or goddesses on lion heads form a group that almost looks acrobatic.[18] The erotic iconography of this forehead piece has close parallels in other Near Eastern horse trappings and in ivory adornment of royal furniture such as, for example, the Nimrud ivories. The subject matter points to the realms of the goddess Astarte and denotes both the erotic and the warlike aspect of this great Oriental goddess. This remarkable find is to be assigned to North Syria on the basis of style and it dates to the late ninth century BC. The Aramaic inscription, incised beside the main representation, is of particular interest. It states, among other things, that this is a present or tribute for the Syrian ruler Hazael of Basan. He is most probably to be identified as King Hazael of Damascus, mentioned in the New Testament and other sources, who ruled over the greater part of Syria in the late ninth century BC. The inscription also throws light on the high social rank of the donors of such votives. It is certainly most unlikely that Hazael sent this piece directly to Samos. In the course of time it may well have fallen into other hands, either passed along as a gift or as war booty and thus by some roundabout way was finally dedicated as a valuable votive offering in the sanctuary of the goddess of Samos. At present the inscription is the earliest example of a west Semitic script in Greece. It can serve as an example of the kinds of documents known to the early Greeks when they devised their own writing in the eighth century BC modelled after the Aramaic–Phoenician alphabet. A bronze blinker from Eretria, which

Figure 7.13
Babylonian bronze figurine, found in the Heraion. Inv. no. B 2087.

Figure 7.14
Babylonian bronze figurine, found in the Heraion. Inv. no. B 2086.

Figure 7.15 Bronze relief for the forehead of a war-chariot horse, found in the Heraion. Inv. no. B 2579.

147

carries an identical inscription, could well have belonged to the same set of trappings for a four-horse team as the Samian piece.

These are only three examples out of the many finds which can be pinned down as coming from, for example, Iran, Assyria, Urartu, Phoenicia or Cyprus. Each one of these pieces tells its own story, each deserves to be discussed *per se*. The discussion here is limited to pointing out aspects which make this set of finds extraordinarily interesting taken as a whole, over and above the sum of its parts. What is the common denominator of these finds? What do they say in their entirety? What can be gathered from the context of these finds in the Samian sanctuary?

The decisive link is that these objects were all found at one and the same place. As votives they provide evidence in regard to the character and significance of the cult and, since the Samian Heraion was not a pan-Hellenic sanctuary, the finds also give us knowledge of the early history of Samos. The strange foreign votives reflect the far-flung trade connections between Samos and the countries of the Near East and Egypt in the seventh century BC. Greek merchants making long voyages will have brought these objects, some of them very valuable indeed, back to Samos and dedicated them to their Great Goddess. But there also will have been visitors from abroad, who brought gifts for the Greek Hera. All of these pieces were found in debris deposited in the late seventh century or at the turn of the seventh to sixth century BC. A large part if not all of the finds must have been previously visible in the sanctuary. As for the architecture of the sanctuary at that time, the Heraion presented a rather modest picture: a narrow temple, 30m long, a simple altar, the South Stoa mostly made out of wood, and a few small *naïskoi* around the area of the altar were the only buildings in the Early Archaic Heraion. The abundance and variety of splendid votives are all the more striking in such a modest setting. In these circumstances one comes to realize what the close proximity of such varied votives from widely different countries meant for the evolution of Greek art. The Greek sanctuaries were collecting points and meeting places for art works of all sorts. Visitors to the great sacred shrines encountered entire museums, since the votives were not behind closed doors, but out in the open for all to see. Greek artists, above all, could go to such places for new stimuli and they evidently made rich use of their opportunities. This is especially noticeable in the period to which our finds belong. In the seventh century BC Greek art opens up with headlong momentum, starting with the abstract draughtsmanship of the Geometric style and unfolding into the delight of telling stories full of life and the plasticity of Archaic art. Themes and pictorial stimuli from the older, more developed cultures of Egypt and the Near East played a leading role in this process. Greek artists copied those models, transformed them and translated them into their own artistic language. The latest finds from the Heraion can serve to summon up a picture of the situation in the so-called Orientalizing period in Greek art: there they were open to view in the sanctuary where the visitors could see them at will, old and new, pieces from local workshops beside foreign offerings. A comparison of the local handiwork in clay and wood, some of which could almost be described as primitive, with the technically perfect figures from Egypt, the Near East and Cyprus, makes clear that there must have been a strong impetus to imitate foreign artworks. Several examples illustrate direct take-overs of eastern compositions and ornamental patterns. These examples point up the role of the sanctuary as the meeting places for the young Greek and old Eastern art. The way in which these particular excavations have revealed that widely different votives were set up side by side yields unique insights into the life of the sanctuary.

Earlier archaeological finds in the Heraion of Samos had already made it clear that Samos had played an outstanding role in the history of Greek art. The finds of large-scale marble sculpture, particularly torsos and fragments found on the 'Sacred Way', pointed to an important school of Samian sculptors in the sixth century BC.[19] In the Archaic period, Samos must have been one of the leading centres for marble sculpture in Greece. The many stone statue bases of the Archaic period found in the Heraion make us realize that the many votive sculptures set up close together must have contributed powerfully to the impression of the sanctuary as a whole, but since only fragments of most figures have been recovered, it takes an act of imagination to summon up the richness, variety and beauty of the sculpture.

Under these circumstances the magnificent find of September 1980 from excavations on the 'Sacred Way' is all the more to be treasured. As in the case of so many of the finest archaeological discoveries, it was not the result of a systematically targeted search, but a matter of chance. The excavation had not been undertaken in order to find sculpture, but rather to find the hitherto unlocated main entrance to the sanctuary. In the process of removing a dumped fill of the Roman imperial period the huge marble torso of a youth unexpectedly came to light north of the Roman paving.[20] In this case the head was missing, but the surface was wonderfully well preserved and the monumental volumes and subtle modelling were revealed even while excavation was still in progress.

After the extremely difficult work of recovering the colossal torso, it swiftly became apparent that several fragments from earlier excavations joined break on break, so that the statue was virtually complete except for the head and feet. The most important fragment is the left thigh found in 1974 about 5m away from the findspot of the torso. The fragment bears the dedicatory inscription in large beautiful lettering: *Isches aneteken oresios*. The left forearm, split in two pieces, was found built into a cistern in 1974. The right lower thigh with knee had been found before the war; although it suffered damage during the war, its original appearance could be exactly reconstructed with the help of remaining fragments and good photographs.

The statue represents a so-called 'kouros', a standing naked youth that forms one of the leading types of Archaic Greek sculpture. The newly found kouros is about three times life-size and is thus by far the largest statue of this type ever found in Greece until now in such an excellent state of preservation. The gigantic size and high aesthetic quality of this figure were first fully appreciated in 1984 after the statue had been set up in the newly built museum (which had to be specially altered owing to the size of the kouros).[21] But this made it all the more painfully clear how incomplete this unique statue was without its head. Since virtually all of the heads of other sculpture from the Heraion are missing, obviously the preferred target of later destruction, one never dreamed of finding the head of this kouros. On the other hand, since joining fragments had been found in the immediate vicinity of the kouros, we wanted at least to exhaust all the possibilities of finding further fragments.

In the autumn of 1984 it became possible to investigate the area directly south of the findspot of the kouros, which had until then been off limits; our work there had, among other objectives, the specific aim of finding more of the kouros. On the second day, while we were still in the process of clearing the area before the excavation proper, we came across a large fragment of marble. It is hard to describe our joy and elation as we turned it over and saw the face of the kouros. Rarely are the most secret desires of an archaeologist so swiftly fulfilled beyond all expectation. With this fortunate find came the awareness of how much vitality and power had been missing from the kouros until then.

This masterpiece of Archaic Ionic sculpture (Figure 7.16), recovered almost complete, will surely occupy an important place in the history of Greek art. The statue comes from a Samian workshop; this is proven not only by the style but also by the black-veined marble of which it is made. This marble is typical for the sculpture and architecture of the Heraion and comes from quarries in the mountains in the northern part of the island. The kouros is to be dated c. 580 BC on the basis of the context and the style of the statue. Hence the kouros is the earliest piece of monumental East Ionic sculpture known until now. This does not make it easier to understand the conditions in which this grandiose work was created, since no earlier gradual development in Samian or East Ionic sculpture can be traced leading up to such a sudden blossoming out of masterly carving. The usual conception of a masterpiece, that it stands at the end of a long development, is not applicable in this case. Here amazing perfection emerges so to speak out of nowhere. Art historical analysis and comparisons (which for reasons of space cannot be set forth here) do, however, indicate that monumental Egyptian sculpture must have been a model of decisive significance for the sculptor of the great kouros from Samos. Of course this is not to be taken as meaning that the Samian sculptor simply copied Egyptian models. What he did was to absorb the monumental conception and the thousand-year-old tradition of rendering the male body and transform it into something

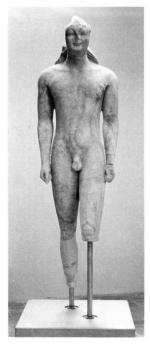

Figure 7.16
Samos, Vathy Museum. Marble kouros, about three times life-size, found at the 'Sacred Way' of the Heraion.

entirely new, purely Greek, in an act of creative synthesis. It is astounding to see how the specific style of Samian-East Ionic sculpture is present in its entirety at the very beginning of large-scale Greek sculpture and thereafter for a hundred years changes or develops further only in small steps. In this connection the Samian giant is comparable with the slightly later huge temple of Hera, which also had no local predecessors and also was created with the earlier Egyptian architecture in mind, standing at the beginning of East Ionic architecture, anticipating its future development.

It is well to bear in mind that the giant kouros was standing on the 'Sacred Way' before the first large temple of Hera was built. At this time the architecture of the sanctuary was still a modest affair and in this context the kouros must have been the most outstanding (in the true sense of the word) monument in the Heraion. This makes it all the more important to under-stand what exactly the kouros meant to the donor and what it meant to the visitor to the sanctuary. The very simplicity of the kouros type and the lack of action and attributes make it hard for twentieth century ways of thinking to interpret. Archaeologists today generally accept that the kouros type embodies ideal concepts of the aristocratic class from which the donors come. In this case, however, the gigantic size of the figure is an additional element. In a way, the size could also be a feature of the content. Such votive sculptures are not only pious gifts to the divinity; they are there to proclaim the prestige of the donor or his family in a prominent place, the sanctuary. The gigantic size of such statues may be linked to the conception widely expressed in Greek literature ever since Homer, that the heroes of earlier times were much larger than the 'people alive today'. For example, Herodotus has a whole set of concrete examples illustrating the belief prevalent in folklore that heroes are larger than lifesize. Here we have, after all, a timeless feature of fairytales, still alive in other cultures until our own times. This idea is so deeply embedded in the Archaic Greek outlook that one may assume that Isches' kouros not only represents an oversize ideal figure, but a specific hero, the ancestor of the donor's family. As we know from the literature, the Greek aristocracy of the Archaic period considered that tracing one's descent back to gods and heroes was an essential element in self-perception. And it would be reasonable to conjecture that Isches as the donor of this gigantic figure set up a monumental statue of his heroic ancestor as a representative votive offering in the main sanctuary of the island.

(Translated by Judith Binder.)

NOTES

1 For the topography, history and excavations of the Heraion in general, see H. Kyrieleis, *Führer durch das Heraion von Samos* (Athens 1981) with bibliography. The author thanks H. Kienast, director of the excavations from 1985 onward, for communicating the latest, as yet unpublished, results of the investigations.

2 H. Kyrieleis, H. Kienast and H. J. Weisshaar, 'Ausgrabungen im Heraion von Samos', *AA* 1985, 365ff.

3 A. Furtwängler and H. Kienast, *Der Nordbau im Heraion von Samos, Samos*, vol. III (Bonn 1989).

4 On the question of treasuries in the Heraion, see Furtwängler (*supra* n. 3) 63ff.; H. Kienast, 'Der sog. Tempel D im Heraion von Samos', *AM* 100 (1985) 122ff.

5 See H. Kienast, 'Zum heiligen Baum der Hera', *AM* 106 (1991) 72ff.

6 A. Furtwängler, 'Heraion von Samos: Grabungen im Südtemenos 1977, I. Schicht-und Baubefund, Keramik', *AM* 95 (1980) 156ff.; *idem*, 'Zur Frage des Grundwasser- und Meeresspiegelansteiges im samischen Heraion seit *c.* 600 v. Chr.', in: J. Schäfer and W. Simon, eds, *Strandverschiebungen. Ruperto Carola. Zeitschrift der Vereinigung der Freunde der Studentenschaft der Universität Heidelberg*, Sonderheft (Heidelberg 1981) 147ff.

7 J. Boessneck and A. von den Driesch, 'Reste exotischer Tiere aus dem Heraion von Samos', *AM* 96 (1980) 245ff.; *idem, Knochenabfall von Opfermahlen und Weihgaben aus dem Heraion von Samos (7. Jh. v.Chr.)* (Munich 1988).

8 See a preliminary notice by the author, 'Offerings of "the common man" in the Heraion of Samos', in: R. Hägg, N. Marinatos and G. C. Nordquist, eds, *Early Greek Cult Practice. Proceedings of the Fifth International Symposium at the Swedish Institute at Athens, 26–29 June 1986* (Stockholm 1988) 215ff.

9 U. Kron, 'Kultmahle im Heraion von Samos archaischer Zeit', in R. Hägg, N. Marinatos and G. C. Nordquist, eds, (*supra* n. 8) 144ff.; *idem*, in: H. A. G. Brijder, ed., *Ancient Greek and Related Pottery. Proceedings of the International Vase Symposium* (Amsterdam 1984) 294ff.

10 See Kyrieleis, Kienast and Weisshaar (*supra* n. 2) 408.
11 See Kyrieleis in R. Hägg, N. Marinatos and G. C. Nordquist, eds, (*supra* n. 8) 215ff.
12 For the finds made out of wood, see D. Ohly, 'Holz', *AM* 68 (1953) 77ff.; G. Kopcke, 'Neue Holzfunde aus dem Heraion von Samos', *AM* 82 (1967) 100ff.; H. Kyrieleis, 'Archaische Holzfunde aus Samos', *AM* 95 (1980) 87ff.
13 See Kyrieleis (*supra* n. 12) 89ff.
14 Kyrieleis (*supra* n. 12) 107ff.
15 The first comprehensive publication of the bronzes: U. Jantzen, *Ägyptische und orientalische Bronzen aus dem Heraion von Samos*, *Samos*, vol. VIII (Bonn 1972). For the ivories, see B. Freyer-Schauenburg, *Elfenbeine aus dem samischen Heraion* (Hamburg 1964).
16 A. Furtwängler, 'Heraion von Samos: Grabungen im Südtemenos, 1977, II. Kleinfunde', *AM* 96 (1981) 107ff., pls 27–30.
17 H. Kyrieleis, 'Babylonische Bronzen im Heraion von Samos', *JdI* 94 (1979) 32ff.
18 H. Kyrieleis and W. Röllig, 'Ein altorientalischer Pferdeschmuck aus dem Heraion von Samos', *AM* 103 (1988) 37ff. For the inscription see further, I. Eph'al and J. Naveh, 'Hazael's booty inscriptions', *Israel Exploration Journal* 39 (1989) 192ff.; F. Bron and A. Lemaire, 'A propos d'une plaque de harnais en bronze découverte à Samos: Réflexions sur le disque solaire ailé', *Revue d'Assyriologie* 83 (1989) 35ff.
19 B. Freyer-Schauenburg, *Bildwerke der archaischen Zeit und des Strengen Stils*, *Samos*, vol. XI (Bonn 1974).
20 For the kouros, see the preliminary publication: H. Kyrieleis, 'Neue archaische Skulpturen aus dem Heraion von Samos', in: H. Kyrieleis, ed., *Plastik*, vol. 1 (Mainz 1986) 35ff.
21 H. Kyrieleis, 'Der Kuros von Samos', *Archäologie in Deutschland* 1988, Heft 1, 18ff.

The evolution of a pan-Hellenic sanctuary: from archaeology towards history at Isthmia

Elizabeth R. Gebhard

The sanctuary of Poseidon on the Isthmus of Corinth (Figure 8.1) was the major extramural shrine of the Corinthians, their most important religious foundation outside the city. Its central location beside one of the main roads linking the Peloponnesus with mainland Greece made the shrine a natural assembly place. It was one of four sanctuaries where Greeks from all parts of the Mediterranean came to compete in pan-Hellenic games. Oscar Broneer discovered the temple of Poseidon in 1952 and then conducted systematic excavations of the central plateau that contained the temple, altar, surrounding buildings, and a Roman hero shrine. He also cleared the theatre, two caves used for dining, and two stadia for the Isthmian Games. In the autumn of 1989 new excavations produced further information about the stages in the shrine's development and their chronology.[1] The following account of the sanctuary should be understood as a preliminary overview that combines the results of Broneer's excavations with the new finds from the 1989 season.[2] The first part is concerned with the monuments and related features of the central area from the period of earliest sacrificial activity until the Hellenistic period; the second section examines evidence for the ways in which the sanctuary was used during those centuries. In the third part the relationship between the sacrificial area and the Early Stadium is discussed, and at the end there is a short account of the hero, Melikertes-Palaimon, who was associated with the games.

As its principal deity, Poseidon presided over the Isthmian shrine, accompanied by Amphitrite and Melikertes-Palaimon. Other gods worshipped with him include Poseidon's children, the Cyclopes, whose altar is mentioned by Pausanias (2.2.1) and Demeter, a divinity frequently linked with Poseidon in cult.[3] Two dedications inscribed to her in the fourth century were recovered in an area about 300m west of the temple of Poseidon.[4] A list of benefactions from the second century AD (*IG* 4, 203) provides us with the names of other deities who had shrines at the sanctuary, but their cult places have not been located. According to the inscription the

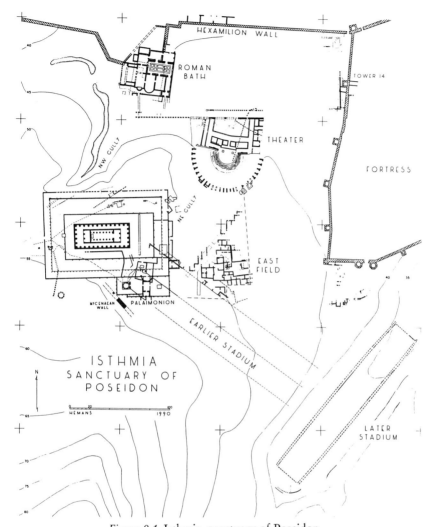

Figure 8.1 Isthmia, sanctuary of Poseidon.

temples of Demeter, Kore, Dionysos and Artemis were grouped within a single walled area called the Sacred Glen (*Hiera Nape*). The other divinities named are the Ancestral Gods, Helios, Eueteria and Kore, and Pluto.[5] Their association with Demeter and the harvest supports the notion that fertility was a major concern for worshippers at the sanctuary. A full discussion of the Isthmian cults, however, must await a future work in which the votive offerings are considered. The role played by Melikertes-Palaimon is briefly surveyed at the end of this chapter.

The temple and altar of Poseidon stood on a small plateau that was the

155

ceremonial heart of the Isthmian sanctuary. It is located in an area riven by valleys, about 1.5km from the Saronic Gulf and 16km due east of Corinth. The triangular plateau lay at the foot of a ridge known today as the Rachi, and the road linking Corinth and the Isthmus ran along a gully at its northwest side (Figures 8.2, 8.5).[6] When the Isthmian Games were founded in the early sixth century, a stadium was added to the shrine, and a century later a theatre and bathing facilities were built on a lower plateau to the north of the temple.[7] In the Hellenistic period the racecourse was moved to the south-east valley where the natural slopes provided space for the increasingly large crowds who attended the popular festival.[8] These monuments occupied the centre of the sanctuary, but there are indications from surface remains and the inscriptions mentioned above, that the entire sacred complex (the *Hieron tou Poseidonos*) stretched some distance to the west, probably reaching the spring at the head of a great ravine about 560m from the temple of Poseidon. All water used in the rest of the shrine seems to have been piped down from that spring, and it must have been in this area that the Sacred Glen was located.

THE MONUMENTS

The Early Iron Age

Evidence for the first ritual activity at the site comes from cups and bowls that were found mixed with ash and burnt animal bones at the south-eastern side of the central plateau. The earliest fragments show that eating and drinking began at this place in the Early Protogeometric period (late-eleventh to tenth century BC), and the unbroken sequence of drinking vessels in succeeding centuries bears witness to the continuity of the practice.[9] The burnt bones came from sheep, goats and cattle that had been sacrificed to Poseidon. The custom, as described by Homer and Hesiod, was to cut off the thigh pieces, wrap them in fat, and burn them for the god. The worshippers feasted on the remainder of the meat accompanied by plenty of wine.[10] Many layers of ash and burnt bones mixed with fragments of pottery cups were recovered in excavations along the eastern edge of the plateau where the long stone altar of Poseidon stood from the seventh century onwards. The material had been used in terracing that, from the eighth through the fourth centuries, enlarged the space along the altar.[11] The worshippers seem to have left their cups, along with pitchers and bowls for mixing wine with water, near the place of sacrifice, possibly after having deliberately broken them in an act of consecration.[12]

On the basis of ritual continuity, we can suppose that the early sacrifices were performed along the eastern edge of the plateau where the altar was later built. Although most of the early remains were cleared away in later times, some soil containing ash and burnt bones mixed with Early Iron Age

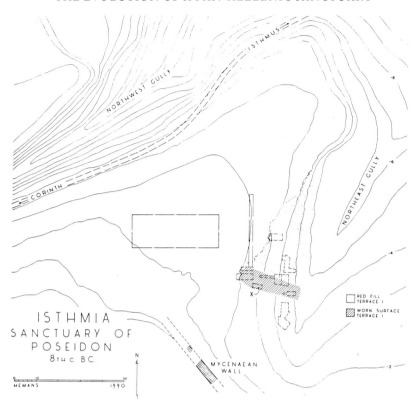

Figure 8.2 Isthmia, sanctuary of Poseidon in the eighth century BC.

sherds was found along the west side of the altar.[13] We cannot know what led the first people to choose precisely this place for their offerings to Poseidon, but it was not unusual for sacrifices at that period to be made on a rock surface without an altar.[14] Mountain-tops were the scene of sacrifices to Zeus, the sky god, and their remains in the form of ash, burnt bones and broken cups are comparable to what we find at Isthmia. In some places the material survives to this day.[15]

A change in the sacrificial area and perhaps in the festival itself took place in the second half of the eighth century. The first large, sloping terrace was laid down along the eastern edge of the plateau, shown by dots in Figure 8.2. The thin layer of fine red soil appears to have been used more to define the sacred area than to modify the natural slope of bedrock.[16] Only one portion of the terrace along the southern edge shows sign of activity. It is indicated by hatching in Figure 8.2. The surface, *c.* 8m wide and 28m long, is covered by a compact layer of small stones, between which we found fragments of dining wares. In a depression at the south edge of the floor more vessels including storage jars were mixed in a dark, soft soil that betrays a garbage

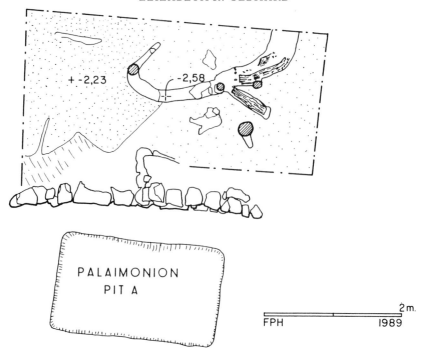

+ -2,23   -2,58

PALAIMONION
PIT A

FPH   1989

2 m.

Figure 8.3 Isthmia, sanctuary of Poseidon. Detail of groove and postholes in the eighth-century terrace shown in Figure 8.2.

dump. It appears, then, that feasting took place on the stone surface and refuse was discarded to one side. The west end of the floor next to the plateau and place of sacrifice lacks the stones and compact surface of the eastern section, and fewer sherds were recovered there although they were of fine fabric and broken into small pieces (most under 0.01m). The difference in quantity and quality of pottery at the two ends of the terrace suggests that some division may have existed among the worshippers, possibly of rank. If so, the less numerous but more privileged persons may have dined next to the plateau where the sacrifices took place. In the same place there are traces of a small feature, marked X on Figure 8.2 and shown in greater detail in Figure 8.3. The remains, not fully excavated, consist of a curved groove and a number of postholes that were covered by three pieces of charred wood (Figure 8.3).[17] The wood may have belonged to a table or container for offerings; the holes could have held supports for a small shelter or tent.[18]

The offerings of the Early Iron Age are simple and few in number, most of them belonging to the eighth century. In addition to these are the drinking cups that may themselves have been left as gifts to the god. Of the other objects most numerous are small, handmade terracotta bovoid figurines, that seem to be unique to the sanctuary.[19] By the end of the century a few richer dedications appear in the form of bronze tripods, arms and armour, but most gifts to Poseidon were simple offerings of Corinthian manufacture that are more likely to have been left by the common man than by aristocrats for the purpose of display. This is in marked contrast to the votives of the same period dedicated to Zeus at Olympia, to Apollo at Delphi and to Hera at Perachora.[20]

Homer's description of the sacrifice to Poseidon at Pylos seems to reflect the kind of occasion that took place at early Isthmia (*Od.* 3.1–384). From the poet's narrative we draw the conclusion that, after completing the burnt offerings, they spent the day drinking and feasting and returned to the city at nightfall. No temple, built altar, or votive dedications are mentioned, and we are given the impression of an open place where an assembly of citizens made public sacrifice to the sea god. There is no indication in the poem whether this was a regular festival or an offering made for some special purpose. If the place of sacrifice at Pylos had ever existed and were now excavated, the remains would be much the same as those found at Isthmia, burnt animal bones and terracotta cups mixed with ash.[21]

The Archaic sanctuary

The construction of the first temple with its altar and lightly built *temenos* wall marks the beginning of the architectural development of the sanctuary (Figure 8.5). Although these monuments had been known from Broneer's excavations, the 1989 season brought to light new evidence for their construction date, for the plan of the temple, and for the course of the *temenos* wall.[22] Within the temple the foundation trenches for the north, east, and west colonnades and for a portion of the south wall of the cella were found to be largely intact. In spite of earlier doubts, we can now be certain that the peristyle was part of the original building.

Along the outer edge of the foundation for the cella wall we discovered a series of ten regularly spaced pits, *c.* 2.26m apart on centres, from which blocks had been removed after the destruction of the building. The sequence had originally extended along the entire wall. Their purpose became clear when we examined the heavily burnt wall blocks from the temple and saw that many of them have strips of unburnt surface crossing the outer face. Evidently an upright member, 0.32–0.37m wide, had protected the wall from fire when the temple was destroyed.[23] The foundations along the wall, then, supported a series of uprights or piers that were standing against the wall at the time of the fire.[24] Since they were probably related to the support system for the roof, their spacing would have corresponded to that of the colonnade and thus gives us the interaxial distance between the columns. Hemans restores a colonnade of 7 by 18 columns. The overall length of the temple was *c.* 39.25m and its width 14.10 to 14.40m; the cella was *c.* 32.28m long by 7.90m wide.[25] In the absence of any suitably large stone columns despite the large percentage of other blocks preserved, it seems likely that they and the entablature were made of wood. There is no apparent evidence for Doric features, such as triglyphs and metopes. A construction date for the temple between 690 BC and 650 BC is revealed by pottery in a construction layer beneath the first floor of the colonnade.[26] Two upper floors show that there were subsequent remodellings, one in the middle of the sixth century and another toward the end of the century. The date of the disastrous conflagration that destroyed the temple can be placed around 470 BC on the basis of the latest pottery vessels that are heavily burnt.[27]

The walls of the cella between the piers were covered with white stucco, traces of which still adhere to the surface along the edges of the unburnt strips. Broneer also recovered small pieces of heavily burnt stone on which there is stucco with painted designs that he restored as panels filling the space between the piers on the outside wall of the cella.[28] Most of the chips are too small to reveal what subject had been represented, but evidently Geometric patterns, animals and probably human figures were included. The one recognizable element is the mane of a horse belonging to a beast that would have been about 0.32m high. It might thus be more likely that the painted decoration took the form of a frieze with a single row of figures and a border at top and bottom. The total height of such a frieze would have been about 0.64m. If it had decorated the outside of the building, it would have run between the piers in panels 1.94m long.[29] On the other hand, none of the painted stucco was found on a wall block, so it is not certain that the painted decoration belonged to the Archaic Temple. If it did embellish the temple, it was very likely on the outside of the building because the inside surfaces of all the wall blocks were completely destroyed by the fire.

At the time of the fire the inside of the temple and its deep eastern porch were filled with offerings, most of which were badly damaged in the blaze. They included figurines of bronze and terracotta, chariots and horse trappings, small oil containers of clay and bronze and large storage vessels whose charred interiors reveal that they too contained oil. It is fortunate that perhaps the most elaborate dedication stood outside the cella in the northeast corner of the peristyle, well away from the centre of the fire. The monument is a great marble basin (*perirrhanterion*) supported on an elaborate stand, the base for which is still in place (Figure 8.4).[30] Broneer recovered many fragments of the stand and basin from the debris of the temple, and the restored monument is now on display in the Isthmia Museum.[31] The bowl, 1.24m in diameter, rests on a ring supported by four women, each standing on the back of a lion and holding in one hand the lion's leash and in the other its tail. The ring between the women is decorated with rams' heads. The exquisite stone carving is further embellished by paint on the hair, face, and clothing of the figures. The worn surfaces of its handles and rim bear witness to the many people that reached into it, presumably for water to purify themselves before entering the cella. The style of the carving makes the

Figure 8.4 Archaic *perirrhanterion* from the temple of Poseidon. Isthmia museum.

monument contemporary with the temple, or a little later. We cannot be certain where it originally stood, however, since its base was moved when the third floor was put into the peristyle, but the absence of weathering tells us that it was never exposed to the elements. Although basins of this type were popular in the seventh century, the Isthmian *perirrhanterion* is outstanding in the intricacy of its design and quality of execution. I think we can safely conclude that it was a major dedication.

The thin *temenos* wall enclosing the temple and altar appears to have followed the contours of the plateau (Figure 8.5). Broneer uncovered remains of it at the north side, and more traces were found in 1989 that showed it bordered the Corinth–Isthmus road and the east side of the altar.[32] At the south, where the temple lay close to the original base of the Rachi, the wall ran along the bottom of the slope within a few feet of the peristyle.[33] At the west no trace of the wall remains, but it may have followed the same line as the Early Roman *temenos* wall (Figure 8.1). When the games were begun and the stadium built in the early sixth century, a section of the wall was removed along the east side of the altar to make way for a ramp leading to the stadium.[34] Later in the century expansion of the eastern terrace moved the limits of the *temenos* still farther east. At that time two formal gateways were built at the entrances to the *temenos*: one on the north for those who

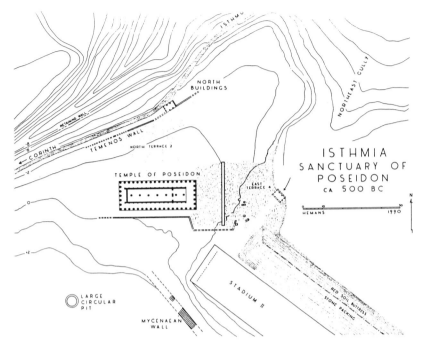

Figure 8.5 Isthmia, sanctuary of Poseidon *c.* 500 BC.

approached the sanctuary along the Corinth–Isthmus road, and another on the east, opposite the temple, for those going directly to the altar and stadium (Figure 8.5). Broneer uncovered the foundations belonging to the north propylon, and we identified the bedding for the east gateway in 1989.[35]

The principal construction of the sixth century was the stadium. In its placement close to the altar it seems to have been modelled on the early stadium at Olympia (Figure 8.5). In both shrines the place of sacrifice and the contest area were linked by an open space that may have been used for ceremonies.[36] At Isthmia, however, locating the stadium near the altar entailed much greater effort than at Olympia. Since the ground at its south-eastern end lay over 5m below the starting line at the west, the Corinthians, in order to create a moderately level track of the appropriate length, were forced to alter the landscape by cutting back the lower slope of the Rachi and hauling in earth for terracing.[37] A construction date in the second quarter of the sixth century is suggested by the traditional date of the first games and by deposits cleared in 1989.[38] We also found that, as part of the same project, a terraced walkway with a concave face was built between the track and the altar.[39] We may imagine that processions of officials and athletes moved along it from the place of sacrifice to the stadium.

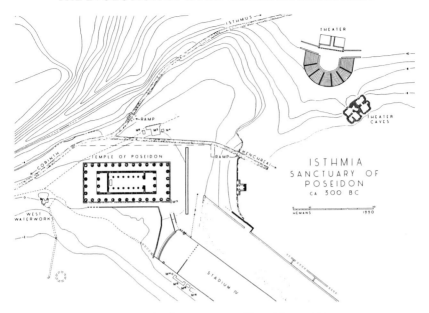

Figure 8.6 Isthmia, sanctuary of Poseidon *c.* 300 BC.

Within a few years more space for spectators was provided by a larger terrace along the track and an extension of the sacrificial area that incorporated the original walkway into a much larger platform stretching across the entire east side of the plateau (Figure 8.5).[40] The Isthmian stadium seems to be an early example of a racecourse that was composed almost entirely of earth terraces, over 100 cubic metres of soil just for the track alone. The labour required to move that amount of soil and rock represented a major investment in the facilities of the sanctuary.

The Classical and Hellenistic sanctuary

After the Archaic temple was destroyed by fire in *c.* 470 BC, a larger temple of the Doric order and Classical proportions was soon built on the same place. Although the building was destroyed in Late Antiquity, Broneer was able to restore its plan. The temple had a peristyle of 6 by 13 columns, a *pronaos* and *opisthodomos* with two columns *in antis*, and, in the fifth century, a highly unusual, single row of columns through the centre of the cella.[41] Fire struck again in 390 BC, apparently causing extensive damage.[42] When the temple was rebuilt, it received a new roof, *sima*, and probably many new columns. The interior colonnade was changed to a conventional double row of supports (Figure 8.6). The long altar was rebuilt and enlarged to conform to the wider proportions of the new building.[43]

The fifth century was a period of great building activity at Isthmia. In addition to the Classical temple and its new altar, the spectator embankment of the stadium underwent a major expansion and the broad terrace along the east side of the altar was raised to make it level with the plateau.[44] The spectator area now encroached well into the space in front of the altar that previously would have been reserved for activities connected with the sacrifices. Two separate entrances were built leading from the altar to the stadium, and the opening to one of them was evidently restricted since it was closed by a special gate. More will be said about these entrances in the discussion of the *temenos* boundaries. Most visitors reached their seats by means of ramps built against the outside retaining wall of the spectator embankment.[45] An elaborate system of starting gates controlled by ropes embedded in a triangular pavement was an early experiment in providing a clean start to the races, but it appears not to have been a success and was replaced in the next century by a conventional starting line.[46] Monument bases, presumably for statues, lined the south-western edge of the track (Figure 8.6).

An early type of simple, rectilinear theatre was built on the lower plateau of the sanctuary some time before the fire of 390 BC.[47] The auditorium was remodelled towards the end of the fourth century in a form that combined a curved centre section with straight rows of seats at either side (Figure 8.6). The wooden, two-storey scene-building of that period included a *proskenion* with 11 movable panels between the uprights. Each panel was provided with a pivot that enabled it to swing open.[48] The second auditorium had perhaps 12 rows of seats that would have accommodated approximately 1,550 persons. To judge from the later programme, the theatre served as a place for musical rather than dramatic contests.[49] Their popularity is attested in the Hellenistic period by the fact that a branch of the performers' guild known as the Artists of Dionysos had its base at Isthmia and Nemea.[50]

The main crowds, however, were attracted to the athletic events, with the result that by the end of the fourth century a larger stadium was constructed. The new racecourse, located in a valley at some distance to the south-east of the central plateau, was much larger than its predecessor. Instead of earthen embankments, the sides of the valley provided natural slopes on which the spectators sat to watch the games (Figure 8.1). The stadium remains largely unexcavated, covered today by orange groves, but through sinking deep trenches and tunnelling between them Broneer exposed enough of the curbs and starting lines to reveal the plan.[51] The terracing for the old stadium was moved away, and it seems likely that some of the fill was used to build up the slopes along the new track.

The principal change in the sacrificial area was the construction of a new, monumental gateway to replace the Archaic propylon at the outer edge of the eastern terrace (Figure 8.6).[52] Only the massive foundations of the portal are preserved, but their size is impressive. The side of the gate facing the temple was 10m long, and it appears to have been free-standing. The location of the new construction towards the south side of the *temenos* is interesting. We might imagine that it would have been more appropriate to move it northward, opposite the centre of the Classical temple, but instead the entrance was built next to its Archaic predecessor. Although the passage in the absence of the stadium was now turned to face the temple, the position of the gate remained fixed. Even in Roman times after the Hellenistic propylon had been demolished, another gate was built in the same location, using the same foundations. Perhaps it was the eastern approach to the plateau that called for the gate to continue in the same place, or the entrance itself was felt to be part of the unchanging tradition of the sanctuary.

On the north side of the sacred precinct we find the same sense of continuity. A large heavily built, T-shaped platform of suitable size and Classical date (marked M5 on Figure 8.6) appears to have supported a gateway that replaced the north propylon after a shift in the Corinth–Isthmus road.[53] The orientation of the foundation with respect to the temple is similar to that of the earlier gateway, but it lies a few metres closer to the temple. No new *temenos* wall seems to have been constructed, but there may have been *horos* stones such as were found at Nemea.[54] The bases that lie on either side of the foundation would have supported monuments lining the road.

The Corinth–Isthmus road continued to be heavily used by wheeled carts, their drivers moving ever farther south onto the temple plateau in search of a firm surface. To aid their passage, two ramps were constructed: one just west of the Archaic propylon for the Corinth–Isthmus route; the other for a branch road that separated from the main track and descended from the plateau at the north-east corner of the sacrificial area (Figure 8.6). In 1989 we uncovered the well-built bedding and four surfaces belonging to the latter ramp. The depth of the ruts and cement-like consistency of the lower layers attest to the amount of traffic that it carried during the fourth century, at least some of it probably related to the reconstruction of the Classical temple after the fire of 390 BC. The road continued in use in later centuries, moving southward after the sanctuary was destroyed in 146 BC, so that it crossed the foundations of the long altar. When the sanctuary was rebuilt again in the first century AD, the road was moved back again to the north side of the plateau where, in the final phase of the *temenos*, it was allowed to pass through the sacred precinct.

ISTHMIA AS A TRADITIONAL GREEK ASSEMBLY PLACE

To anyone sailing westward in the Saronic Gulf or travelling on the old Scironian Road from Athens to the Peloponnesus, the temple of Poseidon, seen with Acrocorinth in the distance, would have been a landmark. The sanctuary itself lay immediately adjacent to the road on the first high ground after the coastal plain. In fact, in all periods of its history the road continued so close to the temple that the sanctuary was a roadside shrine. It seems inescapable that a shrine in this location, easily accessible by land and sea, would have been a natural meeting place. A brief summary of the evidence for foreigners (i.e. non-Corinthians) coming to the shrine will show to what extent natural advantage was indeed utilized in practice. For the early periods we are limited largely to pottery and dedications to reveal who visited the sanctuary, and we can only suppose that they may have come there for regional gatherings. We are on firmer ground for later times, from the fifth century on, when some of the assemblies that took place there are mentioned in the historical records.

Although Isthmia was certainly a Corinthian shrine and everything in the archaeological record points to Corinthian control at all times, at most periods in its history some portion of the vessels that were used and left at the shrine were brought there from outside the Corinthia.[55] In the earliest years of sacrificial activity the imports came from the eastern side of the Isthmus from as far away as Attica. They grew most numerous about 900 BC and continued in lesser quantities throughout the eighth century. Although several possible explanations for them come to mind, it may well be that visitors brought their own cups, bowls and pitchers for use at the sacrificial feast and then left them as dedications. Most of the worshippers, to judge from the simplicity of the pottery and other offerings as described above in the section on monuments of the Early Iron Age, were not aristocrats desiring to make a show but common men. Perhaps on the day of Poseidon's festival the Corinthians joined their neighbours for a celebration at the shrine, or it may be that travellers simply halted their journey to make offerings. If there were organized gatherings, Poseidon was the appropriate divinity since he seems to have been especially associated with assemblies. The Ionian League met at this period in his sanctuary on Mt Mycale, and his shrines were the scene of later regional gatherings on Calauria (modern Poros) and at Onchestos in Boeotia.[56]

Only towards the end of the eighth century did Poseidon begin to receive a few dedications that represent a higher level of investment in the shrine. The armour and weapons are of particular interest in that they were very likely part of soldiers' booty awarded to them after a successful campaign.[57] Isthmian Poseidon was second only to Zeus at Olympia in dedications of arms and armour. During the seventh century the amount of arms and armour increased, and it reached its peak between 550 BC and the temple fire in c. 470 BC. Since the greater part of the fragments was found at the north-west edge of the temple plateau, we can imagine that dozens of helmets, shields and cuirasses were conspicuously set up along the Corinth–Isthmus road. This prominent position suggests that the Isthmian shrine and festival had a political aspect that made it a place for the Corinthians to display their superiority in battle.[58] Such a message would have strengthened the impression of wealth and authority that was conveyed by the Archaic temple.

The decision to celebrate pan-Hellenic games at the Isthmian festival could have been politically motivated, and it certainly attracted more visitors to the shrine. There is some reason to believe that the Corinthians were the first to establish international contests modelled on the famous games at Olympia. The date was 582 BC, the second year of the 49th Olympiad, and within a few months the Amphictionic League held the first pan-Hellenic Pythian Games in honour of Apollo at Delphi.[59] The cycle of games was complete when, some years later (573 BC), the little city of Cleonai, backed by Argos, established international games to Nemean Zeus. The custom that victors in the three new festivals, like those in the venerable Olympic Games, received no prize of value but only a wreath, led to their being known as the holy or crown games. For their wreath the Corinthians selected a crown of pine in memory of Melikertes-Palaimon, for whose funeral, they said, Sisyphos celebrated the original contests.[60] The previously-established role of the Isthmian sanctuary as a central meeting place for neighbouring cities may well have contributed to the early success of the festival.

During the last part of the sixth century and the beginning of the fifth the routes across the Isthmus saw ever greater use, largely by armies marching between the Peloponnesus and mainland Greece. The area was fortified in 480 BC as the final line of defence against a Persian advance into southern Greece, and after the Battle of Salamis in the following year, the victorious Greeks sent Poseidon a captured Phoenician warship as a thanks-offering (Herodotus 8.121).[61] They then gathered at the Isthmian Sanctuary to decide who should be awarded the prize for excellence. Each general placed his vote on the altar, but they found no one had obtained first prize, since each had voted for himself, but all had given Themistocles second place (8.123).[62]

This was perhaps the last grand occasion witnessed by the venerable Archaic temple before the fire. Little is recorded about events during the rest of the century, although the games continued through the troubled years of the Peloponnesian War and its aftermath. In the ensuing conflicts between Argives and Spartans, each supported by a Corinthian faction, control of the prestigious sanctuary and its festival became a prize that was coveted by both sides. Xenophon records an attempted takeover that resulted in a double celebration of the games in 390 BC (*Hellenica* 4.5.4). The Spartan king, Agesilaus, at the head of an army marching towards the sanctuary, surprised the Argives and their Corinthian supporters just as they had completed the sacrifices. After the Argives departed in haste, the Spartans watched their Corinthian allies begin the rites anew and carry out a second performance of the festival. Whether the political strife surrounding the games was connected to the fire that broke out in the temple at the same time is impossible to tell, but the reduced amount of pottery and other objects belonging to the years following the fire suggests a decline in prosperity at the shrine.

Philip II inaugurated a new era. After the Greek defeat at Chaironeia in the winter of 338 BC, he called representatives from the cities to assemble at the Isthmian Games in the following spring to hear the common peace settlement. Shortly afterwards he again assembled them at the sanctuary to gain support for his intended expedition against Persia.[63] His subsequent assassination ended Philip's appearances at the sanctuary, but in the next two years Alexander called two meetings at Isthmia. The use of the sacred festivals for pan-Hellenic assemblies seems to have brought with it renewal of old buildings and construction of new ones. At Isthmia the temple of Poseidon was restored, the theatre extensively remodelled, and a new and larger stadium was provided to accommodate the ever larger crowds. If we are to judge from the pottery and the existence of a flourishing community of dyers and weavers nearby, the sanctuary entered a period of prosperity at the end of the fourth century that was to last for the next 100 years. Although there is no mention of particular occasions when the League again convened at Isthmia, the sanctuary seems to have continued to function as a place of public display since inscriptions recording treaties between the Hellenic League and the Macedonian King, Philip V, were erected at the north side of the *temenos* along the Corinth–Isthmus road. At the end of the third century, however, the sanctuary was caught in the middle of some unrecorded military skirmish, and the temple sustained considerable damage.[64] When Philip was defeated by a combined Roman and Greek army, the victorious Roman general, Titus Quinctius Flamininus, called (in 196 BC) the most famous of all Isthmian assemblies to announce a proclamation of freedom for the Greek cities.

Livy (32.33) introduces his account of the event by explaining that the Isthmian Games were the meeting place and the market of Greece and Asia.[65] At that particular festival, however, not only did the Greeks gather from many places as was customary, but they came full of expectation about what was going to happen to Greece. When they took their seats in the stadium expecting the commencement of the games, the herald with a trumpeter came into the middle of the racetrack and announced that the Greek states would be free from taxes and free to be governed according to their ancestral laws. Plutarch (*Vita Flaminini* 10.3–11) adds that the audience afterwards paid no attention to the contending athletes but shouted so loudly that ravens flying overhead fell to the track. It was this glorious occasion that the emperor Nero tried to recreate at the same festival 263 years later.[66]

From this brief overview of the evidence for inter-state gatherings we can see the extent to which the Isthmian sanctuary served as a meeting place. The small area of its *temenos* enclosing the temple and the apparent absence of elaborate monuments such as are found at Olympia and Delphi emphasize the importance of the stadium as the focus for these gatherings. The connection that Livy made between assembly place and market place is probably significant in explaining the popularity of the Isthmian Games and of the sanctuary as a venue for international meetings. The harbour at the east end of the Isthmus (Schnoinous) and the paved roadway of the *diolkos* that facilitated trans-shipment of goods and sometimes ships, attracted commercial activity to the Isthmus. As was suggested at the beginning of this section, the presence of imported pottery from the Early Iron Age may be an indication that the meetings are as old as the shrine itself. When a leader, such as Philip II, desired to arouse pan-Hellenic spirit for a campaign against the Persians, a general, such as Flamininus, to make an impression on the Greeks, and an emperor, such as Nero, wanted to recreate past glories, they called an assembly at the Isthmian Games.

Sacred space

The scene of Flamininus' proclamation was the Hellenistic stadium, and we can imagine that an avenue (as yet undiscovered) linked the racecourse with the *temenos* of Poseidon. In earlier periods, however, the stadium lay so close to the temple plateau that the spectator embankment, in the second half of the fifth century, extended to within 9m of the altar. At that juncture the Corinthians apparently felt the need to devise a way to separate the stadium from the *temenos* while still allowing free movement between them. From the solutions they adopted we can see something of the honour they accorded the space around the altar and how they sought to provide boundaries for it that would restrict but not exclude passage between the ritual and athletic areas.

Two walkways led into the stadium from the space immediately surrounding the altar. The smaller of the two was a ramp with its entrance only 5m from the temple and its floor sloping down to the north-west corner of the stadium behind the starting pavement (Figure 8.6).[67] Stone walls enclosed the sides of the passage, and at the top sockets cut into bedrock received three wooden posts that formed a double gateway. The ramp's proximity to the temple and altar, narrow width (less than 2m) and gate at the top suggest that it was not open to the public but was reserved for special persons. A clue to their identity comes from a similarly placed passage to the later stadium at Olympia that Pausanias calls the 'Hidden Entrance', through which, he says, officials and athletes entered the stadium (6.20.8).[68] The Isthmian ramp very likely had a similar function.

The second entrance passage leading to the stadium was discovered in 1989. When we found a base with a posthole cut into the upper surface lying opposite the north-west corner of the stadium and saw two similar bases excavated by Broneer, we realized that there had been a line of bases along the outside of the spectator embankment (Figure 8.6). The bedding for a fourth base was uncovered next to the racecourse, showing that the series had extended all the way to the track, and there were very likely more than four in the original row. The blocks would have held tall wooden posts set in place at the time of the festival to separate the space along the altar from the passage into the stadium. The northernmost base is the largest, about 0.75m on a side, with a cutting in the top (0.21 by 0.20 by 0.32m deep) that would have held a wooden post perhaps 3m high. To steady the post and prevent wear on the soft limestone, a collar of hard wood or metal was fitted into a recess in the surface. There is even a notch for a wedge to be fitted into one side of the hole to keep the pole from swaying.[69] Thus, along the entrance to the stadium we can imagine a series of wooden posts that were perhaps decorated with garlands and fillets at the time of the festival. The decorative barrier separated the passage from the space around the altar. The width of the passageway was about twice that of the walled ramp, but only a limited number of persons could have passed through it at any one time. It is likely, therefore, that it too was not open to the general public, but was reserved for a certain group of persons.

At the edge of the racecourse the line of posts turns westward and runs along one end of the starting area. The four bases here are smaller than those bordering the embankment, and the posthole in the top measures only 0.08 by 0.10m and is without a collar.[70] The posts would have been correspondingly slighter and shorter than the other set, but they continued the barrier surrounding the southern end of the altar. The line is completed by the eastern wall of the ramp. Through these arrangements separate entrances into the stadium were provided for special groups of people. Officials and athletes would have processed from the altar to the starting line through the walled ramp, entering it by way of the double gate at the top. The wider and more open passage may have been used by those of lesser rank who enjoyed special seating privileges. Both walkways were carefully set apart from the sacred space surrounding the altar, but each was entered from the area immediately next to it. The temporary installation of wooden posts may be an indication that there were ceremonies at other times for which the posts were unnecessary and perhaps an impediment.

The central portion of the sanctuary in Classical and later times is a space where people gathered for sacrifices but where few monuments, other than the temple, were erected. The popularity of the Isthmian Games, the market at the Isthmus, and the political assemblies held in conjunction with the festival may have overshadowed the ritual activities devoted to Poseidon.

THE CULT OF MELIKERTES-PALAIMON

When a new institution was established, the customary account was that it had originally been founded by a hero or god but had fallen into disuse and was now being revived. The traditional stories surrounding the beginnings of the pan-Hellenic festivals follow this pattern. For Isthmia, the earliest reference to the founding myth occurs in an ode of Pindar that is unfortunately only partially preserved in a later work.[71] The Nereids, sea-nymphs of Poseidon, address the king of Corinth: 'Sisyphos, son of Aeolos, raise up a far-famed prize for the child, Melikertes, who has perished.' Although brief, the fragment makes it clear that Pindar was making Sisyphos the founder of the Isthmian Games as funeral games for the infant Melikertes-Palaimon. Later commentators on Pindar give a fuller account of the story and several variations. Plutarch, in one of his after-dinner conversations, includes a discussion of the Isthmian wreath in which he quotes a number of earlier authors who mention Melikertes and the games.[72] The hero thus appears to have been firmly associated with Isthmia by the first half of the fifth century, and it seems likely that his is the myth that the Corinthians told at the time they started the games.

One founding myth for the Nemean Games was similarly focused on the death of an infant, Opheltes-Archemoros, and his funeral games, in that case celebrated by Adrastus, leader of the fabled expedition against Thebes.[73] At Olympia Herakles was said to have celebrated the first Olympic Games next to the tomb of Pelops (Pindar, *Olympian Ode* 10.24–77); at Delphi, however, Apollo founded his own games after slaying the Python.[74] Heroes at Isthmia, Nemea and Olympia then became patrons of the games and received offerings at the sanctuary. The shrines for Pelops and Opheltes that have been excavated take the form of an open, five-sided *peribolos* located not far from the central area. Since the earliest material associated with them belongs to the sixth century, it is probable that they owe their foundation to the institution of the games and do not represent an earlier cult.[75] At Isthmia we have not yet found a similar enclosure for Melikertes in the Greek period, but, since not all of the central plateau has been cleared, it may yet come to light in a future season.[76] It is probably right, on analogy with the shrines at Nemea and Olympia, to infer that one existed, although it may have been located farther from the central *temenos* than they were.

Melikertes-Palaimon, a child drowned at sea whose body was rescued by a dolphin and deposited on the Isthmus for burial, was a suitable companion for Poseidon. Although his own fate casts a somewhat dubious light on his qualifications as a saviour of sailors, he is invoked as 'protector of ships' in Euripides (*Iphigeneia in Tauros* 270–1). His mother, who became the sea nymph Ino-Leukothea, had a similar function, and her cult was more widespread. In a famous exploit she gave Odysseus her scarf to save him from drowning (*Odyssey* 5.333–5). Another aspect of Melikertes-Palaimon may have been his connection with the fertility of the earth and with the underworld.[77] Poseidon himself had a similar side through his relation to earthquakes, springs and other aspects of the ground, and, as noted earlier, at Isthmia he was associated with Demeter as well as with Kore, Pluto, Eueteria, Artemis and Dionysos.[78]

An alternative myth made Theseus the founder of the games, either in emulation of Herakles at Olympia or in expiation for killing Sinis, the Pine-bender.[79] This story may have been circulated later than the one about Sisyphos and Melikertes, since Theseus was primarily an Athenian hero and the sanctuary, on the basis of the pottery and architecture, appears always to have been firmly under Corinthian control.[80]

In conclusion, we have seen that the Isthmian sanctuary, while the oldest of the pan-Hellenic shrines, seems to have remained relatively simple in terms of its architectural development. The temple of Poseidon stood at its centre, the focal point of the place throughout its history. To travellers by land and sea it was a marker of Corinthian territory, wealth and power. The centrality of the shrine and its location beside the Corinth–Isthmus road made it a natural place for pan-Hellenic games, for a market and for inter-state assemblies. The mass of dedications of arms and armour in the Archaic period reveals its early importance as a political centre, where the symbols of Corinthian achievement were displayed. When the Isthmian Games were founded in the sixth century, they soon attracted crowds that rivalled the famous Olympic festival. Sacrifices, feasting and contests characterized the sanctuary; travellers, embassies and finally the great pan-Hellenic assemblies made it 'the meeting place and market of Greece and Asia'.

NOTES

1 The excavations were directed by the author under the auspices of the American School of Classical Studies at Athens for the University of Chicago and with permission of the Greek Ministry of Culture. They were supported by a grant from the National Endowment for the Humanities and by private donations. The excavation report is divided chronologically, so that Part I includes material from the Mycenaean period to *c.* 470 BC and Part II will cover the remainder through the third century AD. See E. R. Gebhard and F. P. Hemans, 'The University of Chicago excavations at Isthmia: I', *Hesperia* 61 (1992) 1–77; hereafter 'Excavations: I'. For the earlier excavations, see O. Broneer, *Isthmia*, I, *The Temple of Poseidon* (Princeton 1971), hereafter *Isthmia* I; idem, *Isthmia*, II, *Topography and Architecture* (Princeton 1973), hereafter *Isthmia* II; idem, *Isthmia*, III, *Terracotta Lamps* (Princeton 1977), hereafter *Isthmia* III; M. Sturgeon, *Isthmia*, IV, *The Sculpture, 1952–67* (Princeton 1988), hereafter *Isthmia* IV; E. R. Gebhard, *The Theater at Isthmia* (Chicago 1973), hereafter *Theater*. Forthcoming, I. Raubitschek, *Isthmia*, VII, *Metal Objects, 1952–1967, 1989*. Studies in preparation for the *Isthmia* series include: C. Morgan, *The Early Iron Age Sanctuary and the Mycenaean Settlement*; K. Arafat, *Archaic Pottery, c. 700–550 BC*; J. Bentz, *Late Archaic to Early Hellenistic Pottery*; J. Hayes, *Late Hellenistic and Roman Pottery*; A. Jackson, *Arms and Armour*; D. Mitten, 'Terracotta figurines'; L. Houghtalin, 'Coins'. Fritz Hemans, who served as architect and assistant director of the excavations, is preparing a new study on the Archaic temple of Poseidon. In 1976 I succeeded Broneer as director of the

University of Chicago Excavations at Isthmia. I am greatly indebted to my colleagues who are working on the final publications of the Isthmia material for sharing with me the results of their research.

2 Versions of this paper were read at an open meeting of the American School of Classical Studies at Athens in November, 1990, and at the Ashmolean Museum in Oxford in December, 1991. I am grateful to W. D. E. Coulson, to J. J. Coulton and to many others who offered helpful comments and criticisms. I also benefited from discussions with Nanno Marinatos, Christiane Sourvinou-Inwood and George Huxley who suggested the original focus.

3 Pausanias gives several Peloponnesian examples: in Arcadia near Thelpusa (8.25.4–8) and in a cave near Phigalia (8.42.1–3). Their daughter was held by some to be Despoina, worshipped with Demeter at Lycosura in a sanctuary that included an altar to Horse Poseidon as father of Despoina (8.37.1–12). Outside Mantinea a grove of Demeter lies above the sanctuary of Horse Poseidon (8.10.1), while in the Argolid near Troezen a temple to Demeter Law-giver stands above the sanctuary of Poseidon Nurturer. At Eleusis Poseidon appears as Pater (Pausanias 1.38.6) Their association in cult is taken for granted by Plutarch (*Quaest. Conviv.* 4.4.3).

4 *Isthmia* II, 113; *Isthmia* IV, 116. Votives appropriate to Demeter but uninscribed have also been recovered in a settlement south of the sanctuary on a ridge known locally as the Rachi. The earliest belong to the sixth century BC; see V. Anderson-Stojanović, 'Cult and industry at Isthmia: a shrine on the Rachi', (abstract) *AJA* 92 (1988) 268–9.

5 *Isthmia* II, 113–16; most recently D. Geagan, 'The Isthmian dossier of P. Licinius Priscus Juventianus', *Hesperia* 58 (1989) 350–3. The spacing of the letters on the stone suggests that Demeter may have had her own temple, while Kore, Dionysos and Artemis could have shared a shrine. In Athens, Eueteria, 'Good Harvest', was associated with grain and thus Demeter. She was represented by a statue, now missing, whose base bore an honorary decree of 299/8 BC connected with a large benefaction of grain to the city; A. E. Raubitschek, 'Greek inscriptions', *Hesperia* 35 (1966) 242–3. Raubitschek suggests that the statue was perhaps dedicated to Demeter. I am indebted to the author for drawing my attention to the monument.

6 The rectangular area now surrounding the temple was not formed until the second century AD. At that time a level surface for the enlarged *temenos* was created by cutting back the lower slope of the Rachi and filling in the northwest gully.

7 *Theater* 9–25. A Roman bath now covers the Classical pool and other provisions for bathing in the Greek period. The bath was uncovered by Paul Clement; *JHS* 92 (1972), *AR* 1971–2, 7–8; *ArchDelt* 28 (1973) 145–7. His work is continued by Timothy Gregory for Ohio State University. Other buildings related to the games very likely stood on the lower plateau.

8 *Isthmia* II, 46–66.

9 I am grateful to Catherine Morgan for sharing with me the results of her study of the Early Iron Age pottery and for many long discussions about the early days of the sanctuary. She presents a summary of the material in 'Excavations: I', 18–22.

10 The sacrifice at Pylos in *Od.* 3.5–244 is an example of such an occasion.

11 One layer of ash redeposited in the sacrificial terrace and embankment of the Early Stadium amounted to about 1.44 cubic metres. Of a total of 2,439 sherds (fine-wares), 86 per cent belonged to the Early Iron Age, and the remaining were early Archaic. Of the 398 bones, 94 per cent were burnt; of the burnt portion, 27.5 per cent were cattle-sized, the remainder sheep/goat-sized. I am indebted to

David Reese for his analysis of the faunal material. The contents of the early sacrifical ash deposits are summarized in 'Excavations: I', 67, 72, 75.

12 The custom of breaking cups after the meal may have been widespread, since the very fragmentary condition of Early Iron Age pottery at Isthmia is similar to that found at other sanctuaries of the period; J. N. Coldstream, *Geometric Greece* (London, 1977) 332.

13 'Excavations: I', 15–16; 41–2.

14 D. W. Rupp, 'Reflections on the development of altars in the eighth century BC', in R. Hägg, ed., *The Greek Renaissance of the Eighth Century BC: Tradition and Innovation* (Stockholm 1983) 101–7.

15 Three of the shrines are located on the borders of Corinthian territory: Mt Apesas, west of Corinth, J. R. Wiseman, *The Land of the Ancient Corinthians* (Göteborg 1978) 106; fig. 143; Mt Kokkygion, M. L. Zimmerman Munn, 'The Zeus sanctuary on Mt Kokkygion above Hermion, Argolis', (abstract) *AJA* 90 (1986) 192–3); Mt Arachnaion in the territory of Epidauros, D. W. Rupp, 'The altars of Zeus and Hera on Mt Arachnaion in the Argeia, Greece', *JFA* 3 (1976) 261–8.

16 'Excavations: I', 12–18.

17 The groove is 0.12 to 0.16m deep, 0.08 to 0.40m wide, and has a maximum length revealed so far of 2.60m. The postholes range between 0.10 to 0.22m in diameter, 0.10 to 0.30m in depth, and some have a smaller hole cut into the bottom.

18 U. Kron suggests that tents were used for dining near the altar at the Heraion on Samos, 'Kultmahle im Heraion von Samos archaischer Zeit', in R. Hägg, N. Marinatos and G. C. Nordquist, eds, *Early Greek Cult Practice* (Stockholm 1988) 144, nn. 58, 59.

19 David Mitten and Catherine Morgan kindly furnished this information.

20 For a brief survey of early votives, see J. N. Coldstream, *Geometric Greece* (London 1977) 332–8. C. Morgan discusses the economics of dedication in *Athletes and Oracles: The Transformation of Olympia and Delphi in the Eighth Century BC* (Cambridge 1990) 191–203. For the sanctuary of Hera at Perachora, see H. Payne, *Perachora* I (Oxford 1940); T. J. Dunbabin, *Perachora* II (Oxford 1962). Publication of the Isthmian metal votives is forthcoming in the Isthmian volume by the late Isabelle Raubitschek.

21 E. Gebhard, 'Evidence for Corinthian control of the Isthmian sanctuary', in Colloquium, 'Origins of the polis: Homer and the monuments revisited', chaired by Ian Morris, Joint Session of the American Philological Association and the Archaeological Institute of America, Annual Meeting, Chicago, December, 1991; (abstract) *AJA* 96 (1992) 355.

22 *Isthmia* I, 3–56. I am indebted to Fritz Hemans for sharing with me his preliminary work on a new reconstruction of the Archaic temple. His report on the discoveries from 1989 are included in 'Excavations: I', 25–40 (temple); 47–51 (*temenos* wall). See also F. Hemans, 'The Archaic roof tiles at Isthmia, a re-examination', *Hesperia* 58 (1989) 251–66.

23 *Isthmia* I, 35.

24 In the absence of blocks that could have belonged to such piers, Hemans suggests that they were made of wood and stood against the surface of the wall. See 'Excavations: I', 28–30, pl. 11d.

25 F. Hemans, 'New discoveries in the Archaic temple at Isthmia', (abstract) *AJA* 95 (1991) 301–2.

26 We are indebted to Karim Arafat for his analysis of the pottery; 'Excavations: I', 39.

27 Julie Bentz will discuss the evidence in Part II of the excavation report.

28 *Isthmia* I, 33–4, fig. 54, pls A–C.
29 E. Gebhard, 'Early Greek wall decoration and the Doric order', *Résumés, XIII Internationaler Kongress fur Klassische Archaeologie, Berlin, 24–30 Juli, 1988*, 175. The foot and other measures used in the design of the temple will be discussed in detail by Fritz Hemans, but it can be noted here that the cella may have been a hekatompedon, a hundred-footer, thus giving us a foot of 0.3228m, which is close to the foot of 0.3204m proposed by Broneer (*Isthmia* II, 63). The panels would then have been 6 feet long and perhaps 2 feet high.
30 *Isthmia* I, 11–12, pls 3, 8c; 'Excavations: I', 36–7, figs 8, 9. We discovered that, at the time of the fire, the base rested on the 3rd floor of the peristyle.
31 See Mary Sturgeon's description in *Isthmia* IV, 14–61, pls A, B, 1–26, with a discussion of parallel examples and bibliography.
32 *Isthmia* II, 10–11; 'Excavations: I', 47–51.
33 In this section the first course is largely intact. Although Broneer identified it as a terrace wall belonging to the Classical period, the finishing of the surfaces and incipient anathyrosis on the joining blocks so closely resemble workmanship on the Archaic temple and altar that the wall is surely contemporary with them; *Isthmia* II, 14; 'Excavations: I', 49.
34 'Excavations: I', 52–7; fig. 14.
35 North propylon: *Isthmia* II, 10–11; pl. 52a. Broneer assigns it to the Classical sanctuary, although an Archaic date now seems more likely; 'Excavations: I', 47. East gateway: Broneer excavated the bedding but did not recognize it as belonging to a gate. The cutting in bedrock lies at the east edge of the sacrificial terrace, just west of a monumental gateway belonging to the Hellenistic period (Figure 8.6). It is partially covered by the rear wall of the east stoa (Figure 8.1). The gate is discussed in 'Excavations: I', 73–4.
36 A. Mallwitz, 'Cult and competition locations at Olympia', in W. Rashke, ed., *The Archaeology of the Olympics*, (Madison, WI. 1988) 81–6, fig. 6.2.
37 For details, see E. R. Gebhard, 'The Early Stadium at Isthmia and the founding of the Isthmian Games', in W. Coulson and H. Kyrieleis, eds, *Proceedings of an International Symposium on the Olympic Games* (Athens 1992) 73–9; 'Excavations: I', 57–61, pl. 5, fig. 19.
38 Broneer calls it the Archaic Stadium and then the Earlier Stadium, *Isthmia* II, 46–55. We have adopted the name Early Stadium with phases I–IV; 'Excavations: I', 57–61.
39 The walkway is designated East Terrace 2; 'Excavations: I', 52–7, fig. 14.
40 Early Stadium II and East Terrace 3; 'Excavations: I', 61–70, figs 18, 19.
41 *Isthmia* I, 57–173, fig. 66, pl. 4.
42 Burned pieces of marble roof tiles and parts of the entablature and columns are easily identifiable in terraces belonging to the fourth century and later. The fire evidently destroyed the entire roof and upper part of the building, as well as much of the colonnade. Xenophon (*Hell.* 4.5.4) gives an account of the disaster to the effect that, on a cold spring night at the time of the Isthmian festival, Spartan soldiers camping on the heights to the north of the sanctuary saw the temple go up in flames but no one knew who started it.
43 The original altar, contemporary with the Archaic temple, was centred on its façade. An addition was then built on the north end so that it was centred on the Classical temple. The 1989 excavations confirmed a seventh century date for the first altar, thus placing its extension in the fifth century rather than the fourth as Broneer had originally suggested; *Isthmia* I, 98–100; 'Excavations: I', 41–2.
44 *Isthmia* II, 47–55; Early Stadia III and IV and East Terrace 6 will be discussed in Part II of the excavation report.

45 The retaining walls for the ramps, parallel to the outside wall of the embankment, were added shortly after the original construction but before the fire of 390 BC. Although Broneer did not identify them as ramps, the fact that the land drops off abruptly to the east made it necessary to provide some means of access for persons approaching the stadium from that side and ramps would have been appropriate. The walls were built in segments, suggesting that more than one ramp was provided; *Isthmia* II, 52–4, plan II.

46 *Isthmia* II, 49–52.

47 *Theater*, 24–6; E. R. Gebhard, 'The form of the orchestra in the Early Greek theater', *Hesperia* 43 (1974) 428–40.

48 *Theater*, 45–51, pl. VII.

49 *Theater*, 140.

50 A. Pickard-Cambridge, *The Dramatic Festivals of Athens*, 2nd edn, rev. by J. Gould and D. M. Lewis (Oxford 1968) 282–90.

51 *Isthmia* II, 55–64; plan VI.

52 *Isthmia* II, 15–17, plans II, V, pl. 7b. The surface of the final terrace has the same elevation as the floor of the gate. Results from the 1989 excavations in this area (East Terraces 7 and 8) will be discussed in Part II of the report.

53 Broneer mentions the possibility that the foundation may have belonged to a free-standing gate, *Isthmia* II, 12. Plan III shows its relation to the North propylon. Fritz Hemans will discuss new evidence in support of this suggestion in Part II of the excavation report. A base of similar size and shape but different construction is found near the temple of Zeus at Nemea (NU structure). Miller suggests that it held an equestrian monument on the basis of blocks built into a nearby Early Christian basilica; S. G. Miller, ed., *Nemea, A Guide to the Site and Museum* (Berkeley 1990) 85, 155–6.

54 Miller, ed., (*supra* n. 53) 159–60; *Isthmia* II, 69–72.

55 The quantities, derivations and implications of imports will be discussed by Catherine Morgan for the Early Iron Age; by Karim Arafat for the pottery of *c.* 700–550; by Julie Bentz for that of 550–200 and by John Hayes for the remainder to Late Antiquity.

56 For Poseidon as god of assemblies: W. Burkert, *Greek Religion, Archaic and Classical* (Oxford 1985) 136–9; for the Ionians meeting at Mt Mykale: Herodotus 1.141–3; C. J. Emlyn-Jones, *The Ionians and Hellenism* (London 1980) 17. For the Amphictiony at Calauria: Strabo 8.6.14; T. Kelly, 'The Calaurian Amphictiony', *AJA* (1966) 113–21. At Onchestos in Boeotia Poseidon is worshipped on a pass between Thebes and Haliartos where meetings of the Boeotian League were held in Hellenistic times, if not earlier; see Pausanias 9.26.5; A. Schachter, *Cults of Boiotia* (4 vols, London 1981–6), II, 207–21. I am indebted to John Camp for calling my attention to this sanctuary.

57 See A. Jackson, 'Arms and armour in the Panhellenic sanctuary of Poseidon at Isthmia', in Coulson and Kyrieleis, eds, (*supra* n. 37) 141–4. Jackson will further discuss this material in his volume on arms and armour.

58 For evidence of inter-state rivalry at shrines in the Early Iron Age, see A. Snodgrass, 'Interaction by design: the Greek city state', in C. Renfrew and J. Cherry, eds, *Peer Polity Interaction and Socio-political Change* (Cambridge 1986) 47–58; Morgan, *Athletes and Oracles* (*supra* n. 20) 16–25.

59 Solinus, 7.14. A Mosshammer summarizes the evidence but places the first pan-Hellenic celebration of the Pythian Games at Delphi before the first Isthmia, 'The date of the first Pythiad – again', *GRBS* 23 (1982) 22, n.14; pp. 24–5.

60 O. Broneer, 'The Isthmian victory crown', *AJA* 66 (1962) 259–63.

61 J. R. Wiseman, 'A trans-Isthmian fortification wall', *Hesperia* 32 (1963) 248–75;

idem, (*supra* n. 15) 59–62. N. G. L. Hammond, in *Cambridge Ancient History*, 2nd edn, vol. IV, 581–3, suggests that the Persians burnt the Archaic temple in 480, but the latest, heavily burnt pottery from the temple seems to belong to the next decade. Julie Bentz will discuss the evidence in Part II of the excavation report.

62 The account has the sound of a traditional anecdote; see W. How and J. Wells, *A Commentary on Herodotus* (Oxford 1912) vol. II, 276. For the voting procedure, Plutarch, *Per.* 32; Demosthenes, *De Cor.* 134.

63 J. R. Ellis, *Philip II and Macedonian Imperialism* (Princeton 1986) 204–9. The terms of the treaty establishing the Hellenic League prescribe that in peacetime the delegates are to meet at the sacred games; cf. Diodorus 16.89. J. Wiseman lists the international meetings at Corinth and Isthmia before 146, 'Corinth and Rome, I', *ANRW* 2.7.1 (1980) 539.

64 The inscriptions recording relations between Philip V and the Hellenic League appear to have been deliberately smashed. We are grateful to Michael Jameson for providing a summary of the texts before he has completed the final publication.

65 Probably following Polybius 18.44–8.

66 Suetonius, *Nero* 24.2; *Theater*, 85–7. The speech is commemorated on Corinthian coins minted during the year AD 66/67, on which the emperor is shown speaking from a platform with the inscription *ADLO[cutio] AUG[usti]*; see M. Amandry, *Le Monnayage des Duovirs Corinthiens*, suppl. XV of the *Bulletin de Correspondance Hellénique* (Paris 1988) type XXII, 215–21, pl. XXXIX, RIII1–RIV21.

67 *Isthmia* II, 47–52.

68 See A. Mallwitz, *Olympia und seine Bauten* (Munich 1972) 186–94.

69 The bases will be discussed and illustrated in Part II of the excavation report.

70 *Isthmia* II, 48. Broneer suggests that the bases held banners belonging to teams of athletes.

71 The ode is quoted in Apollonios Dyscolos, *Synt.* 2.114 (fr. 6.5(1), Snell). Similar wording occurs at the end of *schol. Isthm. hyp.* a. The full story appears in Pausanias I.44.7–8; II.1.3–II.2.2. See W. Burkert, *Homo Necans* (Berkeley 1983) 196–9.

72 *Quaest.Con.*, 675D–677B.

73 *Schol. Nem. hyp.* a–e; Apollodoros 3.6.4; Pausanias 2.15.2–3; Miller, ed., (*supra* n. 53) 24–30.

74 Pindar, *schol. Pythia. hyp. c*; Pausanias 10.6.5–7.

75 Olympia: Mallwitz, (*supra* n. 68) 133–7; Pausanias 5.13.1–3. Nemea: Miller, ed., (*supra* n. 53) 25–9 (myth); 104–7 (shrine); Pausanias 2.15.3.

76 In the middle of the first century AD when the games were returned to the sanctuary after an absence of two hundred years, a sacrificial enclosure for the hero was built over the western end of the Early Stadium, south of the long altar (Figure 8.1), but there is no trace of an earlier enclosure or sacrifices in that place; see *Isthmia* II, 99–101; East Terraces 1–4 in 'Excavations: I', 12–15; 61–8. The original location of the shrine may not have been known in the first century AD, but only the existence of an heroic cult.

77 See E. Will, *Korinthiaka* (Paris 1955) 169–80 with references; Burkert (*supra* n. 71) 196–9; K. Adshead, *Politics of the Archaic Peloponnesus* (Aldershot, New Zealand 1986) 38–9; 61–3.

78 See *supra* nn. 3, 5.

79 Marmor Parium, *IG* 12, 444, 20; 35ff.; Plutarch, *Thes.* 25,4.

80 See Gebhard, (*supra* n. 37) 73–4.

9

Concordia Discors: the literary and the archaeological evidence on the sanctuary of Samothrace

Walter Burkert

Samothrace[1] is a small and isolated island, yet it was the place of 'Mysteries' that radiated through the whole of the Greek and Roman world; and somehow Samothracian Mysteries have retained their fascination through the ages, mainly by the force of literary tradition.

This special interest saw its peak in the epoch of beginning romanticism, with the rebirth of religious–mythological studies. Articles and books on the mysterious Great Gods of Samothrace were written in quick succession, by Zoega, Creuzer and Schelling; they were read and discussed by the literary élite; and they made an appearance, of course, in Goethe's *Faust*.[2] It was the aura of secrecy that attracted curiosity, of pre-Greek, nay oriental wisdom (Scaliger's etymology of Kabeiroi from Semitic *kabir*, 'great', was generally accepted at the time,[3] while Herodotus (3.37) mentions Egyptian 'Kabeiroi' next to Phoenician 'Pataikoi'), it was the symbolic dimension, and, known to everyone but less commented upon at that time, phallicism. Ithyphallic images in the secrecy of Samothrace, this idea had been broached to the reading public since Herodotus.

In the real world, exploration of Samothrace came later. In 1863 the famous Nike was discovered by Champoiseau, French consul at Istanbul, and transported to the Louvre; closer studies of the site were done by the French in 1865 and by the Austrians in 1873–5, activities which brought further pieces of marblework into the respective museums at Paris and Vienna. Systematic excavation was not started until Karl Lehmann began his life-work in 1938 in connection with New York University. Since then, work on the site has been continuous. It was still the romantic aura of Samothrace, tinged with more recent psychoanalysis, that remained in the background, the prospect of resuscitating Great Gods. Paul and Mary Mellon, friends of C. G. Jung and benefactors of the Eranos centre at Ascona at that time, were found ready to finance the excavations and the exemplary publications through the Bollingen Foundation, established in honour of C. G. Jung.[4]

Archaeological work at Samothrace has been done with great enthusiasm and care. The impressive publication series is far from being finished. No excavations have been made so far within the ancient city next to the sanctuary, the walls of which are well preserved. But it would probably be over-optimistic to expect any great surprises from further explorations, even if interesting inscriptions might still come from the city's archives. As regards the sanctuary of the Great Gods, the limits of archaeological exploration are becoming apparent. Thus it may by now be possible to draw a balance and to ask questions about the interplay of literary tradition and archaeological findings in this case: to what extent did they confirm each other, or are they rather seen to drift apart, each creating circles of its own making, of fragmented information and growing problems?

The earliest characteristic finds within the sanctuary[5] are sacrificial deposits within the so-called *temenos*, dated to the beginnings of the seventh century BC.[6] They prove that religious activities took place, which means that the sanctuary was in existence by then; and they are about contemporary with the beginnings of the Greek settlement on the island, the incipient city. Characteristic are Subgeometric kantharoi of a form that also occurs at Lemnos and at Troy, as well as at Thasos, Lesbos and Chios.[7] This may be understood as pointing to interrelations of pre-Greek and Greek populations. It still does not segregate Samothrace from the common situation in the northern Aegean at the time. Neither does there seem to be anything special about the sacrificial activities that left their traces at the site.

The oldest literary evidence is indirect, it comes in the guise of heroic mythology. In 1915 the Oxyrhynchus Papyrus no. 1359 was published with fragments of Hesiod's *Catalogues* referring to Elektra, her brothers and Troy. This proves that Samothracian mythology was already included in this Hesiodic poem.[8] The *Catalogues* can hardly be attributed *in toto* to the poet whom we date about 700 BC; Martin West came to the conclusion that the composition of the work must have taken place about the middle of the sixth century.[9] This is still Archaic tradition. The preserved fragment from the Hesiodic text is lacunary, but the main argument is clear, and it can be supplemented from later texts: Elektra, the daughter of Atlas and no doubt consort of Zeus, gave birth to Dardanos and Eetion; Eetion died in consequence of his dealings with Demeter, but Dardanos left Samothrace to become the ancestor of the Trojan kings. There seems to be no mention of Harmonia or Kadmos in this context, and nothing about the flood that, according to later texts, made Dardanos abandon his native island.[10] In fact the place name 'Samothrace' does not occur in the preserved relics of the text, but there can be no doubt about the localization of the myth.

There are at least two messages in this fragmentary myth, a double reference to contemporary reality: this myth is about Troy, and about mysteries. The name of Dardanos is telling, as is the mention of his son Ilos, also referred to in the Hesiodic text: the author is all but quoting the text of the *Iliad* 20.216ff., which tells how Dardanos founded Dardanie on the slopes of Mount Ida, because Ilios-Troy down in the plain was not yet in existence; it was left to Ilos to found this city. Thus the Homeric world is presupposed in the Dardanos myth as a reference system, a world seen by Greeks through the medium of epic poetry, in which non-Greeks play a considerable and even a noble role. This is the status of the Trojans. This may well fit the situation of the seventh/sixth century. We know that families of Lesbos claimed descent from Agamemnon, the conqueror of Troy,[11] while putative descendants of Trojans, of Aineias-Askanios and of Hektor-Skamandrios must have been around at the Dardanelles.[12] Myth thus makes Samothrace belong to the non-Greek world; in fact the Thracian town Ainos, whose name has always been connected with Aineias, is quite close to Samothrace. But beyond the stories about other non-Greek settlements, Samothrace is given the status of 'origin' in a special sense: this is the island where gods met men, this is where Dardanos, son of Zeus, came from in the beginning. This singular status of a small and unimportant island must reflect the aspirations of a sacred centre, later known through its Mysteries. The Eetion myth, mixing the divine and the mortal in a story that can intimate catastrophe or bliss or both, points to the same direction. In later tradition this myth is fused with the Cretan story of Demeter and Iasion known from the *Odyssey* and Hesiod's *Theogony*.[13] The name Eetion does not sound Greek, nor does Iasion. 'Original' Samothrace is thus designated to be non-Greek but close to the gods – even if this is expressed through Greek literature in Greek.

Thus the literary evidence, which can be attributed to the sixth century, is compatible with the archaeological data in so far as connections with Troy and pre-Greek Lemnos seem to exist; but it goes far beyond what could be expected from archaeology. A very special claim for the island and its sanctuary is broadcast through the Greek world, a myth of origin, of sex and crime, designating a sacred centre established by Zeus within the non-Greek world.

Archaeology at Samothrace has not much to add during the sixth and fifth centuries. Attic ceramics make their appearance, as everywhere in the region. Sacrificial activities go on, now within the Altar Court; certain rock altars are singled out and used.[14] Still nothing would make us suspect quite special forms of cult. It is only in the second half of the fifth century that the first monumental structure appears at the sanctuary, and it is a very uncommon one indeed: the theatral area at the entrance, a perfect circle enclosed by rising steps, evidently with an altar at the centre.[15] It is a place for demonstrative show to a crowd of people gathered in front of, but not yet entering, the sanctuary proper, connected with some form of sacrifice, no doubt. The structure is in fact blocking the access; special buildings were erected afterwards for even more effective control of the entrance. We can take this building programme as an indication of *aporrheton*, of secret rites, screened from the common worshippers by now – in other words, of Mysteries. We can do this with all the more confidence because we know from the literary sources that Samothracian Mysteries had become famous by then.

Once more what the literary texts reveal goes much farther. The decisive information is part of a most famous and difficult passage in Herodotus – we are thus operating at a date of roughly 440/430 BC.[16] Herodotus maintains the thesis that Greeks learned the names of their gods from the Egyptians, but as an exception to this Egyptian origin he adduces the ithyphallic statues of Hermes:

> But that they make the statues of Hermes to have their members erect, this they did not learn from the Egyptians, but from the Pelasgians, the Athenians being the first among Greeks to receive that custom, and from them the others got it. . . . Anyone who has been initiated into the secret rites of the Kabeiroi, which the Samothracians practise, having derived them from the Pelasgians, this man knows what I say. . . . The Pelasgians have told a sacred story about this, which is disclosed in the mysteries at Samothrace.

For his theory of derivation, Herodotus needs two links: Samothracians are Pelasgians, and Pelasgians were the neighbours of the Athenians for some time; in addition he adheres to the postulate that Pelasgian is older than Greek. In other words: some details from Samothracian Mysteries which must not be directly disclosed but can be alluded to among those who know have given rise, according to Herodotus, to the fabrication of those well-known tetragonal pillars with bearded head and phallus, often ithyphallic, called *Hermai* at Athens, fashioned in that form since Hipparchos son of Peisistratos.[17] Herodotus presupposes that Samothracian Mysteries, in the form of secret rites connected with a 'sacred tale' (*hieros logos*), are not only in existence by his time, but are well known to his public, and that many of them have had their 'initiation into the rites', while, of course, the secret has to be kept. Herodotus is positive that the gods involved are to be called Kabeiroi; Stesimbrotus of Thasos, roughly a contemporary of Herodotus, confirms his indication (*FGrHist* 107 F 20), and he should know, Thasos being rather close to Samothrace.

Herodotus remained a famous and much-read author throughout antiquity; so his phallic intimations did not go unnoticed. In the ninth iambus of Callimachus,[18] an interviewer is made to ask an ithyphallic statue of Hermes in a palaestra about his status; the god answers – the text is preserved only in paraphrase – 'that he is, from farther back, a Tyrsenian, and in accordance with a mystic tale he has got his erection'. Callimachus is alluding to Herodotus, of course; his 'mystic' tale is identical to the sacred tale referred to by the father of history; needless to say, Callimachus is no less discrete as to the contents of the secret myth. Callimachus has replaced the 'Pelasgians' by the 'Tyrsenians': this is the name by which the inhabitants of Lemnos are normally called, but the identity of Tyrsenians and Pelasgians is a thesis that had also appeared in Herodotus.[19]

A glimpse at the sacred tale appears, quite unexpectedly, in Cicero's *De Natura Deorum*:[20] In the list of divine eponyms offered by the sceptic, there appears a 'First Hermes', son of Caelum (Uranos) and Dies (Hemera), 'whose nature was aroused in a rather obscene way, tradition says, because he was moved by the sight of Proserpina (Persephone)'. Here we get an explanation of the ithyphallic appearance through myth: 'Seeing the goddess Kore – Persephone' is the reason. The relation to Samothrace is confirmed by Varro: Caelum/Uranos is one of the great gods of Samothrace in his interpretation.[21] To 'see Kore' seems to have played a role at Eleusis, too.[22] It is hardly a coincidence that in so-called Anodos scenes in fifth century Attic vase painting, the goddess rising from the ground is greeted by Hermes and a grotesquely ithyphallic Pan.[23] Thus the combination of motifs in the sacred tale is documented by the time of Herodotus, though in an indirect way.

The most detailed reference to the facts at Samothrace occurs much later in a curious text, the sermon by the Naassene, a Gnostic author copied by Hippolytus in his 'Refutation of all Heresies':[24]

> There stand two statues of naked men in the Anaktoron of the Samothracians, with both their hands stretched up toward heaven and their pudenda turned up, just as the statue of Hermes at Kyllene. The aforesaid statues are images of the primal man and of the regenerated, spiritual man who is in every respect consubstantial with that man.

In spite of his fantastic interpretation, the author is basically trustworthy – his equally unique indications about Eleusis are to be taken seriously, too. Being a Gnostic, he is personally interested in mysteries but free from obligations of ancient *nomos*, including the law of secrecy. Thus it is here finally that we get details of what Herodotus was intimating: two ithyphallic statues at Samothrace. In fact Varro refers to the same statues, even if he discreetly passes in silence over their ithyphallic status. He says that 'Samothrace has set up two masculine images of bronze in front of the doors', and that these were thought by some to be the Great Gods them-selves,[25] which, according to Varro, is erroneous. The Gnostic is less reticent, and his phantasy makes the ithyphallic status directly prefigure the ascent to heaven due to primal as well as to spiritual man.

It is from this passage that one of the buildings excavated in the sanctuary at Samothrace has been called the Anaktoron.[26] Karl Lehmann had reasons for this identification, but serious problems remain. At first sight there is disagreement between the Naassene and Varro as to the location of the images: 'in' the Anaktoron, or 'in front of the doors'? That they should have been moved in the meantime between Varro and the Naassene is a desperate solution. It is rather to the point to realize that *anaktoron* as used in rhetorical tradition is a word with a very vague meaning: is it a building, or a building within a building (as usually taken at Eleusis), or just a sanctuary?[27] If the Naassene has used the word in its general and vague sense, any foundation for naming a certain building within the sanctuary disappears. This does not invalidate the fact that the so-called Anaktoron is a very uncommon, complicated, 'mysterious' building: a bilingual inscription was found which blocked access to the northern chamber for the uninitiated;[28] hence the initates will have entered this special room. The Anaktoron is of Roman imperial date, but earlier constructions of similar design preceded it. Yet for the exciting *Hermai*, excavation has not produced anything. It is true Lehmann thought for a while he had found something like symbols of *phalloi* and *cunni* within the so-called Anaktoron – and nowhere else.[29] The objects are strange, but it needs a strongly guided Naassene phantasy to detect a sexual meaning in them. 'And one asks whether the brass chest found in the sacristy did not also contain phalloi (Und man fragt sich, ob nicht auch die in der Sakristei gefundene eherne Kiste Phalloi enthalten hat).'[30] What a question posed by reading Herodotus and Hippolytus, which cannot be answered but in fantasy! There remains the representation of a *kerykeion* (herald's staff) and two snakes on the inscription from the Anaktoron, as in some other instances.[31] This could be read as denoting Hermes and phallic power; but it is still a symbol of a symbol. The form of the *kerykeion* itself reproduces coupling snakes, but both images, herald's staff and snake, are so common in Greek cults that nothing special would be surmised, were it not for the literary evidence. Nothing else was found in the excavations to make explicit our phallic fantasies, no statuettes, no graffiti.

Another early indication about the mysteries of Samothrace comes in the form of an anecdote: Diagoras of Melos, the notorious atheist, when confronted with the many votive tablets in the sanctuary at Samothrace, retorted: 'There would be many more of these if those who were not saved had made dedications'.[32] The date would be around 430 BC – if indeed Diagoras is concerned; the anecdote is also attributed to Diogenes the Cynic. The anecdote clearly expresses the main function of the gods of Samothrace: to save the worshippers from the perils of the sea. The role of *euchai* is confirmed by Aristophanes.[33]

The Diagoras anecdote indicates that there was an imposing number of votive monuments to be seen at Samothrace. This would not in fact presuppose mysteries in the sense of special, secret initiations; votive religion and mysteries can be parallel to but independent of one another, they are quite compatible.[34] Be that as it may, the text has been operative in identifying a 'Hall of Votive Gifts' within the sanctuary, and to attribute it to the fifth century.[35] This has remained controversial among specialists. No relics of votives have been preserved. The Hall may just be one of the various *hestiatoria* common in sanctuaries.

The third indication about the mysteries which may come from the fifth century also takes the form of anecdote. It is related three times in Plutarch's *Apophthegmata Lakonika*,[36] referring alternatively to Lysandros, Antalkidas and to an anonymous Spartiate. The date of the testimony thus remains insecure – about 405 BC, if we stick to Lysandros, about 386 BC, if we choose Antalkidas. But it is interesting enough in itself. The priest at Samothrace asks the candidate for initiation 'which was the most lawless deed that he had committed in his life'. The Spartan replies that the gods know and the priest need not know. This is one of the few texts where an officiating priest (*hiereus*) of the Samothracian sanctuary is mentioned. It seems to indicate quite a strange practice in Samothracian cult, and thus has aroused special interest: is this the earliest form of a 'confession of sins' within the Greek world?[37] Karl Lehmann has seen a connection with the fact that initiates of Samothrace claim to have become 'more rightful and pious', as *eusebeis* is the current epithet attributed to the *mystai* in the inscriptions.

Not far from the side entrance at the Eastern wall of the so-called Hieron or 'New Temple' are two stepping stones, apparently renewed from time to time and finally overlaid with a structure of terracotta tiles and concrete; between them a big torch seems to have been put up. This, Karl Lehmann imagined, was the spot where the initiate confronted the priest, made his confession and received purification before he was allowed to enter the Hieron for the higher degree of the Mysteries, *epopteia*.[38] But there is a double problem: re-examination of the archaeological evidence suggests that there was no predecessor for the Hieron that was built after about 325 BC[39] – it had been called the New Temple in earlier literature. This means that the situation at the time of either Lysandros or Antalkidas cannot be reconstructed, but it was probably quite different. In addition, the interpretation of 'confession of sins' is close enough to Christian ideology to raise suspicion. For Christians, confession of sins is the prerequisite for absolution: God is reconciled by humiliation – this is an old and widespread idea.[40] If such was the religion of Samothrace, this would indeed be most remarkable, and, in a certain way, un-Greek. But note that practically all the 'confessions' known from inscriptions, mainly from Asia Minor, concern healing cults, which for all we know was not the specialty of Samothrace. Yet it is striking that the Samothracian priest only enquires about the superlative, the 'most lawless deed'. All the other petty sins seem to be of no interest; in other words, it is not purity in a general sense that is required, but shared knowledge of something important, *conscientia sceleris*. This leads to another interpretation: common knowledge of crime makes for good conspiracy; this is the strongest form of *pistis*, 'to commit together some lawless deed'.[41] What is 'unspeakable' constitutes a closed society. If this interpretation is correct, it is easily integrated in the pattern of Mysteries. Remember that the Mithras Mysteries were said to have originated among Cilician pirates.[42] This still gives an interesting glimpse at the Archaic roots of

Samothracian mysteries. Yet, alas, nothing remains to explain those stepping stones at the Hieron. The archaeological findings and the texts do not meet.

If we look to events of the fourth/third centuries BC at Samothrace, the main fact documented by archaeology within the sanctuary is the advent of monumental architecture. This comes with the reign of Philip II of Macedon, it is continued by Philippos Arrhidaios, Arsinoe and Ptolemy II. In the literary tradition, this is reflected by anecdotes once more: Philip and Olympias first met when they both received their initiation at Samothrace,[43] and Arsinoe, in the desperate crisis of 280 BC, sought refuge at Samothrace.[44] These indications could hardly make us expect the thorough transformation of the sanctuary which was carried out in these years. Philip had the enclosure to the so-called *temenos* adorned with a porticus, the archaizing frieze of which has in a way become the emblem of Samothrace: a chorus of dancing girls.[45] Philippos Arrhidaios added a building at the theatral area at the entrance, and Arsinoe dedicated what must have been the most conspicuous building in the sanctuary, the rotunda, in fact the biggest circular building of Greek architecture. Ptolemy II takes credit for the propylaia.[46] For the modern historian, the motives of Philip, the shrewd politician, are easy to guess. Samothrace was the only sanctuary of pan-Hellenic renown within his reach. While he was establishing his hold on Greece via Delphi and completed it with his family shrine at Olympia, he did everything to raise 'his' sanctuary in northern Greece to a comparable level, inventing as it were Macedonian civilization. Later, when Arsinoe was queen, wife of Lysimachos and later of Ptolemy II, Samothrace remained an outpost of royal propaganda, whether of Thrace or Egypt.

If the outward history of the sanctuary seems to be clearly understandable on these lines, the intrinsic meaning of the rites becomes all the more obscure. The function of Arsinoe's great rotunda is utterly unclear. It had no windows and just one door; crowds could hardly assemble within. Was it a kind of heroon of the dynasty, as the Philippeion at Olympia? Yet it seems to have had a much smaller predecessor, the Doric rotunda from the fourth century.[47] Hero shrines are not easily superseded or moved. There is another tempting combination. Certain mysteries with circular dancing are evoked in a much-quoted text by Dion of Prusa:

> If one were to bring a man, Greek or barbarian, for initiation into a mystic recess, overwhelming in its beauty and size, where he would behold many mystic views and hear many mystic sounds, where darkness and light appear in sudden changes and other innumerable things happen, where they even follow the so-called enthronement ceremony – they have the initiands sit down, and they dance around them – if all this were to happen, would it be possible that such a man should experience nothing in his soul, that he should not come

185

to surmise that there is some wiser insight and plan in all that is going on.[48]

Dion gives no indication which 'mystery hall' he may have in his mind. The first part might well allude to Eleusis, but the 'enthronement ceremony' is out of place; thus Samothrace becomes an obvious guess. A. D. Nock thought of Dion's text when relics of a circular wooden structure were reported to have been found within the so-called Anaktoron.[49] These, however, have subsequently been traced to a much later lime kiln at the spot. If Dion's ceremony has disappeared from the Anaktoron, why not transfer it to the rotunda? It is true only a small number of participants would be allowed there. Unfortunately there is nothing to substantiate such a guess; no special knowledge of Samothrace is attested for Dion, nor has excavation provided the slightest indication for ritual within the rotunda. Once more there is no link between text and topography.

Further building activities are known from the Hellenistic period; by the third century those two uncommon buildings at least partly reserved for initiates, the Anaktoron and the Hieron, had come into existence. They are definitely connected with the mysteries: inscriptions provide that one room of the Anaktoron and the whole of the Hieron should be entered only by initiates (nn. 28, 38). Karl Lehmann has drawn the conclusion that, since the Hieron *in toto* is for *mystai* only, it was used for the second degree of initiation, for *epopteia*, whereas the Anaktoron, by contrast, remains for the first degree, *myesis*. Thus we get a concrete itinerary for ritual within the sanctuary. Should one conclude that *epopteia* was added only with the construction of the Hieron in the fourth century – no earlier lists of *epoptai* seem to exist? Yet Lehmann has also linked the graffito E on a number of sherds found close to the Hieron to *epopteia*;[50] 'one dates from the sixth, three each from the fifth and fourth centuries'. Then *epopteia* must have existed, without any building that could be assigned to it.

Unrelated to this problem are the two most important details about the mysteries we learn from Hellenistic authors. There is the text of Mnaseas, quoted in the scholia to Apollonius Rhodius.[51] He, and only he, gives names of the Samothracian 'Kabeiroi', apparently the secret names of the Great Gods not to be told to the public outside the cult: Axieros, Axiokersa, Axiokersos, Kasmilos, identified with Demeter, Persephone, Hades and Hermes. It is generally accepted that this is the most authentic information we get about the divinities of Samothrace. Hence Mnaseas' gods resound through all that has been written on Samothrace in modern times. Casmilus, if identical with Etruscan–Latin *camillus*, would confirm the Pelasgian–Tyrsenian–Etruscan links.[52] Still this has remained isolated evidence; excavators have found nothing in the sanctuary to correlate with it, except for the idea that an isolated A found on some graffiti might stand for Axieros or another member of the triad. Yet 'the fullest form preserved is *ag*'.[53] Far from Samothrace, at the tomb of the Haterii on the Via Appia in Rome a series of four gods is represented who have been identified with those mentioned by Mnaseas: Hades, Demeter, Persephone and Hermes.[54] This is hardly more than an intriguing possibility; the combination of these four gods in relation to death and the beyond hardly falls outside of normal Greek mythology, such as that contained, for example, already in the Homeric Hymn to Demeter.

The other text equally comes from the scholia to Apollonios Rhodios:[55] 'They say Odysseus, being an initiate and using Leukothea's veil in place of a fillet, was saved from the storm at sea by placing the veil below his abdomen. For the initiates bind fillets below their abdomens (*koilia*).' This indeed is most interesting, as it brings not only a detail of ritual, of magic one might be tempted to say, to our knowledge, but also the intent and context of the ceremony, salvation from the perils at sea, and the mythical precedent claiming connection with Homer. There is no reason to doubt the ritual; it seems to imply that the initiate was stripped naked, as Odysseus has to throw away his clothes before donning Leukothea's veil. It was not strictly secret, as the application of the scholium shows. The suggestion that the Leukothea motif in the *Odyssey* has to do with Samothrace is hardly acceptable in a direct way, but there are intriguing associations: Kadmos looms large in Samothracian mythology, which may be due to the play of names Kadmos–Kadmilos. Still, there is no hint of Leukothea. Unfortunately, we learn nothing that would allow the attribution of the rite to any specific place or building within the sanctuary of Samothrace. Archaeology and literature remain separated.

The last decisive factor in the history of Samothrace was the appropriation of the Aeneas tradition by Rome, which at a stroke made Samothrace the ultimate origin even of Rome. The gods in particular whom *pius Aeneas* had taken out of Troy were identified with the gods of Samothrace, and hence the *Penates* of Rome became Samothracian. This probably became effective when the Romans took over Macedonia in 168 BC – was it an idea put forward by the Samothracians? – and is already established at the time of Cassius Hemina;[56] then the Trojan connection of Rome was heavily strengthened by Caesar and Augustus. This ensured continuing interest in Samothrace among the wealthy Romans throughout imperial times. A direct testimony to this is the rebuilding of the Anaktoron in the early imperial period; it probably had been damaged by natural forces. We also get the inscriptions from *mystai* and *epoptai*, quite a few of them in Latin, which testify to the influence of the Samothracian gods.[57] Yet this brings no more details about the cult; the enigma of the 'Great Gods' remains unsolved.

It is only in Roman authors and in one Byzantine Lexicon that one peculiarity of Samothracian ritual appears which is finally matched by archaeology: the use of magnetic iron, to be more exact, of iron rings.[58] It is not said directly, but intrinsically plausible that the *mystai* received an iron ring, and that the effect of some hidden, moving power was demonstrated with the phenomenon of magnetism. Here in fact confirmation has come from the excavations: iron rings have been found at various locations within the sanctuary[59] – one ensemble found together, probably handled by the priests within the sanctuary, has not yet been published. Here, finally, quite humble literary texts and inconspicuous corroded findings do meet. The rings no doubt were to demonstrate some form of attachment, of religious community. There remains the secrecy, encompassing mysteries, which is not lifted either by our texts or by archaeology.

NOTES

1 See bibliography (pp. 190–1) for clarification of references and for the standard publication and for *Guide*. Among other studies, outstanding are Chapouthier 1935; Hemberg 1950; Cole 1984 and 1989. I owe special thanks to James McCredie, under whose expert guidance I visited Samothrace in the summer of 1990.

2 Zoega 1797; Schelling 1815; Reinhardt 1945, esp. 334–42; Creuzer I³ 15–21, III³ 19–36, 159–65; see also Welcker 1824; criticism in Lobeck 1829, 1105–348 'Samothracia'.

3 J. J. Scaliger, *Coniectaneae in M. Ter. Varr. de lingua Latina* (Paris 1565) 146.

4 W. McGuire, *Bollingen: An Adventure in Collecting the Past* (Princeton 1982, 2nd edn, 1989).

5 There is no need to discuss here the very interesting Minoan finds which come from another site, quite distant from the sanctuary and the Greek city.

6 (*Samothrace*) V 267–9, 317f.

7 *Guide* 116.

8 Hesiodus, fr. 169 ed. Merkelbach-West. This testimony is missing in *Samothrace* I.

9 West 1985, 130–7: 580/520 BC, perhaps 540/20 BC; on fr. 169 and Samothrace, West 1985, 160.

10 Caduff 1986, 133–42.

11 Alkaios on Archeanaktidai = Atreidai, esp. fr. 70; 112.

12 Hellanikos, *FGrHist* 4 F 31. Hellanikos F 23 recounts the story of Samothrace and Dardanos, adding the Theban connection with Harmonia. Cf. Skymnos, *Perieg.* 679–89. The Aineias tradition, esp. the reference of *Iliad* 20.300–8, remains controversial; see Galinsky 1969; Smith 1981; Horsfall 1987.

13 *Odyssey* 5.125; Hesiodus, *Theogonia* 969–71. Eetion is expressly identified with Iasion in Hellanikos, *FGrHist* 4 F 23, with the rationalized version that 'he committed outrage against a statue of Demeter'; cf. Diodorus Siculus 5.48 f. Mystic bliss of Iasion is alluded to in Theocritus 3.50f.

14 *Guide* 61.

15 *Guide* 92–5.

16 Herodotus 2.51 f. = I no. 140; see Burkert 1985.

17 See Wrede 1985.

18 Fr. 199 Pfeiffer; missing in *Samothrace* I.

19 See Lochner-Hüttenbach 1960.

20 Cicero, *De Natura Deorum* 3.56; also missing in *Samothrace* I.

21 Varro, *De Lingua Latina* 5.58 = I no. 175

22 Burkert 1983, 286f.

23 Pelike from Rhodes 12.454, *ARV*² 1218,2, Bérard 1974, fig. 63 (cf. figs 42, 43).
24 Hippolytus, *Refutatio Omnium Haeresium* 5.8.9 = I no. 147. See on this text
    Burkert 1983, 251.
25 Varro, *De Lingua Latina* 5.58 = I no. 175; cf. Servius, *Commentarius in Vergilii
    Aeneida* 3.12 where the two statues are identified as Castor and Pollux.
26 *Guide* 47–53; cf. Cole 1984, 12f.
27 See Burkert 1983, 276f.; general use of the word for any temple or sanctuary,
    e.g., Aelianus, *Varia Historia* 13.2; Plutarchus, *Sulla* 12.5. Deubner 1945, 15f.
    thinks the statues stood within the building, but in front of the inner door, cf.
    note 28.
28 Bilingual stele from the Anaktoron, II,1 no. 63; *Guide* 38; Sokolowski 1962, 75a.
29 See Hemberg 1950, 106 referring to Lehmann, *AJA* 43 (1939) 140; 44 (1940) 355
    with fig. 36.
30 Hemberg 1950, 106 referring to Lehmann, *AJA* 44 (1940) 349 fig. 28.
31 See II,1 no. 63, *Guide* 38.
32 Diogenes Laertius 6.59; Cicero, *De Natura Deorum* 3.89 = I nos 230/1; Diagoras
    Melius, Theodorus Cyrenaeus ed. M. Winiarczyk, Teubner 1981, T. 36/7;
    Winiarczyk, following Jacoby, dates the Diagoras scandal to about 431 BC. Since
    Diagoras is less well known than Diogenes, the anecdote should originally refer
    to him.
33 Aristophanes, *Pax* 277 = I no. 226, cf. 238.
34 Cf. Burkert 1987, 12–17.
35 IV,1. Cf. Cole 1984, 16.
36 Plutarch, *Lac. apophth.* 217cd (Antalkidas, *tí deinóteron*); 229d (Lysandros, *tí
    anomótaton*); 236 d (*Lákon tis, tí asebéstaton*) = I nos 239/40.
37 See Steinleitner 1913, 70–2; 118f.
38 See III,2 17–20; *Guide* 36; the designation 'Hieron' comes from the inscription
    II,1 no. 62 = Sokolowski 1962, 75.
39 Cole 1984, 13–16 following McCredie.
40 See the 'plague prayers' of Mursilis, *ANET* 394–6.
41 Thucydides 3.82.6, cf. 8.73.3 (murder of Hyperbolos); Andocides 1.67 (muti-
    lation of herms); Plutarch, *Cicero* 10.4 (cannibalism of Catilinarians); *conscientia
    sceleris* Minuc. Felix 9.5. In a parodistic romance, the initiator of a new *gallos*
    claims 'common knowledge of everything': 'I know everything, verily',
    'everything shameful that has happened', of the neophyte (Merkelbach 1973,
    esp. 93f).
42 Plutarch, *Pompeius* 24.
43 Plutarch, *Alexander* 2.2 = I no. 193, echoed by Himerius, I no. 194.
44 Iustinus 24.3.9 = I no. 102.
45 V 50–147, 273–6; the frieze, 5–12, 172–262.
46 Dedication of Arrhidaios: *Guide* 93f.; Arsinoe: II,1 no. 10; see VII 231–9; it
    cannot be established whether the inscription designated the building as *naos*,
    oikos or *hieron*. Ptolemy II: II,1 no. 11, cf. pp. 5–7.
47 *Guide* 94–6.
48 Dio Chrysostomus, *Or.* 12.33, attributed to Posidonius by W. Theiler,
    Poseidonios (Berlin 1982) F 368; see Burkert 1987, 89f.
49 Nock 1941, cf. *Guide* 35; *contra*: Cole 1984, 29.
50 II,2, 23f.
51 Schol. A.R. 1.917 = I no. 150; Mnaseas is dated to about 200 BC, F. Laqueur,
    'Mnaseas', *RE* XV, 2250–2. On an amulet from Vindonissa with Mnaseas' names,
    of suspected authenticity, see II,2 9 n. 5. The gods mentioned by Mnaseas seem to
    be identical to 'Iuppiter Iuno Minerva' in Varro (Augustinus, *De Civitate Dei*

7.28: 'Hermes' has been dropped) or 'Iuppiter Minerva Mercurius' (leaving out Axieros: Servius, *Commentarius in Vergilii Aeneida* 3.12, 264; 8.679; Servius auctus Danielis, *Aen.* 2.296). Demetrios of Skepsis denied that the gods of Samothrace were 'Kabeiroi', Strabo 10 p. 472.

52 Cf. Hemberg 1950, 87–9 (who arbitrarily makes Axieros male), 95f., 316f.; Kadmilos has also been provided with a Hittite etymology, Hasammeli, by A. Götze, *Language* 29 (1953) 269f., *Reallexikon der Assyriologie* IV 127; *contra*: O. Gurney, *Some Aspects of Hittite Religion* (1977) 12f.

53 II,2 14 no. 56, cf. 58–61, nos 55–64.

54 Pettazzoni 1908; III,1 325–7; Bianchi 1976, 30f., no. 58.

55 Schol. A.R. 1.917 f = I no. 229 gh.

56 Cassius Hemina fr. 6, *Historicorum Romanorum Reliquiae*, ed. H. Peter, I 99f., Pomponius Atticus fr. 1, *Historicorum Romanorum Reliquiae* II 6; Varro in Macrob. *Saturnalia* 3.4.7; Dionysius Halicarnassensis, *Antiquitates Romanae* 1.68.2–4; St Weinstock, 'Penates', *RE* XIX, 417–57, esp. 435–40, 446–8, 451–5; Kleywegt 1972; Cole 1984, 100–3; 1989, 1580–96.

57 Cf. Cole 1984, 87–103.

58 Lucretius 6.1044 = I no. 212; Plinius, *Naturalis Historia* 33.23 = no. 213; Isidorus, *Origines* 19.32.5 = no. 30; *Etymologicum Magnum*, 'Magnetis' = no. 20. Nonnos 3.65 = no. 219 has nothing to do with this.

59 See V 403f.; *Guide* 25f., fig. 9.

BIBLIOGRAPHY

The standard publication is Karl Lehmann and Phyllis Williams Lehmann, eds, *Samothrace. Excavations Conducted by the Institute of Fine Arts of New York University*, I: *The Ancient Literary Sources*, ed. N. Lewis (Princeton 1958); II,1: *The Inscriptions on Stone*, ed. P.M. Fraser (Princeton 1960); II,2: *The Inscriptions on Ceramics and Minor Objects*, ed. K. Lehmann (Princeton 1960); III,1: *The Hieron*, ed. Ph. Williams Lehmann (Princeton 1969); IV,1: *The Hall of Votive Gifts*, ed. K. Lehmann (Princeton 1962); IV,2: *The Altar Court*, ed. K. Lehmann, D. Spittle (Princeton 1964); V: *The Temenos*, ed. Ph. Williams Lehmann, D. Spittle (Princeton 1982); VI: *The Rotunda of Arsinoe*, ed. J. R. McCredie, G. Roux, S. M. Shaw, J. Kurtich (Princeton 1992). (Hereafter quoted by volume and page number only.)

A preliminary synthesis is Karl Lehmann, *Samothrace: A Guide to the Excavations and the Museum*, 5th edn revised and enlarged by Phyllis Williams Lehmann (New York 1983). (Hereafter abbreviated *Guide*.)

The following works are quoted by author and year:

C. Bérard, *Anodoi. Essai sur l'imagerie des passages chthoniens* (Neuchâtel 1974).

U. Bianchi, *The Greek Mysteries* (Leiden 1976) (Iconography of Religions XVII,3).

W. Burkert, *Homo Necans: The Anthropology of Ancient Greek Sacrificial Ritual and Myth* (Berkeley 1983; first published in German as *Homo Necans. Interpretationen altgriechischer Opferriten und Mythen*, Berlin 1972).

——, 'Herodot über die Namen der Götter: Polytheismus als historisches Problem', *Museum Helveticum* 42 (1985) 121–32.

——, *Ancient Mystery Cults* (Cambridge, Mass. 1989).

G. A. Caduff, *Antike Sintflutsagen* (Göttingen 1986) (Hypomnemata 82).

F. Chapouthier, *Les Dioscures au service d'une déesse* (Paris 1935).

S. G. Cole, *Theoi Megaloi: The Cult of the Great Gods at Samothrace* (Leiden 1984) (Etudes préliminaires aux religions orientales dans l'empire romain 96).

——, 'The Mysteries of Samothrace during the Roman period', in: H. Temporini and W. Haase, eds, *Aufstieg und Niedergang der römischen Welt* II 18,2 (Berlin 1989) 1565–98.

F. Creuzer, *Symbolik und Mythologie der alten Völker, in Vorträgen und Entwürfen* (Leipzig 1810–12, 4 vols, 2nd edn 1819–23, 6 vols, 3rd edn 1836–43, 4 vols).

L. Deubner, 'Zum Weihehaus der Eleusinischen Mysterien', Abh. Berlin 1945/6 2; repr. in L. Deubner, *Kleine Schriften zur klassischen Altertumskunde* (Königstein 1982) 739–57.

H. Ehrhardt, *Samothrake. Heiligtümer in ihrer Landschaft und Geschichte als Zeugen antiken Geisteslebens* (Stuttgart 1985).

G. K. Galinsky, *Aeneas, Sicily, and Rome* (Princeton 1969).

B. Hemberg, *Die Kabiren* (Uppsala 1950).

N. M. Horsfall, 'The Aeneas-legend from Homer to Virgil', in J. N. Bremmer and N. M. Horsfall, eds, *Roman Myth and Mythography* (London 1987) (*BICS* Suppl. 52) 12–24.

A. J. Kleywegt, *Varro über die Penaten und die 'Grossen Götter'* (Amsterdam 1972).

C. A. Lobeck, *Aglaophamus sive de theologiae mysticae Graecorum causis* (Königsberg 1829).

F. Lochner-Hüttenbach, *Die Pelasger* (Vienna 1960).

R. Merkelbach, 'Fragment eines satirischen Romans', *ZPE* 11 (1973) 81–100.

A. D. Nock, 'A Cabiric rite', *AJA* 45 (1941) 577–81.

W. Oberleitner *et al.*, eds, *Funde aus Ephesos und Samothrake*. Kunsthistorisches Museum, Vienna, Katalog der Antikensammlung II (Vienna 1978).

R. Pettazzoni, 'Una rappresentazione Romana dei Kabiri di Samotracia', *Ausonia* 3 (1908) 79–90.

K. Reinhardt, 'Die klassische Walpurgisnacht', *Antike und Abendland* 1 (1945) 133–62; idem, *Von Werken und Formen* (Godesberg 1947) 348–405; idem, *Tradition und Geist* (Göttingen 1960) 309–56 (quoted from this edition).

F. Schelling, *Über die Gottheiten von Samothrace* (Stuttgart/Tübingen 1815).

P. M. Smith, 'Aineiadai as patrons of Iliad XX and the Homeric Hymn to Aphrodite', *HSPh* 85 (1981) 17–58.

F. Sokolowski, *Lois sacrées des cités grecques. Supplément* (Paris 1962).

F. Steinleitner, *Die Beicht im Zusammenhange mit der sakralen Rechtspflege in der Antike* (Ph.D. diss. Leipzig 1913).

F. G. Welcker, *Die Aeschylische Trilogie. Prometheus und die Kabirenweihe von Lemnos* (Darmstadt 1824).

M. L. West, *The Hesiodic Catalogue of Women* (Oxford 1985).

H. Wrede, *Die antike Herme* (Mainz 1985).

G. Zoega, *De origine et usu obeliscorum* (Rome 1797).

10

Twenty-five years of research on Greek sanctuaries: a bibliography

Erik Østby

More than a hundred years have passed since the intensive, archaeological research in Greece had its beginning in the famous sanctuaries of the Athenian Acropolis, Delphi, Delos and Olympia, and the Greek sanctuaries have, ever since, remained a focal point in the study of ancient Greek culture and civilization. There can be no question here of presenting a full bibliography of the enormous amount of publications dedicated to this material. Instead, a representative selection of published works from the last 25 years (since 1965) is intended to provide up-to-date information on the general course and accomplishments of recent research, which are now, to a greater extent than before, concerned with modest, minor sanctuaries as well as with the large and famous ones. References to earlier literature can be found in the cited works, for most sites also in: D. Leekley and R. Noyes, *Archaeological Excavations in the Greek Islands* (Park Ridge 1975); in their *Archaeological Excavations in Southern Greece* (Park Ridge 1976), and D. Leekley and N. Efstratiou, *Archaeological Excavations in Central and Northern Greece* (Park Ridge 1980).

GENERAL STUDIES

The basic study on structural and spacial organization of Greek sanctuaries is B. Bergquist, *The Archaic Greek Temenos* (Lund 1967); see also G. P. Lavos, *Altgriechisches Temenos: Baukörper und Raumbildung* (Basel 1974). An older study by C. A. Doxiadis, *Architectural Space in Ancient Greece* (Cambridge, Mass. and London 1972 and later editions; originally published as *Raumordnung im griechischen Städtebau*, Heidelberg 1937) is controversial, but has maintained its interest. V. Scully, *The Earth, the Temple and the Gods*, 2nd edn, rev. (New Haven and London 1979) focuses on the relations between the sanctuaries and the surrounding landscape.

R. A. Tomlinson, *Greek Sanctuaries* (London 1976) gives a general account of Greek sanctuaries and a more specific discussion on some of them. E. Melas, ed., *Temples and Sanctuaries of Ancient Greece* (London 1973;

earlier German edition) collects essays by Greek scholars on various sanctuaries. Much important material can be found in U. Jantzen, ed., *Neue Forschungen in griechischen Heiligtümern*, papers from a seminar arranged at Olympia by the German Archaeological Institute (Tübingen 1976), cited as Jantzen, ed., *Neue Forschungen*, and in R. Hägg, N. Marinatos and G. C. Nordquist, eds, *Early Greek Cult Practice*, papers from the 5th international symposium at the Swedish Institute in Athens 1986 (Stockholm 1988), the latter also with much interesting material on otherwise neglected aspects of Greek sanctuaries. Note also G. Roux, ed., *Temples et sanctuaires. Séminaire de recherche 1981–1983* (Lyon 1984), with papers on both Greek and Oriental material.

The origins of Greek sanctuaries and possible continuity from the Bronze Age have been much discussed recently; F. de Polignac, *La naissance de la cité grecque. Cultes, espace et société, VIIIᵉ–VIIᵉ siècles avant J.-C.* (Paris 1984) and B. C. Dietrich, 'Die Kontinuität der Religion im "dunklen Zeitalter" Griechenlands', in H.-G. Buchholz, ed., *Ägäische Bronzezeit* (Darmstadt 1987) 478–98, are good, recent treatises of the problem, from opposite points of view. H. W. Parke, *Greek Oracles* (London 1967) remains unsurpassed as an introduction to those cults. Cults and sanctuaries for Demeter have been surveyed by G. Sfameni Gasparro, *Misteri e culti mistici di Demetra* (Roma 1966); hero-cults by H. Abramson, 'Greek hero-shrines' (Ph.D. diss. Berkeley 1978; Ann Arbor 1986). For source-cults in the Greek world there are extensive sections in F. Muthmann, *Mutter und Quelle. Studien zur Quellenverehrung im Altertum und im Mittelalter* (Basel and Mainz 1975), chs III–VI. Late formal developments of representative, statal sanctuaries are sketched by F. Felten, 'Heiligtümer oder Märkte?', *AntK* 26 (1983) 84–105.

The best, general book on the principal category of monuments in most Greek sanctuaries, the temple, is probably G. Gruben, *Die Tempel der Griechen*, 4th edn, rev. (Munich 1986), where more than usual attention is also paid to functional aspects and to the general context within the sanctuary. The origins of temple architecture have attracted much attention recently; after the basic work by H. Drerup, *Griechische Baukunst in geometrischer Zeit*, Archaeologia homerica II O (Göttingen 1969) the subject has been taken up by A. J. Mazarakis-Ainian, 'Contributions à l'étude de l'architecture réligieuse grecque des âges obscurs', *AntCl* 54 (1985) 5–48, and by K. Fagerström, *Greek Iron Age Architecture*, SIMA 81 (Göteborg 1988) A. E. Kalpaxis, *Früharchaische Baukunst in Griechenland und Kleinasien* (Athens 1976) focuses on the seventh century; H. Knell, 'Dorische Ringhallentempel in spät- und nachklassischer Zeit', *JdI* 98 (1983) 203–33, is a morphological study of later Doric temples. One particular problem, the origin and meaning of the peristasis, is the object of two important recent papers: A. Mallwitz, 'Kritisches zur Architektur Griechenlands im 8. und 7. Jahrhundert', *AA* 1981, 599–642 (morphological) and W. Martini, 'Vom Herdhaus zum Peripteros', *JdI* 101 (1986) 23–36 (functional). Functional aspects have also been discussed by P. E. Corbett, 'Greek temples and Greek worshippers: the literary and archaeological evidence', *BICS* 17 (1970) 149–58, concerning the accessibility of the interior of the temple, and for the adyta (also those of temples in Greece) by S. Kallemeyn Thalmann, 'The adyton in the Greek temples of South Italy and Sicily' (Ph.D. diss. Berkeley 1976; Ann Arbor 1980). The functional problems concerning temples without the normal altar in front of the building have mostly been discussed in connection with the Parthenon; G. Zinserling, 'Zeus-Tempel zu Olympia und Parthenon zu Athen – Kulttempel?', *ActAntHung* 13 (1965) 41–80, faces it on a more general basis.

For altars as such, no later study has replaced C. G. Yavis, *Greek Altars* (St Louis 1949); D. W. Rupp, 'Greek altars of the north-eastern Peloponnese *c.* 750/725 BC to *c.* 300/275 BC' (Ph.D. diss. Bryn Mawr 1974; Ann Arbor 1977), and M. Ç. Şahin, *Die Entwicklung der griechischen Monumentalaltäre* (Bonn 1972; dealing mostly with the Hellenistic monumental altars of Asia Minor), are more limited in scope.

Passing to secondary monuments, there is a morphological study of the tholoi by F. Seiler, *Die griechische Tholos* (Mainz 1986); their function remains an enigma. To the general study of the stoai by J. J. Coulton, *The Architectural Development of the Greek Stoa* (Oxford 1976), important conclusions on their function in the sanctuaries are added by G. Kuhn, 'Untersuchungen zur Funktion der Säulenhalle in archaischer und klassischer Zeit', *JdI* 100 (1985) 169–317. Ritual meals and their importance in the cult have recently attracted much attention, and have been studied by M. S. Goldstein, 'The setting of the ritual meal in Greek sanctuaries' (Ph.D. diss. Berkeley 1978; Ann Arbor 1982), and by C. Börker, *Festbankett und griechische Architektur*, Xenia 4 (Konstanz 1983). On propyla, not only of sanctuaries, there is a dissertation by J. R. Carpenter, 'The propylon in Greek and Hellenistic architecture' (Ph.D. diss. Pennsylvania 1970; Ann Arbor 1979). Another study on an important and neglected subject, D. Birge, 'Sacred groves in the ancient Greek world' (Ph.D. diss. Berkeley 1982), is at present available only in microfilm. There is to my knowledge no general study of treasuries.

Votive offerings and dedications are another important aspect of any Greek sanctuary. The only general study of the complex has recently been re-issued: W. H. D. Rouse, *Greek Votive Offerings* (Hildesheim and New York 1976; first edn Cambridge 1902). A succinct, but useful catalogue of votive offerings known from literary or epigraphical sources has been set up by F. Brommer, *Griechische Weihegaben und Opfer (in Listen)* (Berlin 1985). The papers from a symposium at Uppsala have been published by T. Linders and G. Nordquist, eds, *Gifts to the Gods*, Boreas 15 (Uppsala 1987); connections between cult images and votive figurines, and dedications showing gods other than those worshipped in the sanctuary are discussed by B. Alroth, *Greek Gods and Figurines*, Boreas 18 (Uppsala 1989). S. H.

Langdon, 'Art, religion and society in the Greek Geometric period. Bronze anthropomorphic votive figurines' (Ph.D. diss. Indiana 1984; Ann Arbor 1985) provides an extensive discussion of a central group of early votives; W. Gauer, *Weihgeschenke aus den Perserkriegen, IstMitt* Beih. 2 (Tübingen 1968) studies those from a particular historical situation. An enormous amount of votive inscriptions concerning the archaic period has been collected and analysed by M. L. Lazzarini, 'Le formule delle dediche votive nella Grecia arcaica', *MemLinc* Ser. VIII.19 (1976) 47–354; nothing similar exists for later periods.

On early cult figures the work by I. B. Romano, 'Early Greek cult images' (Ph.D. diss. Pennsylvania 1980; Ann Arbor 1982) is now fundamental. An excellent, general survey of the sculptural decorations of temples and treasuries, stressing their function as conveyors of messages rather than the formal aspects, has recently been published by H. Knell, *Mythos und Polis – Bildprogramme griechischer Bauskulptur* (Darmstadt 1990). The papers published by H. Kyrieleis, ed., *Archaische und klassische griechische Plastik* I–II, international colloquium in Athens 1985 (Mainz 1986) cited as Kyrieleis, ed., *Plastik* I/II, deal to a large extent with recent discoveries of architectural or votive sculptures.

On the important economical functions of Greek sanctuaries, prelude in certain ways to modern banking, there are two solid works by R. Bogaert: *Les origines antiques de la banque de dépôt* (Leiden 1966), and *Banques et banquiers dans les cités grecques* (Leiden 1968).

MINOAN AND MYCENAEAN SANCTUARIES

This field has been particularly rich in new discoveries in recent years. B. Rutkowski, *The Cult Places of the Aegean*, 2nd edn, rev. (New Haven and London 1986) provides a thorough and up-to-date survey. Almost all relevant sites are also discussed in R. Hägg and N. Marinatos, eds, *Sanctuaries and Cults in the Aegean Bronze Age*, papers from the first international symposium at the Swedish Institute in Athens 1980 (Stockholm 1981).

Cult functions connected with the Minoan palaces were discussed in many of the papers published in R. Hägg and N. Marinatos, eds, *The Function of the Minoan Palaces*, 4th international symposium at the Swedish Institute in Athens 1984 (Stockholm 1987). Minor, separate sanctuaries have also been identified; see J.-Cl. Poursat, 'Un sanctuaire du Minoan moyen II à Mallia', *BCH* 90 (1966) 514–51, for a structure at Mallia, and Rutkowski, 234–6, for the preliminary notices on G. Sakellarakis' exciting discovery at Anemospilia near Archanes, alleged to involve a case of human sacrifice. Evidence for the Minoan sanctuary at Symi (for which see also next section) has been presented by A. Lebessi and P. Muhly, 'Aspects of Minoan cult. Sacred enclosures. The evidence from the Symi sanctuary', *AA* 1990, 315–36. Cave, peak and rural sanctuaries have been discussed by P. Faure, 'Nouvelles recherches sur trois sortes de sanctuaires crétois', BCH 91 (1967) 114–50, and 93 (1969) 174–213. The cave sanctuaries, including their continued use in later periods, have been studied by E. L. Tyree, 'Cretan sacred caves. Archaeological evidence' (Ph.D. diss. Columbia 1974; Ann Arbor 1977) following the previous work by P. Faure, Fonctions des cavernes crétoises (Paris 1964). Less attention has been dedicated to the peak sanctuaries; for recent work at the Juktas sanctuary by A. Karetsou there are preliminary notices in Prakt (since 1974), and for the entire group short studies by B. C. Dietrich, 'Peak cults and their place in Minoan religion', Historia 18 (1969) 257–75; D. Levi, 'Caratteri e continuità del culto cretese sulle vette montane', PP 33 (1978) 294–313; and A. A. D. Peatfield, 'Minoan peak sanctuaries: history and society', OpAth 18 (1990) 117–31. A large, general study by the latter is forthcoming.

In the Greek islands the publication of a small sanctuary at Phylakopi on Melos by C. Renfrew, The Archaeology of Cult. The Sanctuary at Phylakopi, BSA Suppl. 18 (London 1985) includes a wealth of essential, theoretical reflections. Far-reaching, theoretical issues are also raised by N. Marinatos's interpretation of the houses with wall paintings in the settlement of Akrotiri on Thera as cult centres; see her book Art and Religion in Thera (Athens 1984) and article 'The West House at Akrotiri as a cult center', AM 98 (1983) 1–19, for preliminary accounts. The temple of Hagia Irini on Keos, with its famous group of large-scale terracotta statues, is another important discovery awaiting publication; one volume, M. E. Caskey, Keos II. The Temple at Ayia Irini. Part I: The Statues (Princeton 1986) has appeared.

On the Greek mainland building complexes of clearly cultic character have been discovered at Tiryns and Mycenae; information can be found in Rutkowski and in the relevant papers in Hägg and Marinatos, eds, Sanctuaries, op. cit., for Tiryns also in the reports by K. Kilian in AA 1978, 449–70, and 1979, 379–411. The general survey of the evidence presented by G. E. Mylonas, Μυκηναϊκή Θρησκεία. Ναοί, βωμοί και τεμένη – Mycenaean Religion. Temples, Altars and Temenea (Athens 1977, Greek and English text) remains useful, but is already dated.

CRETE

The Cretan sanctuaries of early historical times are modest, but show interesting connections with earlier Minoan and with contemporary Oriental traditions.

Cult in the cave of Mt Ida, the legendary birthplace of Zeus, has now been shown to go back to the Minoan period, and much Early Archaic material has also been discovered; see preliminary reports by G. A. Sakellarakis in Prakt since 1983; and his papers 'Ἑκατὸ χρόνια ἔρευνας στὸ Ἴδαιο Ἄντρο', ArchEph 1987, 237–63; and 'The Idaean cave. Minoan and Greek worship', Kernos 1 (1988) 207–14. The same continuity has been demonstrated in the open-air sanctuary for Hermes and Aphrodite at Symi, investigated by A. Lembessi; preliminary reports in *Prakt* since 1972, and one volume of her definitive publication dedicated to Early Archaic, cut-out bronze plaques: *Το ἱερό τοῦ Ἑρμῆ καὶ τῆς Ἀφροδίτης στή Σύμη Βιάννου, I.1: Χάλκινα κρητικά τορεύματα* (Athens 1985). At Smari a small megaron temple seems to continue the religious traditions of a Minoan peak sanctuary: D. Chatzi-Vallianou, 'Σμάρι πεδιάδας', *AAA* 13 (1980) 20–60.

The sanctuary on the acropolis of Gortyn, with an early, atypical temple and a monumental cult statue, has what are probably Oriental affinities; publication by V. S. M. Scrinari and G. Rizza, *Il santuario sull'acropoli di Gortina I* (Rome 1968). Phoenician elements are evident in the cult buildings recently discovered at Kommos on the southern coast; see preliminary reports by J. W. Shaw in *Hesperia* 46 (1977) to 55 (1986), and *idem*, 'Phoenicians in southern Crete', *AJA* 93 (1989) 165–83. The problems involved in architectural reconstructions of the uncanonical, early Cretan temples are emphasized by the provocative study of I. Beyer, *Die Tempel von Dreros und Prinias A und die Chronologie der kretischen Kunst des 8. und 7. Jhs. v. Chr.* (Freiburg i.Br. 1976). A modest, conventional sanctuary for Demeter at Knossos has received an exemplary publication by J. N. Coldstream, *Knossos. The Sanctuary of Demeter*, BSA Suppl. 8 (London 1973).

PELOPONNESIAN SANCTUARIES

In the area of Corinth, the principal sanctuary is the Isthmian one for Poseidon with its pan-Hellenic games, excavated by American scholars from the university of Chicago. The first three volumes of the publication are by O. Broneer, *Isthmia I: Temple of Poseidon* (Princeton 1971); *Isthmia II: Topography and Architecture* (1973); *Isthmia III: Terracotta Lamps* (1977), and the most recent by M. C. Sturgeon, *Isthmia IV: Sculpture I, 1952–1967* (1987). Work has recently been resumed, with important results, particularly concerning the early phases of the sanctuary and the reconstruction of the Early Archaic temple: see the preliminary report by E. R. Gebhard and F. P. Hemans, 'University of Chicago excavations at Isthmia 1989: I', *Hesperia* 61 (1992) 1–77. See also E. R. Gebhard, *The Theater at Isthmia* (Chicago and London 1973), and her important note 'The early sanctuary of Poseidon at Isthmia', *AJA* 91 (1987) 475–6; moreover, R. F. Rhodes, 'Early Corinthian architecture and the origins of the Doric order', *AJA* 91 (1987) 477–80, announcing important conclusions on the early stone temples here and at Corinth. At Corinth, recent investigations of the sanctuary for Demeter and Kore (preliminary reports by R. S. Stroud, N. Bookidis and J. E. Fisher in *Hesperia* 34 (1965) to 43 (1974)) are now to be published: E. G. Pemberton, *Corinth XVIII.1: The Sanctuary of Demeter and Kore: The Greek Pottery* (Princeton 1989) has appeared. See also the small guide by N. Bookidis and

R. S. Stroud, *Demeter and Persephone in Ancient Corinth*, Corinth Notes 2 (Princeton 1987). Early, minor sanctuaries in the area of the Roman Forum have been studied by C. K. Williams II, 'Pre-Roman cults in the area of the Forum of ancient Corinth' (Ph.D. diss. Pennsylvania 1978; Ann Arbor 1979). For another important sanctuary in the area, the Heraion at Perachora, J. Salmon, 'The Heraeum at Perachora and the early history of Corinth and Megara', *BSA* 67 (1972) 159–204, R. A. Tomlinson, 'The upper terraces at Perachora', *BSA* 72 (1977) 179–202, and U. Sinn, 'Das Heraion von Perachora. Eine sakrale Schützzone in der korintischen Peraia', *AM* 105 (1990) 53–116, are important, recent contributions.

In the sanctuary of Nemea the University of California has excavated since 1974 with impressive results; preliminary reports by S. G. Miller in *Hesperia* 44 (1975) to 57 (1988), and he has also edited the excellent, brief presentation *Nemea, a Guide to the Site and Museum* (Berkeley 1990). The temple has been published by B. H. Hill, *The Temple of Zeus at Nemea* (Princeton 1966), but further research has been carried out, and there is also an anastylosis project. Note L. Bacchielli, 'L'adyton del tempio di Zeus a Nemea', *RendLinc* Ser. VIII.37 (1982) 219–37, for the curious, recessed adyton which had perhaps oracular function.

A good, recent summary concerning the sanctuary of Asclepios at Epidauros was published by R. A. Tomlinson, *Epidauros* (London 1983). The study on the epigraphical evidence for the construction of the temple of Asclepios, by A. Burford, *The Greek Temple Builders at Epidauros* (Liverpool 1969) is becoming a classic in its field. R. Patrucco, *Lo stadio di Epidauro* (Florence 1976) is concerned also with the function of the stadion in the sanctuary. L. Käppel, 'Das Theater von Epidauros', *JdI* 104 (1989) 83–106, and H. Büsing, 'Zur Bauplanung der Tholos von Epidauros', *AM* 102 (1987) 225–58, are studies of design principles. A paper by N. Yalouris, 'Die Skulpturen des Asklepios tempels von Epidauros', in Kyrieleis, ed., *Plastik* II, 175–86, was dedicated to the sculptural decorations of the temple of Asclepios. For recent investigations in the sanctuary of Apollo Maleatas there have been preliminary reports by V. Lambrinoudakis in *Prakt* since 1974.

The Heraion of Argos, with its very early and important architectural monuments, has not received the attention it deserves. H. Lauter, 'Zur frühklassischen Neuplanung des Heraions von Argos', *AM* 88 (1973) 175–87, is a structural study; J. C. Wright, 'The old temple terrace at the Argive Heraeum and the early cult of Hera in the Argolid', *JHS* 102 (1982) 186–01, is concerned with the origins of the sanctuary and its first impressive monument. I. Strøm, 'The early sanctuary of the Argive Heraion and its external relations', *ActaArch* 59 (1988) 173–203, and C. M. Antonaccio, 'Terraces, tombs and the early Argive Heraion', *Hesperia* 61 (1992) 85–105, discuss the Early Archaic period and the old temple. A re-publication of the Classical temple is needed, and has been undertaken by C. Pfaff.

An excellent, general review of the literary and archaeological evidence from Arcadian sanctuaries has recently been published by M. Jost, *Sanctuaires et cultes d'Arcadie* (Paris 1985); R. Stiglitz, *Die grossen Göttinnen Arkadiens* (Vienna 1967) remains useful for the traditions and rites of the various local Demeter sanctuaries. M. E. Voyatzis, *The Early Sanctuary of Athena Alea at Tegea* (Göteborg 1990) is also concerned with early stages of other Arcadian sanctuaries, with particular emphasis on the votive gifts. In the Tegea sanctuary the Archaic temple has recently been identified by E. Østby, 'The Archaic temple of Athena Alea at Tegea', *OpAth* 16 (1986) 75–102, and an excavation project conducted by the Norwegian Institute in Athens has been taken up. The four temples at nearby Pallantion and the finds from them will be published by A. De Franciscis, M. Iozzo, M. Pagano and E. Østby in *ASAtene*, with a general discussion of Archaic Arcadian temple architecture (by E. Østby). The Despoina sanctuary at Lycosoura has never been properly published and deserves further field work; see G. Orlandini, 'Considerazioni sul *Mégaron* di Despoina a Licosura', *ASAtene* 47–8 (1969–70) 343–57, and I. and E. Loucas, 'The megaron of Lykosoura and some prehistoric telesteria', *JPR* 2 (1988) 25–34, for two interesting, preliminary approaches. Good, general publications exist for the Archaic sanctuary of Athena at Alipheira (A. K. Orlandos, Ἡ ἀρκαδικὴ Ἀλίφειρα καὶ τὰ μνημεία της, Athens 1967–8) and for the later sanctuary of Aphrodite Erycina at Psophis (Ch. Kardara, Ἀφροδίτη Ἐρυκίνη. Ἱερόν καί μαντεῖον εἰς τήν ΒΔ Ἀρκαδίαν, Athens 1988). For the temple and sanctuary of Apollo at Bassae the publication by F. A. Cooper is awaited, to replace the preliminary issue 'The temple of Apollo at Bassai, a preliminary study' (Ph.D. diss. Pennsylvania 1970; London and New York 1978); note also N. Gialouris, 'Problems relating to the temple of Apollo Epikourios at Bassai', in *Acta of the XIth International Congress of Classical Archaeology* (London 1979) 89–104.

For a general, recent survey of Laconian cults and sanctuaries the second part of Ch. Kardara, Οἱ Λακεδαιμόνιοι. Πολιτική, κοινωνική, πολιτειακή καί θρησκευτική ἱστορία τῆς ἀρχαίας Σπάρτης (Athens 1979) can be recommended. Material from the Orthia sanctuary has been studied by E. L. I. Marangou, *Lakonische Elfenbein- und Beinschnitzereien* (Tübingen 1969), and by J. B. Carter, 'The masks of Ortheia', *AJA* 91 (1987) 355–83. On the Apollo sanctuary at Amyklae, where cult continuity from the Mycenaean period is presumed, S. P. Antonakos, Ἀμύκλαι (Athens 1982) is superficial, but useful as an introduction; the last study on the throne is by R. Martin, 'Bathyclès de Magnésie et le "trône" d'Apollon à Amyklae', *RA* 1976, 205–18. N. D. Papachatzis, 'Ποσειδῶν Ταινάριος', *ArchEph* 1976, 102–25, discusses the modest remains of a sanctuary with considerable religious importance.

The Hellenistic sanctuary of Asclepios at Messene is best described by A. K. Orlandos in his contribution to Jantzen, ed., *Neue Forschungen* 9–38; the investigations are now carried on by P. Themelis. The mystery cult in the sanctuary at Andania is known only through an inscription, last discussed by

P. K. Georgouzos, 'Τά μυστήρια τῆς 'Ανδανίας', *Platon* 31 (1979) 3–43. An old, German excavation of a rural sanctuary in Triphylia has recently been published, including the votive material, by U. Sinn, 'Das Heiligtum der Artemis Limnatis bei Kombothekra', *AM* 93 (1978) 45–82, and 96 (1981) 25–71; at another such sanctuary H. Knell, 'Lepreon. Der Tempel der Demeter', *AM* 98 (1983) 113–47, is concerned only with the temple. In Elis, the Early Classical temple for an unidentified deity at Mazi, with a Late Classical pediment decoration, has been studied by A.-I. Trianti: *Ο γλυπτός διάκοσμος του ναού στο Μάζι της Ηλείας* (Thessaloniki 1985), notices in *Prakt* 1978, 125–9, and a paper on the pediment (title as above) in Kyrieleis, ed., *Plastik* II, 155–68. Austrian excavations at Aigeira in Achaia have discovered early temple buildings on the acropole; preliminary reports by W. Alzinger in *ÖJh* from 51 (1976–7) on, and an extensive account by the same author 'Aigeira-Hyperesia und die Siedlung Phelloë in Achaia I: Akropolis', *Klio* 67 (1985) 426–51.

OLYMPIA

The German investigations at Olympia have been going on almost without interruption since 1875 (cf. A. Mallwitz, 'Ein Jahrhundert deutsche Ausgrabungen in Olympia', *AM* 92 (1977) 1–31). The best general account of the sanctuary and its history is undoubtedly H.-V. Herrmann, *Olympia. Heiligtum und Wettkampfstätte* (Munich 1972), with an excellent bibliography of earlier works. L. Drees, *Olympia. Götter, Künstler und Athleten* (Stuttgart 1967; English edn, *Olympia. Gods, Artists and Athletes*, London 1968) is more popular. A. Mallwitz, *Olympia und seine Bauten* (Munich 1972) pays particular attention to the buildings and can be considered as an unusually thorough guide-book to the site. Much recent research was summarized in the exhibition catalogues by B. Fellmann and H. Scheyhing, eds, *100 Jahre deutsche Ausgrabung in Olympia* (Munich 1972) and by A. Mallwitz and H.-V. Herrmann, eds, *Die Funde aus Olympia. Ergebnisse hundertjähriger Ausgrabungstätigkeit* (Athens 1980). The old series of preliminary publications *Olympiabericht* has only been issued twice since 1965: vol. VIII, 1958–62, ed. E. Kunze (Berlin 1967) and vol. X, 1966–76, ed. A. Mallwitz (Berlin 1981); vol. IX has never appeared. The principal publications are now the monographical volumes of the series 'Olympische Forschungen' (OF).

Previous discussions of the prehistoric origins of the Olympian sanctuary, even as recent ones as H.-V. Herrmann, 'Prähistorisches Olympia', in H.-G. Buchholz, ed., *Ägäische Bronzezeit* (Darmstadt 1987) 426–36, or his 'Zum Problem des mykenischen Ursprungs griechischer Heiligtümer. Olympia und Delphi', in *Forschungen zur ägäischen Vorgeschichte. Das Ende der mykenischen Welt* (Cologne 1987) 151–72, must now be revised in the light of the most recent German investigations at the Pelopeion, whose origin can be shown to go back to Early Helladic times; see H. Kyrieleis, 'Neue Ausgrabungen in Olympia', *AntW* 21 (1990) 177–88, for a preliminary account, also concerned with the Geometric and Early Archaic periods. The early historic period is discussed in the recent study by C. Morgan, *Athletes and Oracles. The Transformation of Delphi and Olympia in the Eighth Century BC* (Cambridge 1990). The old oracle of Zeus was discussed by H. W. Parke, *The Oracles of Zeus* (London 1967; also on the oracles of Dodona and Zeus Ammon at Siwa). On the games there are some popular accounts, such as H. Bengtson, *Die olympischen Spiele in der Antike* (Zürich and Stuttgart 1971), M. I. Finley and H. W. Pleket, *The Olympic Games: The First Thousand Years* (London 1976), and N. Yalouris, ed., *The Eternal Olympics* (New Rochelle 1979; also published as *The Olympic Games*, Athens 1980); there is no recent scholarly study, but the papers published in N. Coulson and H. Kyrieleis, eds, *Proceedings of an International Symposium on the Olympic Games* (Athens 1992) and in W. J. Raschke, ed., *The Archaeology of the Olympics* (Madison 1988; also on games generally and elsewhere) are useful and interesting. Note for the female games of the Heraia Th. F. Scanlon, 'The footrace of the Heraia at Olympia', *AncW* 9 (1984) 77–90. Political aspects of the sanctuary have been discussed by A. Hönle, 'Olympia in der Politik der griechischen Staatenwelt' (Ph.D. diss. Tübingen 1968). An account of Olympia in the Roman period is given by A. Mallwitz, 'Olympia und Rom', *AntW* 19.2 (1988) 21–45.

Previous reconstructions of a temple preceding the Heraion have been shown to be unfounded by A. Mallwitz, 'Das Heraion von Olympia und seine Vorgänger', *JdI* 81 (1966) 310–76, but he does not exclude the possibility that some such building existed. Concerned with the Heraion are also A. E. Kalpaxis, 'Bemerkungen zu den Innensäulen des Heraion von Olympia', *AM* 90 (1975) 83–96, and U. Sinn, "Εκτυπον. Der sog. Hera-Kopf aus Olympia', *AM* 99 (1984) 77–87, connecting the famous head with a presumed sphinx in a relief pediment. Recent work on the temple of Zeus has been summarized by P. Grunauer, 'Der Zeustempel in Olympia – Neue Aspekte', *BonnJbb* 171 (1971) 114–31. After the essentially pictorial volume by B. Ashmole and N. Gialouris, *Olympia. The Sculptures of the Temple of Zeus* (London 1967), the more important works on the sculptural decoration have been re-issued with some excellent, original contributions by H.-V. Herrmann, *Die Olympiaskulpturen* (Darmstadt 1987, with full bibliography until 1984, pp. 339–47). Note also J. Fink, *Der Thron des Zeus in Olympia. Bildwelt und Weltbild* (Munich 1967; based on Pausanias' description).

Other buildings and monuments have also been discussed: the prytaneion by S. G. Miller, 'The prytaneion at Olympia', *AM* 86 (1971) 79–107; the Philippeion by S. G. Miller, 'The Philippeion and Macedonian Hellenistic architecture', *AM* 88 (1973) 189–218; W.-D. Heilmeyer, 'Durchgang, Krypte, Denkmal: Zur Geschichte des Stadioneingangs in Olympia', *AM* 99 (1984) 251–63, for the last contribution on this particularly difficult structure; and W. Koenigs, *Die Echohalle*, OF 14 (Berlin 1984). For recent reconstruction and excavation activity in the area of the treasuries: K. Herrmann, A. Mallwitz and H. van de Löcht, 'Bericht über Restaurierungsarbeiten in Olympia. Schatzhaus der Sikyonier', *AA* 1980, 351–67, and J. Schilbach, 'Untersuchung der Schatzhausterrasse südlich des Schatzhauses der Sikyonier in Olympia', *AA* 1984, 225–36; also K. Herrmann, 'Beobachtungen zur Schatzhaus-Architektur Olympias', in Jantzen, ed., *Neue Forschungen* 321–50. For various votive dedications: K. Herrmann, 'Spätarchaische Votivsäulen in Olympia', *AM* 99 (1984) 121–43; F. Eckstein, *ΑΝΑΘΗΜΑΤΑ. Studien zu den Weihgeschenken strengen Stils im Heiligtum von Olympia* (Berlin 1969); H.-V. Herrmann, 'Die Siegerstatuen von Olympia', *Nikephoros* 1 (1988) 119–83; W. Hoepfner, *Zwei Ptolemaierbauten. Das Ptolemaierweihgeschenk in Olympia und ein Bauvorhaben in Alexandria*, *AM* Beih. 1 (Berlin 1971) 1–54; R. Bol, *Das Statuenprogramm des Herodes-Atticus-Nymphäums*, OF 15 (Berlin 1984); K. Hitzl, *Die kaiserzeitliche Statuenausstattung des Metroon*, OF 19 (Berlin and New York 1991). Several studies have been dedicated to the Nike monument by Paionios: W. Deonna, *La Niké de Paeonios de Mendé et le triangle sacré des monuments figurés*, Coll. Latomus 62 (Brussels 1968); K. Herrmann, 'Der Pfeiler der Paionios-Nike in Olympia', *JdI* 87 (1972) 232–57; T. Hölscher, 'Die Nike der Messenier und Naupaktier in Olympia. Kunst und Geschichte im späten 5. Jahrhundert v. Chr.', *JdI* 89 (1974) 70–111.

Most of the volumes in the OF series have been dedicated to votive objects: H.-V. Herrmann, *Die Kessel der orientalisierenden Zeit 1*, OF 6 (Berlin 1966); W.-D. Heilmeyer, *Frühe olympische Tonfiguren*, OF 7 (Berlin 1972); W. Gauer, *Die Tongefässe aus dem Brunnen unterm Stadion-Nordwall und im Südostgebiet*, OF 8 (Berlin 1975); P. C. Bol, *Grossplastik aus Bronze in Olympia*, OF 9 (Berlin 1978); M. Maass, *Die geometrischen Dreifüsse von Olympia*, OF 10 (Berlin 1978); H.-V. Herrmann, *Die Kessel der orientalisierender Zeit 2, Kesselprotomen und Stabdreifüsse*, OF 11 (Berlin 1979). Note for this material also H.-V. Herrmann, 'Kesselschmuck, Nachträge', *AM* 99 (1984) 17–33, and W. Gauer, 'Gerät- und Gefässfüsse mit Löwenpranken und figürlichem Schmuck aus Olympia', ibid. 35–53. Furthermore: W.-D. Heilmeyer, *Frühe olympische Bronzefiguren, die Tiervotive*, OF 12 (Berlin 1979); H. Philipp, *Bronzeschmuck aus Olympia*, OF 13 (Berlin 1981); B. Fellmann, *Frühe olympische Gürtelschmuckscheiben aus Bronze*, OF 16 (Berlin 1984); P. C. Bol, *Argivische Schilde*, OF 17 (Berlin and New York 1989). To the latter publication, including recent finds of Archaic shield-straps with narrative decoration, the paper on Etruscan imitations by A. Moustaka, 'Spätarchaische Weihgaben aus Etrurien in Olympia', *AA* 1985, 353–64, can be added. Evidence for the fabrication of bronze objects in the sanctuary was presented by W.-D. Heilmeyer, 'Giessereibetriebe in Olympia', *JdI* 84 (1969) 1–28, and has been confirmed by the recent discovery of a classical foundry: W.-D. Heilmeyer, G. Zimmer and

G. Schneider, 'Die Bronzegiesserei unter der Werkstatt des Phidias in Olympia', *AA* 1987, 239–99. Similar observations have also been made in other sanctuaries.

DELPHI

Delphi's position as the most prestigious of all Greek sanctuaries, with fame and renown far beyond the Greek world, is well reflected in the steady stream of small and large publications dedicated to it. The excavations and investigations have been going on since 1893, carried out by the French school in Athens; the definitive publications appear in the series 'Fouilles de Delphes' (*FdD*, 34 volumes to date), preliminary reports regularly in the *BCH*. For a general account of the site and the collections in the museums two official guides produced by the French school, on the pattern of their similar guides for Delos and Thasos, have recently appeared: J.-F. Bommelaer, *Guide de Delphes. Le site* and (no named author) *Guide de Delphes. Le musée* (both Athens/Paris 1991). Other general works, with particular emphasis on the oracle function, are P. Hoyle, *Delphi* (London 1967); G. Roux, *Delphes, son oracle et ses dieux*, 2nd edn (Paris 1976); and M. Delcourt, *L'oracle de Delphes*, 2nd edn (Paris 1981). In English there is the heavy study by J. Fontenrose, *The Delphic Oracle. Its Responses and Operations with a Catalogue of Responses* (Berkeley 1978), and another by the same author on the mythical origins of the sanctuary: *Python, A Study of Delphic Myth and its Origins*, 2nd edn (Berkeley 1980). Note for these themes also the studies by C. Sourvinou-Inwood, 'The myth of the first temples at Delphi', *CQ* 73 (1979) 231–51, and 'Myth as history: The previous owners of the Delphic oracle', in J. Bremmer, ed., *Interpretations of Greek Mythology* (London and Sydney 1987) 215–41; and J. Defradas, *Les thèmes de la propaganda delphique*, 2nd edn, rev. (Paris 1972) for various aspects of Delphic ideology. J. Fontenrose, 'The cult of Apollo and the games at Delphi', in W. J. Raschke, ed., *The Archaeology of the Olympics* (Madison 1988) 121–40, is a recent study of the games. For three important phases in the historical development, the studies by C. Morgan, *Athletes and Oracles: The Transformation of Delphi and Olympia in the Eighth Century* BC (Cambridge 1990); H. W. Parke, 'Croesus and Delphi', *GRBS* 25 (1984) 209–32; and S. Levin, 'The old Greek oracles in decline', *ANRW* II.18,2 (1989) 1599–649, should be mentioned. For the early topographical development P. de La Coste-Messelière, 'Topographie delphique', *BCH* 93 (1969) 730–58, is fundamental. *Etudes delphiques*, *BCH* Suppl. 4 (Paris 1977), contains miscellaneous papers mostly on archaeological and epigraphical material. For the inscriptions, which cover an extensive section of the *FdD*, the publications by G. Rougemont, *Corpus des inscriptions de Delphes, 1. Lois sacrées et règlements religieux* (Paris 1977); J. Bousquet, *Corpus des inscriptions de Delphes, 2. Les comptes du quatrième et du troisième siècle*

(Paris 1989); and also by the latter, *Etudes sur les comptes de Delphes*, BEFAR 267 (Paris 1988) should be mentioned.

The progression of the work on the Late Classical temple of Apollo can be traced through inscriptions; G. Roux, *L'amphictionie, Delphes et le temple d'Apollon au IVe siècle* (Lyon and Paris 1979) and J.-Fr. Bommelaer, 'La construction du temple classique de Delphes', *BCH* 107 (1983) 191–216, are concerned with this material, and there is an important section on the temple in the extensive report by P. Amandry, 'Chronique delphique (1970–81)', *BCH* 105 (1981) 673–769. The fragments of the Classical pediment decorations have been studied by F. Croissant, 'Les frontons du temple du IVe siècle à Delphes: esquisse d'une restitution', in Kyrieleis, ed., *Plastik* II, 187–97, and by A. Stewart, 'Dionysos at Delphi. The pediments of the sixth temple of Apollo and religious reform in the age of Alexander', in B. Barr-Sharra and E. N. Borza, eds, *Macedonia and Greece in Late Classical and Early Hellenistic Times* (Washington 1982) 205–27. Date and other problems connected with the altar have been discussed by P. Amandry, 'Chios and Delphi', in J. Boardman and C. E. Vaphopoulou-Richardson, eds, *Chios* (Oxford 1986) 205–32; see also E. Stikas, 'La restauration de l'autel d'Apollon à Delphes', *BCH* 103 (1979) 479–500.

More attention has been devoted to minor buildings and monuments in the sanctuary. The Sicyonian treasury and the Archaic building material in its foundations has now been studied by D. Laroche and M.-D. Nenna, 'Le trésor de Sicyone et ses fondations', *BCH* 114 (1990) 241–84; see J. de La Genière, 'A propos des métopes du monoptère de Sicyone à Delphes', *CRAI* 1983, 158–71, and G. N. Szeliga, 'The composition of the Argo metopes from the monopteros at Delphi', *AJA* 90 (1986) 297–305, for proposals to connect this monument with the western Greek world. The architecture of the Siphnian treasury has now been published by G. Daux and E. Hansen, *Le trésor de Siphnos*, *FdD* II (Paris 1987), and several important contributions have appeared on the sculptural decoration: L. V. Watrous, 'The sculptural program of the Siphnian treasury at Delphi', *AJA* 86 (1982) 159–72; E. Simon, 'Ikonographie und Epigraphik. Zum Bauschmuck des Siphnier-schatzhauses in Delphi', *ZPE* 57 (1984) 1–22; V. Brinkmann, 'Die aufgemalten Namensbeischriften an Nord- und Ostfries des Siphnier-schatzhauses', *BCH* 109 (1985) 77–130; M. B. Moore, 'The West Frieze of the Siphnian treasury: A new reconstruction', *BCH* 109 (1985) 131–56. The traditional date of the monument, about 525 BC has been questioned by E. D. Francis and M. Vickers, '*Signa priscae artis*: Eretria and Siphnos', *JHS* 103 (1983) 49–67, but is fiercely defended by P. Amandry, 'A propos des monuments de Delphes: questions de chronologie', *BCH* 112 (1988) 591–610. The old discussion on the date of the Athenian treasury continues, but there have been attempts at compromise solutions (W. Gauer, 'Das Athenerschatzhaus und die marathonischen Akrothinia in Delfi', in F. Krinzinger, B. Otto and E. Walde-Psenner, eds, *Festschrift B. Neutsch*

(Innsbruck 1980) 127–36); the metope decoration has last been discussed by K. Hoffelner, 'Die Metopen des Athener Schatzhauses. Ein neuer Rekonstruktionsversuch', *AM* 103 (1988), 77–117. The portico of the Athenians has been downdated and re-assessed by J. Walsh, 'The date of the Athenian stoa at Delphi', *AJA* 90 (1986) 319–36. On later treasuries there are studies by J.-P. Michaud, *Le trésor de Thèbes, FdD* II.3 (Paris 1973), and by D. Laroche, 'L'emplacement du trésor de Cyrène à Delphes', *BCH* 112 (1988) 291–305. Ch. Le Roy, *Les terres cuites architecturales, FdD* II.2 (Paris 1967) includes some particularly important evidence for archaic buildings.

Much research, and re-thinking, has recently been concerned with the large sculptural dedications. Cl. Vatin, 'Monuments votifs de Delphes', *BCH* 105 (1981) 429–59, and 106 (1982) 509–25, has studied palimpsest inscriptions and identifies 'Kleobis' and 'Biton' as Dioscuri. H. J. Schalles, 'Zur Deutung der unteren Tarentinerbasis in Delphi', *AA* 1981, 65–75, and L. Beschi, 'I donari tarantini a Delfi; alcune considerazioni', in M. L. Gualandi, ed., *Aparchai P. E. Arias* (Pisa 1982) 227–38, are concerned with the Tarentine dedications. P. Roesch, 'La base des Béotiens à Delphes', *CRAI* 1984, 177–95, is also concerned with the course of the sacred way. Several important monuments have been illuminated and even discovered in the last few years: A. Jacquemin and D. Laroche, 'Notes sur trois piliers delphiques', *BCH* 106 (1982) 191–218, and 'Le char d'or consacré par le peuple rhodien', *BCH* 110 (1986) 285–307; by D. Laroche, 'Nouvelles observations sur l'offrande de Platées', *BCH* 113 (1989) 183–98; again by A. Jacquemin and D. Laroche, 'Une base pour l'Apollon de Salamine à Delphes', *BCH* 112 (1988) 235–46, and 'Une offrande monumentale à Delphes: le trépied des Crotoniates', *BCH* 114 (1990) 299–323. See for the various Delphian tripod dedications also P. Amandry, 'Trépieds de Delphes et du Péloponnése', *BCH* 111 (1987) 79–131. His paper 'Statue de taureau en argent', in *Etudes delphiques*, op. cit., 273–93, presents perhaps the most impressive recent addition to the Delphi museum, Cl. Rolley, 'En regardant l'Aurige', *BCH* 114 (1990), 285–97, a new reconstruction of the most famous Delphic dedication. Minor objects have received less attention, beyond the volumes by Cl. Rolley, *Les statuettes de bronze, FdD* V.2 (Paris 1969), his *Les trépieds à cuve clouée, FdD* V.3 (Paris 1977), and M.-A. Zagdoun, *Reliefs, FdD* IV.6 (1977); add the special study by L. Lerat, 'Trois boucliers archaïques de Delphes', *BCH* 104 (1980) 93–114.

On monuments outside the sanctuary, but connected with it, there are publications by R. Aupert and O. Callot, *Le stade, FdD* II (Paris 1979), and G. Roux and O. Callot, *La terrasse d'Attale I, FdD* II (Paris 1987); and on the Castalia fountain P. Amandry, 'Notes de topographie et d'architecture delphiques VI/VII. La fontaine Castalia', in *Etudes delphiques*, op. cit., 179–228, and *BCH* 102 (1978) 221–41; and H. W. Parke, 'Castalia', ibid. 199–219. The sanctuary of Athena Pronaia at Marmaria has received due attention, with a publication of the late Classical temple by J.-P. Michaud, *Le temple en calcaire*, *FdD* II.4 (Paris 1977), and a note on the pediment sculptures of the Archaic forerunner by P. Themelis, 'Neues über die Giebelskulpturen des Athena-Tempels II in Delphi', in Kyrieleis, ed., *Plastik* II, 153–63; recent studies on the tholos and its decoration by J. Marcadé, 'Les métopes mutilées de la Tholos de Marmaria à Delphes', *CRAI* 1979, 151–70 (updated by *idem*, in Kyrieleis, ed., *Plastik* II, 169–73) and by G. Roux, 'La tholos d'Athéna Pronaia dans son sanctuaire de Delphes', *CRAI* 1988, 290–309; and a discussion of the building with two rooms west of the Classical temple, variously identified as a particular temple building, a *hestiatorion* and a provisory sculptor's atelier (N. Bookidis, 'The priest's house in the Marmaria at Delphi', *BCH* 107 (1983) 149–55; J. Bousquet, 'L'atelier de la tholos de Delphes', *BCH* 108 (1984) 199–206). The precise identification of the various buildings depends on the interpretation of a difficult passage in Pausanias, on which no agreement has been reached; see J.-Cl. Carrière, 'La révolution de Cratès à Delphes et la reconstruction des temples du sanctuaire d'Athéna Pronaia', in H. Walter, ed., *Hommages L. Lerat* (Paris 1984) 145–79, and L. Lerat, 'Les "énigmes de Marmaria"', *BCH* 109 (1985) 255–64, for recent contributions.

CENTRAL AND NORTHERN GREECE

A full and precise general survey of cults and sanctuaries in Boeotia is given by A. Schachter, *Cults of Boiotia*, BICS Suppl. 38.1 (London 1981) and 38.2 (London 1986), 38.3 still to appear, with bibliographical references. The most extensively investigated sanctuary in this region is doubtless the Kabirion at Thebes, where the German institute of Athens has taken up a pre-war excavation; preliminary report by G. Bruns, *AA* 1967, 228–73, and volumes of the definitive publication (following vol. I by P. Wolters and G. Bruns, *Das Kabirenheiligtum bei Theben*, Berlin 1940) by W. Heyder and A. Mallwitz, *Die Bauten im Kabirenheiligtum bei Theben* II (Berlin 1978); U. Heimberg, *Die Keramik des Kabirions* III (Berlin 1982); K. Braun and Th. E. Haevernick, *Bemalte Keramik und Glas aus dem Kabirenheiligtum bei Theben* IV (Berlin 1981); B. Schmaltz, *Terrakotten aus dem Kabiren- heiligtum bei Theben* V (Berlin 1974); B. Schmaltz, *Metallfiguren aus dem Kabirenheiligtum bei Theben* VI (Berlin 1980). The bones have been studied by J. Boessneck, *Die Tierknochenfunde aus dem Kabirenheiligtum bei Theben (Böotien)* (Munich 1973). Much work remains to be done with the sanctuary of Apollo at Ptoon, where the unusually numerous votive kouroi have been published by J. Ducat, *Les kouroi du Ptoion*, BEFAR 219 (Paris 1971).

In the neighbouring region of Phokis, German excavations in the sanctuary of Artemis and Apollo at Kalapodi (ancient Hyampolis) have uncovered an impressive group of Classical and Archaic temples and cult structures, including Mycenaean material; extensive, preliminary reports by R. C. S.

Felsch and his collaborators in *AAA* 8 (1975) 1–24; *AA* 1980, 38–123; *AA* 1987, 1–99.

In the pan-Aetolian sanctuary of Thermon attention has always been attracted to the succession of Early Archaic temples, discussed mostly in the context of general studies on early temple architecture. On temple C there has been some discussion on the frieze construction: I. Beyer, 'Der Triglyphenfries von Thermos C', *AA* 1972, 197–226; T. E. Kalpaxis, 'Zum aussergewöhnlichen Triglyphenfries vom Apollontempel C in Thermos', *AA* 1974, 105–14. On the earlier temple B, with the presumed remains of an ellipsoid peristasis, there are studies by B. Schmaltz, 'Bemerkungen zu Thermos B', *AA* 1980, 318–36, and by B. Wesenberg, 'Thermos B 1', *AA* 1982, 149–57. Investigations have recently been taken up by I. A. Papapostolou (brief notes in *Prakt* since 1983).

On the ancient oracle of Zeus at Dodona there is a section in H. W. Parke, *The Oracles of Zeus* (London 1967), and a general study by L. Treadwell III, 'Dodona; an oracle of Zeus' (Ph.D. diss. Western Michigan 1970; Ann Arbor 1987). S. I. Dakaris, *Archaeological Guide to Dodona* (Ioannina 1971) is a concise guide to the site. On the poorly known athletic games there is a recent study by P. Cabanes, 'Les concours des *Naia* de Dodone', *Nikephoros* 1 (1988) 49–84. For the Greek excavations there are preliminary reports by S. I. Dakaris in *Prakt* 1965–74 and 1981–3. Another unusual and interesting sanctuary of chthonic character in this area, the Nekyomanteion at Ephyra, has also been an object of Greek excavations in the 1960s and 1970s; see S. I. Dakaris in *Prakt* 1975–7 for the most recent, preliminary notices, and his *The Antiquity of Epirus* (Athens n.d.) for a short guide to the site.

At Corfu, the various temples and sanctuaries have received comparatively little attention. J. L. Benson, 'The central group of the Corfu pediment', in M. Rohde-Liegle, H. A. Cahn and H. Ch. Ackermann, eds, *Festschrift K. Schefold*, AntK 4. Beih. (Berne 1967), 48–60, is the only important study dedicated to the famous Gorgon pediment; for another, smaller Archaic pediment recently discovered there is a preliminary notice by A. Choremis, ''Αρχαϊκὸν ἀέτωμα ἐκ Κερκύρας', *AAA* 7 (1974), 183–6. The small temple at Kardaki has been studied, unfortunately without autopsy, by W. B. Dinsmoor Jr, 'The Kardaki temple re-examined', *AM* 88 (1973), 165–74. A full publication of the material from the sanctuary at Mon Repos is much desired; G. Dontas has given a general account in his 'Denkmäler und Geschichte eines kerkyräischen Heiligtums', in Jantzen, ed., *Neue Forschungen* 121–33.

Sanctuaries in Northern Greece are at present few and modest, but more may turn up under the lively excavation activity of the last years. The contribution by E. Juri, 'Τὸ ἐν 'Αφύτει ἱερὸν τοῦ Διονύσου καὶ τὸ ἱερὸν τοῦ "Αμμωνος Διός', in Jantzen, ed., *Neue Forschungen* 135–50, is concerned with small sanctuaries, including a Late Classical, Doric temple, at Kallithea (Aphytis) in the Chalkidiki.

ATHENS AND ATTICA

For sanctuaries and other sites of this region, general information and a full bibliography up to 1985 is provided by J. Travlos, *Bildlexikon zur Topographie des antiken Attika* (Tübingen 1988), also bringing up to date the material on Athens collected in his *Pictorial Dictionary of Ancient Athens* (New York and Washington 1971) 26–33. General studies involving the entire complex of Attic sanctuaries at different periods (mostly including the Acropolis) are J. S. Boersma, *Athenian Building Policy from 561/0 to 405/4 BC* (Groningen 1970); H. Knell, 'Vier attische Tempel klassischer Zeit', *AA* 1973, 94–114; H. Knell, *Perikleische Baukunst* (Darmstadt 1979); F. Kolb, 'Die Bau-, Religions- und Kulturpolitik der Peisistratiden', *JdI* 92 (1977) 99–138. The sanctuaries for the phyle heroes are among the material discussed by U. Kron, *Die zehn attischen Phylenheroen*, *AM* Beih. 5 (Berlin 1976). Various architectural decorations have been assembled by A. Delivorrias, *Attische Giebelskulpturen und Akrotere des fünften Jahrhunderts* (Tübingen 1974).

On the northern coast of Attica, the precise and exhaustive publication of the sanctuary of Amphiaraos at Oropos by V. Chr. Petrakos, "Ο Ὠρωπός καὶ το ἱερόν τοῦ Ἀμφιαράου (Athens 1968) has been followed only by a thorough publication of the stoa (J. J. Coulton, 'The stoa at the Amphiaraion, Oropos', *BSA* 63 (1968) 147–83) and by A. Petropoulou, 'The *Eparche* documents and the early oracle at Oropus', *GRBS* 22 (1981) 39–63. V. Chr. Petrakos has afterwards turned his attention to a long-term investigation at Rhamnous, including the sanctuary of Nemesis, with preliminary reports in *Prakt* since 1975, and two recent, general accounts: 'Το Νεμέσειον του Ραμνουντος' in *Φίλια ἔπη* to G. Mylonas 2 (Athens 1987) 295–326, and 'Οἱ ἀνασκαφὲς τοῦ Ραμνοῦντος (1813–1987)', *ArchEph* 1987, 267–98. On the Classical temple there is a recent and exhaustive publication by M. M. Miles, 'A reconstruction of the temple of Nemesis at Rhamnous', *Hesperia* 58 (1989) 133–249. Much recent work has been done on the fragments of the cult statue and its base. See for this G. I. Despinis, Συμβολή στή μελέτη τοῦ ἔργου τοῦ Ἀγορακρίτου (Athens 1971; the statue), and V. Petrakos, 'La base de la Némésis d'Agoracrite', *BCH* 105 (1981) 227–53; also *idem*, in Kyrieleis, ed., *Plastik* II, 89–107.

At the sanctuary for Artemis and Iphigenia at Brauron, more attention has been dedicated to cult and rites than to the archaeological material. Thorough, general accounts have been given by the discoverer: I. D. Kondis, 'Ἄρτεμις Βραυρωνία', *ArchDelt* 22.A (1967) 156–206; and quite recently by A. I. Antoniou, Βραυρών. Συμβολή στην ιστορία του ιερού της Βραυρωνίας Ἀρτέμιδος (Athens 1990). The principal building in the sanctuary, a stoa, has been studied by Ch. Bouras, Η ἀναστήλωσις τῆς στοᾶς τῆς Βραυρῶνος, *ArchDelt* Suppl. 11 (Athens 1967). For the temple, compared with other temples for Artemis in the region see the contribution by I. Travlos, 'Τρεῖς ναοί τῆς Ἀρτέμιδος: Αὐλιδίας, Ταυροπόλου καὶ Βραυρωνίας', in Jantzen, ed., *Neue Forschungen* 197–205; note, however, M. B. Hollinshead, 'Against Iphigeneia's adyton in three mainland temples', *AJA* 89 (1985) 419–40. For the cult and legends there are studies by L. Kahil, 'Autour de l'Artemis attique', *AntK* 8 (1965) 20–33 (also on the connections with the cult for Artemis Mounychia at Pireus) and her 'L'Artemis de Brauron: rites et mystère', *AntK* 20 (1977) 86–98; W. Sale, 'The temple-legends of the Arkteia', *RheinMus* 118 (1975) 265–84; A. Antoniou, 'Minoische Elemente im Kult der Artemis von Brauron', *Philologus* 125 (1981) 291–6; P. Perlman, 'Plato, *Laws* 833 C – 834 D and the bears of Brauron', *GRBS* 24 (1983) 115–30.

Far less attention has been devoted to the sanctuaries at Sounion. W. B. Dinsmoor jr, *Sounion* (Athens 1971) is a short, but good general guide; H. Abramson, 'A hero shrine for Phrontis at Sounion', *CSCA* 12 (1979) 1–19, deals with a small, particular sanctuary. Rustic sanctuaries in Attica have been published by H. Lauter, 'Ein ländliches Heiligtum hellenistischer Zeit in Trapouria (Attika)', *AA* 1980, 242–55; H. Lauter, *Der Kultplatz auf dem Turkovuni*, *AM* Beih. 12 (Berlin 1985); and M. K. Langdon, *A Sanctuary of Zeus on Mount Hymettos*, *Hesperia* Suppl. 16 (Princeton 1976). For the sanctuary of Artemis Mounychia at Pireus, mentioned above, there is a publication by L. Palaiokrassa, Τό ἱερό τῆς Ἀρτέμιδος Μουνιχίας (Thessaloniki 1983), to which her article 'Neue Befunde aus dem Heiligtum der Artemis Munichia', *AM* 104 (1989) 1–40, is a supplement.

Beyond the works cited in the first paragraph, general information on the sanctuaries of Athens is to be found in R. E. Wycherley, *The Stones of Athens* (Princeton 1978); note also his 'Minor shrines in ancient Athens', *Phoenix* 24 (1970) 283–95. Work on the sanctuaries of Athens, except for the Acropolis, has been comparatively scarce. The date of the temple at the Illissos has been discussed, and tends now to be more closely connected with the temple of Athena Nike; see C. A. Picón, 'The Ilissos temple reconsidered', *AJA* 82 (1978) 47–81, and M. M. Miles, 'The date of the temple on the Ilissos river', *Hesperia* 49 (1980) 309–25 (but note also W. A. P. Childe, 'In defense of an early date for the frieze of the temple on the Ilissos', *AM* 100 (1985) 207–51). See for the frieze A. Krug, 'Der Fries des Tempels am Ilissos', *Antike Plastik* 18 (Berlin 1979) 7–21. The identification of the sanctuary of Aglauros in a cave on the east slope of the Acropolis, due to G. S. Dontas, 'The true Aglaurion', *Hesperia* 52 (1983) 48–63, has had far-reaching effects for the topography of Archaic Athens. S. Walker, 'A sanctuary of Isis on the south slope of the Athenian Acropolis', *BSA* 74 (1979) 243–57, and U. Kron, 'Demos, Pnyx und Nymphenhügel', *AM* 94 (1979) 49–75, also deal with minor sanctuaries. For those of the Agora, a good, general account is provided by H. A. Thompson and R. E. Wycherley, *The Athenian Agora* XIV (Princeton 1972), ch. VI; special studies by G. V. Lalonde, 'A hero shrine in the Athenian Agora', *Hesperia* 49 (1980) 97–105; W. B. Dinsmoor jr,

'Anchoring two floating temples', *Hesperia* 51 (1982) 410–52; and C. W. Hedrick jr, 'The temple and cult of Apollo Patroos in Athens', *AJA* 92 (1988) 185–210, can be added. For the Hephaisteion and its sculptural decoration, attention is drawn to E. B. Harrison's study in three sections in *AJA* 81 (1977): 'Alkamenes' sculptures for the Hephaisteion I: The cult statues', 137–78; 'II: The base', 265–87; 'III: Iconography and style', 411–26. See also S. von Bockelberg, 'Die Friese des Hephaisteion', *Antike Plastik* 18 (Berlin 1979) 23–50, and J. Dörig, *La frise est de l'Hephaisteion* (Mainz 1985).

For the mystery sanctuary at Eleusis and the rituals and religious ideas connected with it, G. E. Mylonas, *Eleusis and the Eleusinian Mysteries* (Princeton 1961 and later editions) remains an unsurpassed introduction, although he is probably too critical toward the literary evidence. This is one of the sanctuaries where the possibility of a continuity from the Mycenaean period must be taken seriously, and has been worked out in detail by J. Travlos, ῾Η ᾿Αθήνα καί ἡ ᾿Ελευσίνα στόν 8° καί 7° Π.Χε. αἰώνα᾿, *ASAtene* 61 (1983) 323–38; note also Ch. Kardara, 'A prehistoric survival in certain Greek telesteria', *AAA* 5 (1972) 119–26. Other scholars, like P. Darcque, 'Les vestiges mycéniens découverts sous le télestérion d'Éleusis', *BCH* 105 (1981) 593–605, remain sceptical to these connections. See J. Boardman, 'Herakles, Peisistratos and Eleusis', *JHS* 95 (1975) 1–12, for a crucial moment in the Archaic period of the sanctuary; T. L. Shear jr, 'The demolished temple at Eleusis', in *Studies H. A. Thompson, Hesperia* Suppl. 20 (Princeton 1982) 128–40 (evidence for dismantling of the Archaic Telesterion before the Persian war); K. Clinton, 'The date of the Classical Telesterion at Eleusis', Φίλια ἔπη to *G. Mylonas* 2 (Athens 1987) 254–62, and Rh. F. Townsend, 'The Roman rebuilding of Philon's porch and the Telesterion at Eleusis', *Boreas* 10 (1987) 97–106, for later stages of the telesterion. Add for some important sculptures from the site: L. Schneider, 'Das grosse eleusinische Relief und seine Kopien', *Antike Plastik* 12 (Berlin 1973) 103–23, and R. Lindner, 'Die Giebelgruppe von Eleusis mit dem Raub der Persephone', *JdI* 97 (1982) 303–400. The vast literature on the rites and on the particular religious ideas behind them can be no more than briefly touched on in this context. As significant, recent contributions W. Burkert, *Homo necans* (German edn Berlin and New York 1972; American edn Berkeley 1983) ch. V; B. Dietrich, 'The religious prehistory of Demeter's Eleusinian mysteries', in U. Bianchi and M. J. Vermaseren, eds, *La soteriologia dei culti orientali nell'impero romano*, EPRO 92 (Leiden 1982) 445–71; and L. J. Alderink, 'The Eleusinian mysteries in Roman imperial times', *ANRW* II.18,2 (1989) 1457–98 (going far beyond what the title suggests), deserve a particular mention. Add, for the priests, K. Clinton, *The Sacred Officials of the Eleusinian Mysteries* (Philadelphia 1974), and W. Geominy, 'Eleusinische Priester', in H.-U. Cain, H. Gabelmann and D. Salzmann, eds, *Festschrift N. Himmelmann* (Mainz 1989) 253–64; and for the social context in the Roman period, well documented through inscriptions, K. Clinton, 'The Eleusinian mysteries: Roman initiates and benefactors, second century BC to AD 267', *ANRW* II.18,2 (1989) 1499–539.

Megara, being now within the territory of Attica (although this was not so in antiquity), should be mentioned here. A. Muller, 'Megarika', *BCH* 104 (1980) 83–92, and 107 (1983) 157–79, has dealt respectively with the cult places for Demeter/Kore and with the sanctuary for Zeus Aphesios.

THE ACROPOLIS OF ATHENS

For the monuments of the Acropolis as for those of Athens, general information and a full bibliography up to 1969 can be found in J. Travlos, *Pictorial Dictionary of Ancient Athens* (New York and Washington 1971), brought up to 1985 by his *Bildlexikon zur Topographie des antiken Attika* (Tübingen 1988) 28–30. For general presentations of the site, at more or less popular levels, R. J. Hopper, *The Acropolis* (London 1971); R. E. Wycherley, *The Stones of Athens* (Princeton 1978) chs IV–V; F. Brommer, *Die Akropolis von Athen* (Darmstadt 1985); U. Muss and C. Schubert, *Die Akropolis von Athen* (Graz 1988); and L. Schneider and Chr. Höcker, *Die Akropolis von Athen* (Cologne 1990; with full bibliography pp. 262–83) are to be mentioned. There are also some important specialist studies dealing with the sanctuary as a whole: H. Büsing, 'Vermutungen über die Akropolis in Athen', *MarbWPr* 1969, 1–30 (an analysis of the Periclean building programme); G. Beckel, 'Akropolisfragen', in Χαριστήριον A.K. Ὀρλάνδου 4 (Athens 1967–8) 329–62 (on the date of the first Parthenon and other problems); J. A. Bundgaard, *The Excavation of the Athenian Acropolis 1882–1890* (Copenhagen 1974; documentary material from the Greek and German excavations in the late nineteenth century); same author, *Parthenon and the Mycenaean City on the Heights* (Copenhagen 1976; fanciful, but suggestive). See for the Mycenaean Acropolis S. E. Iakovidis, *Late Helladic Citadels on Mainland Greece* (Leiden 1983) 73–90.

For the archaic Acropolis there is a recent, general study by S. Bancroft, 'Problems concerning the Archaic Acropolis at Athens' (Ph.D. diss. Princeton 1979; Ann Arbor 1981), and interesting, but controversial contributions by I. Beyer, 'Die Reliefgiebel des alten Athena-Tempels der Akropolis', *AA* 1974, 639–51, and 'Die Datierung der grossen Reliefgiebel des alten Athenatempels der Akropolis', *AA* 1977, 44–74. Note the modest, but incisive studies on the Archaic pediments by B. Kiilerich: 'Bluebeard – a snake-tailed Geryon?', *OpAth* 17 (1988) 123–36; 'The Athenian Acropolis: the position of lions and leopards', *ActaArch* 59 (1988) 229–34; 'The olive-tree pediment and the daughters of Cecrops', *ActaAArtHist* 7 (1989) 1–21; and K. Stähler, 'Zur Rekonstruktion und Datierung des Gigantomachiegiebels von der Akropolis', in R. Stiehl and G. A. Lehmann, eds, *Festschrift H. E. Stier* (Münster 1972) 88–112, for an important study on the Late Archaic marble pediment. On the sculptures of the Acropolis there is now, in addition to the classical volumes by H. Payne and G. M. Young, *Archaic Marble Sculpture from the Acropolis*, 2nd edn (London 1950) and H. Schrader, ed., *Die Archaischen Marmorbildwerke der Akropolis*, 2nd edn (Frankfurt a.M. 1969) the recent catalogue by M. S. Brouskari, *The Akropolis Museum. A Descriptive Catalogue* (Athens 1974). The recent identification of the Aglauros sanctuary has had consequences also for the understanding of the Archaic Acropolis, discussed by N. Robertson, 'Solon's Axones and Kyrbeis, and the sixth-century background', *Historia* 35 (1986) 147–76.

Discussions of the Classical Acropolis tend to concentrate on the Parthenon and its predecessor, which have generated an enormous bibliography collected in E. Berger, ed., *Parthenon-Kongress Basel. Referate und Berichte* (Mainz 1984) 461–95. The state of research on this building, including the sculptural decoration and the vexed problem of its function is well defined by the numerous important contributions to this volume. The impressive, architectural publication by A. K. Orlandos, Ἡ ἀρχιτεκτονικὴ τοῦ Παρθενῶνος Α'–Γ' (Athens 1976, 1977 and 1978) is unfortunately less definitive than one might have hoped; see also, for the restoration programme, M. Korres and Ch. Bouras, Μελέτη ἀποκαταστάσεως τοῦ Παρθενῶνος I–II (Athens 1983 and 1989). Active research on the Parthenon and its decorations, based on scale models and casts, has been carried out in Basle; notes and reports on this activity by E. Berger, *AntK* 19 (1976) 122–42; 20 (1977) 124–41; 23 (1980) 66–100; and as editor, *Der Parthenon in Basel. Dokumentation zu den Metopen* (Mainz 1986). The discussion concerning the date of the pre-Parthenon and its relation to the Periclean building has usefully been summed up by H. Drerup, 'Parthenon und Vorparthenon – Zum Stand der Kontroverse', *AntK* 24 (1981) 21–38; no agreement is in sight. Note for this problem the particularly controversial, but stimulating study by Rh. Carpenter, *The Architects of the Parthenon* (Harmondsworth 1970), and the archaeological observations and material published by A. Tschira, 'Eine Tastung in der Cella des Parthenon', *AA* 1965, 401–28; A. Tschira, 'Untersuchungen im Süden des Parthenon', *JdI* 87 (1972) 158–231; and S. Sinos, 'Zur Kurvatur des Parthenonstereobats', *AA* 1974, 157–68. B. Wesenberg, 'Wer erbaute den Parthenon?', *AM* 97 (1982) 99–125, has proposed an unorthodox solution to another much discussed problem, the name of the architect. The basic works on the sculptural decoration are by F. Brommer: *Die Skulpturen der Parthenon-Giebel* (Mainz 1963), *Die Metopen des Parthenon* (Mainz 1967), *Der Parthenonfries* (Mainz 1977); his *Die Parthenon-Skulpturen* (Mainz 1979) is a more easily accessible concentrate. Minor studies of iconographical character abound, with particular emphasis on the frieze and the south metopes. Note for the metopes E. Simon, 'Versuch einer Deutung der Südmetopen des Parthenon', *JdI* 90 (1975) 100–20; M. Robertson, 'Two question-marks on the Parthenon', in G. Kopcke and M. B. Moore, eds, *Studies P. H. von Blanckenhagen* (Locust Valley 1979) 75–87; B. Wesenberg, 'Parthenongebälk und Südmetopenproblem', *JdI* 98 (1983) 57–86, and *idem*,

'Perser oder Amazonen? Zu den Westmetopen des Parthenon', *AA* 1983, 203–8 (with final evidence for the latter alternative). For the frieze, the interpretation by L. Beschi, 'Il fregio del Partenone: una proposta di lettura', *RendLinc* Ser. VIII.39 (1984) 173–95 (also his contribution 'Η ζωφόρος του Παρθενώνα. Μία νέα πρόταση ερμηνείας', in Kyrieleis, ed., *Plastik* II, 199–224) seems more acceptable than various other, recent proposals. J. Dörig, 'Τὸ πρόγραμμα τῆς γλυπτῆς διακοσμήσεως τοῦ Παρθενῶνα', *ArchEph* 1982, 187–214, attempts a general interpretation of the decoration. On the chryselephantine statue: N. Leipen, *Athena Parthenos, a Reconstruction* (Toronto 1971), and B. Fehr, 'Zur religionspolitischen Funktion der Athena Parthenos im Rahmen des delisch-attischen Seebunds', *Hephaistos* 1 (1979) 71–91; 2 (1980) 113–25; and 3 (1981) 55–93.

Far less attention has been devoted to the Erechtheion. See H. J. Kienast, 'Der Wiederaufbau des Erechtheion', *architectura* 13 (1983) 89–104; E. M. Stern, 'Das Haus des Erechtheus', *Boreas* 9 (1986) 51–64, for a particular interpretation of the building; and N. Papachatzis, 'The cult of Erechtheus and Athena on the acropolis of Athens', *Kernos* 2 (1989) 175–82, for a note on the cult. On the sculptural decoration: P. N. Boulter, 'The frieze of the Erechtheion', *Antike Plastik* 10 (Berlin 1970) 7–28; and H. Lauter, *Die Koren des Erechtheion*, *Antike Plastik* 16 (Berlin 1976); see M. Vickers, 'Persepolis, Vitruvius and the Erechtheum Caryatids: The iconography of Medism and servitude', *RA* 1985, 3–28, for an interpretation of the caryatides. Add J. H. Kroll, 'The ancient image of Athena Polias', in *Studies H. A. Thompson*, *Hesperia* Suppl. 20 (Princeton 1982) 65–76, for the cult image; and K. Jeppesen, *The Theory of the Alternative Erechtheion* (Aarhus 1987), for an original identification of the Erechtheion described by Pausanias with another, smaller building close to the northern wall.

No full publication exists for the Propylaia, but the Late Archaic forerunner has been published by W. B. Dinsmoor jr, *The Propylaia to the Athenian Akropolis 1. The Predecessors* (Princeton 1980). H. Büsing, 'Optische Korrekturen und Propyläen-Fronten', *JdI* 99 (1984) 27–73, is concerned with formal 'refinements'; A. Linfert, 'Die Propyläen der Akropolis von Athen – ein Dach für viele', *AM* 93 (1978) 25–34, with the various minor cults connected with the building; and P. Hellström, 'The planned function of the Mnesiklean Propylaia', *OpAth* 17 (1988) 107–21, with a convincing interpretation of the 'pinakotheke' and the planned, inner halls as hestiatoria. The traditional opinion of the Nike-temple and its relation to the temple at the Ilissos is changing, most scholars now tending to regard them as contemporary creations of the 430–20s; see B. Wesenberg, 'Zur Baugeschichte des Niketempels', *JdI* 96 (1981) 28–54; H. B. Mattingly, 'The Athena Nike temple reconsidered', *AJA* 86 (1982) 381–5; and C. A. Picón, 'The Ilissos temple reconsidered', *AJA* 82 (1978) 47–81. On the sculptural decoration: G. Despinis, 'Τα γλυπτὰ τῶν ἀετωμάτων τοῦ ναοῦ τῆς Αθηνᾶς Νίκης', *ArchDelt* 29.1 (1974) 1–24; E. Simon, 'La decorazione architettonica del tempietto di Nike sull'Acropoli di Atene', *Museum Patavinum* 3 (1986) 271–88.

Secondary monuments and structures in the area of the sanctuary have been discussed by R. F. Rhodes and J. J. Dobbins, 'The sanctuary of Artemis Brauronia on the Athenian Akropolis', *Hesperia* 48 (1979) 325–41 (note also T. Linders, *Studies in the Treasure Records of Artemis Brauronia Found in Athens* (Stockholm 1972), for epigraphical material from this sanctuary); L. La Follette, 'The Chalkotheke on the Athenian Akropolis', *Hesperia* 55 (1986) 75–87; W. Binder, *Der Roma-Augustus Monopteros auf der Akropolis in Athen und sein typologischer Ort* (Stuttgart 1969). Add A. Linfert, 'Athenen des Phidias', *AM* 97 (1982) 57–77, for the Promachos and Lemnia dedications.

THE AEGEAN ISLANDS

For the northern Aegean island of Thasos, where investigations are conducted by the French School of Athens, the various smaller and larger sanctuaries are all discussed in the School's admirable *Guide de Thasos*, 2nd edn, rev. (Athens and Paris 1968). On the old sanctuary of Heracles there is a particularly important study by B. Bergquist, *Heracles on Thasos*, Boreas 5 (Uppsala 1973), where the presumed Early Archaic temple is re-interpreted as an early hestiatorion; other remarks on the same sanctuary by G. Roux, 'L'Heracleion thasien: problèmes de chronologie et d'architecture', in *Thasiaca*, *BCH* Suppl. 5 (Paris 1979), 191–211. Thorough discussions of material from other sites have been offered by J. Servais, *Aliki I, Les deux sanctuaires*, Etudes thasiennes 9 (Paris 1980), and by N. Weill, *La plastique archaique de Thasos. Figurines et statues de terre cuite de l'Artémision 1*, Etudes thasiennes 11 (Paris 1985).

The famous sanctuary for the mystery cult of the Kabeiroi at Samothrace, probably based on pre-Greek, local religion, has been investigated by American scholars. K. Lehmann, *Samothrace, a Guide to the Excavations and the Museum*, 4th edn, rev. (Locust Valley 1975) is a good general introduction; H. Ehrhardt, *Samothrake. Heiligtümer in ihrer Landschaft und Geschichte als Zeugen antiken Geisteslebens* (Stuttgart 1985) is also general, with fine illustrations. The material from Czech–French excavations in the 1920s has recently been published by J. Bouzek and I. Ondřejová and R. Hošek, *Samothrace 1923, 1927, 1978* (Prague 1985). The American publications appear in the *Bollingen Series*; recent issues are Ph. W. Lehmann, *Samothrace 3: The Hieron 1–3* (Princeton 1969), Ph. W. Lehmann and D. Spittle, *Samothrace 5: The Temenos* (Princeton 1982), and A. Frazer, *Samothrace 10: The Propylon of Ptolemy II* (Princeton 1990). See for the propylon to the *temenos*, with its rich, sculptural decoration, also Ph. W. Lehmann, *Skopas in Samothrace* (Northampton, Mass. 1973). Occasional, preliminary reports by J. R. McCredie have appeared in *Hesperia*. On the cult, by no means limited to the sanctuary at Samothrace, there is a general study by S. G. Cole, *Theoi Megaloi: The Cult of the Great Gods at Samothrace*, EPRO 96 (Leiden 1984); see also her 'The mysteries of Samothrace during the Roman period', in *ANRW* II.18,2 (1989) 1564–98. Related to the cults of Samothrace are those of Lemnos, where recent Italian investigations have uncovered an Archaic cult place at Efestia and a sanctuary for the Kabeiroi at Chloi; preliminary notices in *ASAtene* since 55 (1977).

On Euboia, geographically and culturally so close to mainland Greece, cults and sanctuaries of Eretria have been investigated by a Swiss mission since the 1960s. A general account is given by P. Auberson and K. Schefold, *Führer durch Eretria* (Berne 1972), and for the early stages, more up-to-date, by A. Mazarakis Ainian, 'Geometric Eretria', *AntK* 30 (1987) 3–24. The principal sanctuary for Apollo Daphnephoros has yielded not only an impressive succession of monumental temples, from Late Geometric to Late Archaic times (publication by P. Auberson, *Eretria I, Temple d'Apollon Daphnéphoros* (Berne 1968); see also H. Knell, 'Eretria: Zur Grundriss-rekonstruktion des älteren und jüngeren Apollontempels', *AntK* 15 (1972) 40–8), but also an intriguing, early structure thought to imitate the mythical laurel temple of Delphi (Cl. Bérard, 'Architecture érétrienne et mythologie delphique. Le Daphnéphoréion', *AntK* 14 (1971) 59–73, and P. Auberson, 'La reconstitution du Daphnéphoréion d'Erétrie', *AntK* 17 (1974) 60–8; and H. Drerup, 'Das sogennante Daphnéphoréion in Eretria', in *Studien F. Hiller* (Saarbrücken 1986) 3–21, with critical remarks). The fragments of pediment decorations from the Late Archaic temple have been studied by E. Touloupa, 'Τὰ ἐναέτια γλυπτὰ τοῦ ναοῦ τοῦ Ἀπόλλωνος Δαφνηφόρου στὴν Ἐρέτρια' (Ph.D. diss. Ioannina 1983), and the Classical pediment with an amazono-machy which later decorated the temple of Apollo Sosianus in Rome has also tentatively been connected with this temple (E. La Rocca, *Amazzonomachia. Le sculture frontonali del tempio di Apollo Sosiano* (Rome 1985). Other Eretrian sanctuaries of interest include a Heroon (Cl. Bérard, *Eretria III, L'Hérôon à la porte de l'ouest* (Berne 1970); see also the same author in *Eretria VI* (Berne 1978) 89–95), a temple for Dionysos near the theatre (P. Auberson, 'Le temple de Dionysos', in *Eretria V* (Berne 1976) 59–67), and a later sanctuary for Egyptian deities (Ph. Bruneau, *Le sanctuaire et le culte des divinités égyptiennes à Erétrie*, EPRO 45 (Leiden 1975); K. Schefold, 'Das Iseion von Eretria', *AntK* 19 (1976) 59–63).

The island of Aigina, also in many ways closer to the mainland than to the Aegean world, has important sanctuaries for Apollo and for the local goddess Aphaia; both have been recent objects of German research. In the urban sanctuary of Apollo the Late Archaic Doric temple has been published by W. W. Wurster, *Alt-Ägina I.1, Der Apollontempel* (Mainz 1974); the fragments of its pediment decorations, and other material, by E. Walter-Karydi, *Alt-Ägina II.2, Die äginetische Bildhauerschule* (Mainz 1987), and by I. Margreiter, *Alt-Ägina II.3, Die Kleinfunde aus dem Apollon-Heiligtum*

(Mainz 1988). For the better known sanctuary of Aphaia D. Ohly, *Tempel und Heiligtum der Aphaia auf Ägina*, 2nd edn, rev. (Munich 1978) is a good introduction; U. Sinn, 'Aphaia und die "Aegineten". Zur Rolle des Aphaiaheiligtums im religiösen und gesellschaftlichen Leben der Insel Aigina', *AM* 102 (1987) 131–67, is a penetrating study of the origin, function and character of the sanctuary. The recent publication of the Archaic temple by E.-L. Schwandner, *Der ältere Porostempel der Aphaia auf Aegina* (Berlin 1985) is another triumph for German research on early Greek architecture. Of the planned re-publication of the pediment groups in Munich, following their new exposition (without the integrations by Thorvaldsen) in the Glyptothek, only the first part has appeared: D. Ohly, *Die Aegineten I: Die Ostgiebelgruppe* (Munich 1976). Short studies by different authors on various problems and material, under the collective title 'Aegina, Aphaia-Tempel', have appeared since 1970 in *AA* (13 papers to date); most important are those by E.-L. Schwandner on the Late Archaic terrace (*AA* 1970, 48–71, and 1971, 505–38); by D. Williams on the much discussed, Archaic cult inscription (*AA* 1982, 55–68), and by M. Ohly-Dumm and M. Robertson on Archaic sculpture dedications (*AA* 1988, 405–21). Add G. Gruben, 'Die Sphinx-Säule von Aigina', *AM* 80 (1965) 170–208, for the most impressive votive monument of the sanctuary; and D. Williams, 'Aphaia', in *LIMC* I.1 (1981), 876–7, for the cult statue.

In the Cyclades, the rich, but frequently overlooked material of Doric religious architecture has been thoroughly discussed by M. Schuller, 'Die dorische Architektur der Kykladen in spätarchaischer Zeit', *JdI* 100 (1985) 319–98. See also H. Lauter, 'Bemerkungen zum archaischen Tempel von Koressia', *AA* 1979, 6–16, and E. Østby, 'The Athenaion of Karthaia', *OpAth* 13 (1980) 189–223, for such buildings on the island of Keos. The Hellenistic sanctuary of Poseidon and Amphitrite at Tenos has received a full publication by R. Etienne, J. P. Braun and Fr. Queyrel, *Ténos I, Le sanctuaire de Poseidon et d'Amphitrite*, BEFAR 263 (Paris 1986). The results of German investigations of the Archaic and Classical religious buildings at Paros and Naxos have been published in a series of dense reports: G. Gruben and W. Koenigs, 'Der "Hekatompedon" von Naxos', *AA* 1968, 693–717, 'Der "Hekatompedos" von Naxos und der Burgtempel von Paros', *AA* 1970, 135–53 and 'Naxos und Paros', *AA* 1972, 319–85; G. Gruben, M. Schuller, K. Schnieringer and A. Ohnesorg, 'Naxos und Paros', *AA* 1982, 159–290. Add for Naxos the preliminary notices on the atypical temple for Demeter at Sangri (G. Gruben and M. Korres, in *Prakt* 1976 to 1979) and on a recently discovered sanctuary at Iria (V. Lambrinoudakis and G. Gruben, 'Das neuentdeckte Heiligtum von Iria auf Naxos', *AA* 1987, 569–621); and for Paros the Early Archaic sanctuary for Athena at Koukounaries (preliminary notices by D. U. Schilardi in *Prakt* from 1976, and by the same author, 'The temple of Athena at Koukounaries', in R. Hägg, N. Marinatos and G. C. Nordquist, eds, *Early Greek Cult Practice*

(Stockholm 1988) 41–8), constructed on the remains of a Mycenaean settlement.

DELOS

The French excavations at Delos have been going on since 1872; see A. Plassart, 'Un siècle de fouilles à Délos', *Etudes déliennes*, *BCH* Suppl. 1 (Paris 1973) 5–16. Beside the principal sanctuary of Apollo, Artemis and Leto, they have been concerned also with the Hellenistic town and with various, minor (mostly late) sanctuaries. An excellent, general survey is provided by J. Ducat and Ph. Bruneau, *Guide de Délos*, 3rd edn, rev. (Athens and Paris 1983). Miscellaneous papers, concerned not only with the sanctuaries, were published in *Etudes déliennes*; the notes by Ph. Bruneau entitled 'Deliaca' I–VIII (from *BCH* 99 (1975) 267–311, to 114 (1990) 553–91) have the same character. Fundamental for any study of Delos are the volumes by R. Vallois, *L'architecture hellénique et hellénistique à Délos*, BEFAR 157; *1. Les monuments* (Paris 1944; on the topography of the sanctuary), and *2. Grammaire historique de l'architecture délienne* (Paris 1966 and 1978). Only three of the volumes in the publication series *Exploration archéologique de Délos* (*EAD*) published since 1965 involve material from the sanctuaries. Preliminary notices on excavation and other activities appear regularly in *BCH*.

Following the fundamental study by H. Gallet de Santerre, *Délos primitive et archaïque*, BEFAR 192 (Paris 1958), discussions of the prehistory of the sanctuaries have been limited to Cl. Vatin, 'Délos prémycenienne', *BCH* 89 (1965) 225–30 (on the tombs of the Hyperborean virgins) and H. Gallet de Santerre, 'Notes déliennes', *BCH* 99 (1975) 247–65 (on the evidence for cult continuity from Mycenaean times in the Artemision). See also for the Artemision J. Tréheux, 'Retour sur l'Artemision de l'île', in *Recueil A. Plassart* (Paris 1976) 175–204, and R. Etienne and Ph. Fraisse, 'L'autel archaïque de l'Artémision de Délos', *BCH* 113 (1989) 451–66. For the Archaic period in the sanctuary of Apollo, the most important event has been the publication of the 'Naxian oikos' by P. Courbin, *L'oikos des Naxiens*, *EAD* 33 (Paris 1980); his interpretation of the building as the early temple of Apollo, repeated in his paper 'Le temple archaïque de Délos', *BCH* 111 (1987) 63–78, has not been generally accepted (sceptical remarks by H. Gallet de Santerre, 'L'Oikos des Naxiens à Délos était-il un temple?', *BCH* 108 (1984) 671–93). The evidence for an earlier building, accepted by Courbin, has been drawn into doubt by A. E. Kalpaxis, 'Die Pfostenlöcher unter dem Naxieroikos auf Delos. Spuren eines Vorgängerbaues oder eines Baugerüstes?', in F. Krinzinger, B. Otto and E. Walde-Psenner, eds, *Festschrift B. Neutsch* (Innsbruck 1980) 237–42, and again in his note 'Naxier-Oikos I und andere Baugerüste', *AA* 1990, 149–53. Another discussion is concerned with the site and immediate surroundings of the famous 'Altar of

Horns' (*keraton*); the solution proposed by G. Roux, 'Le vrai temple d'Apollon à Délos', *BCH* 103 (1979) 109–35 (the altar inside the temple of Apollo, identified with a large, very ruined structure next to the Artemision) has been opposed by Ph. Bruneau, 'Deliaca IV', *BCH* 105 (1981) 79–125, but has been cautiously accepted by H. Gallet de Santerre, 'Kératon, Pythion et Néorion à Délos', in L. Hadermann-Misguich and G. Raepsaet, eds, *Hommages Ch. Delvoye* (Brussels 1982) 201–26. On the dance performed at the altar, the *geranos*, the most recent contribution is by Ph. Bruneau, 'Deliaca VII', *BCH* 112 (1988) 569–82.

Two other early monuments in the sanctuary have been published by M.-Chr. Hellmann and Ph. Fraisse, *Le monument aux hexagones et le portique des Naxiens*, EAD 32 (Paris 1979); see for the former also M.-Chr. Hellmann, 'Encore des hexagones', *BCH* 113 (1989) 149–60. The last contribution to the discussion on the epigram of the Naxian colossal statue was given by Fr. Chamoux, 'L'épigramme du Colosse des Naxiens à Délos', *BCH* 114 (1990) 185–6. On the *oikoi* or treasuries, which have been almost totally neglected in this sanctuary, there is a recent note by J. Tréheux, 'L'Hiéropoion et les oikoi du sanctuaire à Délos', in J. Servais, ed., *Mélanges J. Labarbe* (Liège 1987) 377–90; on probable hestiatoria there is one by G. Roux, 'Salles de banquets à Délos', *Etudes déliennes*, *BCH* Suppl. 1 (Paris 1973) 525–54. On the ship dedication in the Apollo sanctuary and the unusual building where it was exposed there are recent contributions by J. Tréheux, 'Un document nouveau sur le *Néôrion* et le *Thesmophorion* à Délos', *REG* 99 (1986) 293–317, and 'Sur le *Néôrion* à Délos', *CRAI* 1987, 168–84, connecting it with Demetrios Poliorketes. The sculptures published by A. Hermary, *La sculpture archaïque et classique* I, EAD 34 (Paris 1984; dealing only with Classical sculpture) include the acroteria from the temple of the Athenians. Early, minor votive objects have been discussed by J.-Cl. Poursat, 'Ivoires de l'Artémision: Chypre et Délos', *Etudes déliennes*, *BCH* Suppl. 1 (Paris 1973) 415–25, and by Cl. Rolley, 'Bronzes géométriques et orientaux à Délos', (same publication) 491–524.

For sanctuaries and cults of later periods there is a thorough study by Ph. Bruneau, *Recherches sur les cultes de Délos à l'époque hellénistique et à l'époque imperiale*, BEFAR 217 (Paris 1970), to which his paper 'Le dromos et le temple C du Sarapeion C de Délos', *BCH* 104 (1980) 161–88, E. Will, *Le sanctuaire de la déesse syrienne*, EAD 35 (Paris 1985), and G. Roux, 'Problèmes déliens', *BCH* 105 (1981) 41–78 (sanctuaries for the Dioskouroi and for Asclepios) can be added. Interactions between the sanctuaries and the society are among the subjects of the essentially historical study by Cl. Vial, *Délos indépendante*, *BCH* Suppl. 10 (Paris 1984). The extremely rich epigraphical material from this period on the island is illuminating for the economical aspects of the sanctuary; see studies on this material by T. Linders and J. Tréheux in D. Knoepfler, ed., *Comptes et inventaires dans la cité grecque* (Neuchâtel 1988), and the study by D. Hennig, 'Die "heiligen Häuser" von

Delos', *Chiron* 13 (1983) 411–95, and 15 (1985) 165–86, on the dispositions of the real estate belonging to the sanctuary.

THE HERAION AT SAMOS

For the large sanctuary of Hera at Samos, where the investigations have been conducted by the German archaeological institute in Athens, there are good, recent accounts by H. Kyrieleis, *Führer durch das Heraion von Samos* (Athens 1981), and by H. Walter, *Das griechische Heiligtum dargestellt am Heraion von Samos* (Stuttgart 1990). On the cult there is a dense and provocative study by G. Kipp, 'Zum Hera-Kult auf Samos', in F. Hampl and I. Weiler, eds, *Kritische und vergleichende Studien zur alten Geschichte und Universalgeschichte* (Innsbruck 1974), 157–209. Due attention to the sanctuary is also paid in G. Shipley, *A History of Samos, 800–188 BC* (Oxford 1987). The publication of the archaeological material is proceeding in the series *Samos*, which includes volumes dedicated to material from other sites on the island. Preliminary notices have appeared in *AA* and *AM*.

Only the last of the successive temple buildings at the site has received a full publication: O. Reuther, *Der Heratempel von Samos, Der Bau seit der Zeit des Polykrates* (Berlin 1957). An equally thorough treatise of the earlier temples, including the Early Archaic ones and the evidence for what is presumed to be the earliest known peristasis around a Greek temple, remains as a desiderate. Studies of other buildings include H. P. Isler and T. E. Kalpaxis, *Samos IV, Das archaische Nordtor* (Bonn 1978); H. Walter and A. Clemente, 'Zum Monopteros im Heraion von Samos', *AM* 101 (1986) 137–47 (on an unusual, baldachine-like building constructed between the temple front and the altar); H. J. Kienast and U. Sinn, 'Der sog. Tempel D im Heraion von Samos', *AM* 100 (1985) 105–58 (with an interesting excursus on building sacrifices); A. E. Furtwängler and H. J. Kienast, *Samos III, Der Nordbau im Heraion von Samos* (Bonn 1989). Most of the rich material of sculptural dedications of the Archaic period in the sanctuary has been included in B. Freyer-Schauenburg, *Samos XI, Bildwerke der archaischen Zeit und des strengen Stils* (Bonn 1974); the Geneleos group has also been discussed by U. Muss, 'Bemerkungen zur Phileia der Geneleosgruppe', *AM* 96 (1981) 139–44, and by E. Walter-Karydi, 'Geneleos', *AM* 100 (1985) 91–104. For the exciting, recent discoveries of Archaic monumental sculptures (a kouros of giant dimensions, and a kore similar to the famous Cheramyes statue) see the contributions by H. Kyrieleis, 'Neue archaische Skulpturen aus dem Heraion von Samos', and by U. Kron, 'Eine archaische Kore aus dem Heraion von Samos', in Kyrieleis, ed., *Plastik* I, 35–45 and 47–65.

The harvest of votive objects from this sanctuary has been unusually rich, and includes categories not often represented in other Greek sanctuaries. The rich discoveries from recent excavations in the southern part of the area (for which see A. E. Furtwängler, 'Heraion von Samos: Grabungen im Südtemenos 1977', *AM* 95 (1980) 149–224, and 96 (1981), 73–138, with a full, general account) included Archaic objects of wood published by H. Kyrieleis, 'Archaische Holzfunde aus Samos', *AM* 95 (1980) 87–147; earlier finds of such material were published by D. Ohly and G. Kopcke, 'Neue Holzfunde aus dem Heraion von Samos', *AM* 82 (1967) 89–148. The importance of Samos as a focal point for early trade in the Mediterranean is reflected by Oriental votives (G. Schmidt, *Samos VII, Kyprische Bildwerke aus dem Heraion von Samos* (Bonn 1968); U. Jantzen, *Samos VIII, Ägyptische und orientalische Bronzen aus dem Heraion von Samos* (Bonn 1972); H. Kyrieleis, 'Babylonische Bronzen im Heraion von Samos', *JdI* 94 (1979) 32–48) and by others from the far West (B. Freyer-Schauenburg, 'Kolaios und die westphönizischen Elfenbeine', *MM* 7 (1966) 89–108; H. P. Isler, 'Etruskischer Bucchero aus dem Heraion von Samos', *AM* 82 (1967) 77–88). An unusually fine, Early Archaic bronze relief with a mythological theme was published by Ph. Brize, 'Samos und Stesichoros: zu einem früharchaischen Bronzeblech', *AM* 100 (1985) 53–90. More modest objects have been studied by G. Hiesel, 'Samische Steingeräte' (Ph.D. diss. Hamburg 1967), and by A. E. Furtwängler, 'Zur Deutung der Obeloi im Lichte samischer Neufunde', in H. A. Cahn, ed., *Festschrift R. Hampe* (Mainz 1980), 81–98. Archaic pottery with cultic functions has been the object of a short study by U. Kron, 'Archaisches Kultgeschirr aus dem Heraion von Samos', in H. A. G. Brijder, ed., *Ancient Greek and Related Pottery*, symposium (Amsterdam 1984) 292–7. A professional study of bone material from the sanctuary has been provided by J. Boessneck and A. von den Driesch, *Knochenabfall von Opfermahlen und Weihgaben aus dem Heraion von Samos* (Munich 1988).

ASIA MINOR

Concise information and bibliographies on the Greek sites of Asia Minor can be found in G. E. Bean, *Aegean Turkey, an Archaeological Guide* (London 1966); E. Akurgal, *Ancient Civilizations and Ruins of Turkey*, 5th edn, rev. (Istanbul 1983); or W. Hotz, *Die Mittelmeerküsten Anatoliens* (Darmstadt 1989).

A thorough and readable general account of the German research in the sanctuary of Apollo at Didyma has recently been published by K. Tuchelt, *Branchidai – Didyma. Geschichte, Ausgrabung und Wiederentdeckung eines antiken Heiligtums 1765 bis 1990*, *AntW* Sondernummer 22 (1991; full bibliography p. 54). Preliminary reports, also on the recent discovery of a sanctuary for Artemis in the neighbourhood, have been published by Tuchelt and his collaborators in *IstMitt* 21 (1971) 45–108; 23–4 (1973–4) 139–68; 30 (1980) 99–189; and 34 (1984) 193–344. For another Archaic sanctuary on the road to Miletus there are reports by the same author, *AA* 1989, 143–217, and

P. Schneider, 'Zur Topographie der Heiligen Strasse von Milet nach Didyma', *AA* 1987, 101–29. K. Tuchelt, *Vorarbeiten zu einer Topographie von Didyma*, *IstMitt* Beih. 9 (Tübingen 1973) is concerned with all the periods of the sanctuary. Following the brilliant reconstruction of the Archaic temple by G. Gruben, 'Das archaische Didymaion', *JdI* 78 (1963) 78–182, an interpretation of the unusual plan as a pro-Persian document was ventured by B. Fehr, 'Zur Geschichte des Apollonheiligtums von Didyma', *MarbWPr* 1971-2, 14–59; functional problems concerning the open central court and the naiskos have been touched upon by K. Tuchelt, 'Fragen zum Naiskos von Didyma', *AA* 1986, 33–50. His monograph *Die archaischen Skulpturen von Didyma*, IstForsch 27 (Berlin 1970) is concerned with Archaic votive and architectural sculptures; his paper 'Einige Überlegungen zum Kanachos-Apollon von Didyma', *JdI* 101 (1986) 75–84, with the particular fate of the Archaic cult statue. See for the same incisive, historical moment also by the same author, 'Die Perserzerstörung von Branchidai-Didyma und ihre Folgen – archäologisch betrachtet', *AA* 1988, 427–38, and H. W. Parke, 'The massacre of the Branchidae', *JHS* 105 (1985) 59–68. The period after the Persian wars has been discussed by W. Hahland, 'Didyma im 5. Jahrhundert v.Chr.', *JdI* 79 (1964), 142–240, and by W. Voigtländer, 'Quellhaus und Naiskos im Didymaion nach den Perserkriegen', *IstMitt* 22 (1972) 93–112. The discovery of incised architectural drawings on the walls of the courtyard by L. Haselberger ('Werkzeichnungen am Jüngeren Didymeion. Vorbericht', *IstMitt* 30 (1980) 191–215; 'Bericht über die Arbeit am Jüngeren Apollontempel von Didyma', *IstMitt* 33 (1983) 90–123) is doubtless the most important recent discovery concerning the later temple; it involves problems for the date of the naiskos, discussed by W. Hoepfner, 'ΦΙΛΑΔΕΛΦΕΙΑ. Ein Beitrag zur frühen hellenistischen Architektur', *AM* 99 (1984) 353–64, and by M. Pfrommer, 'Überlegungen zur Baugeschichte des Naiskos im Apollontempel zu Didyma', *IstMitt* 37 (1987) 145–85. The architectural ornaments have been studied by W. Voigtländer, *Der jüngste Apollontempel von Didyma, Geschichte seines Baudekors*, *IstMitt* Beih. 14 (Tübingen 1975) and by S. Pülz, *Untersuchungen zur kaiserzeitlichen Bauornamentik von Didyma*, (same series) 35 (Tübingen 1989). For the oracular activity there are studies by W. Günther, *Das Orakel von Didyma in hellenistischer Zeit*, *IstMitt* Beih. 4 (Tübingen 1971) epigraphical, by J. Fontenrose, *Didyma. Apollo's Oracle, Cult, and Companions* (Berkeley 1988), and H. W. Parke, *The Oracles of Apollo in Asia Minor* (London 1985; discusses also the oracle cult at Claros, where French excavations of the 1950s which so far remain unpublished have recently been taken up again by J. de La Genière). See by H. W. Parke also the note 'The temple of Apollo at Didyma: The building and its function', *JHS* 106 (1986) 121–31. The unusually thorough publications of the bones of sacrificed animals (J. Boessneck and A. von den Driesch, 'Tierknochenfunde aus Didyma', *AA* 1983, 611–51; same authors, 'Schneckengehäuse und

Muschelschalen aus Didyma', *AA* 1983, 653–72; J. Boessneck and J. Schäffer, 'Tierknochenfunde aus Didyma II', *AA* 1986, 251–301) deserve a final mention.

Austrian investigations in the Artemision at Ephesos since the 1960s directed by A. Bammer, have been summarized in his *Das Heiligtum der Artemis von Ephesos* (Graz 1984); preliminary reports in *ÖJh*, and an extensive one entitled 'Forschungen im Artemision von Ephesos von 1976 bis 1981', in *AnatSt* 32 (1982) 61–87 by the same author. See for the monumental altar, discovered during these difficult excavations, also G. Kuhn, 'Der Altar der Artemis in Ephesos', *AM* 99 (1984) 199–216, and A. Bammer, 'Die Entwicklung des Opferkultes am Altar der Artemis von Ephesos', *IstMitt* 23–4 (1973–4) 53–62. For the Archaic and Late Classical temples there are studies by W. Schaber, *Die archaischen Tempel der Artemis von Ephesos* (Waldsassen 1982) and by A. Bammer, *Die Architektur des jüngeren Artemision von Ephesos* (Wiesbaden 1972); for the architectural sculpture U. Muss, *Studien zur Bauplastik des archaischen Artemisions von Ephesos* (Bonn 1983), and A. Rügler, *Die Columnae caelatae des jüngeren Artemisions von Ephesos*, *IstMitt* Beih. 34 (Tübingen 1988). C. Talamo, 'Sull'Artemision di Efeso', *PP* 39 (1984) 197–216, is concerned with mythological and epigraphical subjects; R. Fleischer, *Artemis von Ephesos und verwandte Kultstatuen aus Anatolien und Syrien*, EPRO 35 (Leiden 1973), with the particular type of the cult figure.

In the same central Ionian area, some attention has again been dedicated to the sanctuary of Athena at Priene; see preliminary reports on German investigations at the temple by O. Bauer in *IstMitt* 18 (1968) 212–20; by W. Koenigs, 'Der Athenatempel von Priene', *IstMitt* 33 (1983) 134–75; and on the sculptures from the sanctuary J. C. Carter, *The Sculpture of the Sanctuary of Athena Polias at Priene* (London 1983). For the pan-Ionian sanctuary of Poseidon at nearby Mykale, the publication by G. Kleiner, P. Hommel and W. Müller-Wiener, *Panionion und Melie*, *JdI* Ergänzungsheft 23 (Berlin 1967) remains basic. At Miletus, research in the sanctuary of Athena has revealed an extremely interesting, Early Archaic temple following a Geometric cult site and a Mycenaean megaron: A. Mallwitz and W. Schiering, 'Der alte Athena-Tempel von Milet', *IstMitt* 25 (1975) 87–160; see also A. Mallwitz, 'Gestalt und Geschichte des jüngeren Athenatempels von Milet', *IstMitt* 25 (1975) 67–90, for a new reconstruction of the later temple from the fifth century. The Early Archaic temple and sanctuary of Athena at ancient Smyrna has now been published by E. Akurgal, *Alt-Smyrna I. Wohnschichten und Athenatempel* (Ankara 1983); see also G. Kuhn, 'Der äolische Tempel in Alt-Smyrna', *MarbWPr* 1986, 39–80. For the smaller, Archaic temples in Aeolis (Neandria, Larissa, Lesbos etc.) there is a good section in Ph. B. Betancourt, *The Aeolic Style in Architecture* (Princeton 1977), part II.IV.

In Caria, the Swedish excavations in the Hecatomnid sanctuary of Zeus at

Labraunda are slowly being published; there is, however, no extensive, general account of the site. Publications of architecture: K. Jeppesen, *Labraunda I.1, The Propylaea* (Lund 1955); A. Westholm, *Labraunda I.2, The Architecture of the Hieron* (Lund 1963); and P. Hellström and Th. Thieme, *Labraunda I.3, The Temple of Zeus* (Stockholm 1982). Of pottery: P. Hellström, *Labraunda II.1, Pottery of Classical and Later Date, Terracotta Lamps and Glass* (Lund 1965); M.-L. Säflund, *Labraunda II.2, Stamped Amphora Handles* (Stockholm 1980); J. J. Jully, *Labraunda II.3, Archaic Pottery* (Stockholm 1981). On inscriptions: J. Crampa, *Labraunda II.1* and *II.2, The Greek Inscriptions* (Lund 1969 and 1972); M. Meier-Brügger, *Labraunda II.4, Die karischen Inschriften* (Stockholm 1983). For another Hecatomnid sanctuary at Amyzon there is at present only a general, introductory volume to a French publication: J. and L. Robert, *Fouilles d'Amyzon en Carie I. Exploration, histoire, monnaies et inscriptions* (Paris 1983). For recent, American excavations in the sanctuary of Aphrodite at Knidos there are preliminary reports by I. C. Love in *AJA*, from 72 (1968) to 77 (1973). In the same area, the small sanctuary at Kastabos has been published by J. M. Cook and W. H. Plommer, *The Sanctuary of Hemithea at Kastabos* (Cambridge 1966). Add the recent discovery of an Archaic sanctuary of the Doric Hexapolis, by D. Berges and N. Tuna, 'Ein Heiligtum bei Alt-Knidos', *AA* 1990, 19–35.

THE WESTERN COLONIES

Italian and international archaeological research on the Greek sites of Italy south of Naples has been extremely rich and lively in the last 25 years, and has to a large extent been directed toward temples and sanctuaries. Full, preliminary notices for archaeological field work are given for southern Italy each year at the 'convegni di studi sulla Magna Grecia' at Taranto ('Atti' = *ACSMGr*), for Sicily at the four-yearly congresses arranged by the university of Palermo (acts published in *Kokalos*). The two magnificent and lavishly illustrated volumes edited by G. Pugliese Carratelli, *Megale Hellas* and *Sikanie* (Milan 1983 and 1985), have material concerning temples and sanctuaries in the sections dedicated to architecture and urbanism, with rich and up-to-date information.

The origins of colonial sanctuaries and their relation to the urban system, which they can hardly precede, have been the object of some important general studies, beginning with W. Herrmann, 'Santuari di Magna Grecia e della madre patria', *ACSMGr* 4, 1964 (Naples 1965) 47–57, and G. Vallet, 'La cité et son territoire dans les colonies grecques d'Occident', *ACSMGr* 7, 1967 (Naples 1968) 67–142, continuing with O. Belvedere, 'I santuari urbani sicelioti; preliminari per un'analisi strutturale', *ArchCl* 33 (1981) 122–42 (on urban sanctuaries of Sicily), with Cl. Parisi Presicce, 'La funzione delle aree sacre nell'organizzazione urbanistica primitiva delle colonie greche alla luce della scoperta di un nuovo santuario periferico di Selinunte', *ArchCl* 36 (1984) 19–132 (a very full study of the entire subject, based on a recent discovery at Selinus, see below), and with I. Malkin, 'La place des dieux dans la cité des hommes', *RHR* 204 (1987) 331–52. For minor, rural sanctuaries in southern Italy and Etruria there is a good study by I. Edlund, *The Gods and the Place. Location and Function of Sanctuaries in the Countryside of Etruria and Magna Graecia (700–400 BC)* (Stockholm 1987). On temples and sanctuaries of Sicily there is much material in the volume *Il tempio greco in Sicilia. Architettura e culti*, colloquium Siracusa 1976, *CronCatania* 16 (1977 [1985]), and a full, general survey of smaller temples in I. Romeo, 'Sacelli arcaici senza peristasi nella Sicilia greca', *Xenia* 17 (1989), 5–54. See for the beginning of western Dorism G. Gullini, 'Origini dell'architettura dorica in Occidente', *ASAtene* 59 (1981) 97–126. For the monumental Doric temples of the classical period, in southern Italy and in Sicily, the publication by D. Mertens, *Der Tempel von Segesta und die dorische Tempelbaukunst des griechischen Westens in klassischer Zeit*, DAI Rom Sonderschriften 6 (Mainz 1984) is fundamental and can be considered as replacing the old standard work by R. Koldewey and O. Puchstein, *Die griechischen Tempel in Unteritalien und Sicilien* (Berlin 1899); for the Archaic period, however, the latter work remains indispensable.

Joint German–Italian investigations at Metaponto have, since the late 1960s, uncovered the large, central sanctuary with Archaic temples for Apollo, Hera and other deities; the most extensive report is D. Adamesteanu, D. Mertens and F. D'Andria, *Metaponto I*, *NSc* Suppl. 1975 (publ. 1980), the most recent D. Mertens, 'Metapont. Ein neuer Plan des Stadtzentrums', *AA* 1985, 645–71. The Early Classical Ionic temple discussed in his paper 'Der ionische Tempel von Metapont, Ein Zwischenbericht', *RM* 86 (1979) 103–39, is part of this complex. On the suburban sanctuary of the 'Tavole Palatine' there is a study by F. G. Lo Porto, 'Ricerche e scoperte nell'Heraion di Metaponto', *Xenia* 1 (1981) 25–44; on other material his 'Testimonianze archeologiche di culti metapontini', *Xenia* 16 (1988) 5–28. The terracotta votives from a small, rural sanctuary have been published by G. Olbrich, *Archaische Statuetten eines metapontiner Heiligtums* (Rome 1979).

For Paestum there is a general, recent account of the entire site by J. Griffiths Pedley, *Paestum* (London 1990; including a chapter on the excavations conducted by the author at the suburban sanctuary of Santa Venera), and a re-edition of the classical study on the temples by F. Krauss, *Paestum–Die griechischen Tempel*, 3rd edn, rev. (Berlin 1976). The evidence for the cults has been surveyed by A. M. Ardovino, *I culti di Paestum antica e del suo territorio* (Salerno 1986). German publications of the two principal temples (the 'Basilica' and the 'temple of Neptune') are awaited, and there has in the meantime been some discussion concerning their dedication; see E. M. Stern, 'Zeus und die Tempel von Paestum', *MededRom* 42 (1980)

43–66, and M. Wegner, 'Zur Benennung der Tempel von Paestum', *Boreas* 8 (1985) 33–40, for recent contributions. Minor, sacral structures have been discussed by U. Kron, 'Zum Hypogäum von Paestum', *JdI* 86 (1971) 117–48 (on the religious significance of a strange, subterranean sanctuary near the agora); E. Greco and D. Theodorescu, *Poseidonia – Paestum I. La 'Curia'* (Rome 1980; foundations of an Archaic temple discovered under the later curia); and H. Lauter, *et al.*, 'Ein archaischer Hallenbau in Poseidonia/ Paestum', *RM* 91 (1984) 23–45 (small structure near the 'Basilica'). New interpretations of the relief metopes from the Archaic building in the Hera sanctuary at Sele (probably the first temple of the goddess rather than a treasury) have been offered by E. Simon, 'Die vier Büsser von Foce del Sele', *JdI* 82 (1967) 275–95, and by F. van Keuren, *The Frieze from the Hera I Temple at Foce del Sele* (Rome 1989). See for this material and other figurative finds from Paestum also M. Napoli, *Il museo di Paestum* (Cava dei Tirreni 1969).

In Calabria, the sanctuary of Hera at Capo Colonna near Croton and one for Apollo at nearby Cirò Marino have recently been discussed by D. Mertens, 'I santuari di Capo Colonna e Crimisa: aspetti dell'architettura crotoniate', *ACSMGr* 23, 1983 (Taranto 1984), 189–230; cf. also G. Maddoli, 'I culti di Crotone', ibid. 313–43. But in this region attention has concentrated on Locri Epizephirii, discussed in *ACSMGr* 16, 1976 (Naples 1977), with contributions on the cults by M. Torelli and on the architecture by G. Gullini. The latter has also published a general study of the religious architecture entitled *La cultura architettonica di Locri Epizefirii* (Taranto 1980); most of this material is also covered by A. De Franciscis, *Il santuario di Marasà in Locri Epizefiri I. Il tempio arcaico* (Naples n.d.), by E. Østby, 'The temple of Casa Marafioti at Locri and some related buildings', *ActaAArtHist* 8 (1978) 25–47, and 'Osservazioni sui templi di Locri Epizefirii', *ActaAArtHist* Ser. 2.6 (1987) 1–58. To the sanctuary of the Marafioti temple (probably an Olympieion) belong the inscribed bronze tablets published and discussed by A. De Franciscis, *Stato e società in Locri Epizefiri* (Naples 1972) and discussed in the papers edited by D. Musti, *Le tavole di Locri*, colloquium Napoli 1977 (Rome 1979). Of the most famous votive objects from Locri, the relief plaques of terracotta probably from a sanctuary of Persephone, those in the Reggio museum remain unpublished; the publication of the others by H. Prückner, *Die lokrischen Tonreliefs* (Mainz 1968) is for that reason extremely useful, although his interpretation of their religious meaning has failed to convince. See for another group of votives from the same sanctuary M. Barra Bagnasco, *Protomi in terracotta da Locri Epizefiri* (Turin 1986). Greek cults and sanctuaries in Italy could occasionally be established outside the area under political control by the Greeks. Interesting evidence for this has been observed in the Etruscan harbour of Gravisca near Tarquinia (M. Torelli, 'Il santuario greco di Gravisca', *PP* 32 (1977) 398–458), and in a Late Classical, Doric temple under the cathedral of Ancona on the Adriatic coast (L. Bacchielli, 'Domus Veneris quam dorica sustinet Ancon', ArchCl 37 (1985) 106–37).

Passing to Sicily, the exciting discovery of a Late Archaic Ionic temple alongside the Classical temple of Athena at Syracuse is about to be published: G. V. Gentili, 'Il grande tempio ionico di Siracusa', Palladio NS 16 (1967) 61–84 (preliminary), and P. Auberson, P. Pelagatti and G. Gullini, Il tempio ionico di Siracusa, BdA Monografie 1 (Rome forthcoming). A peculiar, Late Archaic temple for Aphrodite at Palazzolo Acreide (ancient Akrai) has received a slim publication by L. Bernabò Brea, Il tempio di Afrodite di Akrai (Naples 1986). For the sanctuaries at Gela there are two important studies by P. Orlandini: 'Lo scavo del Thesmophorion di Bitalemi e il culto delle divinità ctonie a Gela', Kokalos 12 (1966) 8–35 (on a small, suburban sanctuary for Demeter and Kore), and 'Gela–Topografia dei santuari e documentazione archeologica dei culti', RivIstArch NS 15 (1968) 20–66. A particular class of votive terracottas, frequent in sanctuaries for Demeter not only at Gela, has been studied by M. Sguaitamatti, L'offrande de porcelet dans la coroplathie géléenne (Mainz 1984). At Agrigento, the particular structure of the huge Olympieion (shown to have had a hypaithral central cella) is explained in terms of local, religious and philosophical ideas by M. Bell, 'Stylobate and roof in the Olympieion at Akragas', AJA 84 (1980) 359–72; the small fountain sanctuary behind the eastern spur of the Rupe Atenea has been re-published by A. Siracusano, Il santuario rupestre di Agrigento in località S. Biagio (Rome 1983) and connected with a temple for Demeter immediately above. Much work remains to be done on the impressive and well preserved Doric temples; the general study on their design principles by J. de Waele, 'Der Entwurf der dorischen Tempel von Akragas', AA 1980, 180–241, cannot be considered very successful (see the note by D. Mertens, AA 1981, 426–30).

The extensive ruins of Selinus, which have by a miracle remained free from modern settlements (and can be trusted to remain so, after the recent creation of an archaeological park), hold particularly rich promise for future investigations on western Greek sanctuaries. The large sanctuary on the acropolis with temple C and D is the only one in Sicily whose chronological development through the Archaic period it has been possible to follow; see for this A. Di Vita, 'Per l'architettura e l'urbanistica greca d'età arcaica: la stoà nel temenos del tempio C e lo sviluppo programmato di Selinunte', Palladio NS 16 (1967) 3–60 (including a publication of an Archaic stoa), and his 'Selinunte fra il 650 ed il 409: un modello urbanistico coloniale', ASAtene 62 (1984) 7–68, with full use of recent field discoveries. A monumental altar in front of temple A has been recovered by H. Lauter, 'Ein monumentaler Säulenaltar des 5. Jahrhunderts v.Chr. in Selinunt', RM 83 (1976) 233–59. Notices on recent discoveries by G. Gullini in the temple group on the eastern hill (including an Early Archaic temple with semi-Doric forms under the later temple E) are best found in his contribution to Carratelli, ed., Sikanie, op. cit. A small, suburban sanctuary, probably for Hera, west of the town has recently been discovered by a team directed by S. Tusa; see *SicArch* 17.54–5 (1984) 17–58, and 19.60–1 (1986) 13–88, for preliminary reports, and extensive studies based on this discovery by Parisi Presicce, *ArchCl* 36 (1984) op. cit., and 'L'importanza di Hera nelle spedizioni coloniali e nell'insediamento primitivo delle colonie greche alla luce della scoperta di un nuovo santuario periferico di Selinunte', *ArchCl* 37 (1985) 44–83. The most recent (but hardly the definitive) contribution to the old discussion concerning the dedications of the various temples was given by G. Bejor, 'Problemi di localizzazione di culti a Selinunte', *AnnPisa* Ser. III.7 (1977) 439–57. On the famous relief metopes there are studies by L. Giuliani, *Die archaischen Metopen von Selinunt* (Mainz 1979), by V. Tusa, *La scultura in pietra di Selinunte* (Palermo 1983; including a catalogue of formerly unpublished fragments), and by E. Østby, 'Riflessioni sulle metope di Selinunte', *PP* 42 (1987) 123–53 (and a forthcoming monograph in the *ActaAArtHist*).

On the northern coast of Sicily, the Archaic, urban sanctuary of Himera has been excavated and published by the university of Palermo: A. Adriani, N. Bonacasa, C. A. Di Stefano, E. Joly, M. T. Manni Piraino, G. Schmiedt and A. Tusa Cutroni, *Himera I* (Rome 1970), to which N. Bonacasa, 'Il temenos di Himera', in Bonacasa, ed., *Secondo quaderno imerese* (Rome 1982) 47–60, should be added. Sanctuaries of purely Greek type, but in a semi-Greek environment, have been discovered in the settlement at Monte Iato (H. P. Isler, ed., *Studia Ietina II. Der Tempel der Aphrodite* (Zürich 1984)), and include the famous temple at Segesta (Mertens, *Segesta*, op. cit., with evidence for an earlier structure on the site, and for a regular cella planned for the Classical temple). Material presented by E. De Miro, 'Eredità egeo-micenee e Alto Arcaismo in Sicilia. Nuove richerche', in D. Musti, A. Sacconi, L. Rocchietti, M. Rocchi, E. Scafa, L. Sportiello and M. E. Giannotta, eds, *La transizione dal miceneo all'alto arcaismo* (congress Rome 1988; Rome 1991) 593–617, concerning pre-Greek sanctuaries and sacral buildings in Sicanian territory at Polizzello and Sabucina, and connected with presumed traditions from Greek Bronze Age cultures, is likely to create discussion.

The colony of Cyrene in North Africa is naturally to be connected with the western Greek colonial world. See here S. Stucchi, *Architettura cirenaica* (Rome 1975) for a general survey, and D. White, 'Cyrene's sanctuary of Demeter and Persephone. A summary of a decade of excavation', *AJA* 85 (1981) 13–30, for the American excavations in the Demeter sanctuary, for which four volumes of a final publication have appeared: D. White, ed., *The Extramural Sanctuary of Demeter and Persephone at Cyrene, Libya* (I, Philadelphia 1984; II, 1985; III, 1987; IV, 1990).

11

What were Greek sanctuaries?
A synthesis
Nanno Marinatos

BEGINNINGS

The history of Greek sanctuaries reflects the development of Greek society. Although we have very few tangible elements of their beginnings, an investigation is well worth undertaking because the earliest levels might reveal those cult practices that were most essential.

It seems that right from the start sacrificial meals were the primary activity which took place in sanctuaries. This is attested by bones and equipment for eating and drinking, such as kantharoi and plates. This type of evidence usually comes from the earliest levels but it continues throughout the centuries (see E. Gebhard, pp. 154–77 for Isthmia and W. Burkert, pp. 178–91 for Samothrace). The monumentalization of this activity is represented, in later times, by *hestiatoria*: special buildings which served the needs of ritual dining by the élite.[1] For the sanctuary of Demeter and Kore at Corinth dining is particularly well documented (see N. Bookidis, pp. 45–61).

It must be stressed that eating is a necessary corollary to sacrifice, one of the primary rituals of Greek religion. The importance of animal sacrifice has been stressed by Burkert and others and it is not necessary to discuss its meaning again here.[2] But we can pursue another avenue: let us look, not at the remnants of meals, but at the focus of the cult instead. Christiane Sourvinou-Inwood argues in this volume (pp. 1–17) that, in Homer, sacred space was defined by an altar. Thus, we are led to the altar and sacrifice once more. It stands to reason that one of the primary focuses of Greek religion was sacrifice and eating.

This conclusion might seem rather banal, but it is an important one when we consider that the phenomenon of ritual dining is trans-cultural. Eating was the main cult activity in religious communities as diverse as those of the Minoans and the early Christians.[3]

As to early Greek temples, it seems that there existed neither a homogeneous architectural type throughout Greece, nor a linear architectural development from Bronze Age architecture. In Eretria the earliest buildings attested for Apollo Daphnephoros were probably mere huts, seasonal structures that served as temporary shelters for the cult image and other paraphernalia. In Crete, at Kommos, Prinias and Dreros, the temples were rectangular buildings with a hearth. The purpose was certainly ritual dining, housing only an élite, to judge from the relatively modest size of the structures. At Dreros there was, in addition to the hearth, a triadic cult image symbolically partaking in the meal. In other parts of Greece it may have been the chieftain's house with its hearth that served the cultic needs of the community.[4]

All this goes to show that regional architectural solutions were found to house the cult image or the dining rituals. The invention of the Greek temple *does not represent a drastic change in the cult practice, but rather a decision to monumentalize*. The temple became the emblem of the city state, the very manifestation of its power and prestige. There is little doubt that the inspiration for the architectural form of the Greek temple came from the Near East and Egypt. From the Near East was borrowed the concept of the triad: temple, altar, cult image;[5] from Egypt the technology and the idea of monumentality.[6] The impressive Egyptian colonnades in particular may have acted as stimuli for the conception of the Greek temple.

By the seventh century BC there existed temples in the more-or-less canonical form although we still find some regional variation. But we shall not pursue this here. It is more important for our purpose to stress another fact: temples must be seen as an expression of the identity of the city-state. Since city-states were at war with each other, the temple and indeed the entire sanctuary can be seen as a manifestation of power and prestige within the framework of a competitive culture.

SANCTUARIES IN A COMPETITIVE CULTURE

Recent scholarship has stressed the differences between three categories of sanctuaries.[7]

Urban sanctuaries are often placed in the centre of the city or on a summit of a hill within it. As examples we might mention the temples on the Acropolis at Athens, the temple of Athena at Priene or the temple of Apollo at Corinth; all constitute veritable national monuments representing the power and level of wealth as well as the skill of their respective cities.

Extra-urban sanctuaries are administered by the city-state but are located outside the urban space. They too are national monuments but are destined to mark or expand the territorial influence of the city and to act as regional centres for the cult. They thus unite the rustic population under a national cult. For example, the sanctuary of Artemis Brauronia or that of Poseidon (or was it Athena?) at Sounion served as *foci* of Attic unity under the surveillance of Athens. In Asia Minor, the sanctuary of Apollo at Miletus was located outside the city but was under the control of the Branchiadae, a family of Milesian priests. Catherine Morgan has suggested that it united Greek and non-Greek local populations.

Inter-urban sanctuaries. In this category fall the pan-Hellenic sanctuaries of Olympia, Delphi and Nemea. They were located away from major cities and, although they were under the administrative control of their nearby city-states or amphictyonies, they had an aura of neutrality. They thus formed ideal places for political interaction. They were the places where Greeks could meet other Greeks on equal grounds to compete and to agree, to establish superiority in athletics, to read each other's propaganda in the form of dedicatory inscriptions, to sound each other out. It may not be an exaggeration to state that, without pan-Hellenic sanctuaries, Greek culture would not have achieved the kind of richness which is due to constant exposure to stimuli and regional variation. Greeks could share with other Greeks the latest technology and trends in art which they picked from different parts of the world.

Sanctuaries were a perfect arena for competition. As Snodgrass has pointed out, Greek temples became virtual war-museums.[8] The same could be said of treasuries (often filled with war-booty) the function of which was clearly propagandistic. War-booty, in fact, was to be seen all over sanctuaries with appropriate inscriptions specifying the victor and the defeated. When the large temple of Zeus was dedicated in Olympia, a huge shield (a war trophy won by the Eleans) was displayed prominently on the pediment. For war-booty at Isthmia see Elizabeth Gebhard in this volume (pp. 154–77).

Catherine Morgan discusses in this volume (pp. 18–44) the origins of pan-Hellenic sanctuaries. She sees the competitive element even in the earliest levels of the sanctuary of Olympia: small chieftains establishing hierarchy through display. Later, with the emergence of the city-state, there was a regional division of the pan-Hellenic sanctuaries. Olympia was foremost a Doric and western centre, Delphi catered to northern and eastern Greece. Note that Athens is particularly well represented at Delphi, whereas there is no Athenian treasury at Olympia. Conversely, the western colonies are represented in profusion at Olympia but are marginal at Delphi. Still, we should not underestimate the impact of Delphi for shaping policy throughout Greece. This became especially obvious during the Persian wars when most cities turned to Delphi for advice.

Territorial influence of sanctuaries naturally depends on historical circumstances. Let us take Isthmia. It was a marker for Corinthian territory and, later, an entrance-way to the Peloponnese. It is no accident that it acquired prestige after the Persian wars when the Isthmus became a location of particular significance. We only need to be reminded of the assembly that took place there after the battle of Salamis (see Gebhard in this volume, pp. 154–77).

Another case is the sanctuary of the Kabeiroi in Samothrace discussed by Burkert in this volume (pp. 178–91). It gained prestige in the fourth/third centuries BC. Monumental architecture emerged under the reign of Philip II of Macedon and continued under Philip Arrhidaios and his successors. Buildings at this point were mostly individual dedications by great kings and queens.

Competition in sanctuaries took place in every form ranging from literary and musical *agones* to athletics. The games, which became a feature of all pan-Hellenic sanctuaries, may not go as far back as the eighth century. Some scholars would even tend to view the proposed year 776 BC for the first Olympiad with suspicion and suggest that athletics became a marked feature of the pan-Hellenic sites only in the sixth century. The year 776 BC would then be a fictitious date, a projection into the past for reasons of legitimation.

Whatever the case might be, games provided opportunities for political stardom. It surely is no accident that Olympic victors emerged as major politicians. One need only mention Cylon, the Peisistratids and Miltiades: all eminent Athenian statesmen. Athletics was thus not only a means of establishing inter-state superiority but intra-state prestige as well.

In addition to athletics and war, art was also a means of competition. We have already spoken of the function of treasuries as embodiments of the city-state that had dedicated them. We should note in addition that it was not only the contents of the treasuries but their architectural execution as well that constituted a competitive feature. Even temples could serve this function. Herodotus informs us that the Athenian family of the Alcmaeonids had financed the Archaic temple of Apollo at Delphi.[9] This was a fact well known to all Greeks and helped enhance the Athenian prestige which, at later times, was to be represented at Delphi with a treasury, a stoa and perhaps even the tholos in the separate sanctuary of Athena Pronaia.

As regards sculpture, its prestige could be measured by size as well as execution. I need hardly mention the much appreciated statuary, such as the Hermes of Praxiteles or the Nike of Paionios at Olympia. I will dwell briefly on a pair perhaps less well known: the gigantic kouroi which flanked the entrance of the Heraion at Samos, dedicated by some noble family. One statue bore an inscription with the name of the dedicator on his leg: ISCHES. The kouroi served as permanent markers of the power of a particular aristocratic clan (see Kyrieleis in this volume, pp. 125–53). Note that the Heraion is not an inter- but extra-urban sanctuary. Here the competition was not between city-states but between aristocrats from within the city itself. The establishment of hierarchy amongst the aristocracy was a major concern, especially in the case of large states like Athens or Samos, where there were many competing factions. And here literary evidence comes to our support. For Samos Herodotus gives us plenty of stories of vicious struggles between Polycrates, his brother Syloson and his rival Maeandrius.[10] The setting is the sixth century, precisely the time of the kouroi. That the Heraion provided an arena for competing aristocrats, stands to reason.

SANCTUARIES AS PLACES OF REFUGE (*ASYLA*)

One of the most important functions of sanctuaries was to provide shelter to political refugees. Sinn and Schumacher both discuss this issue in the present volume (pp. 88–109 and pp. 62–87). They point out that the location of certain extra-urban cult sites was ideal for *asyla* or refuge sites. Let us just mention those that were situated on promontories or near the sea: the Poseidon sanctuaries at Tainaron and Geraistos, the Heraion at Perachora, the sanctuary at Sounion. Such places would be accessible both by land or sea, by mariners as well as land-travellers.

It is not to be assumed, of course, that such sanctuaries were specifically founded as *asyla*. Rather, we should suppose that in time certain sites became ideal because of their location. Schumacher stresses that Tainaron fulfilled the role of asylum for helots. In this case, the sanctuary assumes a function related to a specific socio-political situation. At any rate, the presence of *asyla* was necessitated by the constant war and factionalism which so characterized Greek culture. A similar function was fulfilled by monasteries in the Middle Ages.

The spatial organization of sanctuaries lends itself to usage by refugees and campers. Sinn divides the space into two zones. The narrower one is the traditional *temenos*, situated around altar and temple. The second zone is much wider but it too is sacred. Sinn calls it 'cult-meadow'; it is in this area that feasting took place but refugees could also camp if necessary. Sanctuaries with large 'cult-meadows' and a prominent geographic location made ideal *asyla*. Examples are Bassae, Ithome, Maleatas and Thermos in Aetolia. In the last site, argues Sinn, the inhabitants could even bring and protect their livestock. The substantial provisions for water-supplies at the sanctuary of Hera at Perachora can be accounted for if the site was used by refugees during long periods of time.

SANCTUARIES AS CULTURAL CENTRES

Where there is a gathering of people there is also a potential market for new art forms. One should not underestimate the role of festivals and ritual activities in sanctuaries as stimuli for new art forms. I will not speak here about how Attic drama evolved in the context of festivals under the patronage of the Peisistratids. Nor will I dwell on the choruses and musical *agones* which were integral part of festivals; these are well-known facts discussed by many learned scholars. It is worth noting, however, that even Herodotus mentions choruses performing in honour of heroes: 'normally, the tragic chorus belongs to the worship of Dionysus; but in Sicyon it was not so – it was performed in honour of Adrastus, treating his life-story and sufferings.' (Herodotus 5.71, transl. by A. de Selincourt.) In short, sanctuaries provided an ideal setting for performance either within their own theatres or perhaps within the *stadia*.

As mentioned above, sanctuaries were ideal arenas for the display of sculpture, painting, architecture and the performing arts. Artists were inspired by their peers and regional styles cross-fertilized each other.

It is thus obvious that Greek sanctuaries were not mere places of worship and pilgrimage but multidimensional institutions which served the needs of their communities and the needs of the Greek city-state as a whole. The social particularities created a symbiotic relationship between religion and state which we are only now beginning to fully understand.

NOTES

1 R. A. Tomlinson, 'Two notes on possible *hestiatoria*', BSA 75 (1980) 221–8.
2 W. Burkert, *Homo Necans, the Anthropology of Ancient Greek Sacrificial Ritual and Myth*, transl. by P. Bing (Berkeley 1983).
3 N. Marinatos, *Minoan Religion* (New York 1993); W. A. Meeks, *The First Urban Christians* (New Haven and London 1983) 157–62.
4 For a convenient handbook on Greek temples see G. Gruben, *Die Tempel der Griechen* (Munich 1966) 27ff. Gruben uses a mechanical and evolutionist approach and implies that the antecedent of the Greek temple is the Mycenaean *megaron*: 'Das Megaron, seit zwei Jahrtausenden der Archetypos der ägäischen Architektur, steht wiederum am Anfang der erlauchten Reihe griechischer Tempel.' (p. 28) Gruben thus avoids the question of how the temple form was conceived. For a different, non-evolutionist approach: A. J. Mazarakis-Ainian, 'Early Greek temples: their origin and function', in R. Hägg, N. Marinatos and G. Nordquist, eds, *Early Greek Cult Practice* (Stockholm 1988) 105–19.
5 W. Burkert, *Greek Religion: Archaic and Classical* (Oxford 1985) 88–9.
6 J. J. Coulton, *Greek Architects at Work. Problems of Structure and Design* (London 1977) 32: 'One explanation . . . is that the Greeks reacted to the stimulus and technical skill of Egyptian architecture.'
7 See especially F. de Polignac, *La naissance de la cité grecque. Cultes, espace et société, VIIIᵉ–VIIᵉ siècles avant J.-C.* (Paris 1984).
8 A. Snodgrass, *Archaic Greece: The Age of Experiment* (London 1980) 104ff.
9 Herodotus 5.62.2.
10 Herodotus 3.140–50.

Index